'His analysis is shrewd, his judgement sound . . . [the book's] strength is to present stories of the secret service's successes and failures within the political and strategic context of the times'

Adam Sisman, *Sunday Times*

'Tells the history of MI6 in the words of real spies'   *Mail on Sunday*

'A refreshing . . . [and] compelling read'

Christopher Sylvester, *Daily Express*

'Corera, the BBC's security correspondent, has enjoyed privileged access to key spy players from the past few decades and, writing in an engaging style, he picks up the story of the MI6 at the point where the "official" history grinds to a halt after the Second World War'

Annie Machon, *Sunday Express*

'As a good journalist and a reader of spy novels, Corera presents his material as fast-paced stories, from the covert diplomacy of the Cold War to recent and current security concerns in Afghanistan and the Middle East, and he humanises the grand dramas of a duplicitous trade'   Iain Finlayson, *The Times*

'Highly readable and well-researched account of the Service . . . Let's hope the current generation of spooks has learnt from past mistakes'

Con Coughlin, *Daily Telegraph*

'Corera provides a unique insight into how British intelligence has changed since the Second World War and how our spymasters reacted to major crises such as the September 11 attacks and the Iraq war. A fascinating read'   Hanna Tavne, *People*

'Superb new history of British intelligence'

Matthew d'Ancona, *Evening Standard*

'The best post-1949 account of British intelligence I have read . . . this is as good as it gets. And it's a good read'   Alan Judd, *Spectator*

'A fine overview, well told and well documented'

Hayden Peake, CIA Library

Gordon Corera is a Security Correspondent for BBC News. He is the author of *Shopping for Bombs* about the rise and fall of the Pakistani nuclear arms salesman A. Q. Khan. He was educated at Oxford and Harvard Universities and joined the BBC in 1997.

MI6

Life and Death
in the British Secret Service

GORDON CORERA

PHOENIX

A PHOENIX PAPERBACK

First published as *The Art of Betrayal* in Great Britain in 2011
by Weidenfeld & Nicolson
This paperback edition published in 2012
by Phoenix,
an imprint of Orion Books Ltd,
Orion House, 5 Upper St Martin's Lane,
London WC2H 9EA

An Hachette UK company

5 7 9 10 8 6 4

A CIP catalogue record for this book
is available from the British Library.

ISBN 978-0-7538-2833-5

Typeset by Input Data Services Ltd, Bridgwater, Somerset

Printed and bound by CPI Group (UK) Ltd, Croydon, CR0 4YY

The Orion Publishing Group's policy is to use papers that
are natural, renewable and recyclable products and
made from wood grown in sustainable forests. The logging
and manufacturing processes are expected to conform to
the environmental regulations of the country of origin.

www.orionbooks.co.uk

CONTENTS

INTRODUCTION

A former MI6 officer, one of the few to have risen to become 'C' or Chief of the Service, takes pleasure in recounting a story. Framed by a collection of John le Carré's novels on the bookshelves behind him, he tells it with a boyish smile and a playful twinkle in the eye which suggests a mischievousness not entirely lost to age. The story concerns a young officer making his way to a hut somewhere in Africa. It was the first contact MI6 had made with a local tribal chief whose assistance was required in some escapade whose exact details have long since been lost in the retelling. The officer was unsure of what welcome he would find and how receptive the chief might be to his request. He did not even know whether the chief could speak a word of English. But the officer's cautious introduction was met by a wide smile. It turned out the chief knew three words. 'Hello, Mr Bond,' he said, before offering his hand and his help. 'I doubt if he would have received such a warm welcome if he'd been from the Belgian Secret Service,' the former spymaster explains with a touch of pride and with no particular disrespect meant to Belgium or its spies.

True or not – and as with most stories about spies you have to be careful – the tale illustrates how the mythology of the British Secret Service has been spread far and wide and how fact and fiction have commingled to the point where the two have sometimes become indistinguishable in the public mind (and sometimes in that of the practitioner as well). That process has been aided by the cloak of secrecy which has shrouded British intelligence for much of its hundred-year history. The task of the Secret Intelligence Service (SIS) – or to use its more popular name MI6 – is to steal the secrets of others. But it has fiercely protected its own. For most of its existence, secrecy was so prized that MI6 did not even exist. At least not officially. Those in power were trained never to utter a word about it. In the corridors of Whitehall, the head of the service might be referred to as 'C' in hushed tones and a few might occasionally see a note with his distinctive green ink scrawled on it. But the outside world never knew his name.

That era has passed. The modern world, and the threats posed by it, demands greater transparency and accountability. And so, gingerly, the Secret Service has begun to edge out of the shadows, even inviting an official history of its first forty years from 1909 to 1949. This book offers an unprecedented insight into the following years, from the end of the Second World War to the present, a glimpse beneath the covers into the danger, the drama, the intrigue, the moral ambiguities and the absurdities that sometimes come with working for British intelligence.

The story centres on Britain's overseas intelligence service, MI6, but some of the characters find their homes in its sister service, the domestic security agency MI5, its weighty transatlantic cousin, the CIA, and its deadly rival, the KGB. This is emphatically not an authorised or comprehensive history which aspires to tell the complete story of British intelligence over nearly seventy years. Such a work is impossible while access to the files remains closed. It is not *the* history, rather it is *a* history – an attempt to understand the wider issues surrounding intelligence and the evolution of a particularly British organisation through a narrow lens which focuses on a relatively small number of individuals and episodes. The grand dramas of the Cold War and after – the rise and fall of the Berlin Wall, the Cuban Missile Crisis, the 11 September 2001 attacks and the Iraq war – are the backdrop for the human stories of our selected spies. But some of the individuals featured here, in turn, helped shape the course of those events.

At the heart of this book lie the personal accounts of the men and women who have been associated with intelligence work since 1945 in different ways and in different countries. All memories are faulty and spies, in particular, are trained to deceive, and so while this book is, in part, based on first-hand testimony and the memoirs of participants, those stories have been cross-checked against original documents, archives and secondary sources. Through their eyes, this book traces the triumphs and disasters as MI6 has undergone a dramatic transformation from a gung-ho amateurish service into its modern, at times equally controversial, incarnation.

Through its hundred-year history, the enemies the British Secret Service has fought have come in many guises. But in its essential form the work of a British spy has barely changed. It involves persuading someone to betray secrets, a deeply personal, even intimate act, and one fraught with risks. More often than not this involves betrayal, sometimes of a country, sometimes of a friendship. It involves working with the complexities of human motivation and especially its darker paths and traversing a fine line between right and wrong. It also involves breaking laws. 'We act within our own law – British law,' one man who has been chief of MI6 once commented to me. 'Our relationship with other people's laws is' – he paused for a moment before continuing – 'interesting.'

Does spying exist not just beyond other people's laws but also beyond traditional precepts of morality? Some have argued that it does, a few even that it should. Asking someone else to act illegally and, perhaps, unethically by providing secrets also frequently involves asking them to take huge risks, often with their lives. For what purpose? To 'betray something that needs betraying', as one former MI6 Chief puts it.[1] The art of betrayal is one that many countries, particularly Britain, have long nurtured, but it carries a price. 'I have been involved in death, yes,' Daphne Park remarked of her line of work, before adding enigmatically, 'but I can't talk about that.'[2] It is the agent though, not normally the MI6 officer, who faces the greatest risk. For the agent who has been recruited to work for MI6, they are embarking on a dangerous double life, a world of brush contacts, dead-letter drops and clandestine meetings. If they are lucky, there is the possibility of a new life, if not perhaps a bullet in the back of the head. So why spy? This book tries to answer that question by hearing from those who have chosen this path and exploring what drives those involved in espionage.

'I've never found – within the service – people hung up in any way on literature,' John Scarlett, a former C, has claimed. 'It is more interesting doing the real thing.'[3] But as our retired Chief at the start makes clear, even MI6 references itself, in part, by the fictional world, not least because many of the great British spy-thriller writers like Graham Greene, John le Carré and Ian Fleming were former

3

intelligence officers themselves who, to varying degrees, drew on their own experiences. At one extreme lies the lean, aggressive, morally certain and self-confident Bond with his insistence on *doing* things. At the other end is the podgy, donnish Smiley with his desire to *understand* things coupled with a keen awareness of the moral ambiguities of the world he inhabits.

The story of British intelligence since the Second World War can be understood, in part, as the evolving tension between these two poles, between the doers and the thinkers – those who sought to change the world and those who sought to understand it, or, to put it another way, between covert action and intelligence gathering. They are not mutually exclusive and to be successful any spy service needs both to jostle alongside each other in a creative tension. But often one or other strand has been dominant, sometimes too dominant – with disastrous consequences. As our story begins in the early Cold War, working for His and then Her Majesty's Secret Service was not so distant from the fictional life of Fleming's Bond. There may not have quite been a formal licence to kill, but stealing, breaking the law, overthrowing unfriendly governments and parachuting agents behind enemy lines was standard fare. But this was also a service which was clubby, amateurish, penetrated by its enemies and prone to mishap. Its secret wars were betrayed by its most painful traitor in the beguiling guise of Kim Philby. Slowly a new professionalism surrounding the business of collecting intelligence emerged, epitomised by one officer, Harold Shergold, and one agent, Oleg Penkovsky. Out of their time together, the 'Sov Bloc master race' was born within MI6, a group who would transform the service.

MI6 has slowly evolved from a self-selecting and self-perpetuating gentlemen's club for members of the establishment with a naughty streak to something more like a professional, bureaucratic organisation no longer set apart from the rest of government. The early days were marked by a macho culture in which women had their place – normally as secretaries, although even they undertook dangerous tasks on the front line. Only very few women, like Daphne Park – who made her mark in the Congo during one of the great crises of the Cold War – managed to run their own operations. Her story highlights not only the way in which the superpower rivalry intruded into the developing world with deadly effects but also the extent to which MI6 operations in more distant parts of the world offered an alternative tradition of building relationships and influencing events to the spycraft operating within the Soviet bloc.

Old-fashioned attitudes and rivalries once extended to relations with the domestic Security Service. MI5 thought their foreign counterparts were a bunch of cowboys, while MI6 thought their domestic equivalents were glorified policemen. Now, they work closely together. The relationship with the American 'cousins' has also seen a reversal. For many years, some in Britain wanted to see themselves as the smarter, wiser Athens to the CIA's Rome, educating the new arrivals in the ways of spying. But it did not take long before it was clear where the balance of power really lay, creating a complex relationship of trust and anxiety, intimacy and dependence much like that between the two countries as a whole.

The work of an intelligence service acting as the clandestine arm of government in pursuit of the national interest throws light not just on policy but also on the way in which a country – and particularly its elite – sees itself and its place in the world. For many years, Britain's Secret Service was the keeper of the flame, the perpetuator of the illusion of Britain being a 'great power'. Particularly in the early Cold War, MI6 was seen as a means of preserving influence even as economic and military might dissipated, much in the way James Bond could save the world with only a little help from his American friends. The secret world and its mythology helped sustain and shape the illusions of power. And the more self-aware observers of their own world describe the British Secret Service as characterised by a mixture of outward bravado and inner insecurity, perhaps like Britain itself.

Thrillers reflect the anxieties and preoccupations of their age and while Bond harks back to a still powerful Britain, the bleaker, more inward-looking world of John le Carré's Smiley is also rooted in a slice of the truth. British intelligence's darkest hour came in the 1960s when both MI5 and MI6 discovered that they were riddled with traitors and embarked on painful 'molehunts' (a term adopted from fiction) as the services looked inwards and colleagues wondered whether the man sitting next to them might be a traitor. One officer, who walked down the winding paths that became known as the 'wilderness of mirrors', can still recall every step of following a colleague around London nearly half a century earlier, wondering if he was working for the other side. Paralysis ensued as clever men thought too much and the service did too little.

As the Cold War entered its final decade both faces of the service's Janus-like personality were still evident. There was the cautious, careful intelligence gathering involved in running the enormously valuable agent Oleg Gordievsky, culminating in his daring but carefully planned escape from Moscow from under the watching eyes of the KGB. And then there was the more vigorous campaign, reminiscent of the Great Game of Kipling's day, in which teams infiltrated Afghanistan under cover to support the mujahedeen in their battle with the Soviets through the 1980s. Another way of describing the dichotomy in the service's personality was explained by one former officer who says that in the past colleagues could be divided into 'Moscow Men' – those who inhabited the shadows, glancing over their shoulder as they ran agents behind the Iron Curtain and carefully pieced together fragments of precious intelligence – and the 'Camel Drivers' – those whose preferred habitat was a tent out in the desert discussing with a sheikh, over tea, how stirring up the tribes and helping him in some small war might be of mutual benefit (an earthier description of this latter type was often deployed by in-house cynics which revolved around the officers doing something other than driving the camels). Like most stereotypes, it is truer in the abstract than in reality but still captures something of the two different sub-cultures within the service.

Critics would say there are good reasons why spies prefer to operate out of sight and feed off the reputation created by thrillers. A mystique has surrounded MI6. But is it justified? Beyond all the tales of derring-do and disguise, did it actually make any difference? Does dealing in deceit corrupt, and did it fuel mistrust during the Cold War? Or were the spies the final guarantor of peace during dangerous times? In some cases, an individual spy has been crucial. Oleg Penkovsky's intelligence contributed to defusing the Cuban Missile Crisis and Oleg Gordievsky helped London and Washington manage the end of the Cold War. But not everyone is convinced the reality matches the myth, and the end of the long struggle against Communism raised uncomfortable questions about whether the spies were really needed any more.

The early 1990s saw a period of fundamental questioning of the need for the Secret Service of the past. And within its walls, those who favoured cautious intelligence gathering were challenged by modernisers who wanted a service which had impact and could show the rest of government its worth. After 11 September 2001, they would get their chance, but with results they could not have predicted. The attack on the Twin Towers ended the debate about who the new enemy was and what intelligence was for, but it also thrust intelligence services on to difficult ethical terrain. Running agents inside terrorist networks involves all kinds of moral hazards, and so did working with allies, including one – the CIA – whose thirst for revenge led to it playing by different rules.

Protecting the public against terrorist attack made the work of intelligence agencies public in a manner never witnessed in the past, but what really opened up MI6 to controversy was the use of its intelligence to justify a war of choice. Iraq was the lowest moment for MI6 since the betrayal of Kim Philby. Its intelligence turned out to be wrong and the aftermath of the war a disaster. The myth came crashing against reality as MI6's intelligence, on which a case for war was built, was shown to be dud.

A social compact of sorts once existed in which people accepted that it was best not to ask exactly what spies really got up to so long as it was understood they did not cross certain, largely unwritten lines. But a willingness to accept that they might do bad or difficult things so that the rest of us purer souls could sleep easy in our beds at night has lost its hold. Modern notions of transparency and accountability now apply to spies, and revelations of past failures, whether in the early Cold War in the form of the traitors like Philby, or more recently with questions over intelligence on Iraq and allegations of complicity in torture, have eroded the willingness of the public to give spies a free pass. Trust between the public and its spies is hard to earn but easy to lose at a time when the appetite for intelligence – whether on terrorist threats, nuclear proliferation or the actions of unpredictable states – remains as large as ever, as does the public's fascination with the work of spies who produce it.

The stories of individuals – rather than institutions or the evolution of policy – lie at the heart of this book. The intention is to paint a picture of the realities of espionage by drawing on the first-hand accounts of those who have spied, lied and in some cases nearly died in service of the state, from the spymasters to the agents they ran and to their enemies. By focusing on the interlocking narratives of a small number of individuals, the aim is to tease out the wider changes in British intelligence and also to explore the unique and personal relationships that lie behind human espionage – what Graham Greene called 'the human factor' – the motivations and loyalties that go to make up a spy or a traitor and the relationships that are coloured by their actions. And the truth is often more remarkable than the fiction. The story begins as our cast assembles among the ruins of Vienna after the war.

1

INTO THE SHADOWS –
LIFE AND DEATH IN VIENNA

For those seeking to cross it, the Iron Curtain was much more than a political concept or rhetorical device. It was something tangible and often deadly. In the first decade of the Cold War, it was rising mile by mile. Thick wooden posts supported three walls of barbed wire, taller than a man, on the Czechoslovakian border with Austria. A wide clearing lay on one side to make footprints easy to spot, with landmines casually littered around. A touch of one piece of stretched wire might launch a signal flare; at another place it would offer a 6,000-volt shock, the short circuit alerting guards with guns and dogs. Three hundred people were killed trying to cross the Czechoslovak border, some shot by guards, others electrocuted, leaving their bodies caught on the wire hanging at an obtuse angle; one man shot himself after his foot was blown off at the ankle by a mine.[1]

Jan Mašek had somehow made it across. But he had not found safety. These were the dangerous days of the early Cold War, as he was about to discover. A lance corporal in the Czechoslovak army, he was slight of frame, not too tall, with dark hair. His rough-skinned tan came from the twenty-odd years he had spent growing up in a country village, brought up alone by his mother.[2] She had fallen ill and he had asked for compassionate leave from the army. His commanding officer had refused, so he simply left to see her. But as he headed back to his unit, he was warned that he faced a court martial. He decided to flee over the border into divided Austria.

There he had found his way into the welcoming arms of British Field Security in Vienna. These were the men, most just out of their teens, who performed the grunt work for Britain's Secret Intelligence Service, MI6. Among their tasks was the interrogation of the illegal frontier crossers who had come over from Hungary or Czechoslovakia. Once any suspicion that they had been sent by the other side to cause trouble was removed, they were sucked dry of every ounce of usable information. Britain was blind about what was happening on the other side of the Iron Curtain. A claustrophobic fear of imminent war haunted every debriefing. Field Security was under orders to extract every nugget, however trivial, so it could be laid alongside a thousand other nuggets in the hope of revealing something useful and perhaps giving early warning of the Red Army beginning its march. What type of shoulder-boards did the Soviet troops wear in a small village in Hungary? What was a particular factory in Czechoslovakia producing? Even a grandmother might know whether a relative in the army had been moved from one place to another. The purpose was to divine where the enemy was and whether he was on the move.[3]

Mašek was quietly spoken and sensitive. He was questioned for five days at Field Security's Vienna office, a grand five-storey building at Sebastianplatz near the city centre. Bob Steers asked the questions, trying to separate fact from fiction in a small, bare room with only two chairs and a table. He 'fronted' for the Secret Service by advertising himself as a contact in the Viennese underworld, allowing the MI6 men to remain out of sight. He produced a synopsis of Mašek's information, which went up to MI6 at its grand hiding place in the Schönbrunn barracks. Two of their people came over. Mašek had some interesting details on how the Czechoslovak army was being integrated with the Soviets. He was a touch simple minded, and extracting more detail was painfully slow. But after two and a half weeks his life had yielded up forty-five pages of double-spaced typed notes.

Just as his reward of a one-way ticket to Australia was being prepared, one of the MI6 men intervened. A radio set had to be taken urgently to near where Mašek had come from in Czechoslovakia. Mašek was the only person around at that moment to do it. This would normally be a job for a professionally trained courier. But the border was being tightened and a network of 'resistance' couriers had just been rolled up. More than sixty had been arrested. One betrayed his friends by agreeing to work for the other side. MI6 had a training centre for its couriers in Austria and an office back in

London (under the name Kenneth Proud Translation Services, code-named 'Measure') to help organise Czech agents. But these operations were penetrated by the Czechoslovak security service, the StB. Over ten years, the StB would record details of more than a thousand individuals linked to British intelligence.[4]

Adventurous, foolhardy methods were sometimes employed to smuggle couriers across the border as it was tightened. Aqualungs and inflatable rubber suits were used to traverse rivers. Hot-air balloons with canvas folding baskets were another trick – although the discovery of two bodies on a Czech hill bearing the marks of having fallen from a great height bore witness to the dangers. Another method was using the defectors and frontier crossers who had found some way out and who showed some potential. They would be offered a choice: take a message or a radio back and we will get you out of your squalid refugee camp now and give you a ticket to a new life when – or if – you make it out again. Sometimes a radio came with the offer of a gun, one captured from the other side so it could not be traced. One man who appeared tough as nails cried himself to sleep the night before he went back. When he was cornered on the frontier, he shot himself rather than face the secret police.

Mašek did not have potential. 'He's too soft,' Steers protested. He had spent days in a room with him and had promised him he was as good as on the boat. 'If he came out, he can go in the same way,' the MI6 man insisted. It took a few hours to persuade Mašek. His orders were clear. Having buried the radio at the agreed spot, he had to – had to – come back immediately. Under no circumstances should he visit his mother as it would be noticed by the informers who worked in the village on behalf of the secret police.

He got across the border and successfully buried the radio. But then he went home to see his mother. Another agent radioed a message to Vienna. The local press were reporting that a British courier had been caught. Jan Mašek's name was added to the list of those executed for acting as couriers for Western intelligence, joining at least forty others. Many of these were motivated by a commitment to fight Communism. Jan Mašek was just a simple man who wanted to see his mother.[5]

Lives were held in the balance in Vienna after the war. They dangled precariously between life and death and East and West like the city itself. The Iron Curtain that Winston Churchill warned of in 1946 was descending from Stettin in the Baltic in Europe's north to Trieste in the Adriatic to the south. And yet Vienna lay almost a hundred miles behind a straight line connecting those two places, east even of Prague. Austria was the easternmost area of Western influence and Vienna lay in its far corner, making it a crossroads – a route out from those escaping the Iron Curtain and a route in for those seeking to penetrate it.[6] For a decade from the end of the Second World War until Austria gained its independence in 1955 Vienna's narrow, winding, cobbled streets were a stage on which the drama of the unstable, early Cold War was played out and in which the British Secret Service struggled to adapt to a new enemy and a new war. It was a world of bravery and betrayal, of black and white and every shade in between. East and West were colliding and Vienna lay on the fault line.

The words 'cleared of enemy' could still be found stencilled in Russian on the corner of Viennese buildings long after April 1945. They were a reminder of the five days when the Red Army had fought its way from house to house to drive out the Nazis. American and British bombers had done their work from the skies above, burning the roof of St Stephen's Cathedral and gutting the Opera House in the city's medieval centre.

The months following the capture of the city were in many ways more traumatic than the brief but intense fighting that preceded it, leaving deep emotional scars of fear and suspicion. 'People in dark overcoats hurried along with hunched shoulders and blank, shut-down faces,' recalled a British official who visited in those first few months. 'Furtiveness, fear and suspicion were everywhere.'[7] People were constantly on the move, looking for food, trading their treasured possessions on the black market for dried peas and bread.[8] The phones and electricity were down and at night an air of sinister malevolence hung over the deserted roads.

The Viennese learnt to fear the knock on the door. While the Western powers chose to overlook the previous widespread support for Hitler, the Soviets saw the Austrian people as a defeated enemy and had elected to seize the spoils of victory. 'Every day every hour it is the same,' a French occupation official told a visitor that November at a police station. 'The Russians ... have knocked down an old woman in the street and are stealing her clothes. The Russians are pillaging a house ... A man walks home with his wife and sees her raped before his eyes ... Monsieur, it is fatiguing ... The life in Vienna is fatiguing.'[9] The claims were often exaggerated. A deep hatred of the Russians, inculcated by Nazi propaganda, had led to fear among the Austrians of being left to the Red Army and its vengeance.[10] In August 1945, the Soviets unveiled a memorial to the Red Army in the central Schwarzenbergplatz. A small crowd carried banners, one reading 'Saviour of Vienna from the Atom Bomb'. A British Field Security agent reported that the applause was unenthusiastic.[11]

The memorial joined the statues of forgotten emperors on horseback that stared grandly over the broad Ringstrasse which wrapped around the old city. War had left Vienna a hollowed-out shell of its imperial self. The destruction was not as complete as that inflicted on Berlin and so the still-standing but skeletal façades of baroque buildings gave the city the feel of a film or theatre set for the many visitors who stepped out on to it.

The vision of a rubble-strewn city of shadows, statues and ruins in which the darker paths prospered was immortalised by a former, but not entirely divorced, member of the British Secret Service. In the bitingly cold days of February 1948, if you had happened by the Café Mozart on the square near the Opera building, you would have found a man seated at a table beneath the ornate mirrors and lavish chandeliers working on a screenplay entitled *The Third Man* as black-tied waiters served thick coffee. There had been snow on the roofs and driving sleet when Graham Greene arrived in the city. A wry Catholic fascinated by sin, Greene was on his way to becoming England's most famous writer, but one who never quite left the secret world. So powerful would be his evocation of Vienna that those who lived through these years would find it hard to separate their own memories from the world as defined by Greene and the film he helped create.

'I never knew Vienna between the wars,' Greene's British military police narrator explains; 'and I am too young to remember the old Vienna with its Strauss music and its bogus easy charm; to me it is a simply a city of undignified ruins which turned that February into great glaciers of snow and ice.' The mood in the city was as bleak as the weather when Greene had arrived. There was talk of Nazis meeting in *Gasthaus* back-rooms planning sabotage and of Communists preparing putsches. People were simply vanishing into thin air never to be heard of again. Rumours swept the locals that the Allies were preparing to abandon the city to the Russians. 'Listening to conversations in trams and streets, as well as taking part in discussions in family circles of all classes, the impression is being gained that morale has reached a dangerously low level,' a British intelligence report read.[12]

The desire to capture post-war Vienna on celluloid – and especially its moral ambiguities that contrasted so sharply with the black and white of the war – came from the Hungarian-born film producer Alexander Korda, another sometime helper of MI6. His company London Films had been involved in intelligence work since the 1930s – scouting for locations provided excellent access to places otherwise hard to reach. Korda had pulled some strings so that Greene could retreat into the cosy warmth of the Hotel Sacher round the corner from the Café Mozart, normally reserved for British officers involved in the occupation. Before the war the cream of Viennese society had gathered in the Sacher's famous velvet-draped Red Bar. After the war, the bar had become a British officers' canteen, serving baked beans and dried-up rashers on toast with NAAFI tea as full-length portraits of elegant Viennese women and their children and dogs looked on disapprovingly.[13] A warren of rooms and cubbyholes on the ground floor proved perfect for whispered conversations. The headwaiters there and across the city did their best to preserve the airs and graces of Old Vienna, dressing in tailcoats and maintaining their haughty air even as their cafés and restaurants had little food and were cold and dirty and covered in grime.

Greene's tour-guide through the rubble was an unusual character, straight from the pages of one of his books. Peter Smollett, the *Times* correspondent, knew the city inside out. He had been born there before becoming a British citizen in the 1930s and returned after the war. Greene and Smollett would drink until the early hours of the morning in some of the seedier clubs like the Oriental and Maxim's whose floor-shows harked back to pre-war Berlin. Greene would also visit some of the lowest prostitutes. 'I have my ways,' he explained to one of Korda's staff who had asked him how he could do so while remaining a Catholic.[14]

Smollett took Greene into the Soviet sector of the city where the Prater, the famous funfair, used to draw the crowds. 'The Prater lay smashed and desolate and full of weeds, only the Great Wheel revolving slowly over the foundations of the merry-go-rounds like abandoned millstones,' Greene wrote in a letter back home.[15] The wheel gave Greene the defining backdrop for the moment in his drama when loyalties collide. His story revolved around Holly Martins, a cheap thriller writer, coming to visit an old friend, Harry Lime, in Vienna, only to find him recently deceased. A mysterious third man had been seen at the time of his passing and Martins seeks him out. He discovers that the third man was Lime himself, who had faked his own death to try and escape the rap for selling fake penicillin which was killing children. As they meet on the Great Wheel, Lime stares down from the creaking carriage through the steel girders to the broken city below. 'Would you really feel any pity if one of those dots stopped moving for ever?' he asks. 'In these days, old man, nobody thinks in terms of human beings. Governments don't, so why should we?'

Smollett had probably told Greene about the real-life penicillin rackets. He also knew about spies. He had anglicised his name from Hans Peter Smolka and had worked during the war as head of the Russian section in the British Ministry of Information. This rather suited him since he was himself a Communist and, also, from at least the start of the Second World War, passing information to the Soviet Union.

Graham Greene's experience of the world of espionage came after he was recruited into MI6 during the war through his sister who worked for the service. True to the service culture of the time, he had been checked out during a series of boozy all-night parties.[16] His first posting was to mosquito-ridden Freetown in Sierra Leone where vultures clattered on his tin roof and he hunted cockroaches at night by torchlight. He was not a success. A typically Greene-like proposal to open a brothel to try and gather information on German soldiers was rejected by London. He hated being asked to pressure a Scandinavian sailor by warning him that if he did not talk he would be interned and his girlfriend would not wait for him. It was, he thought, 'dirty work' which should really have been done by the local MI5 man and he soon returned to Britain to be immersed in MI6 files.[17]

The setting for the climactic scene of his Viennese screenplay was, Greene claimed, provided on the penultimate day of his first visit by a young British intelligence officer.[18] The officer explained that he had seen a reference to 'underground police' and, thinking that this meant secret police, he had ordered them disbanded. It was then explained that their name came from working beneath the ground in the sewers. Wearing heavy boots and a mac, Greene was taken down by the men in their white uniforms with trousers tucked into boots to protect them from the rats. The main sewer appeared as wide as the Thames. Around a curving iron staircase lay a shallow scum containing orange peel and old cigarette cartons. When a policeman shone a torch it revealed an army of rats – some looked the size of small dogs – originally raised on farms for their fur. The Russians controlled the sewers and refused to lock the entrances, which were disguised aboveground as kiosks. These allowed their agents to disappear from one part of the city and suddenly emerge ghost-like somewhere else.

The rats of the Viennese sewers were close acquaintances of a mutual friend of both Greene and Smollett. They had been witnesses to the birth of his betrayal more than a decade earlier. Kim Philby returned to Vienna for a brief visit after the war.[19] The memories of his earlier life in the city were hidden carefully away in one of the many locked compartments of his mind. He was in the process of submerging the last vestiges of that past and of the journey he had begun in the dank, subterranean paths of the sewers.

Philby had arrived in Vienna in 1933 just down from Cambridge. His formative university years had been marked by three great events: a bleak economic depression which brought social misery, the abject failure of a British Labour government which dashed political hopes, and the rising menace of fascism which fuelled fear. His response was to see Communism as the answer. For the sons and daughters of the privileged elite, Communism offered both an intellectual critique of the current malaise and an emotional rebellion against their parents' complacency. One of Philby's tutors had provided him with the contacts to get to Austria to help those on the front lines of the struggle. Here his intellectual Communism would be blooded. In Vienna the left was holding out against a national government that had turned towards the right. Philby lodged in a spartan flat in the city's ninth district. There he was introduced to a small, vivacious and brave activist called Litzi who would shape his future. She was utterly devoted to the Communist cause. When he explained that he had £100 to last him the year, she performed some quick calculations and told him £25 could be given up for the revolution. 'He was two years younger than me,' she recalled years later, 'and was a very good-looking man. He behaved like a gentleman. And he was a Marxist, a rare combination ... He stammered, sometimes more, sometimes less. Like many people with a handicap he was very charming. We fell in love immediately.'[20] The twenty-one-year-old inexperienced British public-school boy fell for the East European activist and they became lovers in the snow ('surprisingly warm,' Philby would later remark). She would be the human factor that made his intellectual idealism visceral and real. He had discovered a sense of purpose which, in turn, set him on a path from which he could not or would not stray for the rest of his life.

A British passport was Philby's ticket into the clandestine world as he flashed it at the border, couriering Communist messages in and out of Austria. One grey morning in February 1934, the city echoed to the sound of gunfire. Listening to his radio, Philby heard that martial law had been declared in response to an uprising. Through the windows he and Litzi watched lorries packed with soldiers moving swiftly through the empty, elegant streets.[21] The city was plunged into darkness and artillery pounded the workers' housing estates where families and a few men with guns held out. Hundreds were killed. The socialists and Communists who were not killed or captured fled. Many went underground into the sewers to find refuge with the rats. Those who were caught were hanged. Philby went to friends begging for clothes which he could take below to replace fugitives' bloodstained rags as he prepared to smuggle survivors across the border into Czechoslovakia. He married Litzi two weeks after the uprising in Vienna's town hall.[22] He would later say it was just to provide her with a way out. But those who saw the couple at the time were convinced that their love was real.

Two months later Philby returned to London with his bride (who was met with the instant disapproval of her newly acquired mother-in-law). He had glimpsed what he believed was the dark future for Europe if fascism triumphed. It was a danger he believed his countrymen had yet to understand. Others had also noticed how the young man had shown courage in his willingness to fight and risk his life for a faraway country and for ideals in which he believed. So, soon after returning home, one of Litzi's friends from Vienna who had also come to London took him on a long walk to Regent's Park. Edith Tudor-Hart was slim and pale with blue eyes and bobbed blonde hair. She had been under occasional surveillance from MI5 and the police since 1930 when she attended a workers' rally in Trafalgar Square before being deported back to Vienna. They suspected she was already working with the Russian intelligence services. They were right. Like Litzi, a marriage to a British citizen who was a Communist would allow her to come to London after the uprising. An opportunity to change history was lost. MI5 and the police Special Branch were still trying to establish where exactly she lived in June 1934 and so there was no surveillance on her the day she took Philby on a roundabout walk to meet a man on a park bench.[23] He was another Austrian, a former university lecturer who now lived near Hampstead and was ostensibly studying psychology. Cosmopolitan and erudite, he was the perfect recruiter for the forerunner of the KGB, having the right personality to appeal to the fresh, intellectual Cambridge man. His strategy was to cultivate young idealists and then send them into the British establishment. This required a patience that MI6 officers later reflected they did not possess.[24]

Philby's work in Vienna had caught people's attention, the man explained. Would he be interested in working secretly for the Communist cause? 'You are a bourgeois by education, appearance and origin. You could have a bourgeois career in front of you – and we need people who could penetrate into the bourgeois institutions. Penetrate them for us!'[25] A message soon went back to Moscow with news of the recruitment of an insecure and shy young man. He had said there were other 'sons of functionaries' at Cambridge who shared his views and he would soon be providing a list.[26] With his stories of blood and turmoil in Vienna, Philby drew others to his cause. He would only tell Litzi of his recruitment the following year.[27]

Philby was instructed to hide his Communist past and he publicly began to disavow it, flirting with right-wing pro-German politics. One person who knew the truth was Greene's tour-guide around Vienna, 'Hans' Peter Smollett, another friend of Litzi's in Austria who had come to London. Philby and Smollett even went into business for a while running a press agency. Philby thought he 'was a hundred percent Marxist, although inactive, lazy and a little cowardly'. That did not stop Philby using him as an occasional source. One day he said to him, 'Listen, Hans, if in your present job you come across some information that in your opinion could help me in my work for England – and I winked at him – come over to me and offer me two cigarettes. I'll take one, you'll keep the other, that will be a signal you want to tell me something important.'[28] But Smollett's amateurishness irritated the security-conscious Philby, especially once he had made it into the inner sanctum by joining MI6 in 1941. Smollett was like the embarrassing friend from school who followed you to university and knew you were not quite what you pretended to be.

With his easy charm, Philby had skilfully glided up the ranks of the British Secret Service. Betraying those around him, and especially the women who fell for him, came easy. There was the illicit thrill of not just entering the secret world but of subverting the establishment which he held in disdain, of duping the fools around him. Secret knowledge offers the needy a sense of superiority and power over ordinary folk. For the traitor within a service, that extended even to one's colleagues. As the war ended and his career showed no sign of waning, Philby realised he needed to normalise his personal life. His relationship with Litzi was long over but they were technically still married. Philby took the risky step of telling his superiors, explaining that the marriage had been a gallant attempt to rescue a young woman. His superior sent a request over to MI5 for a trace – she was a Communist, now living with a Soviet agent they said. That revelation barely caused a ripple. End it quickly, they said, and Philby did. The two Communist agents agreed to divorce on the pretext of infidelity so that Philby could marry his new partner, Aileen, who by then was expecting their fourth child.[29] The two former lovers never met again and rarely spoke of each other. The few times Litzi mentioned 'Kim', it was with a tone of regret and love but tinged with bitterness. To those who knew them well, the reticence hid the pain aroused by a deeply felt relationship which had been sacrificed for the cause.[30]

Greene was one of the few friends not scarred by Philby's betrayal. Instead it provided a wellspring for his fiction. Philby had been Greene's boss during the war in MI6, the two men lunching and drinking and enjoying each other's company, Philby in his tweed jacket with leather patches. Greene had flirted with Communism in his youth but had eventually sided with Catholicism.[31] 'Of course I couldn't talk to him as a Communist,' Philby said years later. 'But I did talk to him as a man with left-wing views and he was Catholic. But at once there was human contact between us.'[32] Greene had left MI6 suddenly for a far less exciting job in the Ministry of Information. Why? A few have wondered if he might have suspected what his friend was up to and wanted to avoid becoming caught up in it. If so, *The Third Man* takes on a different hue with its story of a hapless writer, shocked at the amoral behaviour of an old friend he had once looked up to and now determined to chase down the charismatic but ruthless rogue. The writer even falls for the rogue's East European girlfriend, who needs a passport to get out.[33] In the screenplay, the writer, torn between conflicting loyalties, finally sides with the authorities over his treacherous friend. Reality, for Greene, was always more complex and beguiling than the fiction.

Spy-fact and spy-fiction intertwined from the earliest days of the British Secret Service when Whitehall's decision to establish what would become MI5 and MI6 was encouraged by ribald thrillers which warned of German spies fanning out across England, stealing its secrets and preparing for an invasion. Sleep safe, the writers told their readers, for the British Secret Service was busy catching the German spies and returning the favour. Except that the bureaucrats knew it was not, since it did not yet exist, and so in 1909 they founded the Secret Service Bureau to catch up. In Vienna, the early Cold War provided the ferment for a new generation of novelists whose work would again shape reality. Greene was foremost among them. It was not long after his visit that the CIA chief could stand on the city's streets and watch Orson Welles film his scenes for *The Third Man*.[34] Once it opened, the British Field Security team trooped en masse to the cinema to watch their world brought to life.

Over in the Austrian town of Graz another twenty-year-old member of Field Security was discerning the cadences of loyalty and betrayal. He would draw on his experiences to create a fictional world that would define the public understanding of the British Secret Service. David Cornwell, later to become John le Carré, plied his trade among the desperate detritus of the refugee camps. Thousands had been swept up in the ebb and flow of Nazism and the Red Army and deposited far from home. Moving through the flotsam were the spies of many nations picking over the remains. Inside the camps could be found every type of person fleeing something, heading somewhere, some perhaps knowing something.[35] In his most auto-biographical novel, *A Perfect Spy*, le Carré has the young Magnus Pym of Field Security trawling the camps asking the questions Jan Mašek was asked. 'Where do you come from? What troops did you see there? What colour shoulder-boards did they wear? What did they drive around in, what weapons did they have? Which route did you take, what guards, obstructions, dogs, wire, minefields did you meet along your way? What shoes were you wearing? How did your mother manage, your grandmother if the mountain pass was so steep? How did you cope with two suitcases and two small children when your wife was so heavily pregnant? Is it not more likely that your employers in the Hungarian secret police drove you to the border and wished you luck as they showed you where to cross? Are you a spy and if so, would you not prefer to spy for us?'[36]

There was the occasional burst of excitement – for instance, carry-ing a loaded Browning revolver while accompanying a senior officer to meet a Czech source who was promising a 'one-time sell' of intelligence. But then there was the disappointment when the clan-destine rendezvous at a pub drew a blank. Later he would wonder if the Czech agent ever really existed and whether his senior officer was not something of a fantasist living out his own dream of the spy-world like so many others. 'He imagined himself at the Spies' Big Table, playing the world's game.' In the fictional world, Magnus Pym is artfully reeled in by an intellectual friend, his own version of Philby's man on the park bench, who draws him into choosing friendship over his country and embarking on a long path of betrayal for the Czech Secret Service. 'What would have bought me, I wonder? What would have turned me?' le Carré later asked.[37]

Le Carré soon afterwards entered the inner sanctum of MI5 and MI6. 'It wasn't long before I, too, was fantasizing about a real British secret service, somewhere else, that did everything right that we either did wrong or didn't do at all.'[38] One day, he bumped into the in-house lawyer. Sitting on his Formica-topped table was a copy of Graham Greene's latest book. *Our Man in Havana* was a savage satire of Greene's former employers in which an MI6 officer recruits a vacuum-cleaner salesman who in turn passes off designs for his latest model ('the atomic') to a gullible and eager service as those of a new weapon of mass destruction being built in the mountains. The sight of the two-way nozzle causes particular consternation in London. 'Fiendish isn't it?' the Chief says, after someone remarks that plans for the weapon of mass destruction bore a passing resemblance to an outsized vacuum cleaner. 'The ingenuity, the simplicity, the devilish imagination of the thing,' he adds. Greene, the lawyer remarked to le Carré, had gone too far and might have to be prosecuted for this outrage. 'It's a damned good book. That's the whole trouble,' he explained.[39]

Vienna was filled with its own tricksters, fraudsters and charlatans on the make. Intelligence was a commodity for sale like everything else on the black market and often just as fake, with refugees running paper mills churning out fabricated documents to satisfy the demands of the spies. There was the high-living, sixty-year-old 'Count' with his bevy of lady friends who claimed to know a Soviet major interested in betraying the latest ciphers in return for $25,000. Washington was so excited that it sent out a team. 'This guy's lying like a rug,' they were told after a polygraph.[40] The British had similar problems. One agent codenamed 'Dandelion' was being run as a double agent against the Soviets until he explained that his Russian case officer wanted him to go to South America and needed money to continue his work there. He was a fraud, one officer warned, only to be overruled. Once safely ensconced in Venezuela, Dandelion vanished. It was clear he had made everything up.[41]

One young MI6 officer, who had warned of Dandelion's flakiness, walked the Viennese stage with all the confidence that came from being the youngest officer then recruited into the British Secret Service. Once a month, the dark-haired Briton, straight out of central casting and with a swagger to match, would turn into an alley and then down some steps into a gothic beer cellar just inside the Russian sector of Vienna. He would take a seat and listen carefully to the music. If the next song that the musician struck up was a popular Austrian song called 'Mamachi' then all was clear and his contact – a Russian official – had also arrived. The musician was in the pay of the British Secret Service. If he didn't play the song, Anthony Cavendish would have a beer and hopefully leave as peacefully as he had arrived.[42] It was risky, perhaps a bit amateurish – typical of the Secret Service culture of the times. Vienna had become a place to take risks and play spy games in because, like its larger German cousin Berlin, the Viennese capital was one of the only places that British, American and French soldiers and spies came into direct, daily contact with their erstwhile allies, the Soviets. Austria had been sliced into four zones – Soviet, British, American and French. Vienna itself was entirely surrounded by the Soviet zone. It was isolated.

The city itself was divided into four sectors, one for each power. The exception was the First District, the old medieval Innere Stadt or inner city. In a decision that could only have been agreed in the opening days of hesitant co-operation, it was policed collectively by 'four men in a jeep', one military policeman from each of the powers with the lead role rotating every month. In their jeeps, suspicions often turned violent. When one patrol passed a Russian checkpoint, the Russian in the jeep forced the vehicle to stop and got his colleagues to drag out a prisoner the Americans had been after.[43] One Sunday in June 1946, British and Russian troops brawled outside the railway station, wielding broken bottles. It began when a group of more than fifty British soldiers charged a Russian jeep. One Russian officer died of his injuries.[44]

Smaller than Berlin and nestled into Eastern Europe, Vienna's intimacy and its location meant that it acted as a place in which to probe the enemy and see what could be learnt and how far they could be pushed before pushing back, a place to divine both Stalin's intentions and those of individual Communists to see if someone from the other side might be encouraged to meet and perhaps to talk out of line. Within months of the war ending, MI6 officers in the city could see the advantages of making Vienna a centre for intelligence gathering for all of Central and South-Eastern Europe. 'I would like to urge the importance of establishing in Vienna a separate long-range SIS bureau, entirely divorced from all existing intelligence organisations, if necessary entirely unknown to any of the latter, and operating directly under London,' wrote one officer in November 1945.[45]

By the time Cavendish arrived in Vienna with its Middle European cold and its grey skies, he was working out of the Schönbrunn barracks on the outskirts of town. His task, like that of every MI6 officer, was the recruiting and running of agents. MI6 officers only occasionally spy themselves in terms of collecting secret information. More often than not, they gather intelligence by recruiting agents – people with access to secrets who are willing to risk their lives by passing it on. They might offer their services (a 'walk-in' or a defector) and do so willingly – for money or to escape. Or they might be 'persuaded' – perhaps they need a passport or they have had their hand in the till or been in someone else's bed.

Cavendish, aged just twenty-one, was imbued with all the brash self-confidence that came from the combination of youth and membership of the secret world. His father had taken the family to Switzerland but then died in a mountaineering accident when his son was only five. His mother decided to stay and the boy attended a village school in the Alps, becoming fluent in French, German and Swiss-German. Cavendish had been commissioned young into the Intelligence Corps aged just nineteen and was posted to Cairo as the war ended. There he had met a plump, owl-faced lieutenant colonel with rumpled khaki shorts, untidy hair and spectacles. Maurice Oldfield, the grammar-school-educated son of Derbyshire hill-farmers, worked for British Security in the Middle East. He was a natural intelligence officer destined eventually to become chief of MI6, and he took Cavendish under his wing.

Cavendish had roared around Cairo on his Twin Triumph motorbike, occasionally posing as a German prisoner of war to infiltrate escape routes. Oldfield went on to join MI6 and Cavendish soon followed. There he worked in R5, Philby's old section ('Call me Kim,' the leading light of the service would say as he popped into the office) and in the department dealing with Austria, Germany and Switzerland – his first assignment was eavesdropping on a Swiss trade delegation in London. Training for new officers was slapdash and had not progressed much from the pre-war days when the new

MI6 officer in Vienna – fresh to the whole game and without any instructions from base – had arrived in town and went to see the man he was succeeding for any tips on how to recruit agents. 'Could you give me some idea of how to begin?' 'You'll just have to work it out for yourself,' he was told. 'I think everyone has his own methods and I can't think of anything I can tell you.'[46]

Cavendish had his own painful introduction into the costs of Secret Service work just before he arrived in Vienna. As he was driving through the North German countryside looking for an evacuation route in the event of the Red Army rolling west, he picked up two young hitchhikers, a boy and a girl in their late teens or early twenties. They came from a town in East Germany called Prenzlau. The Russians had a military garrison in the town and the service wanted a source there. He bought them dinner at a guesthouse. The girl's name was Frieda, his was Alfred, and they both disliked the Russians. To them Cavendish was 'Paul'. He persuaded the girl to undertake some rudimentary training for a few days, while Alfred was given some money to enjoy himself. She was taught how to use a wireless set and a one-time pad that allowed messages to be written in code, then they were both sent home. Three weeks later she filed her first report. Simple. But six months on, Cavendish had received a message that he should come to see Frieda. Over dinner, she said she was scared that her boyfriend had informed on her because he suspected an affair with Cavendish. 'Of course, you'll be safe,' he reassured her. Next time they met, she said she thought she was being watched and wanted to stay in the West. It took a lot of persuasion but she went back. A few weeks later she was caught, put on trial and shot. It was only in his later years that the memory of the young girl would trouble Cavendish as he looked back on his own younger, more ruthless self.[47]

The life of a junior MI6 officer, like Cavendish, in Vienna, was taken up to a large extent with the routine work of maintaining an infrastructure for espionage – looking for locations for dead-letter drops where documents could be stashed by an agent and then picked up by his British case officer or checking out new safe houses to replace old, blown ones (the demand for such apartments must certainly have kept the Viennese property market buoyant, the spies reckoned). There was also the work of recruiting support agents, the musicians in the beer cellars, the hotel porters, the taxi-drivers who could be useful in operations or when it came to meeting the agents from the other side who were passing on secrets.

Attempts to recruit agents who could pass on secrets were painfully difficult and reflect the amateurishness of the service of the time. By the lavish baroque abbey in Melk, Cavendish struck up a conversation with a young Russian artillery captain called Grigori on the terrace of a pub on the banks of the Danube, which led to a drinking competition involving a near-lethal mix of two-litre glasses of beer and vodka. Perhaps they could meet again? A fortnight later they were back at the pub chatting about their background and Cavendish wondered if he had found a source in Soviet Military Headquarters. Two weeks on and Grigori failed to show. The landlord was asked to make some discreet inquiries among a group of Russian officers about Captain Grigori by saying he had left something behind on his last visit. He had been sent back to the Soviet Union, he was told. He was not the only Russian officer whom Cavendish befriended who would soon afterwards disappear. A colonel he encountered at the Opera one evening agreed to meet three days later at a local beer cellar. All went well, and another meeting was agreed in a week's time at a restaurant in the inner city. A team watched the restaurant in case an attempt were made to kidnap Cavendish but the Colonel never showed. A phone call by a third party to his office revealed that he too had been suddenly recalled to the Soviet Union. Something was not quite right, Cavendish sensed, maybe a bad apple was in the mix somewhere. Field Security felt the same. One time a truck carrying an agent was stopped at a checkpoint. The agent was in disguise, with another twelve men in uniform. Yet a Red Army officer held a photo up and spotted the agent and beckoned him out.[48] At one point, MI6 activities virtually ground to a halt amid fears of Soviet penetration, and a senior officer came out from London. Laxness in Field Security was the problem, it was concluded.[49]

Along with recruiting and running agents to look for signs of the impending war, Cavendish's other task was to prepare for the war itself by building a so-called stay-behind network. This consisted of recruiting sleeper agents and burying weapons and communications systems which would be activated only in the event of Austria being overrun by the Red Army. The men and munitions would then provide the core of a resistance network, modelled on those the Special Operations Executive had supported in the Second World War. Setting this up involved acting like pirates on Treasure Island, by finding a quiet spot in the park or the countryside and then counting paces from a tree or other landmark, burying a box three feet deep and then producing a map with instructions on how to retrieve the radio or ammunition. Cavendish purchased a large American Chevrolet car, changed the plates and took it to a garage where a secret compartment was fitted in the boot into which weapons could also be stuffed to get them past Soviet checkpoints as he headed out to Lower Austria. Across Europe and the Middle East, gold ingots were dropped into lakes, guns hidden in caves and radio sets buried as part of these efforts. Some were dug up later. Some were not.

There were other distractions in Vienna, which would get Cavendish into trouble. 'My social activities at this time were devoted mainly to two of the young women working for the CIA, and I have to admit that coping with both of them at the same time diverted some of the energy that I should have been putting into intelligence,' he recalled. When not wooing the American girls, Cavendish would occasionally engage in his own bit of spying by taking a drive out of Vienna through the Russian zone of Austria to get to the British zone. His destination was a little pub by a river where he could go fishing. The route conveniently took him past the Soviet-controlled airport. At just that moment, his car engine would splutter and he would have to stop, lift up the bonnet and rummage around. While doing so, he would aim a long-range camera at the airfield and snap off as many shots as possible of the Soviet aircraft so that some poor soul in London could count whether there were any more or less than there had been the previous weekend and try to work out what that meant.

Scratch beneath the thin veneer of glamour and much of the routine work of MI6 was a form of glorified train-spotting – with a little plane- and boat-spotting thrown in. This was true from the service's inception in 1909 when its primary task was to gather intelligence on the German naval build-up as it recruited people to stroll around harbours. During the First World War, networks of agents behind enemy lines would watch coaches move down the rail tracks as they did their knitting. Drop one for a troop car, purl one for something else. Send the resultant pullover back for analysis. In postwar Vienna, the methods of intelligence gathering had changed only a little.

Recruiting agents was proving hard, so the next best thing was a defector coming over. Every defector from the Soviets, however lowly, was asked the same initial question. 'Did they have any knowledge of an impending attack on the West?' This was because it was the question asked again and again at Whitehall at the weekly meeting of Britain's intelligence chiefs. They demanded the answers from every Secret Service station in the field: 'are there signs of Russian preparations for war?'[50] This was the number-one requirement and the first question dealt with in the weekly summaries of current intelligence. The reason it was asked so often and so urgently at the start of the Cold War is that there was no hard intelligence to summarise. Britain was blind.

When it came to intelligence from inside the USSR, the US and UK both had absolutely nothing. Not one source. Not one agent. The Whitehall mandarins frequently expressed their frustration at the poverty of information as they struggled to understand how far Stalin was willing to push a crisis. A March 1946 Joint Intelligence Committee (JIC) analysis recorded that conclusions on Russian intentions were 'speculative' as 'we have practically no direct intelligence of a detailed factual or substantial nature, on conditions in the different parts of the Soviet Union, and none at all on the intentions, immediate or ultimate, of the Russian leaders'.[51] MI6 had been banned from running agents against an ally during the war and the ban remained in place after the war, much to the frustration of officers who were itching to try.[52]

The blindness was especially painful because it was in sharp contrast to the all-seeing eye that the service had provided in the Second World War. The reputation of MI6 had been salvaged by the box that the Chief hand-delivered to the Prime Minister. Inside it was intelligence derived from the breaking of the German codes (such as those generated by the Enigma machine) at Bletchley Park. That information allowed Britain to get inside German intentions and operations and turn their agents back against them as part of the famous Double-Cross System. But as the gaze shifted from one enemy to another, it lost all focus. The Soviet Union was a giant black hole out of which no intelligence was to come for well over a decade until the combination of satellites and the first spies provided an initial glimpse. Without that insight, train-spotting and snapping pictures of airfields was the only fall-back.

The threat of the Red Army steamrollering into Western Europe was ever present in those first years of the Cold War, before nuclear-tipped missiles and mutually assured destruction. Fear and insecurity were heightened by ignorance. Because of the reliance on scraps and morsels, intelligence estimates were way off the mark. In 1947, the Joint Intelligence Committee thought the Soviets had an army of 170 divisions which could reach the Atlantic coast in forty days while also seizing the whole of the Middle East. In reality at least half those divisions existed only on paper.[53] But no one knew that. The fear that at any moment the Soviets could invade was visceral and real, and the desire to know about it was urgent. If those divisions were to head west some would come through Austria. MI6 was asked to construct an elaborate tripwire to give as much warning as possible of any sign they might be on the move.

The network of train-spotters had been established after the war by MI6's station chief in Vienna, George Kennedy Young, one of the service's most aggressive operators. A tall, independent-minded Scot with red hair and a sharp intellect, Young had served with intelligence in Italy in the Second World War and after a brief spell in journalism had been recruited by an old friend from St Andrews University. Vienna was to mark the beginning of his rapid rise up the ranks of the Secret Service and nurture a profound hatred for Communism which would later draw him to the political right.

Young had a taste for bravura operations, even if they involved a little risk. 'Keeping the Russians annoyed is rather an important part of intelligence work,' he later said. 'We are trying to breed insecurity and uncertainty about their own people.'[54] In Vienna, he learnt that the Germans had carried out photographic reconnaissance of the Soviet Union and that the valuable information had been buried in the Soviet zone of Austria right next to a Red Army checkpoint. He organised for a newsagent run by his team to send its delivery van to the checkpoint and drop off a copy of a girlie magazine to the guard at the post. While the guard thumbed through its pages, the former

Luftwaffe officer who had originally buried the photographic plates frantically dug them up and stowed them in a secret compartment in the back of the van before quickly driving off.[55] 'The professional skill of espionage', Young later wrote, 'is the exploitation of human weakness.'[56]

As head of station, Young's main task was to take a strategic overview. He favoured action to confront Soviet aggression. He would complain that the Foreign Office and politicians were far too cautious when his agents reported that the Soviets were using their proxy secret services to bring Czechoslovakia and Hungary under their heel. 'We were not prepared to take the minimal risks of exploiting internal weaknesses in the Soviet Bloc by active political warfare,' he later recalled. 'In autumn of 1947 it was apparent that the next Communist take-over would be in Czechoslovakia, but nothing was done to bolster up the will of those Czechs who might have resisted what was in fact a skilfully conducted bluff.'[57]

Stalin was reasserting his authority at home and abroad, determined to show that he would not be cowed. Nothing was more dangerous, he thought, than the hint of weakness. Stalin's advantage was a deluge of intelligence about his opponents. This, if it had been adroitly handled, could have allowed him to calibrate even more successfully his mix of pressure and bluff to maximum effect, to know when to push and when to back down. Stalin did not want a war but, as Churchill had said, he wanted the fruits of war, a series of pliant buffer states across Eastern Europe. Crackdowns, purges and coups would deliver Soviet control of Hungary, Czechoslovakia and Romania in the years after the war.

Austria lived in fear of being next. At first, the Soviets had co-operated hesitantly with the other occupiers. But when the Communist Party was trounced in elections in November 1945, the Soviets responded with a slow squeeze, particularly of Vienna, where they controlled all the road and rail access points including to the airports.[58] By 1948 tension was rising. The city watched fearfully as the Soviets blockaded Berlin. CIA officers began preparing escape plans involving donning lederhosen and walking through the Viennese woods.[59] British officers drew up top-secret plans to confront a putsch with military force, leading to arguments about whether such plans were realistic.[60] Britain's military had begun to push for Special Operations in the form of propaganda and the spreading of rumours to try and undermine Soviet influence in Austria and fuel anti-Russian sentiment.[61] Young had tried to recruit agents within Austria's Communist movement and wanted to send Czechoslovak and Hungarian refugees back home to work their way up the ranks of their Communist parties.[62] By the end of 1948, his agents reported that the Kremlin seemed to be pulling back from its most aggressive revolutionary activity in Europe, partly in the face of a tougher line from the West over the Berlin blockade. Young's progress in planting agents was slow. Not many people were willing to sacrifice the best years of their lives to infiltrate Communist parties.[63]

Young had a staff of about twenty officers and secretaries, most of them, he knew, blown to the Russians.[64] Even though it was given extra resources, the MI6 station in Austria struggled to keep up with the demands placed on it. MI6 stations do not decide their own priorities. These are agreed back in London by the different government departments, based on what intelligence they are seeking. By 1953, there were a total of nineteen different 'Top Priority' requirements for intelligence, ranging from Soviet order of battle to intelligence on individuals travelling to the UK. Further down the list were another thirty-nine requirements. The station could 'barely cope with responsibilities', officials noted.[65]

If Young sat at the top of the intelligence tree and Cavendish in the middle, at the bottom were the grunts from Field Security who carried out the mundane tasks. During the Soviet military's spring and autumn manoeuvres, they would wait for a tip-off from a contact who worked on the railways and then stand along the line to count carriages go past in the middle of the night. When two Field Security men went to check out the registration numbers of vehicles in one boxcar, its door was suddenly opened and they were forced to hide behind a hoarding. The Red Army soldiers who emerged proceeded to urinate in the dark against the hoarding, prompting a complicated expenses claim for dry cleaning.

The day-to-day debriefing of the stream of desperate defectors and frontier crossers, men like Jan Mašek, was the domain of Field Security. Up to 160 individuals a month were picked up and every possible scrap of intelligence extracted.[66] The identity documents they had brought with them were also valuable as MI6's forgers could use them as models to create their own sets for people being sent back. When defectors had been sucked dry, they would be put into a 'ratline' out of the country. The British smuggled them out of Vienna past the Soviets to the British zone and the Semmering Pass on a local train. Then they would be housed in a pub until Field Security Graz could pick them up and take them to a Displaced Persons camp where they would wait – often for a year or two – to get a visa and a boat ride from Italy to a new life in Britain, North America or Australia. The chance to see the West up close in Austria provided temptations for Soviet soldiers which the US and UK encouraged. In one twelve-month period, the US handled a hundred Soviet soldiers and officers.[67] US Army intelligence ran one ratline for defecting Red Army soldiers by using a corrupt, fascist Yugoslav priest in the Vatican who was willing to provide visas to South America for deserving Catholics if they were willing to pay $1,500. A motley crew of Croatian war criminals, Nazi collaborators and Red Army soldiers scurried on to freighters bound for Latin America.[68] The same ratline would later be used to get Klaus Barbie, the 'Butcher of Lyons' who had tortured, killed and sent countless people to Auschwitz, off to Bolivia via Austria after he had worked with the Americans. British intelligence also protected Nazis like Horst Kopkow and Friedrich Buchardt who had blood on their hands.[69]

The biggest ratline operating in Austria was also the most problematic for the British. Up to 2,000 Jewish refugees were arriving in Vienna every month from the East in early 1946. Many ended up on board boats from Yugoslavia and Italy and went to fight the British to force them out of Palestine. British intelligence responded by placing spies among the refugees in order to look at these routes and try to close them down.[70] Late in the evening of 19 March 1948, thirty to forty kilos of dynamite exploded at the Park Hotel, where many British officers, including Cavendish, would stay.[71] It followed an attack on the Hotel Sacher a few months earlier and the discovery of a rucksack bomb buried by tracks near where a British military train passed.[72] The suspects were the Jews bringing their fight in the Middle East into Middle Europe. MI6 did not have clean hands either. Approved at the highest political level, it ran Operation Embarrass to blow up ships in European ports due to take Jewish refugees to Palestine. MI6 even planted fake documents in Casanova, a Viennese nightclub believed to be under KGB control (the same club was frequented by Graham Greene while he wrote *The Third Man* and it became Harry Lime's haunt).[73] The documents falsely claimed that the Jewish refugees from the East were providing MI6 with valuable intelligence, in the hope it would persuade the Russians to stem the flow.[74]

Britain's closest ally was not altogether helpful with this problem. The Jewish head of station for the Israeli secret service Mossad LeAliyah Bet, who was masterminding the ratlines using forged Red Cross documents, sheltered in the American zone where he worked under cover as a newspaper reporter.[75] Some American officers conducted clandestine training for the Jewish refugees and there was a semi-official policy of turning a blind eye to Jewish activity including even arms shipments.[76] Jewish groups also began hunting war criminals. One group called the Avengers used British uniforms, documents and vehicles to get inside the POW camps holding SS officers to exact their vengeance.[77]

Scavengers of many different stripes hunted in the bleak human wasteland of the refugee camps. One of the most remarkable was a forceful twenty-three-year-old British woman called Daphne Park.[78] Where Field Security looked for those coming from the East, Park sought out the remains of Nazism and its secrets. Park had grown up on a farm in Africa, digesting the great Edwardian writers of British imperial spy fiction like Kipling and Buchan, and had decided she wanted to be a spy. War had opened up new paths for women and, with a fierce ambition and a willingness to talk directly to her superiors, she had carved out a role with the Special Operations Executive training French resistance agents. She had been rejected by MI6 when hostilities ended and so she joined the closest thing she could find, a body called Field Intelligence Agency Technical. That dull bureaucratic title masked its job of tracking down war criminals in the refugee camps and finding valuable scientists. Its progenitor was a group called 30AU founded during the war by Ian Fleming, a Naval Intelligence officer with an active imagination who maintained an interest in Park's FIAT as it came into being.[79] In the first year or two of occupation British intelligence hunted those who had run the concentration camps, including doctors who had carried out experiments on the living. The woefully under-resourced team would chase down rumours of Nazis holding clandestine meetings in restaurants or of Martin Bormann having been spotted living in the 12th district under an assumed name.[80] One professor committed suicide before he could be handed over for trial in Nuremberg.[81]

It did not take long before the search for Nazi scientists who could help in the future superseded the desire to deliver justice for the past.[82] There were few rules as each of the four occupying powers raced to grab the individuals behind Germany's industrial and scientific advances, many of whom had become members of the SS. Their secrets would be shared openly with commercial companies back home.[83] The top targets were experts on biological and chemical warfare, electronics, guided weapons, aerodynamics and underwater warfare.[84]

Daphne Park had two half-colonels and a major who were specialists in rockets working for her along with a sergeant major and twenty drivers, as well as a terrifying woman from the Auxiliary Territorial Service who bullied Park mercilessly but licked her into shape.[85] Park's lack of German led to a few problems. She was told of one professor who had worked on guided missiles and was now living in the depths of a forest in a Hansel-and-Gretel-type cottage. When she arrived, he proved very excited to see her and enthusiastically started drawing diagrams and talking about flights. Park picked up the word 'Blumen' which she thought meant flowers. So she woke up her dozing sergeant and told him to listen properly and translate. He explained that unfortunately the professor was studying the flight path of the bumble-bee rather than the V2 rocket.[86]

In Germany, where the battle for scientific secrets was fiercest, everyone played dirty. German industrialists were 'invited' to Britain and then interned and not allowed out until they had spilled commercial secrets to their British rivals.[87] The Americans were more than happy to take on for their own rocket programme men who had developed the V2 rockets that had bombed London. In Austria, there were desperate attempts to get rocket scientists and research chemists out of the Russian zone before the Russians got their hands on them. 'It was quite important to get there fast because if the Russians got there first they simply kidnapped them and took them away and they were never seen again,' recalled Park.[88]

Vienna was a lawless city in which the police could not always be trusted and in which the rules of the Cold War espionage game had yet to be codified. As a result, the city was known to spies as 'the shooting gallery' – a body found in a park or floating in the Danube was an everyday occurrence. Amid the darkened alleys of Vienna, one fear in particular haunted not just those involved in the secret world but ordinary citizens. And that was kidnap. It had begun immediately after the war when people suspected of being involved in certain German units or helping the Nazis disappeared (one woman who had allegedly been a Gestapo informer was kidnapped from her apartment rolled in a rug). As the Soviets lost control of the Viennese police, the trend intensified for targeted kidnapping.[89] By 1948 the spate of kidnappings had become a hot political issue with up to three people a day disappearing.[90] Increasingly the victims were those suspected of being spies for the West. One Austrian public official was forced into a waiting car on his way home in December 1947 and never seen again. An English university student was kidnapped after a spurned lover told the Soviets she was the mastermind of an alleged ring of British intelligence agents.[91] In all, 400 people were kidnapped in three years, most by the Soviets, although the Americans were not averse to kidnapping people in the Soviet zone and taking them west.[92]

The US and UK were particularly worried about the pattern of kidnapping, which suggested that Moscow was looking for help in building an atomic bomb.[93] America's bomb was its only counter to the perceived conventional strength of the Red Army. Intelligence officers were sent out with the specific remit of finding out what scientists the Soviets were after as a clue to understanding their progress. MI6 had found intelligence that the Soviets were mining uranium near the Czech border with Germany and there were reports of further deposits sought in Bulgaria, leading to urgent intelligence-gathering operations to investigate further. One of the more popular of the multitude of swindles employed by those on the make in Vienna were those of the 'uranium salesmen' who swamped Britain and America with 'samples' wrapped up in cotton stuffed into pill bottles and the promise of more.[94] The failure to predict the Soviet atomic test of 1949 only increased paranoia about what else lay unknown. What London and Washington would only slowly realise was that the Soviets had help from inside the West's own atomic programme, thanks to Klaus Fuchs and Bruno Pontecorvo, whose Communist pasts had been overlooked or ignored.[95]

Daphne Park watched the Russians' ruthlessness with horror but also with growing fascination. 'Many of the scientists were being kidnapped by the Russians. It was this that made me want to learn Russian and serve in the Soviet Union, and see what it was really like there,' she later recalled. 'I watched them swallow up Czechs, Poles – people I had known. I wanted to meet and understand the people who lived under such a regime.'[96] She would get her chance. Daphne Park's stint in Vienna was short-lived. One day a woman turned up and explained that her friend, who happened to be a Russian major, was being sent home but he was reluctant to return. Would Daphne Park see him? She went to pay a visit to the members of the MI6 station with whom she occasionally worked. They were extremely interested. But they had some trouble finding an escape route fast enough. Daphne used her military contacts to get the Russian out. That got her noticed. George Kennedy Young decided she had what it took. In 1948, in a brief nod to the modern world which would not be repeated for another two decades, she became one of the only women to be allowed to join MI6. She was made the stay-behind officer for Germany, Austria and Switzerland. In a small office, under particularly tight security, she acted as the point of contact for the stations, including the work of Anthony Cavendish, who respected her as capable, if a touch 'unfeminine'. Her year and a half in Vienna was formative for a woman who would eventually rise to become a controller at MI6. Decades later when she was asked where her deep-seated and vociferous hatred of Communism and the Soviet regime – which she always called simply 'the enemy' – came from, she would answer, 'I had seen them on the streets of Vienna and how they behaved and I felt anger.'[97]

As the Red Army had driven west at the end of the war, a vast tide of refugees had pushed before it. And then as the Iron Curtain began to fall, thousands more came. Across Austria at least a million

Poles, Ukrainians, Jews, Yugoslavs, Cossacks and White Russians had settled into huge Displaced Persons camps. Thousands had been collaborators with the Nazi regime, including war criminals who had been part of SS units drawn from anti-Communist elements in local populations. Others were deserters from the Red Army. Others simply did not want to live under Communism. Some, like the White Russians, had been fleeing and fighting the Communists since the Revolution of 1917. The Soviets wanted them all back and, to their later shame, initially the Allies agreed, shoving many of them into boxcars for transportation to the Russians.[98] Some Cossacks killed themselves and their children rather than return. The Soviet Union also sent out their feared SMERSH (the name meaning 'death to spies') counter-intelligence teams to hunt for collaborators and enemies of the state. In one case it even appears that a British officer sold out a group of White Russian generals in Austria to SMERSH in exchange for fourteen kilos of gold.[99]

Vienna's role as a refuge, albeit an insecure one, for those fleeing Communism made it home to a bewildering series of front organisations representing the differing émigré groups. MI6 and the CIA would work closely with these as they scoured the camps in search of agents and intelligence from the East. One of these groups was based at an MI6 safe house at Weyringergasse, not far from the border with the Russian zone. It had the feel of a busy railway station with a constant bustle of young, idealistic Hungarians heading back and forth over the border. Some acted as couriers, others were gathering information and contacting friends, others organising resistance groups. At the centre of the web was Béla Bajomi, a Hungarian who had fled by clinging to the underside of a railway carriage after the Second World War to begin working with MI6.[100] As with other émigré groups, they ran their own intelligence-gathering networks and had knocked at the door of the CIA and MI6 asking for help and offering assistance, promising that the local population was ready to rise up. The Soviets were obsessed with these émigré groups and expended enormous amounts of effort in targeting them. Occasionally, they succeeded. In autumn 1947, a whole MI6-sponsored network in Hungary was rolled up and a hundred people arrested after an 'unfortunate mishap'.[101]

One evening Bajomi received an urgent message from a Hungarian colleague who said he was heading for a safe house. Next morning there was no sign of him. An elderly Austrian taxi-driver said he had seen someone being shoved into a car with Russian number plates. An unknown voice telephoned and asked for Bajomi two days later. The caller said the Russians had been unable to get his friend to their zone and offered information to help organise a rescue. He told Bajomi to meet him one block from the Russian zone. Bajomi took a loaded revolver. He arrived just before 11. In the silence and gloom, he walked past bomb-damaged, baroque flats to a drab grey building. All the windows were dark except two on the top floor. He went through heavy oak double doors into a corridor, lit dimly by a yellowish light, up the staircase to the top floor where the lights were on, drawing his revolver. As he approached the door, he heard Russian voices and began to move backwards to make a run for it. The door crashed open and uniformed Russians ran towards him. Others approached from the other end of the corridor. Two men grabbed him and hit him in the face. A hand was placed over his mouth. A voice said in Hungarian, 'Now we have got you as well. You are the real prize.'

He was bundled into a car and taken back to Hungary. Later, in a Budapest prison, he recounted the story of his capture to members of the resistance network he had helped organise. Many of them were barely out of their teens – his son was one of them. They had been providing the bread-and-butter, low-grade intelligence that MI6 was so eager to consume. But their letters – written with secret ink and posted to the safe house in Vienna – had been intercepted. They had risked their lives to establish the position of a bus terminal, the registration of a Soviet vehicle or the production figures for milk and butter and they were now in jail. Paul Gorka had been passing on details of heavy industry. He had recruited colleagues, friends, relatives and his own girlfriend. In jail, some said they had been ambushed as they crossed the Iron Curtain. One spoke of a British Field Security officer in a small village restaurant giving him a map and telling him to take a particular route. He found the Hungarian Secret Police waiting for him. One day Gorka saw Béla Bajomi through the small inspection hole of his cell. 'We and all of us, here and abroad, have been betrayed by members of the British Intelligence Service at a very high level,' the frail man with blond-white hair and a blue-and-white-striped prisoner's uniform told him. In April 1951, Bajomi was executed, a prison guard gloating about it to his son. The CIA also found that most of its agents were rounded up within a few hundred feet of the barbed wire in Hungary. The remaining few who made it over provided almost no intelligence.[102]

The Americans were newcomers in the intelligence game. But their rising influence, compared to a weary, near-bankrupt Britain, was quickly evident in Vienna, whether in small ways like the ready supplies of chocolate and cigarettes provided to agents or the much more significant largesse of the Marshall Plan, which provided billions of dollars to help reconstruct Europe. MI6 officers noted that in the competition for agents the Americans were 'paying enormous sums as retainers'.[103] Occupation had brought competition for information, and competition drove the market. One Viennese hotel porter worked simultaneously for money for the American, British, Soviet and French services while also working on the side for free for his own country.[104]

The CIA was young but persistent and determined. Even if it was initially naive, it learnt fast. Like the British, it was also desperate. 'What you have to remember is that in the beginning, we knew nothing,' Richard Helms, the official responsible for the region and a future head of the CIA, remembered later. 'Our knowledge of what the other side was up to, their intentions, their capabilities, was nil, or next to it.' Helms later reckoned that at least half the information on the USSR and Eastern Europe in the CIA's files was fabricated and that the Berlin and Vienna stations had become 'factories of fake intelligence'.[105] Until 1952 the CIA did not have a single Russian-speaking case officer in town.[106] 'The Austrian station has one real mission and a bucket of marginal responsibilities, many of them bilge,' Helms told one officer on his way to Vienna. 'Your job is to recruit Russians. Until we've done that, we've failed. I don't care how many reports the station sends in on the Czech Communist Party or Hungarian order of battle. Our basic job is to penetrate the Soviet establishment – that's the only way we'll get the answers the White House is screaming for.'[107]

It was in Vienna that the CIA finally managed their first serious penetration into Russian intelligence anywhere in the world, their first chance to run an agent who was willing to remain in place and provide information rather than just defect. On New Year's Day 1953, a tense man approached a car carrying the American Vice-Consul in the international sector and asked for directions. He dropped a note before leaving. It read: 'I am a Soviet officer. I wish to meet with an American officer with the object of offering certain services.'[108] It offered a location for a meeting and a fall-back if that failed. CIA surveillance teams staked out the location for a blind date and found a stocky officer from a peasant background called Pyotr Popov who worked for Russian military intelligence, the GRU. His motivations were hardly high-minded – he was lonely and out of place, conscious of his illiterate background. He also liked to drink. A Serbian woman from the refugee camps who had been his agent had become his mistress and needed an abortion (the CIA would eventually pay for three terminations). A CIA psychologist would later describe him as a 'delayed adolescent' who had found the opportunity to pursue his impulses amid the relative freedoms of Vienna and its exposure to the West.[109]

The CIA sent out George Kisevalter to handle him, a bear of a man whose fondness for a drink would later get him into trouble. He had been born in Russia but his family had never returned after the Revolution. He was despatched to Vienna where, after a nervous first meeting, he quickly built on a natural empathy with Popov. 'The only thing is treat me like a human being,' Popov told Kisevalter.[110] The two would meet a hundred times in the next six years. Popov had little information on the Soviet leadership or its intentions but did pass on voluminous details of Soviet operations in Vienna including the names of many of the seventy KGB officers stationed there, allowing a huge chart to be drawn up. Photographs were added to the wall (in their absence many sources when asked what someone looked like would normally reply 'like a Russian').[111] CIA headquarters at one point asked the team to have Popov organise a resistance group among fellow Soviets. It was an absurd idea that would have risked exposing his work and underscored the still amateurish approach to running agents adopted by Western intelligence agencies. Popov refused angrily, and for years the phrase 'a small, tightly knit resistance group' became code in the CIA office in Vienna for 'another wildly unrealistic idea from headquarters'.[112]

Vienna was so much smaller than Berlin that rival intelligence teams would often come to know each other by sight, literally bumping into each other in the alleys. Sometimes British Field Security teams would stop at traffic lights and see next to them a team of Russian footsloggers (as their surveillance men were known). There would be a nod of the head between the driver of a smart, new Soviet BMW and that of a clapped-out British Austin. It was only a short walk around the Innere Stadt's Ring Road from the British base at the Sacher to the less cosy and more imposing Imperial Hotel which, along with the Grand Hotel opposite, was the base for the Soviets and the KGB.

Everything was done by the British to get a sense of what was going on beyond the marble and chandeliered reception of the Imperial. At one point, two Austrian cleaners were bribed to bring out all the rubbish, but the Russians soon spotted the danger. A photo-observation point was set up in an office opposite to snap anyone emerging and add them to a bulging file that an intelligence officer would frequently thumb through. One New Year's Eve, some of the junior British Field Security team thought they would share a bit of the festive joy with their Soviet counterparts. They broke protocol and called the Soviet High Command in the Imperial to wish them a happy new year. Their jollity was met with a short reply in a thick Russian accent: 'Don't provoke.' And the line went dead.

One of those KGB officers, an opposite number to Cavendish at the time he was in Vienna, would play the starring role in one of the most tortuous chapters in the history of the British Secret Service. For those coming from the West, Vienna was drab and dreary, but as Anatoly Golitsyn arrived by train, all he could see were well-dressed, happy-looking people and shops – with no queues outside – filled with goods.[113] Golitsyn, possessed of a powerful belief in his own abilities, had been born in August 1926 in a small town in the Ukraine. He had grown up with pigs and chickens roaming around the quiet dusty streets. But when he was four the great famine, heightened by Stalin's collectivisation of farms, left corpses rotting amid the cherry trees and led his family to Moscow.

Too young to fight in the war, Golitsyn had joined the SMERSH academy in September 1945. Like his British counterparts, he had been inspired by stories of heroes hunting down enemy agents. He had been trained in surveillance, the use of informers and the favourite Soviet ploy of 'provocation'. This involved having a Soviet officer pretend to be, say, a British officer in order to meet a Soviet suspected of dangerous tendencies and see what the Soviet would say (in Berlin, the Soviets went so far as to build a replica American base at a castle with fake Americans in uniforms who could speak English to try and trap their own people).[114] In October 1946, Golitsyn joined the Colony Department of the KGB. This spied on Soviet officials abroad, including ambassadors, to check their loyalty. Vienna was one of the hardest places in which to prevent unauthorised contact with the enemy, so almost everyone was asked to watch everyone else right down to the chauffeurs informing on their passengers. One senior counsellor at the Embassy was suspected of being a British spy and put under extensive surveillance.[115]

Golitsyn's first job had been to run agents within the Russian émigré community, planting individuals plucked from the refugee camps within different groups. A prime target was the anti-Soviet, Russian émigré grouping, the NTS, and its local leader Valeri Tremmel. Every month or two his agents would travel by train to different provincial towns in the Soviet zone where Golitsyn would pick them up in a car for debriefing. In the spring of 1954, a senior KGB boss arrived to explain that the KGB was going to step up its work against the NTS by eliminating its leaders. One of Golitsyn's agents was chosen to administer a drug to Tremmel, brought out from the KGB's special laboratory. The agent and his wife were bugged in order to make sure that they were reliable. The agent managed to give two drugged sweets to Tremmel and he was bundled into a car and driven to Baden.

The KGB Residency in Vienna was divided into fourteen sections, and in September 1954 Golitsyn was reassigned to target the British. Among the notes in his predecessor's file he found an old letter from the head of the KGB British Department requesting the kidnapping of Peter Smollett to answer charges that he had been working for MI6. Most likely this was part of a purge against agents of Jewish origins that Stalin had begun but which was abandoned after his death.[116] Another report referred to an abortive attempt to recruit a young English woman who worked in British censorship in Vienna.

She was having an affair with a Soviet lieutenant under KGB control. One evening they were interrupted in bed by a KGB officer threatening blackmail. She told him to get lost. Golitsyn found few other usable agents apart from one driver for Field Security in Vienna whom he kept going.

In February 1954, the KGB in Vienna was rocked by a defection. Major Pyotr Deriabin walked across the city to the Americans. In a panic, the Soviets put armed patrols in the medieval Innere Stadt to look for him. A CIA officer who carried out a quick initial debrief of Deriabin immediately appreciated his value – including the fact that both of them were running the same Chief Engineer of the Soviet military forces as their agent.[117] Deriabin was placed in a coffin-like hot-water tank which some holes for air bored into it. The tank – labelled machinery – was packed on the baggage cart of the Mozart Express train which ran out of the city and through the Soviet zone and into the American zone of Austria. Guards were told to shoot if the Russians tried to force their way on to the train (they were not supposed to board, although neither was the train supposed to be used for intelligence work).[118] The head of the KGB's German–Austrian Department arrived in a fury after the defection. He warned staff that the Americans would 'launch a massive effort to approach, blackmail, recruit or even kidnap our officers and agents'. Purges, fear and denunciations were sweeping through Soviet intelligence. No one could be trusted. MI6 decided to try and encourage more defections, even of low-level soldiers, to heighten the distrust. 'What appears to be a scruffy malcontent may well be the executioner of one or more senior Army or MVD [intelligence] officers whose demise, or banishment, will weaken the Soviet machine by undermining its authority,' suggested a top-secret memo which reached the Chief of MI6.[119]

The Soviets recruited everyone they could from businessmen to barmaids. Clerical and administration staff working in the Western zones would be approached if they had a relative on the Soviet side. Even if they had no access to secrets they could help identify possible targets who had vulnerabilities in relation to money or sex. A few of these staff reported the approach back to the British or Americans who then tried to turn them back against the Soviets to feed false information.[120] The KGB also ran a campaign of seduction in Vienna employing young, handsome East Europeans who spoke good English and had fancy apartments and spending money. British personnel were explicitly warned of such dangers.[121] In one case a secretary to the US Deputy Chief of Staff for Operations was seduced by a man twenty years her junior. 'What about all those officers here whose wives haven't arrived or are still back home who have been shacking up with every woman in town?' she said when confronted by an officer, pointing out that her boss had had an Austrian girlfriend before his wife had arrived and that she herself had not passed on any secrets. She was still sent home.[122] US military intelligence also knew how to exploit human weakness. Operation Claptrap targeted Soviet soldiers who had become infected with venereal disease and persuaded them to betray secrets in return for medication and to avoid the punishment of being despatched back to the USSR.[123]

Although the Soviets blanketed the city with their spies, the British had one prime, unmatched source. But it was not a human agent. If you walked down Aspangstrasse in 1950 near the main railway freight line, you would have found an innocuous-looking boarded-up shop. Walk to the rear and you would find a bell, a steel door and a spy-hole. Behind were three British soldiers with sten guns. Past them, stairs went down to the cellar and into the heart of one of MI6's most secret and successful operations of the early Cold War.

The operation was the brainchild of the man who had taken over from George Kennedy Young as head of the MI6 station in Vienna. Peter Lunn had captained the British Olympic ski team in Bavaria in 1936 and his father Sir Arnold Lunn had established the Lunn Poly travel agents (occasionally put to use by MI6). A slightly built man, he was quiet and spoke in a soft voice with a lisp. Those outward qualities masked an intense, highly effective operator who was as zealous and fervent in his Catholic faith as he was in his anti-Communism. According to a colleague, somewhere in a file is a note in Lunn's spidery handwriting reading: 'Communists and Communism are vile. It is the duty of all members of the Service to stamp upon them at every possible opportunity.'[124] When he took over, Lunn knew that much of his intelligence was low-grade chit-chat from agents and defectors. He was frustrated that MI6 had yet to penetrate the decision-making level of the Soviets in Austria. One day while reading reports from an Austrian official, he noticed that the cables through which the Red Army HQ in Vienna communicated to Eastern Austria ran through the British and French sectors of Vienna.[125] Perhaps there was a technical solution to his problem. He brought a mining engineer and telephone expert from the General Post Office to discuss a plan to tunnel towards the cables and then tap them. Lunn approached the Ambassador in Vienna who gave it a quiet nod without sending the idea to the Foreign Office for approval, fearing that they would say no. 'I couldn't look at myself if there'd been an invasion and I denied the chance of getting the information,' Ambassador Harold Caccia told Lunn.[126]

Soldiers from the Royal Engineers dug the tunnel and were then promptly posted to Singapore to prevent any loose talk. There was nearly an early disaster. A team carrying the recording equipment had been due to arrive by train in the British district. The reception party waited forlornly. A phone call came in explaining that the men appeared to have got out at the wrong station and seemed to be in the Russian zone. 'Don't move, don't look at anyone, don't talk to anyone. In the meantime don't even breathe and we will be out in half an hour,' said the duty officer as he raced over. They found the two engineers in British uniform on the platform with cases full of listening equipment.[127]

That equipment was taken down to the Aspangstrasse cellar. In the twilight a visitor would have found half a dozen men sitting in front of a tunnel about five feet beneath the street. Wires led to the type of switchboard you would see in an old telephone exchange with a series of sockets in which you could insert jack plugs. One of those sitting in the dank cellar with headphones clasped to his ears was a teenage private named Rodric Braithwaite.[128] He had failed his officer exams but made it into the Intelligence Corps by the skin of his teeth. The fact that he had originally been heading for Cambridge to study Russian and French suggested an aptitude for languages which led to his being assigned to work on the tunnel as part of a team of thirteen men – almost all eighteen or nineteen years old. The team worked twenty-four hours a day in shifts. There was little awareness among them of whether it was day or night, and only an underpowered light illuminated the wax cylinders on which their work was recorded. One of the perks was a steady supply of chocolate and cigarettes. The use of the latter coupled with the lack of ventilation in their subterranean lair led some of the inhabitants to nickname it 'Smokey Joe's'.

The eavesdroppers, who did not speak the language, had to listen out for what sounded like Russian voices and then begin recording on the cylinders. 'Most of us didn't know what was Russian and what was Czech. God knows how many mistakes we made, as nobody told us,' recalls Braithwaite. They were led by a captain whom Braithwaite thought drank too much. Meanwhile, the Captain thought Braithwaite posed a security risk because he insisted on reading the leftish *New Statesman* magazine – although Braithwaite also wondered if some of the animosity between the two men might originate in the Captain having once played in an orchestra conducted by Braithwaite's father. After six months, Braithwaite shifted to interview refugees, occasionally brushing up against the spies. That experience left him with a distrust of the betrayals intrinsic to the secret world, so when he was approached at Cambridge, he declined a career in MI6, preferring the Foreign Office. He would carry with him from Vienna a scepticism of spies that would last all the way through the Cold War to its dying days when he was ambassador to Moscow and then Chair of the Joint Intelligence Committee.

The Vienna Tunnel was a success. The headphoned men could hear all Soviet military calls and long-distance civilian calls going out to Bucharest, Sofia, Prague and Budapest. It provided a wealth of material on Soviet military activity. One crucial conversation it picked up was between two Russian soldiers talking about which troops were going to be demobilised. This meant that a war was not on the cards. The tunnel in the cellar lasted until 1951 when the Soviets moved their lines, but more tunnels were built and would survive through to the end of occupation in 1955; one was underneath a bogus jeweller's shop, another located in the suburban house of a British official.

The Americans were not informed at first of this British success, but they had begun to work on their own plan. So Lunn's successor from 1950, Andrew King, brought them into the secret. King had known Vienna from the 1930s when he had travelled around looking for locations as part of Korda's London Film Productions, cover for his role in MI6. He retained an air of flamboyance which might have suited the film industry well but made him rather conspicuous as a spy. He drove around in a fancy green Jaguar, often accompanied by his Pekingese dog.[129] He was both gay and a former Communist. Neither feature had been impediments to Secret Service work in the past, although they would eventually cause trouble for him.

Every morning the product of the tunnel team was picked up in a laundry basket and taken over to the MI6 station at the Schönbrunn barracks. So much material was produced by this operation that the two Russian-speakers based there were soon swamped and a backlog of months' worth of tapes grew. It was decided to send the tapes to London to be processed. The tapes were flown back three times a week by a special RAF plane and then taken to the new Section Y. The translation was undertaken in the grand setting of an MI6 office at 2 Carlton Gardens off Pall Mall by a curious mix of the children of English merchants who had worked in St Petersburg and émigré Russians, as well as some Polish army officers left over from the war. 'There was plenty of Slav temperament and moodiness about and it required a great deal of tact and careful handling to keep the peace and the machine running smoothly,' remembers the MI6 officer who became deputy head of the team from September 1953. That officer was handsome and his rather exotic background, mixing Jewish, Turkish and Dutch, not to mention a recent experience as a hostage in Korea, led to his being seen as a 'pet' by the secretaries in the office. He was anything but tame.

Just after six o'clock one evening in October 1953, that officer took a leisurely walk through Soho to Oxford Street. He had a cup of tea and some cake and then caught the Underground at Charing Cross. When the Northern Line train came in he boarded at the last moment. At the next station he jumped off just as the doors were closing. He let two trains pass and got on the third. He alighted at Belsize Park and walked towards the exit clutching a newspaper nervously in his left hand. The streets were quiet. 'A man came slowly out of the fog walking towards me,' he wrote many years later, 'also carrying a newspaper in his left hand. In his grey, soft felt hat and smart grey raincoat he seemed almost part of the fog.' The man, a Russian, had had few problems evading MI5 surveillance in London. The KGB knew from its sources in MI5 exactly what procedures were used to monitor the Embassy. It even listened to MI5's radio communications and knew when its watchers had their breakfast.[130] Even so, a Russian intelligence officer was trained to spend five hours on foot and public transport to evade surveillance. The MI6 man handed over a folded piece of paper. It contained, he said, the precise details of the telephone tapping and microphone operations in Vienna, as well as other microphone operations undertaken elsewhere. The two men agreed to meet in a month's time. An hour later, George Blake was home having dinner with his mother. His overwhelming feeling was of relief. He had passed the point of no return. He would later claim that during his time in Korea his own religious faith had been supplanted by a new faith in Communism. 'I came to the conclusion that I was no longer fighting on the right side,' he would say. There was another, more human reason that Blake never mentioned. He had been dating a secretary from the office. Her father, a traditional type, made a remark along the lines that he would never have a daughter of his marrying some foreign Jew. Later in Seoul when another officer paid a visit to the station, Blake again encountered the casual anti-Semitism that was endemic in much of the English establishment at the time. He never felt particularly British, perhaps because he was not particularly British, and with his capture in Korea a combination of alienation, idealism and sheer pragmatism had led to his offer to switch sides. And when MI6 and the CIA held a joint meeting to plan a far more ambitious tunnel in Berlin, Blake took the minutes. The British would bring their experience from Vienna, the Americans would bring the money, and, thanks to Blake, the KGB would know all about it.[131]

The KGB top brass decided to allow extensive communications from their colleagues in the Russian military to continue in Berlin, for a while at least, without telling them that they were being intercepted. This was because it was considered more important to preserve the secret of Blake's treachery – even if that meant allowing the CIA and MI6 to collect valuable intelligence – rather than risk his exposure by issuing a warning. When Blake was eventually transferred to a position where the trail would be harder to follow, the KGB decided to 'discover' the Berlin tunnel, making out that this had happened by chance. In Vienna too, belated warnings were given by Moscow to colleagues on the ground. In the spring of 1955 a letter from Moscow explained that British intelligence had been intercepting Soviet military telephone communications. Enclosed was a document of ninety to a hundred pages giving details of conversations between Soviet generals and other officers. The KGB Resident, or head of station, was told to show it to the chief of Soviet military counter-intelligence under strict conditions.[132] By that time, the tunnel's work had largely been done. Vienna's time at the frontline of the intelligence war was about to pass, although it would remain a playground for spies of all sides.

The Viennese had not expected a ten-year occupation in 1945. But the Russians blocked moves towards independence until Stalin's death in 1953. His successor Nikita Khrushchev accepted the notion of Austrian neutrality, a policy aimed at winning over Third World countries, and this opened the way for a treaty reviving an independent Austria signed in May 1955. The Cold War's final demarcation lines between East and West in Europe were being drawn.

The signing led to a final, frenetic burst of activity for the spies. Most had operated under cover of the occupation and knew they would have to depart. The CIA managed to pay off an estate agent helping a senior KGB officer find a house and had the property promptly wired for sound.[133] The KGB tried to place agents in positions of strategic influence in Austrian public life and buried 'burst' radio transmitters which could send compressed messages around the suburbs in plastic containers.[134] The departing powers all deposited their wares in preparation for the next war, which they still thought would be fought like the last. The KGB trained its men in surveillance, small arms and ju-jitsu before placing them deep under cover to prepare for 'partisan' activity.[135] It left caches of arms in villages across the Soviet zone as well as in a monastery and two ruined castles.[136] Britain and America buried modern weapons, explosives and money in underground caves as part of Operation Gladio, which co-ordinated activity across all of Western Europe. MI6 sent out officers to prepare caches and recruit agent networks to lead the resistance. 'It doesn't take much imagination to work out that the Russian army would have hunted us from pillar to post,' one of those MI6 men said decades later. 'It would have been a short but interesting life I suspect.'[137]

In October, a vast crowd gathered to cheer as each of the four flags which had hung over the Allied Control Commission building was lowered. The Soviet flag fell last. After ten years, the occupation was over. A few weeks later, the State Opera House, that symbol of Viennese pride, was reopened. Vienna had survived. The war had moved on. But the loyalties and betrayals nurtured in the crucible of Vienna were also moving on to play out on a larger stage.

2

THE COST OF BETRAYAL

A violent banging on his front door summoned Anthony Cavendish from a deep slumber. It was three in the morning. He
was MI6's liaison officer with the Royal Navy in Hamburg in the
British zone of Germany, a city out of which operations at the northern end of the Iron Curtain were run.[1] At the door he found one of
his radio operators in a visibly distressed state. There was a problem
that required his urgent attention. The previous night, Cavendish
and a fellow officer had taken three Baltic agents to the red-light
district of Hamburg. The men, plucked from refugee camps, had
been offered a last indulgence before embarking on a secret mission.
It should have been relatively safe since they had been led to a bar
in the Reeperbahn where the manager was an informant for Field
Security. When Cavendish had retired for the night, the men had still
been enjoying themselves, knocking back a peculiar German brandy
drink and talking to some over-made-up girls while they watched
the floor show. But the radio operator explained that, although two
of the agents had made it back to their own secluded safe house, the
third and the MI6 officer 'looking after him' had got into a fight.

Cavendish threw on some clothes and headed for the bar. He
found it smashed up. The police had taken everyone involved to the
station. Cavendish persuaded them to release his two men, but there
followed a long, painful post-mortem to ensure that the agents' cover
story as visiting businessmen had not been blown. This was the
inauspicious prelude to one of MI6's most aggressive and ill-fated
operations of the early Cold War, which, along with many others,
would be betrayed.

A day or so later, when the weather had improved, the agents were
taken down to a jetty at a nearby harbour. Waiting for them was a
German called Helmut Klose. During the war he had captained

E-boats which dropped Germans behind Russian lines to carry out acts of sabotage. He knew every nook and cranny of the stretch of coast along the Baltic. A German boat had been purchased by MI6 and taken back to Portsmouth to be kitted out with a new engine which offered fifty knots with barely a sound. Klose's cover was as part of the British Control Commission's Fishery Protection Service.

Cavendish's job had been to establish a safe house, look after the agents and liaise with the Royal Navy. His naval contact was Anthony Courtney, a bluff officer whose remarkable career would take him back and forth between Moscow and London, from the netherworld of intelligence to the bright lights of parliament, and end in disaster at the hands of the KGB. Courtney was perhaps unique among British intelligence officers in having donated blood to the Red Army.[2] His father had once sold machine tools to the Russians and would return from trips to the Soviet Union with beautifully carved wooden bears and books full of fairy stories. They were impenetrable to his son but had contributed to an abiding fascination with all things Russian, including its women.

After joining the navy, Courtney was one of the few Westerners to visit the Soviet Union in the mid-1930s, a period when he was also in touch with MI6. He wrote up long reports for Naval Intelligence with details ranging from the battleships he saw to how many roubles a month a waiter earned. He also drafted papers on what operations could be mounted against the Soviets in the Arctic and Black Sea in the event of war. 'I'm afraid I have rather violent ideas on what we really could do to the USSR if we tried,' he wrote in a 1936 report.[3] His experience led to a posting as deputy head of the Naval Mission in Moscow during the war, sailing the Arctic to Murmansk through storms violent enough to detonate mines around the boat. Those years in Moscow were filled with frustration and obstruction but he managed not only to donate blood in an act of solidarity but also to embark on an affair with a Russian dancer at the Bolshoi, which lasted until the secret police warned her off.[4]

After the war, he advised MI6 on the use of fast surface craft and special submarines for operations in the Black Sea. In 1948, he had been made chief of intelligence staff to the Flag Office in Germany, living with his wife in a house with a pool and tennis court, although he repeatedly complained of a lack of money. Germany offered him the chance to run his own front-line operations as he learnt how German fast boats could be adapted to slip quietly and quickly out of smaller harbours.

Courtney had approached Helmut Klose in May 1949. Klose had not been a Nazi, but Courtney explained to him that his wartime activities had been discovered and suggested he might like to undertake similar work again.[5] No pressure was needed since Klose proved happy to resume his duel with the Bolsheviks. Courtney's deputy was John Harvey Jones, later chairman of ICI and TV troubleshooter, who had joined Naval Intelligence after studying Russian at Cambridge.

After a few false starts, Klose's white E-boat, *S-208*, carrying Cavendish's Baltic agents finally headed out from the harbour on 31 October 1949. Its destination was Latvia, which had been swallowed up by the Soviet Union during the war. The men included former members of the SS whose past had been conveniently overlooked. MI6 was fighting the new war as if it were the last one, finding exiles to drop behind enemy lines. These men had been trained in weapons and secret inks back in Britain, including at a firing range in Chelsea. They carried a brown suitcase containing radios, machine guns and pistols. In watertight plastic bags they had codebooks and false passports. They had money belts full of gold coins and each carried a cyanide pill in case of capture.[6]

The Latvian drop was not the first. The Baltic coast, MI6 believed, was a weak point in the Iron Curtain. British intelligence had studied it closely. They knew it was guarded by camouflaged watchtowers, concealed lookouts and guard patrols, but these were at irregular intervals. The area closest to the shore had been evacuated and islands declared prohibited zones. Fishing vessels had informers placed on board and were scrutinised by coastal cutters, which guarded the boundary with the British sea zone.[7] MI6 had already tried similar missions to Lithuania but these had ended in disaster with a KGB ambush on the beach.

Klose dropped the men at an isolated spot. They made their way to the house of a priest and gave him their password: 'Can I buy some beer here?' The agents radioed back to Hamburg that their mission had started well. They headed for Riga and knocked on another door. They had arrived to help the resistance in the forests, they explained.

The next day, their contact said he was going out to get food. Instead he got in touch with a man called Janis Lukasevics. 'They're comfortable and feel quite at home,' he told Lukasevics.[8]

The Baltic operations were masterminded by a brooding, secrecy-obsessed MI6 controller in London called Harry Carr. With an arched nose, intense eyes and straight black hair, Carr was the leading member of a group of MI6 officers for whom the Second World War had been only a brief interruption in their single-minded struggle against the real enemy. Back in the nineteenth century, the Russians had been Britain's rivals as the first intelligence skirmishes were fought as part of the Great Game in Asia. The imperial roots of anti-Russian sentiment in the Secret Service were then supplemented by a deep distaste for Bolshevism and its class struggle. For Harry Carr, the appropriation of property was also personal. He had been born in the northern Russian port of Archangel in the last weeks of the nineteenth century. His father managed timber mills and Carr grew up in luxury with a grass tennis court and servants before everything was taken away by the Bolsheviks.[9] A remarkable number of MI6 officers had links to the old Russia either personally or through marriage. This created a highly motivated faction who were emotionally committed to confronting the Soviets. In the 1920s they had fallen foul of a Soviet deception called the Trust – a fake émigré group which acted as flypaper to trap agents. But Carr and his like had not learnt their lesson. A doer, not a thinker, Carr demanded aggressive operations. 'There was a philosophy which affected almost everything they did which was "We must do something. Never mind what – but something,"' recalls a colleague who worked in Carr's department just after the war.[10]

Carr was among those itching to start operations against the Soviets after the Second World War and chafing at the restrictions initially imposed by the government on operating inside Russia. Eventually, the leash was loosened and it was agreed that operations could be launched from outside the Soviet Union into its perimeter.[11]

One of those was the effort to support the partisans in the Baltic forests. But an ambitious KGB major called Janis Lukasevics was waiting. He had interrogated a group of Latvians who had landed as early as 1945 and by the time more groups landed in 1949, including those shepherded by Courtney and Cavendish, he was ready to enmesh them in his web of deception.[12] The real partisans had been almost totally crushed by the Soviet secret police, and six of his KGB officers would pose as fake partisans. 'We put them in a safe place,' Lukasevics recalled decades later of the team dropped in October. 'There was a decision not to touch them.'[13]

The newly arrived agents were hidden under fish boxes in a truck and taken to meet their fellow 'forest brothers'. Deep in the woods, the MI6 agents spent months training the 'partisans' and gave them codenames. They told them they would receive £20 a month paid into a London bank account. At one point, one of the MI6 agents put his arm around the shoulders of a 'partisan' and confided that in the first few weeks he had been worried it was all a KGB trap. They began to supply information back to London – profiles of people, troop movements and factory production – nothing special but good enough to be included in MI6's weekly intelligence summary for the Foreign Office. More agents arrived, including another undercover KGB man planted to report back on every element of the operation.[14] Over five years, Klose would drop many more agents into the Baltics. The KGB would capture and in some cases torture and kill them. MI6 had been ensnared. It had been betrayed. Who was to blame?

At the same time as the Latvian operation was under way at the northernmost reaches of the Iron Curtain, an even more ambitious, but equally ill-fated, covert action was being undertaken by MI6 at the southern end. On the moonless night of 3 October 1949, a boat called the *Stormie Seas* lay 200 yards off a cove on the Albanian coast. A group of men climbed into a rubber dinghy and rowed ashore.[15] Hidden by darkness, the landing spot was a remote ravine at the bottom of cliffs with a goat track leading up the scrub-covered mountain. One of the men thought he spotted a light, but a few seconds later it disappeared. When a British marine brought the second half of the team over in his dinghy, he found the first arrivals still waiting, unsure of what lay in store for them in the dark. He ushered them up the hillside. 'They all just mooched off,' he later recalled. 'We'd let them down very badly.'[16]

The nine men again split into two groups. Within hours, one group was ambushed and three of its four members killed. The others made contact with villagers who told them that soldiers had been in the area for several days. The Albanian security forces had been preparing for weeks. Their networks of informers had been told to be on the lookout.[17] At a radio station in Corfu the MI6 team running the operation began to panic as days passed with no contact. Slowly messages trickled back and a few survivors made it into Greece to report the bad news. A second team that went in had likewise been expected and had fallen into a trap.

These teams' objective was to get a feel for the population in preparation for toppling the Albanian government.[18] The losses were bad but not bad enough to put off those who had decided that this was the way in which the Cold War was to be fought. There were late-night conferences to work out what had gone wrong. Sitting in a secure office in the Pentagon, monitoring those first drops, one American said there had to be a leak. His counterpart, the newly arrived liaison from MI6, whom the Americans found comfortingly English and only mildly eccentric by his colleagues' standards, remained quiet.[19] The culture of the times, one MI6 officer recalled, was to meet every setback with the cry 'not to worry, bash on regardless'.[20]

The USSR was seen by Britain's Joint Intelligence Committee in 1948 as a 'hostile, messianic state, with a world-wide mission of hastening the elimination of capitalism'.[21] Albania had been identified by both MI6 and the CIA as a weak spot in the Communist front and in February 1949 the decision had been taken to make it the test case to 'roll back' Communism, a policy in many ways as aggressive as anything the KGB was attempting. All means short of war were on the table.

Britain had one problem. Money – or a lack of it. The country was broke. The solution was obvious: the Americans. They did not take much persuasion. Britain was retreating from centre-stage and passing the baton. In February 1947, London had informed Washington that its economic and military aid to Greece and Turkey would have to stop because Britain was approaching bankruptcy. Given the danger that those countries would fall to Communism, the US President announced the Truman Doctrine offering support to all 'free people who are resisting subjugation'. This was followed by the Marshall Plan to offer economic aid to prevent Communist influence. It was accompanied by a vast increase in propaganda and covert action, including the backing of émigré groups and the financing of anti-Communist political parties in places like Italy where enormous effort had been expended to 'win' the election in 1948. The vogue phrase to describe this was 'political warfare'. It ranged from propaganda to manipulating commodity prices, from counterfeiting currency to sabotage, from bankrolling émigré front organisations to dropping leaflets from hot-air balloons (some of which, destined for Czechoslovakia, were discovered by Scottish farmers, much to their bemusement).[22]

Albania was a test case for the most aggressive end of the political-warfare spectrum. The British Foreign Secretary Ernest Bevin, a fierce anti-Communist thanks to his battles inside the trade unions, was a supporter. There were differences in emphasis between London and Washington, particularly over who to back. In one discussion with US Secretary of State Dean Acheson, Bevin uttered that great British battlecry: 'Are there any Kings around that could be put in?'[23] Not everyone in the Foreign Office and State Department was keen on the plan, but MI6 found an enthusiastic backer in Washington in the form of Frank Wisner, known as 'the wiz'. A former corporate lawyer from Mississippi, he was smitten with the idea of using covert operations to take on the Soviets. From an office known as the 'rat palace' because of the vermin scuttling through its corridors, he ran the Office of Policy Co-ordination, which was tasked with fighting the secret war, a role he continued after the OPC was absorbed into the CIA in 1950. By 1951, Wisner was spending more than $200 million a year on his covert operations, three times the money spent on collecting and analysing intelligence.

MI6 and the CIA have always had two functions – information gathering and covert action. The latter involves engineering outcomes with the hand of government hidden. For Wisner and his people, intelligence was about doing things, not finding out about things. 'The central and decisive battles of the secret war are fought in the vast realm of covert political operations,' wrote James Mc-Cargar, who led the American side of the Albanian operation. 'The ultimate national aim in the secret war is not simply to know; it is to maintain or to expand national power.'[24] Not everyone agreed. 'The operational tail will wag the intelligence dog,' one American spy chief warned.[25] But the CIA, even more than MI6, came to be infused with a paramilitary culture and enthused by the possibilities that covert action offered. The US was deciding there was only one way to play against an implacable, deadly new enemy hell-bent on domination. 'There are no rules in such a game,' an official report argued in language that would be echoed after 9/11. 'Hitherto acceptable norms of human conduct do not apply. If the United States is to survive, long-standing American concepts of "fair play" must be reconsidered ... We must develop effective espionage and counterespionage services and must learn to subvert, sabotage and destroy our enemies by more clever, more sophisticated and more effective methods than those used against us.'[26] ('We cannot afford methods less ruthless than those of our opposition,' a fictional British intelligence man argues in John le Carré's *The Spy Who Came in from the Cold*.)

Bankrolling Britain's Albania plan was no problem for the cash-rich American spies who operated a slush fund siphoned out of the Marshall Plan money with almost no oversight.[27] How the cash-strapped British Secret Service housed in the Broadway buildings by St James's tube station, with its brown linoleum floors, grotty furnishings and bare lightbulbs, must have gazed in envy at the wealth of its younger, brasher cousin. Beneath the surface, a few in Washington detected a sour resentment of the Americans, particularly among some upper-class Britons, who disliked the passing of the baton and the anti-imperial instincts of their cousins.

The awareness of no longer being top dog and of being reliant on American largesse was expressed in the fictional writings of one of Anthony Courtney's friends and former colleagues from Naval Intelligence who, just as the Albania operation reached its zenith, was writing his first book. 'Our people are definitely interested. They think it's just as important as your friends do and they don't think there's anything crazy about it all. In fact, Washington's pretty sick we're not running the show,' the CIA man explained to James Bond. Just as Bond's British operation, fought at the baccarat table of Casino Royale rather than in the Albanian mountains, looked lost, CIA man Felix Leiter slides an envelope across the table, 'thick as a dictionary', with the words 'Marshall Aid. Thirty-two million francs. With the compliments of the USA', allowing Bond to win the day and bankrupt his enemy. In Ian Fleming's fantasy world, the British were still in charge even if they did need American money. This was an escapist alternative reality in which the British reader could be consoled by the thought that, even as the days of Empire and greatness were passing, Britain was still good at something, a world in which the illusions of power and influence could be preserved in the form of a cool and ruthless superspy.[28]

In the real Albanian operation, the exchange was not quite so one sided. In return for American cash, Britain could offer two things – a claim (only partly true) to have wisdom and expertise on Albania and also, crucially, real estate from which to run the operation. Leftover bits of Empire, from Cyprus to Hong Kong and later Diego Garcia, always came in useful and the Americans' propensity for favouring decolonisation certainly had its limits. 'Whenever we want to subvert any place,' Frank Wisner confided to an MI6 officer he wrongly believed was on his side, 'we find that the British own an island within easy reach.'[29] For Albania, the island was Malta.

The cultural differences between the two countries' spies are captured in McCargar's account of attending planning meetings on either side of the Atlantic. In Washington, he arrived to find an intricate bureaucratic, organisational chart on the wall for the Albanian operation. 'A colleague pointed at it and said we'd need 457 bodies. I didn't think we could find 457 bodies and said that I would happily settle for six brains,' McCargar recalled. A week later he went to London to confer. After an hour or two someone said, 'I say, why don't we get old Henry up here? He knows about this.' 'A day or two later old Henry showed up from down in Sussex and when the problem was put to him, finally agreed to undertake the task, although, as he said, "This will wreak havoc with the garden, you know. Just getting it into trim."' He then said he needed a grand total of six people to report to him.[30]

The 'old Henrys' of the Albania operation were a group of Special Operations Executive (SOE) veterans who would become known as the Musketeers. During the war, the SOE had sent in men and weapons to support Albanians fighting first against the Italians and then against the Germans. There had been a sharp and bitter division between those who favoured the Communist-allied partisans and those who worked with the nationalists and royalists and who favoured the exiled King Zog (who had been ensconced for much of the war in the front line of Henley-on-Thames). The partisans had proved more willing to take on the Germans and eventually their pudgy leader Enver Hoxha had emerged triumphant, installing a Communist government which, in turn, distrusted the British for their backing of his rivals. 'Another King down the drain!' Churchill wrote to his Foreign Secretary Anthony Eden when Hoxha's victory became apparent.[31]

The SOE veterans who had worked with the nationalists were bitter at the turn of events. They talked angrily of treachery and of the machinations of the Communist sympathisers among their rivals within SOE. The key figures included Julian Amery, later a Conservative minister, Billy McLean and David Smiley – 'the Three Musketeers'. After the war Amery had worked the overlapping worlds of Whitehall offices and the clubs of St James's in which the demi-monde of British intelligence and its hangers-on lived, telling everybody who would listen that the Albanian people were 'seething with discontent against their Communist masters'.[32] The Musketeers believed that their SOE experience of training and supporting resistance groups was the way to fight the new Cold War, without realising that this time the enemy was playing a different game. SOE had been swallowed up by MI6 which in turn had absorbed its gung-ho culture. New recruits into MI6 were trained, in classic SOE style, to place explosives by a railway line as much as to recruit agents. A divide had emerged in the culture of MI6, just as it had among their American counterparts, between those who wanted action and those who wanted intelligence. The men of action, who believed in continuing the paramilitary methods they had enjoyed in the Second World War, had the upper hand in these years. These were the men who had 'had a good war' and could not let go. The Chief of MI6 was unsure about the Albania operation, saying there was no point in undertaking it unless it was followed through, but he also saw it as a way of keeping the SOE 'stinks and bangs people' happy.[33]

Colonel and Musketeer David Smiley was in charge of training the Albanians. His name crops up again and again in accounts of the clandestine wars fought by Britain from the Second World War onwards (making it perhaps ironic that a man of action not dissimilar to Bond coincidentally enjoyed the same name as le Carré's pudgy, cerebral spy). He had been commissioned into the full plumage of the Royal Horse Guards – a world of strict formality in which he was once reprimanded for being seen at the Café de Paris wearing a dinner jacket when he should have been in white tie and tails.[34] As the Second World War began, he sold his racehorse and private aeroplane and moved into irregular warfare. In 1943, he had been recruited to work for SOE in Albania, parachuting out of a Halifax bomber. He first worked with Hoxha, whom Smiley, being an old-fashioned British imperialist, argued with incessantly, before switching to the more amenable nationalist Abas Kupi. A few years after the war, an old SOE colleague now with MI6 explained that the old crew was getting back together for one more adventure.[35]

In the summer of 1949 Smiley arrived at the base of operations in Malta, an isolated hill-top fort, equipped with drawbridge and moat. He lived under cover and spent the mornings at an office being as conspicuous as possible. Summer afternoons were for playing polo, sometimes with Admiral Mountbatten and his nephew Prince Philip accompanied occasionally by his wife, the then Princess Elizabeth, who stayed on the island for a while. When the Princess was crowned queen a few years later, Smiley rode alongside as commander of her escort.[36]

The Albanian agents had been recruited from Displaced Persons camps and were trained by Smiley's team of weapons experts, wireless operators and even an Oxford don who was a scholar of classical Persian. The technology was equally quirky. The batteries for the old Second World War radio sets they had were too large so they used a type of collapsible bicycle without wheels. Someone would have to pedal furiously to generate enough power to send a signal.

By July 1950, a specially fitted private yacht, the *Henrietta*, had replaced the *Stormie Seas*. 'We would be alongside in Malta and a taxi [with] four hooded characters would arrive,' remembers Eric Walton, who sailed the boat.[37] 'They arrived on board blindfolded ... We would take off and disappear knowing full well that the Russians or some other spies would know we were going. But what they didn't know was that we could do 25 knots and we had long-range tanks.' The team acquired a local reputation as top-notch smugglers, and a Greek shipping magnate even asked them to smuggle some gold in return for 10 per cent of the proceeds. The team declined.[38] Walton, like many involved, felt growing sympathy for the hooded men, who came to be known as the pixies. When one died in Malta, they had to dispose of the corpse without any records and dumped the body at sea. But it was their fate on landing in Albania that really elicited sympathy even among the hard-headed MI6 men.

The mood soured as the pixies were repeatedly ambushed on arrival. And yet the operations continued. Tony Northrop, a young MI6 officer who trained the pixies in Malta, became depressed as he watched them sail off. Lives were being thrown away, he thought.[39] When one pixie disappeared from training, Northrop found him sitting on a bench in the town square. As Northrop approached, the man put his hand to his mouth. Northrop realised he was trying to swallow the cyanide pill he had been given for the mission. Northrop grabbed him by the throat and rushed him to hospital to have his stomach pumped. Northrop became so disillusioned that he told his superiors the whole thing was doomed. But still the drops continued. Too much had been invested to admit failure and turn back. 'They had no country and no future,' Smiley later recalled. 'I feel very sad, to be quite frank. Looking back knowing the result, it is just heartbreaking.'[40]

The Americans began in 1950 to drop their men into Albania by parachute, the planes coming in at just 200 feet to evade radar before rising to 500 feet for the jump. Washington's political strategy had fallen apart amid interminable Albanian feuds and their agents' fate was the same as the British. They had been expected and were surrounded, some burnt to death in a house, others shot, others captured. The Albanians, like the Latvians, began running a deception operation, forcing agents to broadcast the all-clear, leading to more agents being lured to their deaths. 'Our famous radio game brought about the ignominious failure of the plans of the foreign enemy,' Hoxha later boasted. 'The bands of criminals who were dropped in by parachute or infiltrated across the border at our request came like lambs to the slaughter.'[41]

In London, they knew something was going wrong. George Kennedy Young, back from Vienna, began post-mortems on the Iron Curtain operations, 'the pride and joy' of some parts of the office.[42] Using so-called 'barium meals' in which false information is fed into a network to see where it ends up, he became convinced they were being run by the KGB. This led to furious rows with Carr and his allies who simply did not want to accept that they had been duped.

The Chief, John Sinclair, who was out of his depth, ignored the warnings. The British began to pull back, realising that the Albanian operation – codenamed 'Valuable' – was anything but and risked fuelling Stalin's paranoia. Britain, having initially feared American disengagement from Europe and a return to isolationism, was also beginning to worry that perhaps the Americans were a bit too reckless and might start a war, a war in which London, not Washington, would be obliterated.

Covert operations had fanned out beyond the Baltic States and Albania to the entire periphery of the Soviet Union including Ukraine and the Caucasus. And they all seemed to be going wrong at enormous cost in terms of lives, manpower and money.[43] Eventually, the Albanians revealed their hand in a Tirana show-trial, providing the perfect pretext for Hoxha to tighten his grip. The game was up. It had gone on too long. And at the cost of many lives, maybe 100, maybe 200. But these were foreigners and volunteers who knew the risks, the British and American intelligence officers said. And this was a war.

There were recriminations. The British thought that the Americans had been a bit amateurish. 'I was quite convinced our security was very, very tight,' reckoned Smiley. But the Americans thought there had been a leak. The operation had been betrayed. Who was to blame? There was an elusively simple answer to the conundrum of not just Latvia and Albania but all of the other failed MI6 operations of this period.

As the first team were setting sail from Malta, an MI6 officer was on a much more comfortable boat journey, heading towards New York and enjoying a crate of champagne that had been delivered to his cabin. It had taken just half an hour for Kim Philby to agree to accept the position of British liaison to American intelligence which took him to the fulcrum of the secret world. He knew it was precisely what his masters in Moscow would have wanted. He had spent September inside MI6 HQ at Broadway in London being briefed on current operations, including Albania, ahead of his new posting. When he arrived, he was taken to a hotel overlooking Central Park. As he gazed out of the twenty-fifth-floor window, Philby felt sick and broke into a sweat.[44]

On the day the second team landed in Albania in October 1949,

Philby formally took up his job. The US no longer wanted to be as reliant on the UK as it had been in the Second World War, but the British were still the 'big brother' who had been in the game much longer. Philby met frequently with the head of the CIA and its staff gossiped freely with him. 'Philby was a great charmer,' McCargar recalled. 'He came to us with an enormous reputation. He was known as a young Turk ... and the American bureaucracy sometimes admires that kind of thing ... one had the feeling one could have confidence in him.'[45]

Every week, Philby would lunch with James Jesus Angleton, an increasingly influential figure in American intelligence. A wiry man with thick glasses, who grew orchids and studied poetry, Angleton cultivated an aura of being cleverer and better at playing the game of intrigue than anyone else. Educated in England and at Yale, he had known Philby during the war and, like others, admired him as a 'professional'. In Washington, the two men drank Martinis and ate lobster at Harvey's Restaurant as each cultivated the other and traded secret information, Philby even going to Angleton's house for Thanksgiving dinner.[46] The famous Philby charm worked on most, although a few sensed the driving ambition and coldness that lay beneath the surface. His house in Nebraska Avenue was the site for many a late-night party fuelled by pitchers of Martini. 'They were long and very, very wet,' McCargar recalls of those evenings. 'We really were all afloat on a sea of drink.'[47] How much did Philby know? 'The sky was the limit,' a CIA officer from the time later remarked. 'He would have known as much as he wanted to find out.'[48] One day, Ted Kollek, a visiting Israeli official, bumped into Philby in a corridor at CIA headquarters. 'What is Philby doing here?' he later asked Angleton. 'Kim is a good friend of ours,' Angleton replied. Kollek had been at Litzi and Philby's wedding in Vienna back in 1934 when it was clear he had Communist sympathies. Don't trust him, he warned Angleton. The warning was ignored.[49]

Philby was one of four people co-ordinating the Iron Curtain operations to prevent agents running into each other and getting in each other's way. He navigated the disputes between London and Washington over which exiles to back (the British liked kings, the Americans the republicans, and both argued over the use of war criminals). There was a particularly vicious battle between Harry

Carr and Wisner's people over factions in the Baltics which Philby had to smooth over.[50]

'Do we know which of these operations is already under Russian control?' a CIA officer asked Carr as they struggled to understand what was going wrong.

'Ours isn't,' Carr replied.

'How can you be sure that your agent isn't under control?' snapped the CIA officer.

'We're sure.'

'But how can you be?' persisted the American.

'Because we've made our checks. Our group is watertight,' Carr said.

'So's ours', the American replied. 'But one group is penetrated.'[51]

Philby was taking the minutes, cool as ever, knowing the answer. When their Albanian operations began to go wrong, Frank Wisner apologised to Philby and said, 'We'll get it right next time.'[52]

Angleton, according to those who worked on the operation, gave Philby over drinks the precise co-ordinates for every drop zone for the CIA in Albania.[53] He may also have briefed Philby about all the other infiltration programmes behind the Iron Curtain. So everything was down to Philby.

That is the belief those involved clung to later. 'What had happened was that bloody man Philby was tipping off,' Smiley would say years later with a deep bitterness in his voice.[54] 'The Americans had to tell us what they were doing and I had to tell the Americans what we were doing. This was all done through Washington and the go-between was this fellow Philby, who was told by the Americans what to tell the British, told the British what to tell the Americans. And told the Russians as well. It was a disaster.' For Harry Carr too, it all must have been Philby. For a decade almost all the émigré operations into the USSR – from the Baltic to the Adriatic, with Poland and Ukraine along the way – had been run by the KGB. Everyone knew where to lay the blame. And the same for the Hungarian activists who ended up betrayed and jailed. And for the MI6 officers ambushed at dead drops. And for every other ill-conceived operation that ended in disaster during those years, the answer was always the same. It was all Philby. 'We'd have been better off doing nothing,' one CIA officer said of the years from 1945 to 1951.[55] One officer who worked on the operation said all of those involved in Albania at the agency were left 'psychologically devastated' when they eventually discovered what Philby had done to them.[56]

Philby, it was true, was perfectly placed. Through a ruthless power play, he had manoeuvred himself to become head of the newly formed Section IX in 1944. While Britain was still allied with the Soviet Union, this section was designed to prepare for MI6's return to battle against Communism. Philby was the leading expert on Communist ideology in MI6, critiquing MI5's papers on the USSR. 'To my mind, the purge and the struggle against Fascism and collaboration is the current tactical expression of the class struggle,' he wrote knowledgeably to his counterpart Roger Hollis at MI5, leading to a curious exchange between an MI6 man spying for the Soviets and a future head of MI5 who would be accused of doing the same.[57] Philby was able to use his position to report back to his controllers that the British were already thinking of the Soviets as a potential enemy during the war. He was fully aware of Harry Carr's early plans for covert action. Intelligence derived not just from Philby but from his Cambridge cohorts reached Stalin personally and may well have further convinced him of the hostile intent of the West and the need to build up his own protective buffer of pliant states.

Philby had been engaged in a high-wire act of dizzying complexity. He had staffed his new section with officers who were good – but not too good. Every day he had to decide which operations to sabotage and which to let run in order to foster his own career. He did not pass everything to Moscow, not out of any residual patriotism but because he feared that his masters would not be careful enough in using it and it might lead back to him.[58] But he certainly betrayed the existence of the Albanian operations. Philby would later show no remorse over this. 'The agents we sent into Albania were armed men intent on sabotage, murder and assassination,' he told a biographer years later. 'They were quite as ready as I was to contemplate bloodshed in the service of a political ideal. They knew the risks they were running. I was serving the interests of the Soviet Union and those interests required that these men were defeated. To the extent that I helped defeat them, even if it caused their deaths, I have no regrets.'[59] So it was all that bloody man Philby. Was it?

The truth is that the malaise affecting British intelligence was much greater than one man. Philby's betrayal masked far more fundamental problems in the specific operations and in the whole culture of Anglo-American intelligence. The problems with the operations continued long after Philby had left Washington and when he was in no position to know the details. Cavendish, McCargar and others intimately involved knew he could not have been aware of all the landing times and places in the Albanian and Baltic operations. The operations were deeply flawed and compromised from the start, even without Philby. Security was lax. The Soviets had informers in all the refugee camps, in the front movements and in the networks themselves. Everyone everywhere knew what was happening inside the leaky émigré community where agents were recruited.[60]

Not just the execution but the very concept of the operation in Albania was fundamentally flawed. The Musketeers were personally committed to backing their men against the Communists. But they failed to appreciate that much of the support for Hoxha was based on real sentiment among the populace. And even as that sentiment began to sour, the strength of the secret police left others fearful of joining what always looked like a small-time attempt at revolution. The Soviets had much more to go on than just Philby.

The same was true for the Baltic operation. Philby may have kept the KGB informed of MI6's deception plans but the operation had been organised separately. He had very little involvement with Carr's work after 1947 apart from during his trips to Washington and knew almost none of the detail. All across Eastern Europe, the CIA and MI6 had begun to support resistance movements which had peaked in 1947 and by the time the parachutes and boats arrived they had dwindled to nothing, or worse, had become KGB traps. The methods of the last war were simply not up to the job this time round. MI6 did not yet have the measure of the new enemy it was facing.

It was all too convenient to blame every disaster on Philby in those years. He was a scapegoat who could be cast into the wilderness bearing the sins of Britain's and America's spies, leaving them free of blame. A few knew that it was not so simple. Philby's betrayal was enormous. But it did not account for everything. His greatest damage lay in what his betrayal did to Washington's perception of British intelligence and particularly in the manner of his departure.

In the summer of 1950, Philby received a letter from his old Cambridge friend Guy Burgess. He had been posted by the Foreign Office to Washington and wanted to stay at Philby's house. This was a problem for Philby. He had first introduced Burgess to Russian intelligence in the 1930s and Burgess had repaid the favour by helping Philby into British intelligence during the Second World War. But Philby had been unsure about Burgess from the start and the once lovable rogue was becoming increasingly dissolute and dangerous.[61] He left a trail of destruction wherever he went, from Tangier to Dublin, involving drunkenness, young men and occasional boasts of espionage.

At the same time, Philby had been briefed about an FBI investigation hunting for a spy who had been at the British Embassy. The FBI's knowledge was only partial, based on a decrypted set of Soviet communications, and its officers had been inclined to think that the culprit was a junior or a local member of staff. A charlady with a Latvian grandmother had a fifteen-page report compiled on her private life. But Philby watched nervously as the investigation began to lead to another of his Cambridge contemporaries whom he had talent-spotted for the Soviets fifteen years earlier. Donald Maclean, once the golden boy of the Foreign Office, was by then back in London. After his time in Washington, he had begun to self-destruct in Cairo, thanks in part to a poor KGB handler looking after him. Fifteen years of deception had taken its toll. He wanted out. But it was too late. He trashed an American's flat by smashing a large minor on to a bath after a drinking binge. However, after a brief spell with the Foreign Office shrink he had been made head of the America desk. Now Philby, who never showed the same signs of cracking that his fellow spies did, could see the net closing in on Maclean.

Burgess would go back home to warn Maclean, he and Philby agreed. At the last dinner they would share, Burgess and Philby sat in a booth at a Chinese restaurant where music could mask their conversation. 'When I drove him to the station next morning, my last words, spoken only half-jocularly, were "Don't you go too."'[62] A few days later Philby was called in by a colleague at the Embassy who had just received a 'Most Immediate' telegram from London. Could Philby's secretary help decrypt it? When the work was complete, the man looked grey. "'Kim," he said in a half-whisper, "the bird (meaning Maclean) has flown … there's worse than that … Guy Burgess has gone with him."' Philby did not need to feign distress at the news. There was panic in London, where they had been waiting until the weekend was over to interrogate Maclean. The Soviets believed that the MI5 surveillance team did not work weekends and had taken advantage of this by sending their two agents on a weekend cruise to France which did not require passports. From there, they fled east.

Philby realised that the Cambridge connection between Burgess and Maclean would also lead to him. So he returned to his Washington home, went down into his basement and wrapped his secret camera and accessories into waterproof containers and drove out to Great Falls. He parked his car on a deserted stretch of road and began digging with a trowel to bury evidence of his deceit. But rather than panic and flee Philby decided to hold his nerve. He understood the Americans and the British spy-hunters in a way his two colleagues did not and he knew that any evidence would be circumstantial. He also understood that many senior people in London would not want to face up to the possibility that they had been duped, and that his many friends would give him the benefit of the doubt.

The summons to London soon arrived. On his way back, Philby went to see Angleton and they passed a 'pleasant' hour in a bar. He even saw CIA chief Allen Dulles, who acted as if it was business as usual and asked Philby to follow up some business back home.[63] But while Angleton, despite what he later claimed, never had any doubts about his friend, other CIA colleagues did. One, Bill Harvey, wrote a memo outlining the circumstantial case that Philby had gone bad and sent it to Dulles. Washington had insisted to London that Philby leave and not come back.[64] Back in London, the first of many interrogations began. The initial task fell to the capable MI5 officer Dick White. Philby was a cool customer and knew that since his former friends at MI5 had no evidence they were counting on a confession. He toughed it out. He was asked to resign but was handed a fat pay-off. Ministers and other officials were not told of MI5's investigation.

The Americans were unhappy, in some cases furious, with the failure to resolve the issue and pressured the British to do more, especially in the wake of the Albanian failures. As a result, Philby was hauled in for another three-hour questioning. The interview was led by a lawyer and ex-Security Service officer, H. J. Milmo. Sitting in with him was a quiet young MI5 officer who would become Philby's chief pursuer. His name was Arthur Martin. 'He remained silent throughout, watching my movements,' Philby recalled. Martin was intense and focused, determined to expose the traitor for what he was. He had been recruited into MI5 and knew Philby well but now he burned with anger at the way Philby had got away with it for so long and at the way MI6 protected him.[65] Much of the evidence Martin had carefully pieced together was admittedly circumstantial. There had been a spectacular rise in the volume of Soviet radio traffic at just the moment in 1945 that Philby had been informed about a defector offering his services in Turkey. Philby had been assigned to follow up the offer and, sensing the danger to his own position, had played for time until the would-be defector could be spirited back to the Soviet Union on a military aircraft, presumably to his death.

Litzi and the Vienna connection were a weak spot and Martin zeroed in on it to search for proof to support his conviction. Those who had known Litzi were summoned to Room 055 of the War Office to meet a man named Morley, Martin's cover-name.[66] He began one interview in October by explaining that the inquiry was about Litzi and asked what the interviewee knew. The interviewee had only known her in London during the war but said she never seemed to want for money and now seemed to be living a surprisingly comfortable life in the Soviet sector of Berlin. Martin focused on Edith Tudor-Hart, who had walked Philby to the park bench to be recruited. The day before the interview in Room 055, a full telephone tap was placed on her in addition to the existing mail check and surveillance. She realised that she was being watched and became increasingly neurotic, waiting for her house to be raided.[67] She also received a phone call – from whom is unclear – and destroyed a picture she had taken of Philby back in the 1930s.[68]

The investigation into Philby generated a painful fracture within British intelligence. Almost everyone in MI5 – and especially those who had watched him being questioned – was convinced of Philby's guilt. The two agencies were rivals in the way many sister services can be, expending untold energy in petty bureaucratic squabbles, but there were also deeper distinctions. MI5 were seen as little more than policemen – many were ex-Colonial Special Branch officers – and their well-tailored relatives from MI6 certainly never left them in any doubt that they did not move in the same circles or inhabit quite the same world as MI6 did with its gentlemanly values. Philby's friends in MI6 thought it impossible that one of their own could have been working for the other side. He had been the victim of a McCarthyist witch-hunt by those fanatics in Washington, they said.

The misplaced loyalty to Philby reflected the culture of the Secret Service and its cherishing of 'gentlemanly conduct'. Security and vetting had been lax at MI6 for decades. This was because the service recruited incestuously from within small circles in the tight-knit British elite. Fathers recruited sons, officers married secretaries and they all socialised with each other, partly because it alleviated any security concerns and partly because of the sense of superiority it provided. MI6 was a gentlemen's club and a gentleman could always be trusted. Intelligence, to the old-school types, was a game like cricket where alongside some cunning there were still rules of gentlemanly conduct to be observed ('It's such a dirty business that it's only suitable for gentlemen,' a spy once said of his work).[69] The KGB, whose culture was very different, exploited this weakness by recruiting young idealistic agents who were rebelling against the smug certainties of their parents' generation. There had been a distrust of intellectuals before the war by the men of action, property and Empire who ran MI6. The service's number two had boasted that he 'would never willingly employ a university man'.[70] But after the war things began to change. Philby, though recruited through the club, had managed to style himself as a man of the future, representing the rise of the professional. In 1950, one new recruit was told that he should 'model' himself on Philby, the 'star of the service'.[71]

Philby's close friend in MI6 was Nicholas Elliott, son of an Eton provost and a classic establishment man: 'he was everything you would expect an Etonian to be,' recalled Anthony Cavendish, who knew him well. A thin man who would glance over his round glasses in a donnish manner, he had two joys in life, Ascot and dirty jokes. Elliott's recollection of a conversation with a security officer on his return to London from the Middle East in 1945 gives a taste of both Elliott himself and of the closed world of MI6 and the establishment:

Security Officer: Sit down, I'd like to have a frank talk with you.

Nicholas Elliott: As you wish, Colonel.

Security Officer: Does your wife know what you do?

Nicholas Elliott: Yes.

Security Officer: How did that come about?

Nicholas Elliott: She was my secretary for two years and I think the penny must have dropped.

Security Officer: Quite so. What about your mother?

Nicholas Elliott: She thinks I'm in something called SIS which she believes stands for the Secret Intelligence Service.

Security Officer: Good God! How did she come to know that?

Nicholas Elliott: A member of the War Cabinet told her at a cocktail party.

Security Officer: Who was he?

Nicholas Elliott: I'd prefer not to say.

Security Officer: Then what about your father?

Nicholas Elliott: He thinks I'm a spy

Security Officer: So why should he think you're a spy?

Nicholas Elliott: Because the Chief told him in the bar at White's.[72]

Elliott, like many of the new generation, looked up to Kim Philby. He became his greatest defender, paving the way for a very personal betrayal. Philby too had been recruited through knowing the right people, culminating in lunch with a senior MI6 officer accompanied by his father St John Philby. 'When Kim went out to the lavatory, I asked St John about him,' the officer later recalled. '"He was a bit of a communist at Cambridge, wasn't he?" I enquired. "Oh, that was all schoolboy nonsense," St John replied. "He's a reformed character now."'[73] That was enough for the MI6 man, who had known St John from India and who later said, 'I knew his people.'[74] St John Philby was an oddity, a member of the imperial establishment who had begun in the Colonial Service in India but ended up converting to Islam and receiving as a second wife a slave girl from King Ibn Saud. All the way through this strange journey, he kept his membership of the Athenaeum Club in Pall Mall and tried to catch the cricket test match scores. When his young son Harold talked to the locals in India, the father said of him, 'He's a real little Kim,' after the Rudyard Kipling spy-boy who could blend in with the locals. The nickname had gone with him through Westminster School and Cambridge and then to the service. On one hand, there could hardly have been a less apt nickname for a man who so utterly rejected the flag-waving, imperial patriotism that Kipling had espoused and that had lured many others, like Daphne Park, to join the Secret Service. On the other hand, Kipling's Kim was a boy who could pretend to be someone else (Indian rather than English) and above all, 'what he loved was the game for its own sake – the stealthy prowl through the dark gullies'. Philby too loved the game of espionage but was also trapped by it.

For all his success, Philby had not always been trusted by his KGB mentors. They had refused to believe him when he said that MI6 had no agents in Russia, and the fact that MI6 appeared so incompetent in failing to spot his Communist past added to suspicions that he might be a double agent whose allegiance remained with Britain and who was being used against them. At one point contact with him was terminated and a rather inept surveillance team sent out to see if Philby and those he recruited (with the possible exception of Maclean) really were loyal to British intelligence.[75] Although he hid them carefully in his untrustworthy memoir, Philby himself had doubts, particularly when he was abandoned and at the start of the war when the Soviet Union signed a short-lived pact with the Nazis. But, once embarked on, the path of treachery is almost impossible to leave. Philby remained steadfast. Some say it was deceit itself and the thrill of the double life which drove him rather than a faith in Communism. In later life he denied that his commitment was anything other than ideological. He had chosen his side and then stuck with it, he said, quoting a line from his friend Graham Greene's book, *The Confidential Agent*, in which the agent defends himself for backing the poor even when their leaders commit atrocities like those of the other side. 'You've got to choose some line of action and live by it. Otherwise nothing matters at all … It's no worse – is it? – than my country, right or wrong. You choose your side once and for all – of course, it may be the wrong side. Only history can tell that.'[76] Philby particularly hated being called a 'double agent' in the popular sense of the term implying someone who had changed sides. He always saw himself as a 'Soviet intelligence officer' for whom the struggle against fascism extended into a struggle against imperialism.

'All through my career, I have been a straight penetration agent working in the Soviet interest.'[77] The burden of betrayal, however, did not perhaps sit as lightly on Philby as he, and his critics, would make out.

He was so successful as a penetration agent that some thought Kim was destined to become chief of MI6. That was partly because the competition was not up to much. 'Sometimes, in the early weeks, I felt that perhaps I had not made the grade after all,' Philby says of his early days in the Second World War. 'It seemed that somewhere, lurking in deep shadow, there must be another service, really secret and really powerful.' Fellow wartime MI6 officer Hugh Trevor-Roper thought Philby a candidate for the top. 'Who else of his generation was there? . . . I looked around the world I had left, at the part-time stockbrokers and retired Indian policemen, the agreeable epicureans from the bars of White's and Boodle's, the jolly, conventional ex-naval officers and the robust adventurers from the bucket-shop; and then I looked at Philby.'[78] McCargar says Angleton told him that Kim might yet become chief even after the first allegations had surfaced.[79] Philby himself was more realistic, understanding that the number-two spot was more likely thanks to his complicated personal life, which featured women and too much drink even for the 1950s.

But then in 1951 he found himself out of a job and without a purpose. He floated around the City and journalism for a few years. Then a Russian defector in Australia revealed that Burgess and Maclean had been long-term penetration agents, leading to speculation about a 'third man'. The pressure was back on. The Americans, especially FBI Director J. Edgar Hoover, who had been a guest at Philby's house, were convinced of his guilt and angry about their British cousins' perceived protection of him. Along with some MI5 officers, they made sure that friends in the newspapers got hold of his name. Ironically, MI6 officers would be furious with the Americans for the leaking of Philby's name, seeing it as the unacceptable smearing of one of their own. Philby was on a train, undertaking the long process of getting rid of any surveillance in preparation for meeting his Soviet contact, when he saw a copy of the *Evening Standard* newspaper. In October 1955 an MP had asked the Prime Minister Anthony Eden 'how long he was going to go on shielding the "dubious Third Man activities of Mr Philby"'.[80] By a strange quirk of fate, the title of Graham Greene's screenplay was now applied to the man who, unbeknown to anyone, may have helped inspire it.

The establishment rallied round. Philby had survived another bout of questioning by his former colleagues at MI6, one which his pursuers at MI5 thought absurdly polite and non-confrontational as if MI6 were trying to help him clear his name. 'To call it an interrogation would be a travesty,' said an MI5 officer.[81] The Foreign Secretary, Harold Macmillan, stood up in the House of Commons in November and said there was no evidence that Philby had betrayed the interests of his country. Philby hosted a bravura press conference in his mother's flat in London. For five minutes flash bulbs illuminated the scene almost continuously before the questioning began.

'Were you in fact the Third Man?'

'No, I was not.'

'Do you think there was one?'

'No comment.'

Each question was met with a brief, clipped answer.

'Mr Macmillan said you had had Communist associations. Is that why you were asked to resign?'

'I was asked to resign from the Foreign Office because of an imprudent association with Burgess and as a result of his disappearance.'

'Can you say when your Communist associations ended? I assume they did.'

'The last time I spoke to a Communist knowing he was a Communist was some time in 1934.'

There was no sign of a stammer. The only suggestion of something amiss were a few hairs which had not quite been Brylcreemed into position.

'Would you still regard Burgess, who lived with you for a while in Washington, as a friend of yours? How do you feel about him now?'

'I consider his action deplorable. On the subject of friendship I'd prefer to say as little as possible because it's very complicated.'[82]

He then served the assembled hacks beer and sherry. The following day his friends from MI6 called to congratulate him. The next summer Philby, now effectively in the clear, received a phone call from Nicholas Elliott.

'Something unpleasant again?' Philby said

'Maybe just the opposite,' Elliott replied.

Philby's old chums, George Kennedy Young and Nicholas Elliott, had got him a job in Beirut. Officially he was a journalist for the *Economist* and the *Observer*.[83] But he was also a salaried agent of the service (an agent who would be handled by an officer rather than an officer in his own right who could recruit agents). The Americans were never told he had been put back on the payroll and were unhappy when they later found out. Philby arrived in the Lebanon in August 1956. He would find a new life as a spy in a city which lay at the centre of much of the plotting and scheming of a turbulent Middle East. But, even without being aware of their grievous error in sending him there, Philby's two friends in MI6 were going through dark times.

The mid-1950s came to be known as 'the horrors' by the MI6 officers who lived through those years. The wildmen known within the service as the Robber Barons championed aggressive covert operations but were coming unstuck in a spectacular and occasionally grisly way. The emerging myth of James Bond met its counterpoint in the sad tale of Lionel 'Buster' Crabb. In April 1956, the Soviet leader Nikita Khrushchev made a high-profile trip to Britain on board the state-of-the-art cruiser the *Ordzhonikidze*. This was an important visit for Anthony Eden who wanted to play the statesman in the new, friendlier, post-Stalin era. The MI6 London station – run by Nicholas Elliott with Andrew King as his deputy – decided that the visit was too good an opportunity to miss and ten days beforehand put up a list of six operations to MI6's Foreign Office adviser. The Admiralty had been particularly keen to understand the underwater-noise characteristics of the Soviet vessels.[84] The placing of a Foreign Office adviser inside MI6 was part of a drive to put the service on a somewhat tighter leash, but when an MI6 officer ambled into his office for a ten-minute chat about the plans, the adviser, who had just learned of his father's death, later claimed he expected plans to be cleared higher up while Elliott and his colleagues assumed that the quick conversation constituted clearance. The problem was that the Prime Minister had explicitly ordered that no risky operations were to be carried out and had already vetoed a number of plans (including bugging Claridge's Hotel where the Soviets were staying and another operation involving a catamaran).[85]

The operation bore all the hallmarks of the over-confident amateurishness of the period. Crabb was an ageing frogman who had an impressive, but increasingly distant, war record foiling attacks on Allied shipping with daring dives. He was now, like others, well past his prime and living on the legends of the past. His private life was a mess with a failed marriage, gambling, drink and depression. Diving and secret work were his escape and he begged to be allowed to undertake one more mission.[86] Crabb and a young MI6 officer checked into a local hotel under their real names and Crabb slugged back five double whiskies the night before the dive.[87] Where Bond battled the bad guys in the crystal-clear Caribbean, the diminutive Crabb plunged into the cold, muddy tide of Portsmouth Harbour just before seven in the morning. He had about ninety minutes of air and by 9.15 it was clear something had gone wrong. For a while, it looked like the whole affair might be hushed up. The MI6 officer went back to the hotel to rip out the registration page. The hotel owner went to the press, who sniffed a good story.[88] The disappearance of a well-known hero could not be covered up.

The Prime Minister, who for weeks was not even told of Crabb's disappearance, was furious when the story broke, taking MI6's recklessness and amateurishness as a personal affront.[89] He was so angry that he broke with the normal 'neither confirm nor deny' rule over intelligence operations and told the Commons, 'I think it is necessary, in the special circumstances of this case, to make it clear that what was done was done without the authority or knowledge of Her Majesty's Ministers. Appropriate disciplinary steps are being taken.'[90] Elliott, to cover his own failings, blamed the politicians. 'A storm in a teacup was blown up by ineptitude into a major diplomatic incident ... he [Eden] flew into a tantrum because he had not been consulted and a series of misleading statements were put out which simply had the effect of stimulating public speculation.' Others thought Elliott was responsible for a veritable 'one man Bay of Pigs'.[91] A few wondered whether there had been a leak about the operation and if so from where. Just over a year later, a fisherman saw a black object floating thirty yards away in the water which looked like a tractor tyre. When he pulled it out with a hook he realised it was a headless, decaying corpse in a black frogman's suit.[92] Crabb's ex-wife could not even identify what was left, fuelling wild speculation that Crabb had defected or been abducted and taken to the Soviet Union. Decades later, a Soviet frogman would claim that a tip-off from a British spy meant that he had been lying in wait. Fearing that Crabb was planting a mine to blow up the ship, the frogman says he swam up from below to slash Crabb's air tubes and then his throat with a knife. The body was so small he at first thought it belonged to a boy. But he then found himself staring into the dying eyes of a middle-aged man. According to his unconfirmed account, he pushed the body away into the undercurrents, leaving a trail of blood.[93] The reflection in the mirror held up before MI6 by the Crabb incident was not lean Bond but a drink-addled frogman doing something stupid on a semi-freelance basis. It was not pretty.

The scandal was the last straw for the hapless Chief of the Service, John 'Sinbad' Sinclair. His weakness had led the Robber Barons to bypass him and all effective oversight: 'Where I felt if [a proposed operation] went any further somebody would say no – and I was quite certain of my judgement to carry out the operation – [you] simply tell them afterwards,' George Kennedy Young later said.[94] In a sign of just how far patience had worn thin with the cowboys, the service suffered the ignominy of having the head of MI5 sent to straighten things out. The new C, Dick White, walked down the dusty, decaying corridors of MI6 headquarters in Broadway and found a place haunted by the ghosts of the past. 'We're still cloak and dagger. Fisticuffs. Too many swashbuckling green thumbs thinking we're about to fight another Second World War,' one of his senior officers told him.[95] With the penchant for risk-tasking came an arrogance – a belief that they were the true guardians of the nation and its values – epitomised in a statement attributed to Young. In a world of increasing lawlessness, cruelty and corruption, he said, 'it is the spy who has been called upon to remedy the situation created by the deficiencies of ministers, diplomats, generals and priests ... these days the spy finds himself the main guardian of intellectual integrity.'[96]

The pendulum had swung too far towards risky, gung-ho operations and White began a purge to instil more professionalism. To protect his flank he later promoted Young to be his deputy, a move he would regret. Young, as head of the Middle East desk, had been involved in plotting the 1953 coup in Iran to remove the nationalist, but democratically elected, Prime Minister Mohammad Mossadegh, in concert with the CIA, a task which seemed to confirm that aggressive, covert political action could be a powerful tool. Mossadegh had thumbed his nose at the British by trying to reclaim control of his country's oil and the British had managed to persuade the Americans to help get rid of him. In the long term, like almost every action of its type, the coup proved to be a disaster as the Shah of Iran subsequently veered towards authoritarianism and the Iranian people blamed, and continue to blame, the British and Americans for their plight, both powers gaining a reputation for conspiring and manipulating in the Middle East (a reputation which British intelligence continues to have in many countries, in part thanks to Britain's colonial history of such entanglements). But at the time the taste for covert action had become intoxicating, a tempting panacea to mask the bitter reality that both political and economic power were rapidly ebbing away from Britain.[97] The spies hoped that with their tricks and coups they could magically preserve Britain's status through a kind of clandestine sleight of hand.

Twelve days after White took over MI6, President Gamal Abdel Nasser of Egypt nationalised the Suez Canal and so began a farcical campaign which would lead to the shattering of the illusions of power. Prime Minister Eden took it personally. Beyond the threat to oil supplies and the concern that Nasser was taking arms from a Soviet Union challenging Britain in its old playground, the idea that some jumped-up Arab could thumb his nose at *Great* Britain was too much for him. Eden was all handsome, polished charm on the surface. But beneath that he was highly strung and physically and mentally under strain with gout and nerves plaguing him, feeding on delusions of British grandeur. At Downing Street on the night of the nationalisation he ranted and raged. A kind of fever took hold of him in the coming days as he became obsessed with destroying Nasser. And he was unusually explicit about what that meant. There were no euphemisms or talk of ridding him of turbulent priests. One of his ministers recalled Eden calling him up on an unsecure line and saying, 'I want Nasser murdered, don't you understand?'[98] This was the licence to kill.

George Kennedy Young was left in little doubt about what he was being asked to do, nor did he harbour any moral doubts about such a course of action. 'It's not a Sunday-school picnic,' he later commented. 'Acts of government are not choices between good and bad. They are between two evils – the lesser of two evils. Someone is always going to get hurt by a decision of government ... absolute morality, absolute ethics just does not exist in affairs of the state.'[99] Before and after the war, Young drew up plans to kill Nasser, ranging from using dissident military officers to kitting out an electric razor with explosives, to using poison gas and sending out hit teams, all very redolent of the CIA's attempts to 'take out' Castro a few years later, which were equally hapless. Others in the service were reluctant to engage in that kind of behaviour, concerned that they would create a martyr.[100] (Other serious requests for assassination would include President Sukarno of Indonesia, which was ignored for fears of the consequences, and later to kill Idi Amin of Uganda.)[101] Nasser learnt of the plans and the KGB provided him with increased security, including a caged bird to warn of poison gas.[102]

But the debate about assassination was a sideshow to the real action. Young would later reflect that the problem with the whole Suez plan, in which he had the lead role within the service, was that it was a last play at Empire, at pretending that Britain did not have to live in the shadow of the Americans. The conspirators concocted a secret plan in which the Israelis would first invade part of Egypt and then the British and French would intervene as 'peacekeepers', leaving the Canal in their hands. 'It was the last self-conscious fling of the old British Style. Its failure may even have been mainly due to this style having become over self-conscious: the play and not the reality was the thing,' Young later wrote. 'As the old wartime basements in Whitehall were opened up for the task-force planners, they all flocked in ... rather too puffy of face and corpulent of body to play wistful roles. They were nevertheless delighted to see each other again, swap old memories, and once more sport their DSOs, MCs and Croix de Guerre.'[103]

The decrepitude of the old-school British intelligence establishment was all too clear to the CIA's representative on the Joint Intelligence Committee staff. The new boy from out of town, Chester Cooper, arrived in London just before Suez. At his first meeting, he found everyone to be very tall and wearing identical black suits (Savile Row), identical blue striped ties (Eton) and identical spectacles (National Health). As well as the latest intelligence documents, they also proceeded to hand round some Greek verse. At one point someone stuck his head through the door to announce the latest cricket score. There were groans. Cooper was then proudly shown a Latin translation of the Greek verse which had occupied someone's attention rather than the more formal documents at hand.[104]

In a situation more than a little reminiscent of another Middle Eastern war nearly half a century later, when British intelligence chiefs were asked what would happen after Nasser had been removed and who would run Egypt, 'there was a collective shrug'. They displayed little understanding of the force of Arab nationalism.[105] The experts failed over Suez to see what was going on in the Arab street and to understand the resentment the presence of foreign troops created.[106] MI6's intelligence on Egypt had also been fatally compromised. An entire network run under journalistic cover was penetrated by the Egyptians and in August was broken up, with thirty agents arrested and two British officials expelled.[107] This was a crippling blow whose impact would spur the desire for a new approach within the service. What the intelligence said did not matter much anyway, since the few warnings that were given were ignored.[108] The whole plot had been undertaken by a tiny cabal, including parts of MI6, around the Prime Minister with even some members of the JIC out of the loop (one transferred his life savings into American investments in fear of Britain's economic future when he found out).[109] The noises from the Soviet Union were sufficiently threatening for Daphne Park, by now stationed in Moscow, to be sent out of the Embassy with the Defence Attaché to look for any signs that the Soviets might respond with force.[110]

The disaster of Suez was blamed by Young, in true blustering style, on timidity in Whitehall and that old canard of failing to follow through on a good plan. 'There is a total collapse of will here,' he says he told his contact in Israel's Mossad during the operation.[111] The failure roused American fury (although the US may also have sensed an opportunity to quash British pretensions of power in the Middle East). The real fury came not just because of London, Paris and Tel Aviv planning their operation in secret and then executing it ineffectively but because of what was happening in Eastern Europe at exactly the same moment.

As the crisis reached its apogee, Cooper of the CIA was woken by a phone call before dawn on Saturday 3 November. He drove to his Embassy in Grosvenor Square, on the way waving to the prostitutes with whom he was now familiar from these trips. There he took a call from CIA Deputy Director Robert Amory. 'Tell your friends', an exasperated Amory shouted so loudly that Cooper thought he could have heard him across the Atlantic without a telephone, 'to comply with the god-damn cease-fire or go ahead with the god-damn invasion. Either way, we'll back 'em up if they do it fast. What we can't stand is their goddamn hesitation waltz while Hungary is burning.'[112]

From his prison cell in Budapest, Paul Gorka, the youthful resistance agent from Béla Bajomi's rolled-up network, had sensed a change of mood through October 1956.[113] One day came the sound of gunfire in the distance, the next that of heavy weapons and artillery followed by helicopters. The guards claimed it was 'just an exercise'. Then a captured tank smashed through the prison main gate. The freedom fighters on board released the prisoners, who stepped out to find bloodstained sandbags, smashed tanks and corpses littering the streets and a fully fledged anti-Communist uprising under way. Surely, with the promised resistance at last showing its strength, the West would come to its aid?

The first Western journalist to make it into the city during those violently hopeful days was Anthony Cavendish. On his way back from a late-night party in Vienna a few years earlier, his motorbike had skidded into a cyclist. This had been one run-in too many with Andrew King, then head of the MI6 station. Cavendish had been pushed out of MI6 and joined the UPI press agency. As he arrived in Budapest the Soviets were still in retreat from the outskirts of the city. 'On the back of one tank lay the corpse of a Soviet soldier, his eyes staring vacantly at the Hungarian capital ... A Hungarian peasant spat at one tank as it passed him an arm's length away,' he wrote.[114]

In the city, people asked Cavendish what the British and Americans were doing and when their help would arrive. There had been no advance warning of the uprising – another failure for British and American intelligence gathering. The CIA had only one officer in Hungary, who spent almost all of his time keeping his cover up and was under orders not to take an active role.[115] For a few, tense days Budapest was liberated. The Russians, for the first time, had been rolled back. And it had been done not by the CIA or by MI6 but by the Hungarian people. Then in the early hours of Sunday 4 November, Paul Gorka and his fellow fighters heard the voice of Imre Nagy, the leader of the uprising, say on the radio that Soviet tanks were on their way. As refugees headed over the border, the CIA station chief in Vienna received a stream of agent reports indicating Soviet preparations to crush the uprising. He knew there would be no cowboys riding to the rescue as the Soviet juggernaut primed itself.[116] In London, officials noted uneasily that they could not protest about Russians attacking Budapest when they had just attacked Egypt.[117]

Frank Wisner arrived in Vienna and watched as the final messages came over from the Hungarian partisans. 'We are under heavy machine gun fire . . . Goodbye friends. God save our souls.'[118] Wisner felt utter impotence as the full might of the Red Army descended on Budapest. He drank heavily that night. On Vienna's pavements people listened to the bleak news on outdoor speakers installed on lampposts.[119] 'It was desperate youngsters who sprung up as fast as others were cut down: it was flaming bottles of gasoline against armour and big guns,' wrote Cavendish in his despatch as the guns opened up on the city.[120]

As he listened to the news of the Soviet tanks entering the city, James McCargar was in a Viennese hotel room. 'My anger was vented on the British and French, whose adventure at Suez I wildly blamed for giving the Russians the pretext for the action in Hungary,' recalled McCargar. All the 'political warfare' and propaganda had led the Hungarians to believe they would not stand alone. They were wrong. There were no plans. There was no help. The Soviets had shown they were willing to use overwhelming force to maintain control of their European satellites and that the attempts to prise them away – whether through covert action or through supporting resistance groups – were likely to lead to nothing.[121] Roll-back was dead.

In London, George Kennedy Young was also angry at a betrayal by an ally. 'Although for ten years the United States government had always hoped for, even where it had not tried to propagate, a spirit of active resistance to Communism behind the Iron Curtain, when the moment came it was not prepared to lift a finger,' he wrote a few years later, perhaps overlooking the fact that lifting a finger over Hungary might have meant Armageddon. He also railed against

America's lack of support over Suez. 'When its own Allies acted in pursuance of what they believed to be their national interests, the United States government took the lead in preventing them.'[122]

Britain had continued to live and labour under the illusion that it was still a great power. Suez exposed the truth. After the initial flare of miserable anti-Americanism had subsided, some would look to a close relationship with Washington to exercise influence and power, wherever that took them; others looked to Europe. But no longer could it be done alone. The relationship with the US would never be quite the same again. It was clear who was in charge. Eden emerged broken, his eyes staring vacantly, his hands twitching and his face grey. In a piece of sublime irony, he set off for Jamaica to recuperate at Goldeneye, Ian Fleming's simple, shuttered, cliff-top home where the former Naval Intelligence man was writing the James Bond books, his own antidote to the reality of post-imperial decline. Eden and Fleming may not have been amused if they had known that the Egyptian intelligence service bought up copies of the Bond books for their training courses.[123]

The deaths in Budapest put paid to the idea that, with Stalin gone, the Soviet Union had fundamentally changed. It helped undermine much of the international appeal of Soviet Communism and there was disillusion from within as well, including for KGB officer Anatoly Golitsyn. The Hungarian uprising was, he claimed, the moment when he understood that the system could not be reformed.[124] Philby in Beirut watched the events faraway in Hungary and closer by in Egypt with a detached air. At the time he was going through one of his phases of feeling rather lost. His betrayals had left him in a strange halfway place between his two lives. His trail of personal devastation continued to grow. His second wife Aileen, who was back in Britain, had been self-harming for some time as her marriage disintegrated and perhaps also as she suspected her husband's dark secret. In Beirut, he received a telegram informing him of her death, news which caused him no distress. By then he had moved on. Just six weeks before Suez, he had been in the crowded bar of the St George's Hotel when he met Eleanor Brewer, the wife of the *New York Times* correspondent. He began to escort her around the souks and cafés and she left her husband. Before long Philby went to tell her ex-husband that he planned to marry Eleanor. 'That sounds like the best possible solution,' Brewer said. 'What do you make of the situation in Iraq?' he added, returning to the political issue of the day.[125] By 1959, Philby and Eleanor were living in a fifth-floor apartment full of her sculptures and his trinkets collected on travels around the region. For most who betray, falling in love is a risk, a vulnerability. But, after Litzi, Philby always managed to separate out his lives and Eleanor saw only the smile, never suspecting what it masked.

After Budapest, Anthony Cavendish went on to Beirut in the late 1950s with UPI, working from the top floor of a seafront hotel. There he filed despatches on bloody gun battles, lounging by the pool with a telephone cable stretched out to the side and a tray carrying beer next to him.[126] Every now and again he would have a 'drink or ten' with Philby for old times' sake at one of the hotel bars. Drinks would stretch on into the afternoon with Philby showing no ill effects. He never lost control or gave himself away no matter how much he consumed. Despite the accusations against him, Cavendish thought it was right to give his old colleague the benefit of the doubt. 'I thought he was a charming and excellent man and never had the least thought of him turning out to be what he turned out to be,' he recalled. 'I suppose I thought he must be very clever and we were very stupid.'[127]

At a Beirut restaurant in 1960, things began to look up for Philby. Nicholas Elliott had arrived as the new MI6 station chief and their friendship resumed and with it Philby's usefulness to the Soviets.[128] He also kept close to the CIA officers. 'Philby was friendly with all the Yanks in Beirut. A lot of them blabbed. He was pretty good at getting them to talk,' said George Kennedy Young, focusing on others' failings rather than his service's own.[129] Philby was still part of the old gang and the source of much interest. When Ian Fleming passed through town later that year, he too dined with his old chum Elliott, and the conversation inevitably turned to Philby.[130]

Philby's father St John had settled in a simple stone house outside Beirut near the mountains, allowing the father and son's strange relationship to resume. Philby looked up to him but never seemed too close and would sometimes blame his stutter on his father for unspecified reasons. The father had, though, impressed on his son the need to have the guts to go through with what one believed whatever others thought, a lesson the son certainly learnt.[131] Philby senior gave a speech at the American Women's Club in the city and told the audience the Americans had ruined Arabia. 'And who brought the Americans to Arabia?' he asked. He paused and then, full of contradictions to the end, said 'I did.'[132]

Elliott had lunch with both Philbys one day. St John was agreeable company. 'He left at tea time, had a nap, made a pass at the wife of a member of Embassy staff in a nightclub, had a heart attack and died early next morning. His last words were, "Take me away, I'm bored here."'[133] Philby junior went out of circulation for days afterwards. As 1962 progressed, Eleanor began to sense a change. The drinking was getting heavier with an edge of desperation, a desire to escape. When a pet fox he kept on his balcony was found dead, Philby plunged into a strange depression. On New Year's Eve he smashed his head against a radiator in a bathroom, leaving himself splattered with blood. A doctor said any more booze might have killed him that night. The denouement approached.

Elliott returned to Beirut for a very different kind of visit in January 1963. He had finished his time as head of station just three months earlier and been replaced by Peter Lunn, formerly of Vienna. Elliott was there to see Philby once more but no longer as his protector. Anatoly Golitsyn had defected with talk of a 'ring of five'. And Flora Solomon had told MI5 that Philby had tried to recruit her for the Soviets in the thirties. Arthur Martin now had enough evidence to convince Dick White. Martin was originally the man who was to be sent out but at the last minute Elliott took his place. The belief was that an old friend would be more likely to secure the deal that White had in mind. Remarkably, White felt he had to lie to Elliott to convince him of his friend's guilt by saying a KGB source had confirmed the exact identity of the traitor, which was not strictly true.[134]

Lunn telephoned Philby and asked him over to a flat which had been wired up for the occasion. Philby arrived at four in the afternoon still bandaged from his drunken fall. He walked in to find his old friend. Elliott got up from a chair.

'I rather thought it would be you,' said Philby. The meaning of these words would be the source of much pain for the British Secret Service.

'I'll get right to the point. Unfortunately it's not very pleasant,' said Elliott. 'I came to tell you that your past has caught up with you.'

Philby laughed. 'Have you all gone mad once again?' he said. 'You want to start all that? After all these years? You've lost your sense of humour! You'll be a laughing-stock!'

'No, we haven't lost anything,' Elliott responded. 'On the contrary. We've found additional information about you. And it puts everything in place.'

'What information? And what is there to put in place?'

Elliott stood up, paced the room, went to the window and looked out. Without turning, he said: 'Listen, Kim, you know I was on your side all the time from the moment there were suspicions about you. But now there is new information. They've shown it to me. And now even I am convinced, absolutely convinced that you worked for the Soviet intelligence services. You worked for them right up until '49.'[135]

Philby did not know what the new information was but would have suspected it was a defector. He knew they had something. But not everything. Why 1949? he might have wondered. So would others later, and some of those would suspect that this was a convenient way for his old friends to signal to Philby that he needed to confess only to crimes committed before he went to Washington that year, in order to keep him out of the clutches of the FBI. Of the Cambridge Five, Philby was the most hard headed, the one who never cracked under pressure, who found deception came easy to the end. It was not over yet.

'You stopped working for them in 1949, I'm absolutely certain of that,' Elliott explained. 'I can understand people who worked for the Soviet Union, say before or during the war. But by 1949, a man of your intellect and spirit had to see that all the rumours about Stalin's monstrous behaviour were not rumours, they were the truth ... you decided to break with the USSR ... Therefore I can give you my word, and that of Dick White, that you will get full immunity, you will be pardoned, but only if you tell it yourself. We need your collaboration, your help.'[136] As Philby prepared to walk out, Elliott added, 'I'm offering you a lifeline, Kim.' There was another line which Elliott later recalled saying but which Philby never recounted when he talked of the meeting, perhaps because it cut a little too close to the bone: 'I once looked up to you, Kim. My God, how I despise you now. I hope you have enough decency left to understand why.' Elliott told him they would meet again the following day. The whole encounter lasted about five minutes. Once he had left, Elliott told Lunn, 'Kim's broken. Everything's OK.'

Philby went back the next day and began to talk. He talked for two hours, saying he had worked for the Soviets until 1946 and had only tipped off Maclean as a friend in 1951. Elliott believed Philby had cracked. But he was still playing the game. Philby went back home and had a whole bottle of whisky. Elliott left for the Congo. Lunn, it was agreed, would take over and finish off the debrief.

In London, the initial 'confession' led to confidence that it would all be wrapped up soon. Roger Hollis, the head of MI5, wrote to Hoover at the FBI to say there was no evidence that Philby had worked for the Russians after 1946. 'If this is so, it follows that damage to the United States will have been confined to the period of the Second World War,' he explained, with more than a hint of plead-ing.[137] But after his meeting with Elliott, Philby had gone to his balcony to signal to his Soviet contact in Beirut – he held a book rather than a newspaper to indicate that it was urgent.[138] 'I think your time has come,' his contact told him. 'There's room for you in Moscow.'

On Wednesday, 23 January 1963, Kim and Eleanor Philby were due to go round to friends from the British Embassy for dinner. A violent storm had swept into Beirut and late in the afternoon Philby took his raincoat and told his wife he had a meeting and would be back at six in time for the party. An hour later, one of his boys told Eleanor that Philby had called to say he would meet her at the party. So she went alone, apologising for her husband's lateness and promising he would be there soon. The hours passed, and eventually everyone agreed to eat without him. Eleanor headed home through the storm, waves breaking against the corniche. At midnight, she called Peter Lunn. He was not there. Philby had been due to meet him and, when he failed to turn up, Lunn had gone straight to the Embassy, panic mingling with despair. Eleanor passed a message to Lunn's wife and ten minutes later Lunn called. 'Would you like me to come round?'

'I would be most grateful,' she said.[139]

She asked whether they should check the hospitals, fearing a car accident. She also suggested that perhaps he had gone off on a 'lost weekend' as he sometimes was wont to do. Lunn already feared a far worse truth and asked if anything was missing. Frantic search parties were sent out. It did not take long for him to realise that it was too late. As the sun rose over the mountains Eleanor knew he had gone. It was their wedding anniversary.

Elliott was about to cross the Congo River when he got the message and rushed back. Philby had the last laugh on the bungling Elliott in Beirut, the last laugh on the British ruling class and its old-fashioned notions of friendship and how 'gentlemen' behaved. He had left Beirut on a freighter and eventually arrived before dawn at a small Soviet frontier post. There were a few tables and chairs and a charcoal stove. Soldiers were brewing tea on the stove and the air was thick with cigarette smoke, he later recalled.[140] One man was waiting for him and in English said, 'Kim, your mission is concluded.'

Despite never having known or suspected he was a spy, Eleanor followed him in September to Moscow. 'He betrayed many people, me among them. But men are not always masters of their fate,' she wrote a few years later when it had all fallen apart and she had returned home. 'Kim had the guts, or the weakness, to stand by a decision made thirty years ago, whatever the cost to those who loved him most, and to whom he was deeply attached.'[141] It was a view echoed by the man himself. 'I have always operated at two levels, a personal level and a political one,' he later reflected.[142] 'When the two have come in conflict I have had to put politics first. This conflict can be very painful. I don't like deceiving people, especially friends, and contrary to what others think, I feel very badly about it. But then decent soldiers feel badly about the necessity of killing in wartime.'

'What a shame we reopened it all. Just trouble,' White told Elliott.[143] Some MI6 officers – and Philby himself – wondered if he had been allowed to flee to avoid the embarrassment of a trial at a time when the government was already reeling from a torrent of spy scandals, including in the Admiralty and MI6 itself.[144] A few came to believe that Philby had been tipped off by a mole within MI5. Most believe that, lacking evidence that could be presented in court, MI6 was hoping an old friend could be used to draw him home and find a quiet way of dealing with this through the exchange of immunity for information. That way no one would be embarrassed. Even when Philby had fled to Moscow, his old colleagues believed he must surely be a double agent 'run by a most secret section' within MI6. Or had he been bundled at gunpoint on to the ship? And everyone was asking: if Philby, then who else?[145] Arthur Martin at MI5 was furious. He had been supposed to go to Beirut to confront Philby using the evidence he had painstakingly built up. But 'they' had chosen one of their own instead, foolishly hoping to play on any vestiges of friendship that Elliott's presence could muster. Even the tapes were flawed because Lunn and Elliott had left the windows open, allowing traffic noises to drown out some of Philby's precious words. Typical MI6 amateurishness, Martin fumed, as he screwed up his eyes and pounded his knees with frustration, listening to what was left. 'It was no contest,' a colleague of Martin said when he listened to Elliott take on Philby. 'By the end they sounded like two rather tipsy radio announcers, their warm, classical public-school accents discussing the greatest treachery of the twentieth century.'[146]

The heyday for the 'wildmen' and the old timers was coming to an end. The old Russia hands were moved on through the 1950s. Harry Carr was sidelined after the Baltic disasters had been exposed and he left MI6 in 1961. At the end of his days, listening to Russian folk songs, he would blame Philby for everything. George Kennedy Young headed for the City the same year that Carr left and continued a long drift first to the right and then beyond to the political fringes, railing against the way in which non-white immigration was endangering Britain while the failure to check left-wing subversion was destroying it from within. When there were whispers in the 1970s of individuals with close connections to MI6 plotting a coup to overthrow the British government, it was Young whom they were talking about. In Washington, Frank Wisner went mad, literally. He was given electroshock therapy for six months in 1958 before being 'cured' and sent as station chief to London. Four years later he relapsed, and in 1965 he put a shotgun to his head and pulled the trigger.[147] Philby's friend and drinking buddy in Washington, James Jesus Angleton, also went mad, but in a different way. He saw himself as Machiavelli. Yet he had been fooled. His colleagues were sure he must have woken in the night remembering yet another secret he had shared with Philby over a Martini. The result in Angleton's mind was a paranoia about the Soviets and their deviousness, which when allied to the ideas of the KGB defector Anatoly Golitsyn would take the CIA and MI6 into a dark place.

Suez had revealed to Britain what it had become – a once great power in decline increasingly incapable of changing the world on its own terms – but Philby had compounded the problem by sowing distrust between Britain and the now dominant United States. When his successor took over as liaison to Washington he found the relationship virtually paralysed.[148] The same officer thought the impact on relations with Whitehall and the Foreign Office was even worse, 'cataclysmic' he thought, with a general perception of incompetence hanging over the service.[149] Philby's betrayal revealed that, for all the myths spun around MI6 by its own members as well as in the fictional world of Bond, its clubby amateurishness had been outwitted by its enemy. Philby tore the service's guts out and then held up the messy entrails he had exposed. A classified damage assessment of the Philby affair was carried out by an MI6 officer. Some officers when interviewed continued to resist the truth and lashed out at the Americans. The full extent of the carnage he wreaked, the agents blown, the operations compromised was truly shocking, according to those who read the report.[150] But it was his introduction of the cancer of betrayal and suspicion into an organisation and its relationships which was hardest to assess but perhaps most lasting in its effect.

The depth of the pain was largely hidden from public view. It would be years before the public at large began to understand that the 'mid-ranking civil servant' who was described as having defected was something far more. Some like Sir Stewart Menzies, the wartime head of MI6 on whose watch Philby had been recruited, knew all too well what had happened and felt haunted. When his son-in-law briefly moved in to stay with Menzies, the thin walls revealed that Menzies was 'suffering from the most appalling nightmares. There was one recurrent theme in these nightmares, which were awful to hear. That was there was a Russian defector who was taken up in a helicopter over the English Channel and given the choice – talk about Philby or be chucked out without a parachute. They chucked him out.'[151] Philby knocked the self-confidence of MI6. Even in the mid-1970s, new recruits remember wondering why certain operations and capabilities were not employed against the Soviets and they slowly realised that it was the legacy of Philby's betrayal and the fear of its being repeated.

As the 1960s got under way, old social conventions were breaking down and the establishment was increasingly being satirised in popular culture. This made Philby an anti-hero to some for exposing its failings. When George Blake was uncovered as a spy in 1961 there was anguish in the service over the secrets lost, but not the sense of personal betrayal associated with Philby. Blake was not one of 'us'. He was virtually a foreigner. 'But Philby, an aggressive, upper-class enemy, was of our blood and hunted with our pack,' wrote John le Carré.[152] Philby became the benchmark for treachery and his story would inspire le Carré to write his own study of betrayal, *Tinker, Tailor, Soldier, Spy.* Philby would be transformed into Bill Haydon, motivated initially to betray even his closest friend by anti-Americanism and a belief that 'the political posture of the United Kingdom is without relevance or moral viability in world affairs', the latter being a sentiment with which his pursuer Smiley half agreed. Haydon too became caught up in the game, unwilling or unable to leave.[153] Where Bond was depoliticised fantasy, le Carré rooted his vision in the mundane, sometimes brutal, realities he had observed from the inside.

Many individuals exert a fascination over the public, but rarely has one individual held such a fascination for so many years for a country that they betrayed. The obsession with Philby is a very British brand of masochism. If a country gets the spies it deserves, then perhaps its spies also get the traitors they deserve. Philby himself always denied being a traitor to anything. 'To betray, you must first belong,' he told a British journalist who confronted him in Moscow. 'I never belonged.'[154]

In the spy's world, patriotism allied to loyalty is the only insurance against treachery. It is a world in which deceit is part of everyday life, whether in protecting one's own cover or in encouraging someone else to betray their country. For a service which encourages betrayal by others, patriotism to country and loyalty to friends is the only guarantee against those skills being turned inwards. While spies trade in treachery, they find it utterly unconscionable among their own. Like the police who need to guard against an understanding of crime turning into a temptation to pursue it, the spies need to draw stark lines to deter subversion from within.

Probe deeper and there is a hint of admiration, though, for the way in which Philby managed to remain consistently loyal to an ideal and carried off his deceit so coolly. 'I differ from my British colleagues who hated him,' CIA man Miles Copeland later said. 'How could I hate him for being a double agent when we were doing the same thing to the other side ... He was one of the best intelligence officers this century. The way he kept one step ahead of the hounds was masterful. I wish we had some like him operating for us.'[155] One former MI6 officer turned writer also thought Philby 'may be regarded as a real-life James Bond. His boozy amours, his tough postures, his intelligence expertise, are directly related to the same characteristics in Fleming's hero.'[156] For Cavendish, Philby was simply doing a job. Young too retained a grudging professional respect.

It is said that new recruits who have arrived at MI6 in recent years, fresh-faced and eager to spy for Britain, have been sat down as part of their training and shown a film of a man many have barely heard of from the distant past. They watch his performance in front of the TV cameras at his mother's flat in 1955. They watch him lie and try to spot the signs that he is lying. Perhaps this is training them in how to get away with it. But it is also a warning of what betrayal looks like. The film runs to the end and there is silence in the room.

3

A RIVER FULL OF CROCODILES –
MURDER IN THE CONGO

It was only her second week in the Congo but Daphne Park was
sure she recognised the thin young African standing in the visa
queue outside the British Consulate General. With short hair, glasses
and a goatee beard, he carried the air of an intellectual with perhaps
a touch of arrogance. As Park struggled to place the scrawny figure,
she might have been surprised to know that the future of the country
lay in his hands, that through him the Cold War would arrive in
Africa and that those she counted as her friends would plan his
murder.[1]

Africa held no fear and few surprises for Daphne Park. She might
not be able to blend in, but this was no strange, alien land. Jack Park,
her father, had been sent to South Africa as a young man in the
hope the climate would improve his health. During one of his many
hospital stays, he had advertised in a magazine for a penfriend, and
a teenager named Doreen, also living in South Africa, had replied.
She hid her gender, signing only with an initial, but eventually Jack,
in his late thirties, would marry the eighteen-year-old girl. Their life
was far from easy. Daphne Park used to say that her father was 'a
man who could not spot a rogue at six inches' and he was repeatedly
fleeced, his tobacco farm struggling towards bankruptcy in the early
1920s. In a desperate attempt to reverse his fortunes, he headed for
Tanganyika, chasing news of a gold strike. Panning the river for
alluvial gold, he dreamed of buying out the coffee farm where Doreen
toiled. But his luck never quite turned. From the age of six months,
their daughter Daphne grew up in a mud-brick house with no
running water and no electricity. The nearest white family was a ten-
mile walk away. The only time Park was beaten by her father was
when she was rude to an African man.[2]

Park's mother was going blind and her daughter read Rudyard

Kipling's *Kim* and John Buchan's spy stories out loud, plunging the two of them into a world of Empire, adventure and spies, a world which captivated the young girl and from which she never quite emerged. Kim Philby may have despised Kipling's creed and the novel which provided him with his name, but for Park these stories of the guarding of Britain and its Empire instilled an unstinting belief in spies as the last line of defence. Far away in Africa, this child of Empire had an uncomplicated faith in her country, right or wrong. By the time she reached the age of eleven, it was clear she needed schooling. Doreen sold her last pieces of jewellery to allow her daughter to make a journey which began with a three-day walk through the bush to reach a lorry which in turn took her to Dar es Salaam to catch a boat to take her to England and then eventually to school in South London. Daphne did not see her parents for twelve years and she would never again see a younger brother, David, who died and was buried in Tanganyika (late in life Daphne Park's unsuccessful search for his grave would weigh heavily on her). The Special Operations Executive, training French fighters, had led to the Field Intelligence Agency Technical in Vienna, hunting Nazi scientists, which in turn had delivered her to MI6. From there she was thrust into Moscow during the Suez Crisis. After a subsequent stint as the London co-ordinating officer for MI6's German stations, her superiors decided to post Park to the increasingly important intelligence battleground of Africa. Their first thought had been to send her to Guinea. The country had just become independent from the French and the Russians were moving in. But knowledge of Africa was extremely limited in MI6. 'You must all be mad,' the Foreign Office's Consul General in Dhaka said when he was consulted on her appointment. 'It's a Muslim country. She will never meet anybody but women behind the veil.' A hasty look at the map led Park instead to be sent as consul to both the French and Belgian Congo in 1959. The timing could not have been better.

A fourteen-day boat journey took Park into the sweltering heart of Africa past a lush green country of rolling hills, their monotony broken only by the occasional isolated village. Rather than talk to the other, rather dreary colonial Europeans on board, Park made her way down to third class where a group of Africans were returning from a world youth conference in her old hunting ground of Vienna.

Down below decks were the bright young men of the future, fired up by the hope of a new Africa free of colonialism. This was a time of rapid change across the continent as white and Western rule was being challenged openly. More than a dozen states would become independent in the coming year. Many of the young men below decks had been enticed by Communism and looked towards Russia as the future. Park, fresh from Moscow, did her best to draw back the veil of Soviet life. The men's faith may not have been dented but a few would remain in touch with the young English lady who was willing to take them on in debate. On the way, the boat had stopped in Accra and Park bought a local newspaper. In the paper there was a photograph of another group of young Africans who had attended a conference organised by Kwame Nkrumah, who had led Ghana to its independence from Britain two years earlier. He was the leading light of a rising pan-Africanism which aimed to spread anti-colonialism among fellow Africans with a view to uniting them in a 'United States of Africa' which would reject economic as well as political exploitation. One of the men in the picture was from the Congo. His name, the paper said, was Patrice Lumumba. Two weeks later, Daphne Park twigged that the man in the visa queue outside the Consulate General was the man in the newspaper photograph.

'Are you Monsieur Lumumba?' she asked.

'Yes, I am.'

'Well, come with me, we'll have a cup of coffee and get your visa in due course.'

She asked one of the local Africans employed at the Consulate General to bring two cups. He brought only one and placed it in front of Park with a glare. He disapproved of a young European woman sitting down with an African man to share coffee. Park, who cared little for social conventions that stood in her path, especially relating to gender, gave Lumumba her coffee and asked for another.

Lumumba was a rising star in the chaotic firmament of Congolese politics. Born to a poor family in a small village, he had become a post office clerk, educated himself and quickly became the leading Congolese voice for radical, pan-African nationalism.[3] He was a volatile, passionate orator who knew how to whip up a crowd but whose judgement could be erratic. The political party he had founded, the National Congolese Movement (MNC), demanded independence from Belgium.

Park talked politics with Lumumba for a while. She asked how long he would be away for on his visa because she would like to talk more. She happened to be heading for the provincial capital of Stanleyville in ten days' time. This was the location of Lumumba's power base. Could she meet the Central Committee of his party? Of course, Lumumba said, offering an introduction to his adviser, a Croatian émigré.

Park called on the Croat during her visit to Stanleyville. After a useful chat, she inquired about meeting the Central Committee.

'Do you like fishing?' he said.

'Yes, I do,' she said.

'Would you like to come for some night-fishing?'

'Of course. When?'

'Tonight.'

Daphne Park and the Croat sat in a small canoe illuminated by a bright nightlight. At two in the morning, the boat pulled into the bank. Some men were sitting around the fire. She was introduced to them one by one as a sharp knife neatly filleted the fish. She produced a bottle of whisky. After talking for a while, she got back into the boat and headed off.

'Well, I enjoyed that very much but I still want to meet the Central Committee,' she told the Croat.

'You have just met them,' he replied. 'They're under surveillance and you're under surveillance. But the Belgians don't go surveilling at night on the river.'

Three of the men seated around the fire that night eventually became ministers in the future Congolese government.

The British Consulate General in which Park worked was a tiny building in the untidy hotchpotch of the capital, Leopoldville. Here a model Belgian colonial city with wide boulevards and tall residential buildings struggled forlornly to assert itself against the Africa in which it had been implanted. There were perhaps only 250 Britons in the country, and traditionally the Consulate General's job had been as much to serve the interests of British big business which had invested in the Congo including BP, Unilever and British American Tobacco. There was a particular British interest in the mineral-rich southern province of Katanga which the colonial adventurer Cecil Rhodes had tried to capture for Britain in the late nineteenth century until he had been outmanoeuvred by the Belgians. Katanga bordered British Rhodesia, and the Belgians were always convinced that the British were playing their games down there to try and steal it back.

The same year Park arrived a senior MI6 officer had gone on a tour of what had been a neglected continent for the British Secret Service. Inside MI6 there had been limited interest in Africans or in what they thought. Africa did not even merit its own controller, instead being lumped in with the strategically more important Middle East. But in the summer of 1956, as Britain and France were mired in Suez and the Hungarians were being crushed, the first real stirrings of nationalism were evident in the Congo as a group of Africans launched a manifesto calling for independence. The following year after Ghana had become independent under Kwame Nkrumah, the Russians were glimpsed lurking in the background. A Foreign Office memo from May 1959 warned of a Soviet strategic objective to remove Western influence from Africa. Under Khrushchev the USSR was taking on a more active role, exploiting anti-Western sentiment and racial tension.[4]

The MI6 officer who traversed the continent in 1959 wrote a detailed report which was passed up to the Prime Minister. The report warned of a kaleidoscope of local struggles, particularly against colonial powers, each of which could fuel the others. Thanks to Britain's imperial past and legacy, MI6 always had more of a global interest than many other intelligence services, and what happened in Africa mattered directly to London. The MI6 officer found the situation in the Belgian Congo among the most worrying. 'One cannot help being struck by the apparent abdication of the will to govern by the Belgian authorities. The country is now wide open to subversion from every quarter and it may well be that the Belgian Congo in its present geographical form will not survive much longer.'[5]

On his last day, the Belgian Director General for Security in the Congo approached the MI6 man with a message. 'I should know that the majority of senior officials in the Belgian Congo believed that the British government had a long-term Machiavellian plan for West

Africa,' he was told. 'They believed that, when the dust from their present nationalist troubles in Africa had settled, the world would find the French and Belgian Empires disappeared and the British still in position, having taken over all the valuable trade concessions.' The MI6 officer contested the view but was met with a wry smile. The Soviets were watching closely, the officer warned London, knowing that 'they have a very good chance of filling to a considerable extent the power vacuum being created by the withdrawal of the Western powers'. They were looking for bases from which to operate and trying to gain control of pan-African nationalist movements. The Congo was likely to be a major target, he warned presciently.[6]

When she arrived, Park had been determined to be close to the Africans and so rejected the first house she was offered, an elegant air-conditioned villa with a pool, because it was located in the special area reserved for diplomats, patrolled by Dobermans and armed guards. The city was segregated, with Africans needing a pass to get through police cordons at night. 'I thought to myself no African is ever going to come and see me and have to pass through all that.' Instead she chose a villa six miles out of town on the road to the airport and not far from the university. No pool. No air conditioning. No guards watched the house at night. Only once did she feel threatened, when she heard robbers at the window. She bellowed out of the window that she was a witch and that their extremities would drop off if they continued to bother her. She slept alone in her house in Africa, as she had often done as a girl when her parents were away. The Belgians thought she was mad. But the Africans came to visit.

The Congolese would drop in on their way to the village or en route to the airport. Mostly they arrived on bicycles or on foot. They would come to gossip or borrow books from her. Few black Congolese had ever had a normal, non-professional conversation with a European and her openness made Park a novelty. Gradually she built a unique network of contacts. She made her first agent recruitment when she provided an individual with what appeared to be sensitive information to strengthen his position (which in fact derived from the BBC summary of world broadcasts, though she did not mention that to him). But this was an exception. None of the other men she got to know were signed up as agents of the Secret

Intelligence Service. 'I never said "Will you work for SIS?" I never needed to say I was an intelligence officer and I never did. And I never recruited anybody in that way. I never sat down and said, "Sign on the dotted line and I'm going to pay you tuppence." It was understood that I had power ... I never said to them, "Please tell me a secret." I talked to them until they told me a secret.'

Agents come in different shapes and sizes, singles, doubles, occasionally triples, conscious and unconscious, each case unique. In Park's line of business and in much of MI6's work in Africa and the Middle East, the classic agent betraying secrets was complemented by a more complex breed, so-called agents of influence or confidential contacts. These are people with whom Secret Service officers like Park will have relationships but who may not necessarily be betraying their own governments, indeed they may often be acting with their knowledge and permission. In some cases they may even be the rulers themselves. These contacts offer the opportunity for back-channel talks and for each side to sound the other out and also, perhaps, persuade each other to go in one direction or another when it comes to policy. In some parts of the world, notably the Middle East and Africa, this was a crucial aspect of MI6 officers' work and it was the aspect at which Daphne Park would excel throughout her career.

For Park, Secret Service work was about trust, not betrayal. For that reason she had a deep loathing of the bleaker fictional portrayals of her world. 'John le Carré I would gladly hang, draw and quarter,' she would say later. 'He dares to say that it is a world of cold betrayal. It's not. It's a world of trust. You can't run an agent without trust on both sides. Of course it is limited. Of course there are things he won't tell you, of course there are things I won't tell him – that's understandable. But if you are actually considering whether the agent is telling you something of vital interest, you need to know that this is somebody who has worked for you and you have to know that he has been trustworthy in other matters before ... And he, for his part, knows that what he tells me I'm not going to go and chat about in the nearest bar and I'm not going to talk about it to anybody. What he says is going to be protected and his identity is going to be protected.'[7]

Building relationships with men was never a problem for Park.

More matron than Mata Hari though, she scoffed at the idea of using feminine charms. 'I wasn't a particularly sexy person,' she explained. 'It's been a huge advantage during my professional career that I've always looked like a cheerful, fat missionary,' she once remarked. 'It wouldn't be any use if you went around looking sinister, would it?'[8] She had never been encouraged by the service to use her femininity to extract information. 'I'm sad to say they only had to look at me to know there wasn't much point in that.'[9]

Sexism pervaded the British Secret Service (as it did the CIA and the KGB). In that sense, at least, James Bond's attitudes were not too far divorced from reality. 'A woman's chief weapon in obtaining information is sex; having once secured an agent or informer by this means, she may easily over-reach herself and fall in love,' warned one MI6 station chief of the old school, noting that 'English women as a rule have little knowledge or experience of foreigners and are less capable of handling them than, say, a Frenchwoman.'[10] During the war, another officer (later to be Daphne Park's boss) noted that 'most of the male officers are fairly pudding-like and are either misogynists or else consider that a woman's place is the bed and the kitchen, certainly not the mess'.[11]

Daphne Park subscribed to the idea that the only thing that stood in the way of a woman succeeding was her own determination. She had made it into her beloved Secret Service through sheer force of personality despite the fact that women, on the whole, were not allowed to be officers. They were, however, given real operational responsibilities as secretaries in the overseas stations, particularly in the smaller offices where there was only one male officer. 'If you were right off in the bush somewhere', explained Park, 'and you had to go travelling, you went away knowing that the secretary would run the agents, would pick things up, would look after things, would pretty well do what you would have done provided you had a good one ... I think we took it for granted quite a lot, I'm sorry to say.' One secretary in Africa was considered far superior to her boss, and there were at least three countries where she could not appear without being taken out for dinner by the head of state. Yet she was never made an officer. After the brief post-war window in which Park was recruited, no more women were made full MI6 officers until the

1960s when just one or two were allowed in before the door was once again slammed shut until the late 1970s.

Female spies had to convince the men that just because they could not hand over an envelope in a men's lavatory, as their male colleagues took such perverse joy in doing, that did not mean they were unable to find some other way of operating. They did occasionally face a different problem. Some men open up more to a female spy, but female MI6 officers also have to be on the lookout for their targets making a pass at them. Occasionally, a recruitment pitch may have to be launched pre-emptively to prevent the target thinking that the friendliness is for a personal rather than professional motive. 'You must have realised I work for MI6 we would say,' one female officer recalls. 'They always say, "Oh yes of course".' In some cultures, a woman having lunch with a man may raise suspicions, but not necessarily suspicions of espionage, and this can provide useful cover. In Africa, though, such contact could be difficult. Only once did an African – a close aide to Lumumba – try it on with Park. 'I pushed him out of the car and I said get out.'

'All the Belgian women love it,' he said.

'Well, I'm not Belgian,' she replied.

'I'll tell Lumumba that you are anti-black,' he countered.

'You go ahead and tell him.'

The next time she went to see Lumumba she wondered what would happen. Lumumba gave a broad grin. 'Your little friend has just put a crate full of the very best eggs in your car and he will not be seeing you again,' he said.

Park also had occasionally to fight off unwanted attention from the Foreign Office. One problem was that the Foreign Office wanted to keep what it saw as the troublemakers of MI6 off its patch. The Secret Service was already banned from operating in British colonies – that was technically 'internal security' and therefore the domain of MI5. And elsewhere on the continent the Africa hands of the Foreign Office disliked spies interfering (George Kennedy Young called one wheelchair-bound Foreign Office official who tried to keep MI6 away 'a crippled mind in a crippled body ... They don't understand communist manipulation'.)[12] Before Park's arrival, the Foreign Office and MI6 had squared off over how long the Belgians would remain in control of the Congo.[13] It was eventually agreed that

MI6 would cultivate relationships rather than aggressively recruit spies.

Daphne Park was not immune from the clashes which often occurred in the field between an ambassador, keen to keep relations ticking over, and a spy, there to steal secrets and generally get up to no good. From its inception, the Secret Service was seen as a grubby relation who had to be tolerated by Britain's snooty diplomats who liked to keep their distance ('A diplomatist has as much right to consider himself insulted if he is called a spy as a soldier has if he is called a murderer,' wrote one Foreign Office man).[14] MI6 officers are supposed to seek sign-off from the ambassador for their operations. 'They would say we're going to get this wonderful intelligence and, if it goes wrong, we need your advice on what the consequences would be,' recalls one former ambassador. 'Well, it is perfectly obvious what the consequences would be – there's going to be a huge bloody great row.'[15] Cultivating a relationship with an ambassador can be nearly as important as doing so with an agent, as Daphne Park discovered. Just as things were beginning to get interesting in the Congo at the start of 1960, Park received a telegram from London asking where she would like to go next. She did not want to go anywhere, she replied. The reply came that a new ambassador, Ian Scott, had been appointed and he had decided he did not want to have a 'friend' – the Foreign Office's occasionally ironic euphemism for a member of MI6.[16] The new man thought it risked destroying his relationship of trust with the Congolese to have MI6 going round spying on people. Park was despondent. But when Scott arrived she threw some parties for him to introduce him to all the new ministers whom she had got to know. At the end of that week Scott, known for his direct manner, asked Park to see him.

'You know that I wanted you withdrawn.'

'Yes, I did.'

'You know I would be happy for you to stay as head of Chancery.'

'Look, I'm already doing head of Chancery, but that's not what I'm here for. I'm here because I'm an SIS officer.'

'Yes, but I can't have that. All sorts of things might happen. However, I might consider it if you would engage to tell me the names of all your agents so that I can decide.'

'I'll go and pack my bags,' replied Park.

'What do you mean?'

'We have an agreement when we recruit people. They are not told about to anybody. There is an absolute rule about that and I wouldn't dream of breaking it. So even if I wanted to do what you suggest I couldn't. It's against our entire ethos.'

'Well, don't you think I'm trustworthy?'

'No. I don't actually.'

'What do you mean?'

'What would happen would be that you would meet one of them – because I don't waste my time recruiting people who are not import-ant – you would meet one of them and you wouldn't be able to resist saying to one of them, "Most interesting idea of yours about such and such," which you remembered from having read his report and he would instantly know that you knew. And that would be the end of that. That is the rule: we do not give the names to anybody outside the service.'

'Well, perhaps I could see your reports first?'

'You do see all my intelligence reports – they are not circulated in Whitehall without being able to say the ambassador agrees or dis-agrees. So that already happens.'

'You're quite sure?' Scott asked, probing to see if she would give a little ground.

'I'm very sorry but I'm quite sure,' Park replied firmly.

'Oh well. Let's leave things for a bit then.'

In the weeks after that conversation, the Congo was to be thrust on to the front page of the papers and to the top of the diplomatic in-tray. Park would prove herself to be indispensable and the Ambas-sador would become a close ally.

Seventy years before Daphne Park took her boat to the country, the writer Joseph Conrad had set out on his own journey up the Congo River, fictionalised in his novel *Heart of Darkness*. The dark-ness was not Africa but the horrors of the colonial mind and its violent outpourings. In 1885, the Congo had become not a Belgian colony but a personal possession of King Leopold II, acquired with the assistance of the British explorer Henry Stanley (two of the largest cities were named after the men). Colonialism in Africa did not have a good record, but Leopold's and Belgium's record in the Congo was the most wretched. Leopold never set foot in the country, but during the twenty-three years that it was his personal fiefdom an estimated ten million Congolese died from disease or starvation or at the hands of the death squads led by the feared Force Publique. A whip made from thick hippopotamus hide was used to keep the locals in line. Entire villages would be massacred if they did not accede to colonial demands and agree to act as slaves to extract rubber and other resources to feed the King's greed.[17] The heads on poles which Conrad wrote about outside the house of the mad colonist Kurtz were a reflection of a culture in which killing was a sport. In 1908, the King sold the colony – eighty times the size of Belgium – to the government in Brussels as if it was a toy he had tired of.

By the mid-1950s, the Belgians could see which way the wind was blowing and started to think about possibly one day granting independence in the distant future, perhaps after a few decades. They did little to prepare the country for that possibility and failed to develop any effective political institutions. There were few ties that bound the six provinces and the myriad tribes together. There were only around twenty African university graduates by the end of the 1950s out of a population of fourteen million, and no doctors or engineers.[18] But then in 1959 riots erupted in Leopoldville's broad streets and Belgium lost its nerve (Graham Greene, in the country at the time to research his book on a leper colony, remembered colonial Belgians sleeping with guns beneath their pillows).[19] Brussels feared being drawn into the kind of violent struggle that was engulfing France in Algeria and so decided to grant independence in a rush, even though the country was woefully under-prepared. Elections were held in May 1960 with independence scheduled absurdly soon afterwards – at the end of the following month. The man who took the second highest tally of seats, the weak-willed and highly influenceable Joseph Kasavubu, was offered the ceremonial role of president. The man who won most seats and would become prime minister was the man from the visa queue, Daphne Park's friend Patrice Lumumba.

Lumumba had already been singled out as trouble by some Westerners who had taken part in a conference on independence in Belgium in January that year. He had been released from jail especially to attend, having been convicted of making inflammatory speeches the previous October when he addressed 2,000 people, talking of death for liberty.[20] The American Ambassador to Brussels observed him at the conference and reported him as having 'a highly articulate, sophisticated, subtle and unprincipled intelligence' – someone who told people what they wanted to hear.[21] 'He gave the impression that he was not a man who could be dominated,' a friend recalled. 'And a man who could not be dominated was dangerous.'[22]

It had been hot and humid as independence approached, the tense atmosphere heightened by the discovery of bodies every morning, the product of tribal or political murder. In June, the British Consul General Ian Scott (who would become an ambassador after independence) threw the traditional Queen's Birthday Party at his house on the banks of the river.[23] On an overcast evening, a Salvation Army band played a tune everyone recognised. It was called 'We are drifting to our doom'. The lights in the garden fused and a fine drizzle began.

The gloom had lifted by the morning of 30 June – independence day – as Patrice Lumumba strode confidently into the imposing Palais de la Nation, originally built to be the residence of the Belgian governor general. An exuberant smile played on his face and he wore a bow tie with a sash across his smart suit. The Prime Minister waved to his supporters. Dignitaries from across Africa and further afield had gathered for the occasion. King Baudouin had come from Belgium and stood before a bronze statue of Leopold II, promising a wonderful future for the former colony – so long as it did not turn its back on those who had looked after it for so long. 'Don't be afraid to come to us. We will remain by your side,' he told the crowd. The absurdity of the speech reflected the grotesqueness of the colonial experience. Even Ian Scott thought it went just a bit too far.[24] 'It's now up to you, gentlemen, to show that you are worthy of our confidence,' the King proclaimed. 'The independence of the Congo is the culmination of the work conceived by the genius of Leopold II.'[25]

Kasavubu, the country's new president, pronounced a few words. Scott thought them 'sensible, moderate and flavoured with a certain humility'. Lumumba had not originally been scheduled to speak. But he had decided he would have his moment. He stepped forward and played to the gallery, speaking directly and angrily to and for the Congolese people rather than addressing the diplomats. 'Fighters for independence today victorious, I salute you in the name of the Congolese government', he began. 'We have known sarcasm and insults, endured blows morning, noon and night, because we were niggers,' he told them. 'Who can forget the volleys of gunfire in which so many of our brothers perished, the cells where the authorities threw those who would not submit to a rule where justice meant oppression and exploitation?' Scott thought the speech, which was as interrupted eight times by applause, 'hard, bitter, accusatory and xenophobic, directed against the Belgians'. The man sitting next to Scott leant over and said he thought the King would walk out.

The Belgians' moustaches trembled with rage as they listened to Lumumba. The King turned to Kasavubu halfway through. 'Mr President, was this planned?' 'Of course not, no,' the new President replied.[26] When Lumumba had finished, a band played an upbeat tune known as the 'Independence Cha-cha-cha'. Across the country, people listened to their radios in wonder. Belgian officials were outraged and humiliated by this young upstart and his lack of respect. A formal lunch was delayed for two hours while the King and the Belgian cabinet deliberated whether to attend or not (they did). Afterwards Lumumba told Scott that he had made the speech to 'satisfy the people' and to reflect his own anger at the Belgians' attempts to prevent him becoming prime minister in the preceding weeks.[27] When the British representative from London had a fifteen-minute meeting with the new Prime Minister the following day, he came out saying 'He is a no-good.'[28] Like Nasser, Lumumba was a national liberationist who wanted to assert sovereignty against the West. He warned that he would not allow political colonialism to be replaced by a new form of indirect economic colonialism. This was an unwelcome message for countries which had large investments in the mining business as they extracted the country's rich deposits of copper, cobalt and diamonds. The Congo held its breath, especially the 20,000 Belgians who remained in the country. For the first few days, the streets were quiet.

Ten days after independence, a sharply dressed American with his thin black hair slicked back in the fashion of the time stepped on board the ferry for Leopoldville. Daphne Park's newly appointed opposite number from the CIA was heading into town. 'There are a lot of black-tie dinners,' a colleague had reassured Larry Devlin before he left. 'You'll be on the golf course by two o'clock every afternoon.'[29] Reality soon hit him in the face, nearly fatally. As he stepped off the ferry, Devlin was faced with soldiers waving machetes in his face. 'We will kill you,' one said to him. Devlin had been recruited into the CIA from Harvard where he had been destined for the academic life. He had been enticed by the idea that the CIA would fight Moscow's ambitions without the US having to engage in the type of open warfare he had witnessed as a soldier in the Second World War. Africa had been left to the Europeans for many years and the CIA had created its Africa division only in 1959. A cool customer in his dark suit, white shirt and shades and with a cigarette rarely out of his hands, Devlin would relish the chance to take on the Soviets in this important new Cold War arena as he became the arch-puppeteer of Congolese politics.

By the time Devlin arrived, the calm of independence a few days earlier had evaporated and the country had been plunged into chaos. The Force Publique was renamed the Congolese Army, but all of its senior officers were white and, like many Belgians, they believed that independence would not change the way things worked. To make the point, a general scrawled on a blackboard in front of his men, 'Before independence = After independence'. That – followed by the announcement of a pay rise for civil servants but not for the army – was too much. A mutiny began in Thysville and unrest spread among soldiers throughout the country, including in the capital.

Daphne Park had a lucky escape in the midst of the violence thanks largely to an incident a few weeks earlier. She had been driving at night through the city when she was flagged down by a distressed African member of the Force Publique. She assumed it was some kind of accident. 'My comrade is in trouble. Please come and help me,' the man said. The streets were pitch black, bereft of lighting, which made the deep storm drains on either side particularly treacherous. Finally, they reached a group of men fighting on the ground. At the bottom of the pile was a friend of the man who had stopped Park. She halted the car and flashed the lights. She then climbed out and banged on the car until she had got everyone's attention.

'I'm very sorry but I'm a very bad driver and if I reverse I shall fall in the ditch, so I have to drive forwards. Would you mind all getting up and getting out of the way?' she said.

The men roared with laughter at this woman who was not even able to reverse her car. They fell about, slapping each other on the back, crying, 'She can't reverse!'

'And by the way, can I have that soldier?' she added. 'I'm going past the barracks.' And so she drove off with the soldier and took him and his comrade home.

When the mutiny began, Park was driving back into town in the evening with an American. As she passed through the rubbish-strewn streets she turned a corner to be met with a scene of anarchy as drunken troops went on a rampage. People wandered around dazed, with battered and bleeding heads. Park was dragged out of her car.

'He is American, I'm British,' she said.

'No, you lie, you are Flemish,' they replied, identifying them as their real enemy.

At length, after arguing over their nationality, they were allowed back into their car.

Park eventually returned home to find an array of British nationals, mainly from the colonies, waiting outside her house in hope of some assistance from the British Consul. On 8 July, the British and French embassies had ordered the evacuation of all non-essential personnel. Stories of rape and murder by the Congolese troops had spread through the white community like wildfire. Everyone wanted to be taken to the ferry to get out to Brazzaville, the smaller and scruffier capital of the French Congo which lay just over the river from Leopoldville and acted as a refuge for those fleeing. Park explained that the ferry did not run before six in the morning and said that everyone should return just before then and without any weapons. Some protested that they needed to defend themselves. She pointed out that the troops had machine guns.

As their convoy headed for the ferry in the morning, soldiers high on drugs were stopping people at makeshift checkpoints and roughing them up. But Park navigated her way through. They seemed to be looking for Russians or Belgians, but not for Britons. A queue of abandoned cars a quarter of a mile long led up to the jetty. Once the ferry was in sight Park's heart sank. Half a dozen cars were burning and there were bloodied people wandering around. Park walked up to the largest soldier, who looked to be in charge.

'I am the British Consul and these are British subjects,' she said.

To her astonishment she was embraced by the man, who said, 'You are my friend. Don't you remember me? You're the one who can't reverse.'

Park could not remember him at all.

He turned and said to all the others, 'This is my friend – she can't reverse you know.' There were roars of laughter. 'You are my friend when I wasn't important, so what do you want?' he asked.

'I'd just like these people to get on the ferry to Brazzaville. They have all got business there.'

He looked at her. 'You can't go.'

'I don't want to go. I've got work here.'

'All right. They are all your friends?'

'They are all my dearest personal friends.'

Park saw them on to the ferry and headed back to the Embassy. A few weeks later, a telegram came from the Foreign Office stating that there had been a question asked in parliament about a British diplomat who had fraternised with the murderous Congolese soldiers. The Ambassador sent back a beautifully crafted but sizzling reply which ended the matter.

Devlin had his own close call. He was picked up by a band of mutinous soldiers in the centre of Leopoldville. Five of them took him to a hot, stuffy room filled with hemp smoke and proceeded to interrogate him, ignoring protests that he was a diplomat. One of the men demanded that Devlin kiss his feet. Devlin refused. He had seen how soldiers had stamped on people's heads as they leant down.

'Ever played Russian roulette?' the soldier asked, putting a gun to his head and spinning the chamber. 'Kiss my foot.'

'Merde!' Devlin replied.

The soldier pulled the trigger. Click. Nothing. He cocked the gun without spinning and demanded again that his foot be kissed.

'Merde!' shouted Devlin again.

Another click. The pattern was repeated until the soldier came to pull the trigger for the sixth and – Devlin assumed – the last time.

Again Devlin shouted 'Merde!' and then he heard the click.

The gun had been empty. The soldiers laughed and offered him a drink before dropping him back in the centre of town.[30]

'The Crisis in the Congo' was fast becoming the big global news story of its day. Fleet Street's finest headed into town for the show amid lurid, and almost entirely false, tales of the rape and murder of white women. The only time Park herself was subject to any kind of attack was in the imagination of the visiting British press pack. One day they gathered at the Embassy asking for the truth about the stories.

'Well, Daphne, you'd better cope with this one,' Ambassador Scott said playfully.

'I have not been raped and no, I am not likely to be,' she told the disappointed hacks.

'Oh but you must have been,' they replied. 'Everyone's been raped.'

'I'm very sorry to disappoint you but I haven't.'

'Why don't you tell them your story,' the Ambassador said with a smile.

Park lived alone in her large house and had woken one morning to the sound of shuffling on the veranda. She had opened her door to find five stark-naked young warriors with spears. She explained that she did not have any work but would get them a drink. Eventually her servants arrived. 'Who are these people on the veranda?' she asked.

'The chief is going to be very angry with us.'

'Why?'

'Because you don't have a gun and you don't have a dog and don't have a nightwatchman, we were all afraid that somebody who didn't know you would come and break in and do things to you. So we have been putting a guard on the house every night. You were not meant to know that it had happened because we knew you wouldn't like it.'

Anticipation mounted among the ravenous pack as she told the story, and they steeled themselves for a front-page tale of a British female diplomat trapped, and treated who knows how by angry spear-wielding Africans. They listened attentively until she explained they had come only to guard her.

'Oh. But then they came back and raped you?' the hacks asked.

'Don't you ever listen to anything!' exclaimed an exasperated Park.

'There's no story in that,' they said, crestfallen. Park certainly made an impression on one of the more serious journalists who covered the crisis. 'One of the most active and effective figures on the Leopoldville scene at the time,' recalled Richard Beeston. 'She was to be seen everywhere, a large bespectacled lady, usually with cigarette ash on her ample bosom.'[31]

As the mutiny continued, Lumumba's problems multiplied. On 11 July, the southern province of Katanga seceded. Katanga was not just any province. It was where the bulk of the mineral resources lay and its leader, Moise Tshombe, based in the provincial capital of Elisabethville, hated Lumumba. He was also close to the Belgians, who saw a chance to use their man to build an alternative power base. A nasty breed of white mercenaries, some Belgian, a few British, bearded and wielding knives and guns, aided Tshombe. Stripped of Katanga's riches, the Congo would not be a viable state. In London, the Prime Minister Harold Macmillan came under strong pressure from the business lobby and from the right of the Conservative Party to recognise the secession and back the Katangans.[32] Secret delegations from Katanga had been approaching British officials from the previous year asking if they might be absorbed into the neighbouring British-led Central African Federation, whose leader in 1960 was also pushing Downing Street to help carve Katanga out of the Congo.[33] The final challenge to Lumumba's authority came when, only two weeks after granting independence, the Belgians responded to the escalating violence by sending in paratroopers to protect 'Western interests' and their citizens' lives. This was a 'humanitarian' intervention, they explained, and explicitly modelled their rationale on that used by Britain and France in Suez in 1956.[34]

The secession of Katanga and the arrival of Belgian troops was beginning to look like a deliberate pincer move on Lumumba, who was now faced with the break-up of his country and its effective recolonisation.[35] Lumumba stopped the army mutiny but in doing so took another step on his fateful journey. He asked one of his closest aides to become chief of staff to the army, a man he trusted like a brother. His name was Mobutu. Mobutu had been expelled from school and sent to the Force Publique as punishment. The experience was the making of him as his hard-working, risk-taking style brought him admirers, including Lumumba. What Lumumba did not know was that his friend had also become a friend of Larry Devlin. The beginnings of a long alliance had been forged at the conference in Belgium in January which Mobutu attended as an aide to Lumumba. Devlin had watched the Soviets working the delegations of locals looking for recruits and he had conducted his own inquiries as to who might be worth getting to know. The name of Lumumba's personal secretary kept coming up. 'I can remember him as a dynamic, idealistic young man who was determined to have an independent state in the Congo and really seemed to believe in all the things Africa's leaders then stood for,' Devlin later recalled.[36] He denied that Mobutu became a recruited agent to whom he could give orders. 'He was a co-operator, not a pussycat,' he explained.[37] Mobutu had an air of almost impossible bravery which was useful when, aged twenty-nine, he walked up to soldiers pointing their guns at him and slowly pulled down the barrels to quell the mutiny. He persuaded the men to return to their barracks, promising them a pay rise and so becoming their hero.

Lumumba needed help to deal with a country that was falling apart. He was also determined to crush his rival, Tshombe. He turned first to the United Nations. They sent in a large international force, but Lumumba was angry that they saw their role as one of strict neutrality and non-intervention and were unwilling to help him bring Katanga to heel (an outcome that was partly the result of British pressure behind the scenes to prevent such a role).[38] UN officials found Lumumba increasingly erratic. 'His dealings with the UN quickly deteriorated into a bewildering series of pleas for assistance, threats and ultimatums,' recalled a UN official. 'He issued improbable demands and expected instant results.'[39]

He began to look elsewhere for help in confronting the secessionists. At one point, members of his cabinet asked the US for 2,000 troops, but President Eisenhower said they could not provide military support unilaterally and Lumumba disavowed the request.[40] So Lumumba made the next of his ruinous decisions. He first asked the Soviet Union to 'follow' the situation, a move designed to put pressure on the UN and the West to persuade the Belgians to get out.

But fearing that the Katangan secession was about to become a fait accompli with Belgian help, a few days later he formally asked Khrushchev for assistance. He did not realise what a dangerous game he was playing. It was a time when Cold War tensions were at a high and he was introducing the superpower conflict into the Congo. After those initial fears of tanks rolling through Austria, the confrontation in Eastern and Central Europe had settled into stasis, especially after the crushing of the Hungarian uprising in 1956 had made it clear that roll-back was over. So increasingly East and West had begun to project their struggle further afield, seeking allies and proxies against each other in the Middle East, Asia and now Africa. Khrushchev in Moscow had seen an opportunity to use decolonisation as a means of winning influence and introducing Communism in the developing world, making his overtures with the offer of military and economic assistance to those leaders like Nkrumah who were socialist in orientation and who disliked Western attempts to perpetuate economic dependency. In the summer of 1960, just as the Congo crisis began, the KGB opened up its first department to specialise in sub-Saharan Africa.[41]

Daphne Park had reported back to MI6 that after independence Lumumba might turn to Moscow.[42] Now, the Congo crisis rose quickly to the top of the agenda, not just for the spies but for the British cabinet. On 19 July, the Foreign Secretary reported that Lumumba was threatening to accept an offer of military assistance from the Soviet Union unless the UN called on all Belgian forces to withdraw in three days.[43] Lumumba made a disastrous visit to the US soon afterwards. One State Department official who met him described him as having an almost '"psychotic" personality'. 'He would never look you in the eye. He looked up at the sky. And a tremendous flow of words came out ... And his words didn't ever have any relation to the particular things that we wanted to discuss ... You had a feeling that he was a person that was gripped by this fervour that I can only characterize as messianic ... he was just not a rational being.'[44] Scott in Leopoldville at first cautioned against listening too much to the Americans. 'Lumumba is not mad,' he cabled home; 'we have to deal with Lumumba.'[45]

But the CIA and Washington were becoming alarmed, fearing that the Congo crisis might be the trigger for war. Devlin never trusted Lumumba. He believed that the Prime Minister's staff included known KGB agents and others under their influence. While he did not think Lumumba himself was a Soviet agent, he did believe he was getting too close to Moscow. 'The ambassador and I concluded that while Lumumba thought he could use the Soviets, they were, in fact, using him,' Devlin later recalled.[46] If the Soviets intervened in force, then the Americans would go in against them. 'We would all be in the fight,' as President Eisenhower put it.[47] In London, Harold Macmillan mused apocalyptically in his diary: 'I have felt uneasy about the summer of 1960. It has a terrible similarity to 1914. Now, Congo may play the role of Serbia. Except for the terror of the nuclear power on both sides, we might easily slide into the 1914 situation.'[48] George Kennedy Young believed that the Congo was the first test for a new Russian strategy of 'revolution by proxy'. The Joint Intelligence Committee in London began work on a paper on the Russian capabilities for intervention, and military planners undertook 'preliminary work' on a response.[49]

Hundreds of KGB men, Devlin believed, were flooding into the country during July and August. His agents at the airport counted anyone white coming off a Russian plane as a citizen of the Soviet Union and quite possibly KGB. The Soviets had backed away from a full-scale military intervention but they were offering extensive support. Devlin was sure that arms and ammunition were also arriving, packed in Red Cross boxes, as part of a Soviet strategy to make Lumumba dependent and ultimately ensure that he was under their control.[50]

The White House was watching closely. When Devlin went back to Washington to brief CIA chief Allen Dulles he told him that the US 'could not afford to lose the Congo to the Soviet Union'.[51] Devlin said he thought the Soviets were planning to use the anarchy in the country to establish a strategic foothold in Africa. If they controlled Lumumba and the Congo, they could use it as a power base to influence nine neighbouring countries. Devlin painted an incredibly dark picture in which the Soviets would try and outflank NATO by extending their influence from the Congo up through Africa and via Nasser in Egypt to the Mediterranean. The Joint Chiefs of Staff at the Pentagon were likewise determined to prevent Soviet control of key airfields and bases.[52] Control of the Congo could also give the

Soviet Union a near monopoly on the production of cobalt, a critical mineral used in missiles and weapons systems, putting the United States' own weapons and space programmes at a 'severe disadvantage'.[53] Sixty per cent of the world's cobalt supply came from a single Belgian company in the Katanga. The Soviets did send people to try and obtain uranium ore for their nuclear programme at one point.[54]

Suddenly, the Congo was being drawn into the heart of the Cold War. This was a pattern replicated across Africa and Asia as local struggles were sucked into the battle for influence between the two superpowers. 'Poor Lumumba. He was no Communist,' Devlin recalled years later. 'He was just a poor jerk who thought "I can use these people." I'd seen that happen in Eastern Europe. It didn't work very well for them, and it didn't work for him.'[55] At the time there was no sympathy, though. This was a man who could not be dealt with. He was 'a Castro or worse', said Allen Dulles. 'It is safe to go on the assumption that Lumumba has been bought by the Communists.'[56] Only the State Department's intelligence arm stood against the consensus by saying he was an opportunist not a Communist.[57]

Daphne Park and Larry Devlin knew each other well and became lifelong friends. To Devlin, Park was 'an absolutely charming young woman and one of the best intelligence officers I have ever encountered'. Britain and America were not always easy allies in the developing world, where America's distaste for colonialism often clashed with British history and investments. In the Congo, American officials were suspicious that the British were manoeuvring to support the Katanga secession.[58] Devlin maintained that while he and Park worked separately (formal liaison was supposed to go through the capitals and not be undertaken in the field) and did not carry out joint operations, they 'had come to similar conclusions' about Lumumba and the other key players.[59]

Daphne Park had remained in touch with Lumumba despite, or perhaps because of, her suspicions about him. 'Lumumba got used to finding me useful and he used to send people to see me. And it was completely cold blooded – he had no illusions. He knew I wanted to know what he was doing and I was perfectly happy that he should know.' He knew she worked for MI6, but it was never discussed explicitly. 'I remember one day having a conversation with Lumumba about it and he said more or less "What's in it for you?" And I said, "Oh knowing the ideas and the thinking of an important man." And he said, "So you would put my interests first?" and I said, "No, certainly not – I put my country's interests first, yours next, but if things go well it will be identical." Months later he said to me that I had impressed him, that I hadn't attempted to say that I loved him best. I'd said outright what I stood for, what I believed in.' Like others, Park watched as Lumumba became increasingly autocratic and mercurial under the pressures of office and of being at the epicentre of the Cold War, alienating and frightening some of his closest colleagues, occasionally employing thugs and violence.[60]

If Devlin was her ally, then Daphne Park's nemesis was Andrée Blouin, one of Lumumba's closest advisers. Madame Blouin was Lumumba's protocol chief and companion to his deputy and she exerted considerable influence. She was half African, half French, and after being abandoned by her parents grew up in a brutal orphanage in the French Congo. The experience turned her into a steely character, fiercely anti-Western, and she became close to a number of African nationalists and to one of the travelling leftists who had gathered around Lumumba. Always well dressed in Parisian haute couture and a touch aloof, she was, Devlin thought (despite working against her), 'tantalising' and 'glamorous'.[61] Those were not words people used about Daphne Park, who had her own views about her opponent. 'Madame Blouin was a very powerful and rather wicked Guinean who was right in the pocket of the Russians.'

Devlin sat in his office on 18 August 1960 encrypting one of his most important and alarmist cables: 'EMBASSY AND STATION BELIEVE CONGO EXPERIENCING CLASSIC COMMUNIST EFFORT TAKEOVER GOVERNMENT ... WHETHER OR NOT LUMUMBA ACTUALLY COMMIE OR JUST PLAYING COMMIE GAME TO ASSIST HIS SOLIDIFYING POWER – ANTI-WEST FORCES RAPIDLY INCREASING POWER – THERE MAY BE LITTLE TIME LEFT IN WHICH TO TAKE ACTION TO AVOID ANOTHER CUBA.'[62] The reference to Cuba, where a pro-American regime had fallen to Communist Fidel Castro the previous year, was designed to ring alarm bells in Washington as loudly as possible. The fear was that key strategic states were beginning to fall to nationalist, anti-Western forces, friendly to the Soviets.

Devlin's cable convinced Washington that action needed to be taken. A National Security meeting at the White House began with a discussion of the 'grave situation' and fears were expressed that Soviet officials were now pulling Lumumba's strings.[63] It looked as if he might be trying to force the UN out in order to allow the Soviets to intervene in force, it was said. Officials around the table predicted that Lumumba would use the Force Publique to drive all whites out, apart from Soviet technicians. According to the official note, the President stressed that the UN had to be kept in at all costs, 'even if such action is used by the Soviets as the basis for starting a fight'.[64] Something else was said which was never written in the formal note of the meeting. At one point President Eisenhower turned to CIA Director Allen Dulles and said he wanted Lumumba 'eliminated'.[65] The man who took the notes at the meeting could not quite believe what he had heard. There was a silence and then the meeting continued. A week later at a meeting of the so-called Special Group which co-ordinated covert action, Dulles presented a plan to bribe parliamentarians to vote out Lumumba. In response, a presidential adviser said that Eisenhower had 'expressed extremely strong feelings on the necessity for very straightforward action in this situation and he wondered whether the plans as outlined were sufficient to accomplish this'.[66] Dulles personally cabled Devlin the next day: 'WE CONCLUDE THAT HIS REMOVAL MUST BE AN URGENT AND PRIME OBJECTIVE AND THAT UNDER EXISTING CONDITIONS THIS WOULD BE A HIGH PRIORITY OF OUR COVERT ACTION. HENCE WE WISH TO GIVE YOU WIDE AUTHORITY.'[67]

Devlin was offered $100,000 in funds for any operation, without anyone back in headquarters signing off. He was told that if need be he could act without referring to either his Ambassador or most of his CIA seniors. Devlin and his team began to work actively against Lumumba, employing the full panoply of political warfare techniques and tapping up the CIA's network of agents and contacts. Newspapers were used to spread stories attacking Lumumba. Rallies were organised. Opposition members of parliament were ordered to work to get him dismissed in a vote of no-confidence and papers drafted for President Kasavubu on the best way to remove Lumumba from power.[68] Eventually in early September, the largely ineffective Kasavubu, encouraged by both Devlin and the Belgians, tried to sack Lumumba. In turn Lumumba tried to remove Kasavubu, creating political deadlock. The city was quiet but the countryside was slipping out of control with murders and refugees spreading anarchy.

One of Park's most important contacts was Lumumba's aide de camp, Damian Kandolo. He was from the same tribe as Lumumba and was trusted by him, so his conversations with her were invaluable. He was particularly helpful in explaining what Madame Blouin and the Guineans around Lumumba were up to. But that group had decided they wanted to get rid of Kandolo, possibly because they had learnt of his relationship with Park. One day he was seized under Lumumba's orders. He was beaten up and his arm broken. He was then put in a car and driven away to be killed. But the people who were driving him were drunk and it was raining and dark. They had an accident and Kandolo managed to roll out of the car into a ditch. They searched for him but after a while simply gave up. Kandolo managed to get himself to a small mission hospital which was not too far away and he went to ground there. He sent a message to Park to ask for help to get his wife and child across the river to Brazzaville because he thought that the thugs would go and look for him at his house and attack his wife if they did not find him. Park went to collect her and put her on the ferry to Brazzaville. Then she went to see Kandolo under cover of night. The hospital was no more than a few small huts and she knew which one he was in. But because it was dark when she entered, Kandolo thought it was the thugs who had come to finish the job, and he attacked Park fiercely. 'It's me!' she cried, bringing a halt to the rain of blows. She explained that she had a plan to get him out stuffed into the rear of her tiny car. 'The great thing about having a Citroën DC is that people never think you are going to hide anything in it. I mean if I'd had a great big car with a boot I'd have had problems ... I was an appalling driver, but I always had the back of my car piled up with blankets and boxes and all sorts of things, so it was quite easy to put him in and pile a few boxes and blankets [on top of him].' Park was nervous but fired up by adrenalin.

She eventually made it to the ferry and placed her grateful passenger on board. Kandolo would not be out of the Congo for long.

During the stand-off between Kasavubu and Lumumba, Mobutu went to see Devlin. The two men were extremely close. Devlin had personally wrestled a gunman to the ground who had been trying to assassinate Mobutu, pulling the pistol back to break the man's finger. Mobutu was grateful and became a regular dinner guest at Devlin's expansive villa with its six bathrooms and foyer the size of a hotel lobby.

'I'm anxious to talk to you,' Mobutu told Devlin. Mobutu understood better than Lumumba how to play the Cold War game. He knew to whisper quietly into the ear of the Soviet-obsessed CIA man exactly what he wanted to hear. 'The Soviets are pouring into the country. You must know that, Mr Devlin?' Devlin nodded. 'We didn't fight for independence to have another country re-colonize us.' Mobutu complained that Lumumba had failed to keep the Soviet influence out of his army.[69] He said he was prepared to overthrow Lumumba if the US recognised a temporary government, which in turn would remove the Soviets.

'And Lumumba and Kasavubu, what happens to them?' asked Devlin.

'They'll both have to be neutralised.'

Devlin, knowing that he had not yet received specific authorisation but had been given wide latitude to act, held out his hand with the words: 'I can assure you the United States government will recognise a temporary government composed of civilian technocrats.' Devlin drove to see his Ambassador at 2 a.m. to tell him what had happened. He then cabled back to the CIA to say they could still call it all off if they disagreed with his decision to offer support. In true bureaucratic style, Devlin says he never received a reply, providing Washington with deniability for having backed the coup if something went wrong. UN liaison officers reported seeing Western military attachés visiting Mobutu 'with bulging briefcases containing thick brown paper packets which they obligingly deposited on his table'.[70]

It was not just Washington that wanted something done. Covert action was London's preferred option as well. Ambassador Scott had become increasingly concerned after visiting Lumumba in

August. He found the Prime Minister's phone ringing a dozen times in ten minutes and files piled up on his desk. He looked as if he had not slept. 'It was by then widely known that he could only carry on by taking drugs. There was a kind of glaze in his eyes,' he recalled, also noting Madame Blouin hanging around the margins.[71] In early September, the Foreign Secretary, Alec Douglas-Home, reported to the cabinet that Lumumba had been 'successful in obtaining considerable support, probably including some military personnel, from the Soviet bloc'. Eleven Soviet military transport aircraft arrived in Stanleyville, heightening fears that a conflict was on the way. London believed they had an African Nasser on their hands. Douglas-Home proposed and the cabinet agreed that 'open support of Colonel Mobutu or opposition to Mr Lumumba was likely to prove counterproductive, though it would be right to follow this course privately'.[72] Prime Minister Macmillan at the end of August had ordered MI6 to work with the CIA to remove Lumumba from power. MI6 chief Dick White, never a great proponent of aggressive action, was not overly keen on the idea but passed the order to Daphne Park.[73]

On 14 September Colonel Mobutu's voice crackled on to the radio. He announced that the army was 'neutralising' politicians until the end of the year and installing a College of Commissioners to run the country. Publicly, the coup was directed at both the President and the Prime Minister, but it was primarily directed at Lumumba. As he heard the news, Devlin was at a party. He watched with some satisfaction as Madame Blouin took a phone call and then rushed away. He reflected that his efforts were at last 'bearing fruit', especially once Mobutu set about expelling Soviet officials.[74] The Russian Ambassador turned up in the middle of the night at UN headquarters asking for protection and saying he feared he might be sent to Siberia by his superiors for having failed.[75] Devlin personally made sure that the visas of Soviet diplomats were cancelled, forcing them to leave the country. He also took a lead role in advising which politicians Mobutu should appoint. Kandolo, whom Park had smuggled out of the country in her car, ended up as a commissioner running part of the Security Service. An even more powerful figure was the head of intelligence, Victor Nendaka, another former colleague of Lumumba, who had been persuaded to switch sides. 'He was Larry Devlin's man,' recalled Park. 'But between us we had it sewn up more or less.' Madame Blouin fled first to Ghana. A few weeks later, Allen Dulles told the National Security Council in Washington that the agency had 'succeeded' in 'neutralising Mme. Blouin, who now wants to come to the US. She is writing her memoirs, which, Mr Dulles observed, should make interesting reading.'[76] How they succeeded in 'neutralising' her is not discussed.

Lumumba had been trapped with two concentric rings of troops around him. There were Congolese troops who wanted to arrest him on the outer perimeter and closer to him a UN force which said it could guarantee his safety only so long as he remained where he was.

But Lumumba was still dangerous in the eyes of the West. He had the support of a significant section of the country as well as the makings of an alternative government with a small army out in Stanleyville. That made him a threat, especially if he ever got out or if parliament was recalled. Soviet-backed African countries began to pressure Mobutu to return Lumumba to office. The Americans were unsure that Mobutu had the nerve to hold out. They worried he might have a breakdown.[77] The CIA wanted a permanent solution to the one man whom it saw as the source of all the problems. Lumumba remained 'a grave danger as long as he was not disposed of', said Dulles at a National Security Council meeting.[78]

Five days after the coup, Devlin got a cable with the codeword 'Prop'. It was from Richard Bissell, the CIA's Deputy Director of Plans. Only four people at CIA headquarters had access to Prop messages and Devlin alone in the Congo received them. His orders were to keep the messages hidden from colleagues and give them priority over all other traffic. The cable said a senior officer whom Devlin would recognise would arrive in Leopoldville around 27 September. He would identify himself as 'Joe from Paris'. Devlin was to carry out his instructions.[79] A week later as he left the Embassy, Devlin saw a man he recognised get up from a table at a café across the street. They got into Devlin's car and he turned up the radio. As they drove away, the man turned to Devlin. 'I'm Joe from Paris,' he said. 'I've come to give you instructions about a highly sensitive operation.'

The man's real name was Sidney Gottlieb, known to some as the 'dark sorcerer' for his conjuring in the most sinister recesses of the CIA. With his club-foot, he was perhaps too easy to caricature as a cross between a Bond villain and Dr Strangelove, a scientist who always wanted to push further without worrying about the morality of where it all led. He masterminded the sprawling MKULTRA programme which had begun in 1953, without any oversight, to experiment on mind control using an array of medical and scientific experiments on Americans, including the use of electroshock and LSD (which Gottlieb himself claimed to have taken 200 times).[80] At least one person involved in his experiments died under suspicious circumstances and others went mad. Gottlieb was also the go-to man when it came to eliminating America's enemies. These were busy times. He was looking at ways of removing Fidel Castro using exploding cigars and poisoned wetsuits, as well as removing the leader of the Dominican Republic. The two men in the car in Leopoldville remained quiet until they reached a safe house. Then Gottlieb said he had brought Devlin poison to kill Lumumba.[81]

'Isn't this unusual?' Devlin said. He had never been asked to kill anyone before. 'Who authorised this operation?'

'President Eisenhower,' Gottlieb said. 'I wasn't there when he approved it but Dick Bissell said that Eisenhower wanted Lumumba removed.' Had Eisenhower meant the phrase 'elimination' on 18 August to be an order for assassination? Later some of those present at the meeting said they were not sure that he had. But CIA chief Dulles, as well as others, believed they knew exactly what the President meant even if he had been careful not to say it too directly. Dulles had begun to put a plan into effect through his Deputy, Richard Bissell.

Devlin lit a cigarette and stared down at his shoes.

'It's your responsibility to carry out the operation, you alone,' Gottlieb said 'The details are up to you, but it's got to be clean – nothing that can be traced back to the US government.' There was silence. Then he pulled out a small package. 'Take this,' he said, handing it over. 'With the stuff that's in there, no one will ever be able to know that Lumumba was assassinated.'

There were several different poisons which had come from the US army biological warfare institution at Fort Detrick. Gottlieb had explored using rabbit fever, undulant fever, anthrax, smallpox and sleeping sickness. One poison was concealed in a tube of toothpaste and was designed to make it look as if Lumumba had died from polio. Grimly Devlin took the poisons and the accessories, including needles, rubber gloves and a mask.

Devlin always says that after accepting the poisons he threw them in the Congo River, neglecting to mention that he only did this months later when their potency had expired. In the meantime he kept them in his safe. When one officer visited Devlin, he mentioned he had a virus in the safe. 'I knew it wasn't for somebody to get his polio shot up to date,' recalled the visitor later.[82]

Devlin maintained that he had no intention of going ahead with this plan. 'To me it was murder,' he said on his deathbed. 'I'm not a 007 guy.'[83] He said he knew that refusing the order outright would lead to his recall and someone else being appointed who would carry out the order, destroying his career in the process. So Devlin says he decided to play it slow. He had only one agent with access to Lumumba's living quarters, where he was effectively imprisoned, but Devlin said he was not sure the agent could get in. He looked at having another agent take refuge with Lumumba to administer the poison but that did not work. He also had conversations with Congolese contacts interested in killing Lumumba.[84]

Headquarters became impatient. It offered to send out another officer to help in case Devlin was not able to devote enough time to the plans. Devlin replied that, if that were done, the officer should be supplied through the diplomatic pouch with a high-powered hunting rifle which could be kept 'in office pending opening of hunting season'.[85] A shady stateless mercenary, willing to do anything, was provided with plastic surgery and a toupee by the CIA and sent off to the Congo to help, but he never got close to Lumumba.[86] The CIA even suggested using a 'commando type group' to abduct Lumumba by assaulting his residence.[87]

On 19 September, Alec Douglas-Home talked to President Eisenhower. 'Lord Home said the Soviets have lost much by their obvious efforts to disrupt matters in the Congo,' the minutes recorded. 'The president expressed his wish that Lumumba would fall into a river full of crocodiles; Lord Home said regretfully that we have lost many of the techniques of old-fashioned diplomacy.'[88] A week later Home, along with Prime Minister Macmillan, met President Eisenhower in New York. 'Lord Home raised the question why we are not getting rid of Lumumba at the present time,' the American note-taker recorded. 'He stressed now is the time to get rid of Lumumba.'[89]

Murder was on the minds of some in London. Ian Scott sent a telegram to London, including Downing Street, on 27 September: 'It seems to me that the best interests of the Congo (and the rest of us) would be served by the departure of Lumumba from the scene either to jail (and sufficient evidence exists to convict him of treason and of complicity in attempted murder of Colonel Mobutu) or abroad,' he wrote, calling for pressure to be brought on Mobutu, who was looking 'irresolute' ('he has not the makings of a dictator', Scott wrongly predicted).[90] One response, in a secret document which could only travel in a locked box, came from H. F. T. Smith, a Foreign Office official who would later be appointed head of MI5. He agreed that pressure should be brought to bear to prevent Lumumba's return. But Smith doubted Scott's remedies would solve the problem. Mobutu was too weak and other African leaders would support Lumumba in jail or abroad. There were only two solutions. 'The first is the simple one of ensuring Lumumba's removal from the scene by killing him. This should in fact solve the problem, since, so far as we can tell, Lumumba is not a leader of a movement within which there are potential successors of his quality and influence. His supporters are much less dangerous material.' The other solution offered was a constitutional change to reduce the Prime Minister's powers so that he could return to office but weakened. 'Of these two possibilities, my preference (though it might be expressed as a wish rather than a proposal) would be for Lumumba to be removed from the scene altogether, because I fear that as long as he is about his power to do damage can only be slightly modified.' Comments added to Smith's memo include 'There is much to be said for eliminating Lumumba', although others voiced scepticism.[91]

Killing people, Daphne Park maintained, was not on MI6's agenda. 'We didn't have a licence to kill,' she explained years later. 'Much as I hated people I don't think I actually would have felt easy killing them or even having them killed. It was much more important to deal with the people who were alive. And fight the others by any way you can, of course, including destroying their reputation if you can – if that's going to do the damage.' Park, who was not told of the CIA plan, always believed that Devlin was too honourable and sensible to carry out his plan.

MI6 did contemplate murder at times – notably against Nasser – but even as it feared Nasser's hand in the Congo, it also knew that in this case the nastier side of the business could be left to others.[92] Daphne Park might not have been given a licence to kill, nor Devlin's killer toothpaste, but she did have her own gadgets, courtesy of Q, the quartermaster for MI6. 'Q used to produce the most wonderful gadgets for almost anything you could think of,' explained Park. 'Sometimes they didn't totally succeed.' Most gadgets supplied to field officers were designed to hide or pass information. These ranged from the typically British – a hollowed-out cricket ball – to the more painful – a bullet-shaped 'rectal concealing device'. In the Congo there were concerns about crowds storming embassies and attacking cars, and so it had been decided that Park needed some protection. Head Office first of all gave her a gun, which Park put in the office safe fearing it would be stolen from her home. She was then informed that Q had come up with a device that had worked wonders in the Sudan in terms of crowd control and was 'absolutely infallible'. It was a capsule which when thrown broke apart and emitted a smell guaranteed to send a gathered throng reeling. In other words it was a large stink bomb. A man was sent out to Leopoldville with a box of tricks to demonstrate. Q had clearly spent some time in the joke shop looking for inspiration because with him also came some itching powder (Park duly applied some of this to a Foreign Office official in the Embassy whom she loathed).

Daphne Park's counterpart from Nairobi happened to be visiting. 'Now, Daffers, we must test these things,' he said, volunteering to try out the stink bomb.

'Oh no you don't. This is my patch,' Park replied, unwilling to miss out on the fun. They drove out of town in her car to a quiet spot with a large storm ditch. One person would have to be the guineapig.

'It has got to be me,' said her counterpart. In true buccaneering style, both wanted to volunteer for the trenches.

'We'll toss for it,' replied Park. Hugo won.

The capsule was duly opened and thrown in and he went down into the ditch. There was a long silence. It's knocked him out, thought Park. She crept to the edge of the ditch and peered over and there he was crawling about in the mud.

'Hugo, what the hell are you doing?' she said.

'Looking for that bloody thing – I can't find it anywhere.' It must have been a dud, they concluded.

'Get out. It's my turn now,' she said. After they had used four of the stink bombs they faced facts and telegraphed London. 'One of the things might just have been confused with a little smell of armpit but that was as far as it got. We do not think it would have made much difference to angry Congolese.'[93]

The Belgian government, like the CIA, was willing to entertain darker ambitions. It had made clear that it wanted Lumumba's 'Elimination definitive', a phrase employed by their Minister for African Affairs. The Belgian codename for Lumumba was 'Satan', a reflection of how they worked to portray him in the media and internationally. Their plan to kill him was called 'Operation Barracuda'.[94] It is unclear if they co-ordinated with the Americans. Three days after a meeting in the White House on 21 September, Dulles sent a personal cable to Devlin. 'WE WISH GIVE EVERY POSSIBLE SUPPORT IN ELIMINATING LUMUMBA FROM ANY POSSIBILITY RESUMING GOVERNMENTAL POSITION.'[95] By November, the CIA had focused on a plan to lure Lumumba out of his refuge and then hand him over to the Congolese authorities who could take care of the rest. Events intervened before they had a chance to try.

An almighty thunderstorm struck Leopoldville on the night of 27 November 1960. Lumumba exploited it as cover to stow himself away in a Chevrolet used to take servants home. He began to make his way to Stanleyville, one of his bastions of support. He managed only slow progress through the driving rain, stopping to speak to supporters en route while Mobutu's men, aided by the Belgians, pursued him.[96]

Around midnight on 1 December, Lumumba was captured at a river crossing just before he reached friendly territory. The local UN garrison was given orders not to place him in protective custody or to get in the way of his arrest.[97] He was taken by aeroplane back to Leopoldville the next day. He emerged with his hands tied behind his back. A soldier lifted his head to show his face to the waiting cameraman, who could see blood on him. He was driven in the back of a truck through town. His hair was dishevelled and his glasses lost. The truck drove right past the UN headquarters.[98] Images of his mistreatment led to a wave of anger internationally, directed at the UN among others for failing to intervene. As the UN found in later years, maintaining a policy of neutrality and non-interference often meant becoming passive observers to tragic, sometimes violent events.[99] Although there was a sense that some in the UN had taken sides or at least were willing to play both sides, the Secretary General of the UN had told a British diplomat a few months earlier that Lumumba was 'already clearly a Communist stooge' and that he hoped to prevent the Soviet penetration of Africa.[100] Next Lumumba was driven to Mobutu's house where his old friend paid his respects. He was then taken to a paratrooper camp at Thysville a hundred miles from the city. A soldier read out a statement he had written in which he said he was head of the government and then stuffed the paper into his mouth. But the dilemma remained over how to eliminate him definitively from the political scene. The US and Belgians both realised that it was better to have the Congolese do the dirty work for them now he was in their hands.

Lumumba's powers of oratory had not deserted him and on 13 January 1961 there was a mutiny at the paratrooper camp. This led to immediate fears that Lumumba might escape again. He had to be dealt with. 'I assumed, particularly after the Thysville mutiny, that the government would seek a permanent solution to the Lumumba problem,' said Devlin. 'But I was never consulted on the matter and never offered advice.'[101] He may not have been consulted, but he was told it was going to happen by Victor Nendaka, his man who ran the Security Service, a subtle, largely semantic difference. Devlin would later write a cable to CIA headquarters outlining what would happen next but delayed sending it for reasons that remain unclear.[102] The incoming Kennedy administration in Washington was divided over whether to continue the hard line over African nationalists or to appeal to the newly independent countries. There were fears in the CIA that the new administration was going 'soft'. Kennedy himself wondered after his election whether or not to 'save' Lumumba and to work with him. Devlin had cabled Washington just before the mutiny desperately trying to maintain a firm line by providing the most alarmist possible take on the situation. 'PRESENT GOVERNMENT MAY FALL WITHIN FEW DAYS,' Devlin said. 'RESULT WOULD ALMOST CERTAINLY BE CHAOS AND RETURN LUMUMBA TO POWER ... REFUSAL TO TAKE DRASTIC STEPS AT THIS TIME WILL LEAD TO DEFEAT OF UNITED STATES POLICY IN CONGO.'[103] The Belgians also made clear that they wanted Lumumba transferred to Katanga and delivered into the hands of his enemies. The job had to be finished quickly.

Just before dawn on 17 January, Lumumba was taken from his cell by Victor Nendaka, his former comrade and now Devlin's man as head of the Security Service. He was brought to a plane. On board his goatee beard was torn out and he was forced to eat it.[104] A debate had been held within the Congolese Commission on how to end the instability. A collective decision was reached to send Lumumba to Elisabethville, the Katangan capital. Among those taking the decision was Damien Kandolo, a member of the College of Commissioners, Daphne Park's man, as well as Devlin's man Nendaka. On arrival, Lumumba was dragged out and thrown on to a jeep under watching Belgian eyes. A small Swedish detail of six UN troops at the airport also witnessed him being driven away. Lumumba was conveyed to a colonial villa, owned by a Belgian, where he was beaten again. The UN knew he had landed but did nothing to intervene. Katangan ministers, including Moise Tshombe, joined in the beatings at the villa.[105]

That night he was led to a clearing in the wood. With Katangan ministers and a number of Belgians present, Lumumba was put up against a tree and executed by a firing squad (the squad included Belgians, who were either mercenaries or working for the Katangan gendarmerie). The corpses of Lumumba and two aides were hacked to pieces and plunged into a barrel of acid by two Europeans. 'We were there two days,' recalled one of the men years later. 'We did things an animal wouldn't do. And that's why we were drunk, stone drunk.'[106]

A few days later it was announced to the world that Lumumba and two aides had escaped from custody and then been killed by villagers. A Katangan minister held a press conference at which he produced a death certificate. It read 'died in the bush'. 'There are those people who accuse us of assassination,' he said. 'I have only one response – prove it.'[107] No one believed the story. Demonstrations erupted in many countries and Belgian embassies were attacked. The crowds may not have known the detail but they understood that Belgian complicity ran deep. Lumumba became a martyr, his death a cause célèbre around the world which Moscow adeptly exploited, even establishing its own university named after him to train and recruit African leaders of the future. 'It was Belgian advice, Belgian orders and finally Belgian hands that killed Lumumba on that 17 January 1961,' according to one detailed study of events.[108]

Mobutu, once Lumumba's ally and trusted friend, almost certainly knew of the killing of the comrade he had betrayed. 'I can't believe he wasn't involved,' confessed Devlin. 'But it was just one of those questions you didn't ask at the time.'[109] Did the CIA know? No direct link to Larry Devlin or the CIA was ever proven, although it is clear that those who ordered the killing were close to both the CIA and MI6 in the Congo. Oddly, one disaffected CIA man claimed that during his training in 1965 another officer had described driving around with Lumumba's body in the boot of his car. When, a decade later, the disaffected officer again encountered the man who had made the claim, that man went to the bathroom twice during dinner to spend fifteen minutes scrubbing and drying his hands, cleaning his fingernails and staring at himself in the mirror. No evidence has emerged to back up the man's claim and the issue of who pulled the strings remains obscure.[110]

Mobutu's rise to power was complete in 1965 as he launched his final coup. Devlin was there in the background, advising him on whom to appoint.[111] 'He had shuffled new governments like cards, finally settling on Mobutu as president,' according to one former CIA officer.[112] Colonel Mobutu eventually mutated into Mobutu Sese Seko Kuku Ngbendu Wa Za Banga, 'the all-powerful warrior who goes from conquest to conquest, leaving fire in his wake', a strange leopardskin-clad character who began to retreat from reality. He was the archetypal African 'big man'. Again the Congolese saw nothing of their country's wealth, as it ended up in Swiss bank accounts.[113] The Congo – or Zaire as it was renamed – was a key US ally, a base for a covert CIA war in Angola, and Mobutu was supported personally with money, guns and intelligence from Devlin's successors. His regime received something like a billion dollars over three decades.[114] When the Cold War ended in the 1990s, Mobutu was quickly abandoned. As in so many other countries, the superpowers came to the Congo, played out their conflict and then left, leaving nothing of value behind.

Devlin says he was haunted by the assassination plan which he never carried out. One of the problems for him was that it became public in the mid-1970s when the US Congress unearthed the CIA's secret assassination programmes to kill foreign heads of government, including the schemes to poison Lumumba and to use the mafia to kill Fidel Castro at around the same time. The CIA emerged from the process chastened and circumscribed, at least for a few years until President Reagan unleashed it again. Sidney Gottlieb tried to atone for his past by helping young children with speech impediments and volunteering at a hospice.[115] For Devlin, the exposure proved difficult. At parties, there would be whispers and people would edge away from him. At one point he was even warned that Carlos the Jackal wanted to kill him to avenge Lumumba. He grew tired of accusations that he was a murderer. But he never really left the Congo. He completed a second tour and then became head of the CIA's Africa division. In 1974 he retired but went on to work for a financier who was investing in the Congo's mineral resources, and he remained close to Mobutu.

Daphne Park left the Congo in 1961. On her last night Kandolo came to dinner at her house. He fidgeted throughout the meal before asking her whether she really did not see Africans as different from white people. She did not, she explained. Some she loathed and some she loved. Park, who would always be fascinated by the riddle of power, went on to spend three years as station chief in Lusaka, working closely with Kenneth Kaunda of Zambia. MI6, like Britain, struggled with post-colonial Africa, and among a certain breed of officers, though not Park, there was a sense that they could not quite come to terms with the end of the Empire. Rhodesia proved a particularly painful chapter, with much sympathy among some old-school officers for the white settlers. Africa remained important for

MI6 as a place where it found it easier to target Soviet bloc officials than it was on their home turf, and so it became an important testing ground for the best new officers to learn the ropes. It also became a place in which MI6 did much work in countering Soviet ideology by supporting academics, trade union leaders and journalists. While operations in the Soviet bloc would become the dominant strand of MI6 work in the coming years and the field where ambitious officers headed, Africa, like the Middle East, would remain an important sub-culture within the office in which specialists operated and a more buccaneering style, evidenced by Park, persisted just beneath the surface.

As the 1960s progressed, Daphne Park moved across to the next hot spot of the Cold War as consul general in Hanoi, North Vietnam, during the country's struggle against the United States. Her movements were highly restricted (when told she could not even have a bicycle she offered to ride a tandem with a Vietnamese officer), but the intelligence she supplied on her trips out of the country was almost the only source that the US and UK had on what was happening in the North and her work brought her many friends in Washington.[116] Asia was becoming another crucial zone of conflict in the intelligence war. Maurice Oldfield had become Controller for Asia and had taken MI6 into Indonesia and Indo-China in the 1950s to fight Communism, working closely with the Americans. Graham Greene paid the occasional visit to Indo-China during Oldfield's time, still it seems doing the odd bit of intelligence work while writing. His Europe of *The Third Man* was now giving way to the Asia of *The Quiet American*, charting the flow of the Cold War east and with it Greene's, and Britain's, unease with American power. Not everyone was convinced by the quality of MI6 work in Asia. A new recruit to cover the region was Gerry Warner. Fresh from St Peter's College, Oxford, he had been invited to see an admiral at Buckingham Gate who recruited for MI6. He found the service a disappointing place. He had learnt Mandarin and so was able to compare the reports coming in from the service's top agent in Hong Kong with those available in the local newspapers. The correlation was obvious but the revelation that Our Man in Hong Kong was a fabricator was not well received by the office. Posted to Burma, Warner found an ineffective station chief (with a taste for skinny-dipping parties) who was fighting the last war by burying radio sets in villages and not recruiting agents or collecting intelligence. He decided he wanted to return home and quit.

Daphne Park eventually rose to become a controller at MI6. If it had not been for the sexism that pervaded the organisation, some say, she would have risen to the next level up, to become a director, or perhaps even have reached the summit as Chief or C. It would not be until the next century that a woman would rise to director level. Park retired from MI6 in 1979 but not from public life, as she became principal of Somerville, one of the last all-women colleges at Oxford University, and a member of the House of Lords where she retained the habit of speaking her mind irrespective of what she was supposed to say. She never married. 'I had four or five love affairs,' she recalled. 'But only one that really mattered, and that ended in death, unfortunately.'[117] There was a loneliness to Park that her colleagues understood and which was sublimated in her work and in her professional friendships. She remained close to Larry Devlin, talking frequently with him on the phone until they both died within a year of each other.

The Congo crisis also played its part in the ongoing debate within the service over covert action versus intelligence gathering. Chief Dick White disliked the type of political action which involved removing governments and wanted to focus on recruiting agents and collecting information. But one section of officers – particularly those who worked in Africa and the Middle East (the so-called Camel Corps) – argued that the two had to go together. For Daphne Park and those like her, intelligence was about building relationships with people, including top politicians, not spending countless months looking for a disaffected fourth secretary or cipher clerk with a drink problem in an embassy. The former kind of work, which many officers relished, offered a chance to understand the wider strategic direction of a country and to sway or even manipulate it. This in turn, they argued, provided intelligence. Only by supporting activists in their political goals would you learn about a country and what might happen. 'Unless we show we're prepared to help influence events, we won't get intelligence and it is questionable if it is worth operating,' the first Controller for Africa argued.[118] Others in the Secret Service, especially those targeting the Soviet Union and its allies, favoured a more purist approach to intelligence gathering, focusing on the collection of information rather than the influencing of events. Back in London, only three months after Lumumba had been killed, a Russian was to offer the service the opportunity to begin rebuilding its capacity and its confidence for recruiting agents against the hardest target and its main enemy. He would pay with his life.

4

MOSCOW RULES

It was just before ten in the evening when the door to Room 360 swung open. A taut, straight-backed man with deep-set eyes and red hair flecked with grey walked in and sat down across a coffee table from two Britons and two Americans. They introduced themselves with false names.[1] Apprehension and expectation hung in the air at the Mount Royal Hotel in London's Marble Arch as the Russian guest lit a cigarette to calm his nerves. It was 20 April 1961 and the Cold War threatened to flare hot.

The man had many identities. His first was as a Soviet official leading a trade delegation to London. His second was as an intelligence officer, there to collect technical secrets for the Soviet Union. But as he sat down he embarked on a third, brief and fateful life as a reckless and driven spy, betraying his country. The five men around the coffee table would go on to spend 140 hours in each others' company. The intense and forceful Russian would become the most important spy for the West in the early Cold War and would help the British Secret Service kick the worst habits of its past.

'Would you prefer to speak Russian or English?' George Kisevalter asked. Kisevalter, the bearish CIA officer who had handled Popov in Vienna, had the easy-going manner and fluent Russian which ensured that he would take the lead in the conversation out of the four. 'I would much rather speak Russian because I can express myself much better in Russian,' replied the well-dressed Soviet official, explaining that his English was rusty. 'Well, gentlemen,' the visitor continued, trying to wrestle back control, 'let's get to work. We have a great deal of important work to do.' He was hungry for betrayal and there was not a moment to waste in disgorging his secrets. 'I have thought about this for a long time.'

Desperation had driven the Russian to undertake ever greater risks to reach this point. He had watched and waited for the right moment, experiencing many false starts. Nearly nine months earlier in Moscow, two American students had been walking on a bridge leading away from Red Square when a man approached them. 'I have tried to get in touch with other Americans but so few of them speak Russian,' he told them cautiously. 'I have some information I wish to give directly to the American Embassy.' They walked on with him. 'Do not open it or keep it overnight in your hotel. Go immediately to the American Embassy with the letter.' The man explained how an American U2 spy plane, piloted by Gary Powers, had been brought down a few weeks earlier after surface-to-air missiles exploded around it. A few streets from their hotel, he entrusted a white envelope to the students. One of the students went to the Embassy with it, fearful every step of the way of a hand on his shoulder.

The letter made its way back to the CIA. It included the first details of how the U2 had been downed. There was also a photograph of a Soviet and an American colonel at a party with the Soviet's head cut out and the words 'I am' written in its place. Tracking down the American was easy, and he explained that the Soviet colonel was a man who had served in Turkey in the mid-1950s called Oleg Penkovsky.

More secrets could be left in a dead drop, Penkovsky explained in the students' letter. The act of physically passing secret information is the most dangerous because it is the most vulnerable. If caught in the act, both agent and officer are finished, the agent as good as dead. A dead drop is one solution. Material is deposited in an agreed hiding place and later picked up, the two parties never having to meet in person. Penkovsky wrote that he would look for a chalk mark in a particular phone booth before loading the drop. Everyone knew that the KGB's home turf was the hardest place to operate, requiring the most rigorous methods. The phrase 'Moscow Rules' would come to be used as shorthand to refer to the type of procedures or tradecraft an intelligence officer would have to employ to carry out his trade in the city's streets.

This might be a provocation, the Americans thought as they looked at the letter – the old Soviet trick of dangling a fake agent to tempt the other side. Whoever took the bait would be identified as an intelligence officer and could be expelled, watched or perhaps targeted to be turned. But the chance of this being a real offer – the chance to run the first top-level spy inside the Soviet Union – was too good to pass by. However, the CIA had a problem. It had no operational presence in Moscow. An officer had been posted to Moscow a few years back to try and work with Popov, but the American had been seduced by his maid, who worked for the KGB. When they tried to blackmail him using pictures taken from a camera in her handbag, he had approached the Ambassador, who had been furious to find that the CIA were operating in his Embassy without his knowledge.[2] Since then, the State Department, which controlled the cover slots that CIA officers would use, had resisted further deployments to avoid upsets. So how could the CIA contact Penkovsky?

A young, inexperienced officer was their first and utterly disastrous answer. Codenamed 'Compass', he arrived in Moscow in October 1960 with cover as a cleaner.[3] The city was a grey, unforgiving place to foreigners. Days would go by without seeing a smile on the streets. The traffic was light because almost all cars were official, but a vehicle belonging to a foreigner would be followed and surveillance would continue on foot on the streets, often in a manner designed to be obvious and enough to put someone on edge. Any conversation with an ordinary Russian would be quickly interrupted. There were few restaurants for foreigners, tickets for the Bolshoi were hard to come by and formal meetings would be stilted and unwelcoming. The only fresh vegetables for American diplomats were those flown in from the US once a week. They said you could tell how long someone had been in Moscow because newcomers headed for the caviar at diplomatic receptions while veterans quickly snaffled fresh lettuce or celery. Life was isolating and Compass could not cope. He became depressed by the cold, dark winters and turned to drink. Like many who served in Moscow, the ever-present surveillance began to play with his head. He became paranoid and came up with increasingly ludicrous schemes to establish contact with Penkovsky. Perhaps, he suggested to headquarters, Penkovsky could practise throwing snowballs and then hurl his material over the wall into the house where Compass lived, pretending he was getting rid of dirty pictures. Not exactly Moscow Rules.

As Christmas approached, Penkovsky had become frustrated that he had heard nothing. He decided to try another route. On 21 December, an American businessman who lived in London reported to the CIA what he thought had been a provocation in Moscow during a recent visit organised by the State Scientific and Technical Commission.[4] A friendly Russian from the Commission had gone back with him to his hotel and asked for cigarettes. He spoke English with a heavy accent but was jovial company. Once they were in his room, the Russian locked all the doors, turned up the radio as loud as he could and produced a folded pack of paper from his coat pocket. These were secret documents, he explained, and needed to go to the American Embassy. The businessman refused. At the end of the trip, the Russian approached him again at the airport and asked him to contact American officials on his return. The Russian gave his phone number and said he would be waiting every Sunday at 10 a.m. for a call.

Penkovsky had picked the wrong member of the delegation to approach. But there would still be time for his path to cross with that of an unusual British businessman who had been on the same trip. Suggesting to a businessman, over a good lunch at a club, that he might like to do his bit for Queen and country has always been par for the course for MI6. Businessmen could move behind the Iron Curtain in a way spies found hard. And surely if they saw something interesting, overheard something interesting or – best of all – met someone interesting, then it would not hurt to report back, would it? MI6 ran a large team out of an office in Queen Anne's Gate, milking the salesmen and industrialists for every drop of intelligence, and the plush Ivy Restaurant in Covent Garden was the venue where MI6 officer Dickie Franks, a future chief, had made just such a suggestion to Greville Wynne, a consultant for British companies. In November 1960, Franks suggested it might be worth getting in touch with a particular committee in Moscow.[5]

The well-groomed moustache, well-cut suits and well-oiled hair gave Greville Wynne the appearance of a well-bred, public-school-educated businessman. But it was a façade he had carefully constructed. Wynne had endured an unhappy childhood in a small Welsh village. When he was a young boy, his mother, who liked to dress him up to impress the neighbours, had taught him how to pretend to be something else, a trick accentuated by his dyslexia which he worked hard to hide. His father, by taking him down the mines to see where most local boys ended up, gave him the urge to escape.[6] When he was eleven his mother died. The overwhelming emotion from father and son was relief, Wynne would later say. As a young man he scrimped and saved to pay for evening studies in electrical engineering and eventually made his way into business, deliberately adopting the clipped tones of the upper class to acquire some social polish, marrying Sheila and stretching to pay for a house in Chelsea. In the stratified world of the English class system his origins could not be entirely hidden, however. 'He was a dapper little figure in his dark suits, what a lower-middle-class Englishman thinks of wearing to put himself up a class,' observed an English journalist who met Wynne.[7] Wynne was a bon vivant, but there was also something fragile about him. When he arrived in Moscow, the Commercial Counsellor at the Embassy thought his trade promotion visit 'ludicrously worthless' and the man 'a silly ignoramus'.[8] But he did not know about the secret life in which Wynne was revelling. The world of spying offered the chance to join a club even more exclusive than those notionally offered by the British class system and with it the opportunity to escape, to be different and to have a secret from others. Exposure to the margins of this world would eventually plunge Wynne into a fantastical Bond-like landscape of the mind.

During the December visit when Penkovsky had approached the American, Wynne had visited the Russian's office. His first observation, true to form, was about the women. 'Buxom healthy girls, but with bad complexions and no make-up. Brassieres and deodorants are unknown to them,' he noted.[9] One of the men at his meeting struck him as different. 'He had a very straight back and did not wriggle or slouch. He sat quite still, his pale firm hands resting on the cloth. His nails were manicured. He wore a soft silk shirt and a plain black tie. His suit was immaculate.' Penkovsky had circled round Wynne during the December visit but never made his pitch, opting instead for the American. At the ballet on the last evening, Penkovsky did suggest to Wynne that perhaps he might like to ask for a Soviet delegation to come to London.

Wynne returned to Moscow in April, just a few weeks before the Marble Arch meeting, to discuss the proposed London trip which he would host. As late snow fell around them, Wynne and Penkovsky walked across Red Square to a hotel. The Russian revealed a hidden pocket in his trouser which he cut with a razor blade to produce documents that he insisted on handing over to a wary Wynne. The Briton was non-committal. At the airport at the last minute Penkovsky offered Wynne an envelope for the American Embassy in London. 'Look, Penkovsky, you are a likeable guy, but I want to go to London, not Vladimir or some damn jail place,' the businessman said. 'I want nothing like that on me when I go through your customs.'[10] Wynne eventually relented and took a letter back, but handed it to MI6. He had become a courier.

The letter was addressed to Queen Elizabeth and President Kennedy among others. 'I ask you to consider me as your soldier. Henceforth the ranks of your armed forces are increased by one man,' it read. American and British intelligence realised that they had both been contacted by the same man and, after edging around what the other side knew, agreed to work jointly. Penkovsky had wanted to talk to the Americans, but the British had the contact in the form of Wynne as well as more people in Moscow. From Wynne they had learnt that Penkovsky was coming to their home turf within days. Neither side had known if he was for real or not. Soon afterwards Penkovsky had arrived in London with his delegation in tow. He greeted Wynne formally at the airport. Later, once the two men were at the Mount Royal Hotel, he gripped Wynne's shoulders. 'I can't believe it, Greville, I just can't believe it.'[11] That evening, Penkovsky had waited until after dinner before making his excuses and heading first for his room and then for Room 360 to begin his betrayal in earnest and deliver to the CIA and MI6 a rich seam of intelligence at a critical moment in international affairs.

The relationship between agent and officer is normally conducted one on one. But Penkovsky was unusual. He was assigned no fewer than four officers, partly because of his importance, partly because meetings could take place in the controlled environment of London and partly because this was a joint operation. This created an unstable mix which would eventually combust.

On the American side, there was Kisevalter. He was the obvious choice to try and make a connection with the unknown officer while also trying to judge whether he was genuine. Kisevalter thought he should be the branch chief in the CIA's Soviet Division.[12] But he was not and the man who had the job made up the other half of the CIA team in the room. Joe Bulik's family was originally from Slovakia and he spoke Russian fluently, having served in Moscow as an agricultural attaché during the war. With his black wavy hair, close cropped at the sides, he was a details man, secretive even with his own colleagues. Kisevalter would rather not have had Bulik around. Bulik knew it, but he was the boss. Working with a fellow CIA officer was one challenge, working with another country – even the old ally Britain – was a totally different ball-game. Neither American had wanted to do it, least of all Bulik. He had been overruled.

The junior member of the British team was a fresh-faced thirty-four-year-old called Michael Stokes. Kisevalter thought he was capable and enthusiastic. Bulik did not, later saying that he thought he was a 'fill-in' and 'hopeless' and was annoyed at his relaxed manner in the hotel room. 'I could have kicked his ass,' the confrontational Bulik remarked.[13]

The senior member on the British side was, many say, the most important officer in MI6's history never to have become chief. Harold Shergold was known to everyone as Shergy. Before the war, he had been a master at Cheltenham Grammar School. Short and well built but slightly bookish, he was intrinsically a shy man but one whose pupils benefited from his keen sense of discipline. In the war he ended up in the Intelligence Corps running forward interrogations of German prisoners in the Middle East with an expertise that impressed those around him.[14] After the war, he went to occupied Germany and learnt the skills of agent handling, winning the respect of his peers for his persistence in getting the information he wanted. He was quietly forceful and he was not of the small, clubby world of the old-school-tie men who had previously dominated MI6. In 1954, he returned to MI6 headquarters at Broadway and picked over the bones of the Baltic operations, learning from the disastrous experience just how capable the Soviet enemy was. He was among the few to fight the battle within the office against those who refused to believe that they had been misled. He realised MI6 had nothing in terms of intelligence in the Soviet Union, just ashes.[15] Daphne Park was one of many young officers who would benefit from his patronage. He would be the man who would instil a sense of professionalism in the British Secret Service and its work against the

Soviets in the wake of the horror show in Albania and the Baltic States and the recurrent discovery of traitors. It is the business of agent runners to turn themselves into legends, John le Carré's Smiley suggests at one point.[16] Shergold and Kisevalter were both legends within their own services.

Shergy was taking the service through an intense period of triumph and disaster. Precisely two weeks before he waited for Penkovsky in Room 360 he had been waiting for another betrayer of secrets down the road at MI6's Broadway headquarters. But this traitor was a colleague. 'There's a few things we'd like to discuss with you about your work in Berlin. Certain problems have arisen,' Shergy said to George Blake as he arrived back from language training in Beirut.[17] The two men proceeded to walk across St James's Park from Broadway. Dick White had chosen the cool Shergy to try and break Blake, who had been identified as a possible spy thanks to a Polish defector. At the MI6 safe house in Carlton Gardens, where Blake had taken the minutes for the Berlin tunnel, he was now carefully probed by Shergy. The morning was spent dancing around the subject, but in the afternoon Shergy began to lay out documents which the Polish defector had identified as compromised, all of which had been handled by Blake. Blake denied everything. Shergy said he was a Soviet spy. Blake denied it. At six o'clock Blake was allowed home (though he was followed by an MI5 surveillance team). He was asked to return for more questioning the next day, and then again the day after that. Shergy knew there was no admissible evidence since the files could not be produced in court. Without a confession, Blake would walk. 'After another half-hour', Shergy later said, 'Blake might have been free.'[18]

According to Blake's own account, it was only when Shergy confronted him with the accusation that he had only become a spy because he had been blackmailed that he broke. 'Nobody blackmailed me! I myself approached the Soviets and offered my services to them of my own accord!'[19] he claims he blurted out in response. Others dispute this as a self-serving story designed to reinforce the impression of a man motivated by ideals. Instead, they say, Shergy actually confronted him with the fact that he had been spotted by surveillance at a telephone box making a plea to his Soviet masters for help. This left Blake with no time to think and he decided to confess to all that he had done. Every other spy who confessed had secured an immunity deal, but Blake did not ask for one. He revealed how in Berlin he had copied station chief Peter Lunn's card index of agents. Blake later said he had perhaps betrayed 500 or 600 agents. Scores had been killed, though this is a truth Blake has always sought to hide from. He clung to a naive faith that the KGB had been telling the truth when they promised they would not harm people based on his intelligence, a move which would have been utterly out of character. Shergy concealed the horror he felt at what he was hearing and barely skipped a beat. 'Am I boring you?' Blake asked at one point. 'Not at all,' Shergy replied. Then it was six o'clock and time to go home.

The next day Shergy drove Blake to a cottage in Hampshire, where they stayed for three days in order to set down a formal confession. Surreally, Blake cooked pancakes with Shergy's wife and mother-in-law. It was like a weekend house party except for the Special Branch outside and the MI6 officer inside confessing to being a traitor. On the Monday, Blake was taken back to London and arrested. An enciphered telegram was sent out to every MI6 station across the world. It was in two parts. 'THE FOLLOWING NAME IS A TRAI-TOR,' read the first part. Every MI6 officer, whether Daphne Park in the darkest Congo or the new man in Laos, remembers deciphering the five letters of the second part which spelled out 'B-L-A-K-E'.[20] Dick White sent over a report, admitting not quite everything, to the Americans. They were furious. One American said he had 'sweated blood' on the Berlin tunnel. 'Here we go again. We should never trust the Brits.'[21]

The revelation that there had been another traitor was not the ideal context for the most sensitive of joint operations between the two nations. But Shergy's temperament and professionalism won the two Americans over as they prepared to meet Penkovsky. At dinner at his house in Richmond his vegetarian wife (a former Olympic athlete) cooked a meal that pleasantly surprised the two carnivorous CIA officers. 'You are sitting opposite me just the way George Blake did when he confessed,' Shergy told Kisevalter and Bulik at the table.[22] Two weeks after Blake, other less sure-footed officers might have run a mile from a Soviet walk-in, fearing another plant or that if he was for real he would be compromised by yet another traitor, but Shergy persisted. Both MI6 and the CIA, rocked by the failure to overthrow

Castro at the Bay of Pigs that same week, needed a success.

And now the four sat across from Penkovsky. He was an unknown quantity to them. Once he had expressed his relief at finally meeting, he vented his annoyance that it had taken nearly a year to get there. 'If you knew how many grey hairs I have acquired since that time.'[23] One of the Americans pulled out the original letter given to the students to show that it was in safe hands and explained that the delay had been needed purely to find a secure way of communicating.

'Between friends, admit that you did not trust me,' replied Penkovsky. 'That is most unpleasant and painful to me.'

The team were beginning to understand that their agent would require careful massaging. 'No, it is quite the opposite,' lied Kisevalter.

Kisevalter asked if the Russian had received a telephone call. The hapless CIA man Compass had called Penkovsky in February. But he had bungled it. Penkovsky said he had received a call but it had come at the wrong time. It was in English and he had hardly understood a single word. His wife and daughter had also been in the room.

'Is your wife absolutely unwitting of your intentions?' asked Kisevalter.

'She doesn't know a thing,' replied the Russian.

With that, Oleg Penkovsky, an extremely well-connected colonel in Russian military intelligence, began to recount his life story. Biography is crucial with all spies: the team needed to understand why he knew what he knew and why he was telling them what he was telling them. Only by understanding that could they hope to determine whether the information he would pass was real or had been planted. Every detail would be checked to assess its originality and veracity. The team had decided to let him speak. They all took notes. This was a charade since they knew a secret recording device was in Shergy's briefcase, but they did not want to reveal that to Penkovsky. Penkovsky spoke in rapid-fire sentences, often jumping from one subject to another without completing his thoughts. The team interrupted as little as possible to allow him to unburden himself of the words he had kept trapped inside for so long.

Penkovsky explained that he had been born in 1919 in the Caucasus. He was an only child brought up by his mother. His father, it was clear, was the key to unlocking his story. He had disappeared without trace just after the 1917 Revolution. 'I was four months old when he last held me in his arms and he never saw me again. That is what my mother told me.'[24] The real truth was deeply troubling and dangerous for the spy. Penkovsky's father had been a White Russian who had fought the Bolsheviks and who was presumed dead. It was dangerous in the Soviet Union to have a White father who was unaccounted for. So Penkovsky's mother had created what spies call a legend – a false back-story to hide the truth. She said his father had died of typhus in 1919. With the truth obscured, Penkovsky joined the Communist Party and the Red Army.

At this point, Kisevalter asked how long Penkovsky could stay in Room 360 without raising suspicion. About two hours, Penkovsky replied. If anyone called his own room while he was with the team, he would say he had disconnected the phone to get some sleep. He continued with his story.

During the Second World War he was at one point the youngest regimental commander on the front line. He had married the daughter of one general and had managed to secure the patronage of another important figure, General – later Marshal – Sergei Varentsov. When he was recovering from an injury, Varentsov asked Penkovsky to take care of one of his daughters whose husband had been shot for participating in a black-market ring. The daughter was distraught and killed herself. Penkovsky sold his watch to pay for her funeral. When he reported back to the father, Varentsov took the younger man under his wing. 'You are like a son to me,' the Marshal had said to Penkovsky. The son had found the father figure he had never had. Now, in a hotel room in Marble Arch, he was turning against him.

Thanks to Varentsov's patronage, Penkovsky was admitted to prestigious military academies and then into military intelligence, the GRU, working on Egypt and the Far East before becoming acting military attaché in Turkey. He had been a colonel by the age of thirty and may well have made general. He was a member of the elite and he knew it. But he had been involved in a nasty bust-up with a superior whom he had informed on. It had meant he gained an unhelpful reputation for intriguing against colleagues. He could be 'vengeful', he admitted. The steep upward trajectory of Penkovsky's career had peaked and then fallen back. A posting abroad as a military attaché had been blocked. Perhaps he had rubbed too many people up the wrong way with his ambition and powerful friends, but a year ago he had learnt of another reason which he believed explained it all. The Chief of Personnel in military intelligence had summoned him and asked him questions about his father. 'You said your father simply died,' he said, going on to explain that the KGB had been going through the archives and had found out more about him, including a possible Tsarist past.

'I have never seen my father and never received a piece of bread from him,' said Penkovsky.

'But evidently you have concealed the fact,' said the inquisitor.

He had been deemed politically unreliable. The KGB were unsure about him rather than convinced of any real wrongdoing, but that was enough to end any hopes of advancement. This was the moment when he had begun to reach out to the West. Frustrated ambition and a desire for revenge is, after money, the most common motivation for an agent. The State Scientific and Technical Commission was the best posting Penkovsky could get now: it required him to operate under cover and look for technical secrets from the West. And even there the KGB expressed reservations about letting him go abroad. It was only a push from Varentsov at the very last minute which had made it possible for him to come to London and to be in the room.

'They will never make me a general,' he told the four attentive listeners, a theme he would return to again and again. 'Maybe I will become a general in another army,' he joked. He talked briefly about being disaffected politically with the Soviet Union, but it was clear that this was a thin veneer masking frustrations relating to his career.

The men sipped on a mild Liebfraumilch as they talked. That was, they noted later as if to justify the presence of wine to their superiors, only to quench thirst because the room became increasingly hot and stuffy, filled with cigarette smoke. The windows could not be opened for fear of someone overhearing.[25]

Penkovsky began to canter through intelligence that the CIA and MI6 team would previously have been scrabbling around to try and piece together. The blindness that had afflicted British and American intelligence since the Cold War had not yet lifted and the years of Penkovsky's espionage were to be the tensest and most dangerous of the Cold War when many believed a conflict and perhaps even a nuclear exchange were imminent. Penkovsky began with details of the structure and personalities of the GRU, and then revealed which brigades were being equipped with atomic warheads. He explained that the rocket troops for use against Britain were located north of Leningrad and that secret tunnels connected the Ministry of Defence to the Kremlin. He roamed backwards and forwards, around and about as the team became almost dizzy. Missiles and rockets were the latest weapons of the Cold War and were becoming the defining technology in the nuclear race as each side tried to show that the future was on its side. Washington had become obsessed with the idea that there was a growing 'missile gap' in which the Soviet Union was perceived to be streaking ahead in terms of both numbers and the power and extent of its arsenal, a concern London shared, although not quite to the same extent.[26] John F. Kennedy had just been elected on a promise to close the gap. Exactly a week before Penkovsky appeared in London, Yuri Gagarin had become the first man in space, spurring a panic among the American public that they were falling behind. (Newly arrived in prison, George Blake found the news an enormous morale boost.) Penkovsky disclosed an important secret. There was no gap. The Soviets had fewer weapons than Khrushchev claimed and their programme had weaknesses in key areas like electronics and guidance systems. 'You know, Oleg, with respect to ICBMs [intercontinental ballistic missiles], we don't have a damn thing,' Varentsov had said to him.[27] It would take some time for everyone in Washington, especially those with a vested interest in talking up the threat, to believe Penkovsky, but he would provide ammunition for some officials, including the President, in their argument with the air force and others who lobbied for more and more missiles.

Penkovsky also offered a unique glimpse into life behind the Iron Curtain. Only around two million of the seven or eight million Communist Party members were really committed Communists, he explained. Visits by British businessmen to factories outside Moscow had been cancelled so they would not see the starving cattle. There had been food riots in some cities and people were resorting to horsemeat sausages. The younger generation was disaffected, he said.

Penkovsky captivated the men as he turned to high politics. 'As your soldier I must report to you that the Soviet Union is definitely not prepared at this time for war.' He told them that the USSR should be sharply confronted. Khrushchev was not going to attack now but he was preparing for the time when a 'rain of rockets' would bury imperialism. The Soviet leader had to be faced down in the next two or three years before he was ready.

'What I would like to do is to swear an oath of allegiance to you,' Penkovsky said as the first meeting came to an end. The men discussed plans to meet again the following night. 'I want to have a clear soul, that I am doing this irrevocably.' He stopped. 'All I ask is for you to protect my life,' he said prophetically. He offered to do what every spy service wants from an agent – to stay in place for a year or two rather than defect, giving himself the opportunity to gather more secrets to fit London's and Washington's requirements.

Penkovsky left Room 360 at three minutes past one in the morning after three and a half hours. He lay in his bed for another two hours with thoughts of missiles and betrayals spinning through his mind. He left behind four intelligence officers who had been almost winded by the ferocity of the intelligence tornado in which they had just been caught up. And it was only the beginning. He would be back the next evening and then again night after night to spill secrets. On the second night, he signed a formal contract. This is standard practice to take an agent beyond the point of no return and bind them into their betrayal. Penkovsky needed no persuading. 'Henceforth I consider myself a soldier of the free world fighting for the cause of humanity as a whole and for the freeing from tyrannical rule of the people of my homeland Russia.'[28] He went on to explain what intelligence he had been asked to collect during his time in London – for instance, about the chemicals for solid fuel for missiles – which revealed Soviet weaknesses. He had also been told to collect any information on MI5 surveillance methods. Did they use watchers in vehicles or on foot, for example? In the course of these meetings, Penkovsky looked at a staggering 7,000 photographs from the files of MI5, MI6 and the CIA, identifying nearly one in ten of the faces staring out at him, including hundreds of KGB and GRU officers.[29] This included almost all the spies operating out of the Soviet Embassy in London, although he warned the team not to put any surveillance on them to avoid pointing the finger at him.

Penkovsky's delegation was touring the country and he went up to Leeds with Wynne. During a car journey on the way north,

Kisevalter read from the details that Penkovsky had provided on missile systems while the other members of the team compared notes.[30] What struck the team most was Penkovsky's access to top military figures, especially Marshal Varentsov. He also had access to the classified library of Russian military intelligence and through Varentsov could look at pretty much anything on missiles.

In Leeds on 23 April 1961 the whole escapade nearly descended into farce. After visiting British businesses in the city, Penkovsky stopped at a small restaurant and downed a litre of cold beer. This led to stomach cramps for about two hours until Wynne called a doctor, who diagnosed an extreme kidney irritation caused by drinking the beer too quickly. 'I feel all right now except that I'm a little weak from the anxiety of this ordeal,' Penkovsky explained as he walked into Room 31 of the Hotel Metropole at around 10.30 p.m. to meet the team. If he had been taken to hospital, he might have come under suspicion, he said.[31] On another occasion, more reminiscent of Austin Powers than James Bond, Kisevalter met Penkovsky and took him towards the hotel. Kisevalter went through the revolving doors only to realise that the Russian was not with him. He then stepped into them just as Penkovsky did the same and they ended up revolving to opposite sides. They then entered the doors again, neither knowing when the other would get out. Eventually they both emerged into the lobby watched by curious guests.[32]

The team were beginning to suspect that there was something unbalanced about their prize agent. In Leeds he elaborated on a suicidal and almost comical plan he had begun mentioning at the first meeting. All he needed, he explained to the stupefied audience, was for suitcase-size nuclear bombs to be smuggled into Moscow in diplomatic bags. He would hide these in his dacha and then bring them into the city and place them in dustbins where they could be used to destroy the Soviet military command in a pre-emptive strike just before it launched a war on the West.[33] 'Here is a note about target number 1,' he said, handing over a piece of paper, 'which must be blown up by a bomb of one or two kilotons.' The target was the General Staff complex in Moscow. The bomb should be detonated between 10 and 11 a.m. to maximise casualties. He had clearly spent a lot of time thinking about how to do this. The team listened patiently without interruption, both awed and embarrassed by this scheme. Three days later, Penkovsky would sit in front of a blown-up map of the centre of Moscow with a red pen and plot a total of twenty-four targets to be sabotaged in this way. 'I could run around and set all these in the proper places.'[34] 'Your intentions are very fine,' replied Bulik, 'and when the time comes to consider this, your proposition will not be ignored.' There was no more revealing sign of the deep bitterness Penkovsky harboured against the Soviet elite which had stymied his career. A psychologist might have had something to say about the fatherless spy who decides, in an attempt to prove his new allegiance, that he wants personally to kill and destroy the institutions which have become his family.

Like a priest in a confessional, listening is important for a case officer. Penkovsky was a loner. He had few close friends and so, as with many spies, the relationship with his case officers was intense. He could not talk so frankly with anyone else, including his wife. The spy–officer relationship is close but also fundamentally deceptive. After all, the spy often never knows the true name of the officer he is spilling his heart out to. The intensity of those first meetings and of Penkovsky's desire to betray startled even the seasoned intelligence professionals in the team. As they listened to him talk, they were all asking the questions every case officer asks when they first meet an agent. What makes him tick? What did he want? How far was he willing to go?

Penkovsky's frustrated ambition was at the core of his fissile personality. This had been compressed into a thirst for vengeance. But lurking in the background, the team soon realised, were other motivations. For many, though not all traitors, money provides an additional incentive. In some cases, it will be the prime mover. For instance, the official who has got into debt and needs a way out might be offered money for secrets. Penkovsky did not spy for the money, but he certainly kept asking about it from the very first meeting. The references began carefully. He wanted to live better and provide luxuries for his family, he said, including a new dacha outside Moscow. Kisevalter explained that monthly payments would be deposited in a bank account. Could they be backdated to when he first began to collect information and before he actually began meeting the team? Penkovsky inquired. At the end of the second meeting, he admitted he had got into debt. Perhaps the team could supply a one-carat diamond he could smuggle back, he suggested.

He also began to reel off a long list of Western luxuries he needed, including fountain pens, ties, nail polish and lipstick. After one meeting had finished he had returned to the room ten minutes later with a jacket over his underwear explaining that he had left a notebook down the side of an armchair. The notebook contained a beautifully presented list of items his wife had prepared, written out in red ink and itemised. It contained magazine clippings of fine ladies' clothes and outlines of the feet of both Penkovsky's wife and his daughter so that he could purchase the right-size shoes for them. His wife, he said, had become very impressed by Western life and consumer goods while in Turkey. Penkovsky himself was also partial, spending three hours with Wynne in Harrods. At one point, Stokes, who was vaguely the same size, was sent to Oxford Street to get measured for a suit for Penkovsky. The Russian liked good clothes – smart white shirts and two red ruffled umbrellas were purchased for him at one point. Not all the gifts were for him or his family. Many were for his mentors in the Soviet elite (including medication to improve their sex lives). The team appreciated that the consumer goods would help smooth their spy's access to the centre of power. The thirst for Western goods among those who ruled the country was a little-noticed sign that, even though the Soviet machine was churning out missiles, rockets and military hardware, it was failing to keep pace in the field of consumer goods which people actually wanted. Only the top officials who travelled abroad understood this, but it revealed a weakness which would eventually help undermine Communism.[35]

Penkovsky would often ask the team to value the intelligence he was providing.[36] Payment had been raised in the first letter he passed to Wynne. He mentioned he had heard that some spies had been paid $1 million. The team tried to avoid too many specifics. They would pay $1,000 a month into an escrow account, but there could be more, they said. It was not just money. His repeated pleas for his worth to be acknowledged were as much about boosting his ego and affirming his self-image as a hugely valuable individual as they were about boosting his bank balance. He quite simply wanted to be the best. 'I wish to do great things – so that I will be your "Number 1",' he declared. 'I consider that I am not just some sort of agent – no,

I am your citizen. I am your soldier ... I am capable of great things. I want to prove this "as soon as possible". Those last four words he spoke in English as if to emphasise the urgency of his desire to prove his allegiance.[37]

Lust, like money, often motivates spies, and satisfying that lust is a way of rewarding them. It is also often the expression of the risk-taking, ego-driven personality. At their meeting on 1 May in London, Penkovsky said Wynne had promised to take him to a 'very big nightclub'.[38]

'And you are not going to take us with you?' asked Bulik.

The issue of entertaining women, as it occasionally can, overlapped with that of money at this point.

'Now I will spoil Mr Harold's mood,' said Penkovsky, looking at Shergy who controlled the purse-strings tightly. 'I was told that it costs £50 to go to a nightclub. I was told that it costs £10 to dance with the girls and the tables cost a lot. He [meaning Wynne] said £50 so that I would pay for him also.' At half-past midnight, having done a day's work as Soviet spy followed by an evening's work as Western spy, Penkovsky headed off to party.

When the five reconvened the next afternoon, Penkovsky was still nursing a sore head but one adorned with a smile. He had left a girl at 4.30 in the morning after two hours at her apartment, he explained, before getting up again at 7 a.m. to go to the Soviet Embassy.[39] 'I was at a most luxurious cabaret. Could you extend my leave for about another ten days?' he quipped. He had met a twenty-three-year-old girl and proudly told the whole team her telephone number. 'She was a nice girl, somewhat experienced in her line of work,' the sated spy remarked.

'The phone number was what, once more?' joked Shergy.

She had been paid £15 by Wynne and told he was Alex from Belgrade. In a rather awkward moment, the team then inquired whether he had been 'careful'. He assured them he had washed himself properly and there was no chance of disease. Her apartment was nicer than his in Moscow, he added appreciatively.

Penkovsky's hunger for recognition also expressed itself in his repeated request to see a government representative to present himself officially. The British were initially at a loss how to deal with this, much to the Americans' amusement until Penkovsky asked to be flown to Washington to see the President. Eventually, a solution was found to appease him. At their fourteenth meeting, Shergy turned to him. 'Now listen attentively. In ten or fifteen minutes a high-ranking representative of the Ministry of Defence of Great Britain will come here. He is personally speaking for Lord Mountbatten, the Minister of Defence [Mountbatten was actually Chief of Defence Staff at the time]. The most important thing for you is to realise that he is in a position to give you complete assurance for your future, for the promises given to you, and to confirm what we have told you.' Shergy left the room to bring in the special guest.

The man who walked in that night – the same night that Blake was taken to Wormwood Scrubs to serve a forty-two-year sentence – was C, Dick White. Chiefs of MI6 do not normally meet agents, but White knew this was not just any agent. Penkovsky was crucial for MI6 as an organisation. He offered a chance to overcome the disasters of Philby and Blake and restore the relationship with the Americans and the service's reputation in Whitehall.[40] White explained that Lord Mountbatten regretted he could not meet Penkovsky personally but he had a message: 'I am filled with admiration for the great stand you have taken, and we are mindful of the risks that you are running. I have also had reported to me the information which you have passed on. I can only tell you that it would be of the highest value and importance to the Free World.'

'I have hoped for this for a long time now,' replied Penkovsky. 'I did the best I could to prove my faithfulness, my devotion, and my readiness to fight under your banners until the end of my life.' Penkovsky then said he wished to swear fealty to Queen Elizabeth II and President Kennedy whose soldier he had become. 'I hope that in the future I will be blessed by this fortune personally by the Queen.'

'I beg that he proceed with caution in view of the great risk,' White said, asking Kisevalter to translate. 'But I want him to know that should the time come when he must leave Russia and make his home in the Western world, the obligations that we undoubtedly have towards him will be firmly and clearly fulfilled.'

'This is clear to me and I think you,' said Penkovsky. 'Please fulfil my request that the Lord at some convenient moment state to Her Majesty the Queen, that her forces have been increased by one member – this colonel who is located in Moscow on the Soviet General Staff and who is fulfilling special assignments, but actually is a colonel in Her Majesty's Service.'

Wine was served for a toast. White then made his excuses to be escorted out by Shergy. When Shergy came back in, Kisevalter explained that Penkovsky was keen to know what impression he had made. 'Oh very good indeed,' said Shergy. That was only part of the truth. After the very first meeting, Shergy had reported back to White that Penkovsky was unstable and motivated by vanity. White believed that Penkovsky was 'neurotic, highly risky and crazy' but he also knew the material was gold dust and set about skilfully using it within Whitehall to try and restore his service's standing.[41] At later meetings, Penkovsky would say that he had appreciated the visit but wondered why he had not met the Queen yet.

Shergy and the others knew they were on to a winner with Penkovsky – a fantastically well-placed spy who was willing to remain in place and collect more and more information rather than defect. Penkovsky himself asked for a small Minox camera to photograph documents which he was trained to use during the meetings. His enthusiasm and his willingness to take risks was astonishing. But that posed a problem, the same one the CIA had faced months earlier and failed to overcome – how were the secrets to be passed in Moscow?

One answer was to use Wynne as a courier. The great advantage of the businessman was that Penkovsky was authorised to meet him for work, so there would be no suspicion or need for illicit contact. But Wynne was only in Moscow occasionally. There needed to be a means of making regular contact. No one had ever successfully run an agent in Moscow.[42] In previous years, opportunistic spying rather than real running of agents was all that had been possible for MI6 officers, like Daphne Park who had been stationed there in the mid-1950s. When she arrived, her Ambassador had warned her that any Russian who talked to her was either a fool who was risking his life and liberty by doing so or else a KGB plant.[43] During a visit to Kalinin with the Assistant Air Attaché, Park had located the local KGB HQ and, finding the door open, walked in, up the stairs to a landing where all the offices of the officials were situated. Each door had the name and position of the person who worked behind it. Park and the Attaché got out their pens and their notebooks and spent twenty minutes writing down every detail. When they later found themselves being watched, they put on swimming costumes and escaped by crossing the Volga.[44] This was not the same as running a high-level Russian military intelligence official. But at least MI6 was able to get its people into the city: the CIA remained barred by its own State Department. 'What do you have?' Shergy asked Bulik at one point, meaning resources and people in the Soviet capital. 'We have zilch, with a capital Z,' Bulik replied.[45]

During the debriefing Kisevalter did most of the talking, but when it came to arranging the tradecraft, Shergold, the details man, took the lead. Options were thrown around including a controlled dead-letter drop in which the material would be left in place for a matter of seconds or minutes before being picked up. Could they meet at a football match and brush past each other at a crowded buffet when getting a glass of beer? The team pored over every detail of Penkovsky's daily routine and movements to look for opportunities.

Shergy came up with a plan. Why not use the wife of the MI6 man in Moscow? The two could meet in a park. Penkovsky would drop material into her pram without saying anything. Penkovsky suggested it would be better to make some small talk with her. It was agreed that the next time Wynne arrived in Moscow the two men could pass material and messages back and forth. Within Wynne's message would be details of how to organise a meeting in the park. Bulik later claimed he was not keen on using this method regularly. 'You can do this once or twice, but beyond that you are gambling,' he said to the British. He recalled (perhaps with a touch of paraphrasing) the British reply as 'And what do you have, American, beside a big mouth?' 'They [were] just about as nasty as that.'[46] The Americans were working to get a CIA officer into the Embassy under cover, but it was taking time.

On the last day of his trip Penkovsky, true to form, mentioned that he had asked for a picture of the receptionist at the hotel, one Valerie Williams She told him she did not have one. So he gave her £5 and asked her to take one for him. She did so and gave it to him the next day with a 'nice' letter in which she said staff were forbidden to go out with guests. 'You see how I spent the last of my pounds!' he told the team.[47]

Penkovsky returned to Moscow on 6 May laden with gifts and secret instructions. He went to a payphone two days later, rang a number and hung up, and then did it again. It was a sign he was in place.[48] His trip was seen by his Soviet superiors as a success, partly thanks to the gifts he brought back and partly thanks to the low-level intelligence he had been supplied with by the team. A few weeks later Wynne returned for a trade show. As they drove from the airport, packages were exchanged including camera film. Wynne went on to the British Embassy and handed them – unopened and without saying a word – to Rauri Chisholm, MI6's station chief. The two men exchanged notes rather than speak in case they were bugged.[49] At dinner that evening, Wynne showed Penkovsky a picture of Rauri's wife, Janet, whom he said was called Anne. They would meet in a park along Tsvetnoy Boulevard. If she had a pram he was to approach and give her a sweet box for the children in which the films could be secreted.

Janet Chisholm was taking on a risky role. But she was capable and smart. Being the wife of an MI6 officer in the field is not easy. Your husband will often be working late doing his real job long after the working day of his cover job is over. You may not be able to ask him what he was doing. And your female friends may gently question why your husband has not been promoted to ambassador and is still only a first secretary. Perhaps that is one reason why, especially in the early days, many relationships remained in-house with officers marrying secretaries who understood the game and who could be trusted. Janet had been one of those secretaries. After learning Russian she joined the service aged twenty and then met and married Rauri. To her dying day, she retained the most important quality for an MI6 secretary – discretion. She never spoke a word about her work with Penkovsky.[50]

Janet Chisholm and Penkovsky made their way separately to the small, narrow city park on 2 July. It was busy and Penkovsky waited for the rain to come and the crowd to thin before approaching. Janet was wearing a brown suede jacket as agreed. He gave the children a box of sweets. Inside were two sheets of paper and seven rolls of film. The material was so important that parts of it would be communicated personally to the President of the United States nine days later. It would be the first of a dozen such brush contacts between the two in the coming months. Her husband was under heavy surveillance, but she believed hers was minimal

The good news from Penkovsky's note was that on 18 July he was returning to London for an exhibition at Earl's Court. This time he was staying in Kensington. Stokes met him and took him to a nearby flat. The first topic was how the meeting with Janet had gone. 'Did I work correctly with this lady, or not?' he asked, seeking approval. Penkovsky found Shergy harder to read and colder, but, as was his nature, he wanted to impress him. 'You stayed a little bit too long with her,' said Shergy, ever the perfectionist. 'Excuse me, I also am a clever man. It's impossible to sit, give and vanish. It is impossible . . . The place is bad.' Penkovsky evidently disliked not like not being showered with approval. But then again his life was the one at stake, he was a professional spy and he knew Moscow better. The team were beginning to understand that he was not going to be easy to direct. Who was leading this dance? they wondered.

Penkovsky's reputation as one of the most important spies of the Cold War comes partly thanks to timing. As well as the mountains of technical information about rockets and spies, he was also able to provide the first insights into the thinking of Soviet leaders at a time when tensions were running high. In June 1961, the newly minted President Kennedy had met the wily Premier Khrushchev at a disastrous meeting in Vienna. The bullying Khrushchev was determined to push the new boy around and the Cold War playground of Berlin was to become the site for their clash of wills. The Soviets were looking at settling the city's status by the end of the year and preventing the flow of people west (100,000 had fled in the first half of 1961). They were considering concluding their own peace treaty with East Germany which would effectively hand over control of the city to their Communist allies. There would be war if America interfered, Khrushchev said in Vienna. 'Then, Mr Chairman, there will be war,' replied Kennedy. The White House was unsure whether the Russian leader was all bravado and bluff or whether, as Washington's hawks claimed, he wanted war. Penkovsky could help them find out.

Berlin dominated Penkovsky's second round of meetings. The question which everyone looked to him to answer was whether the Soviet Union was really prepared for war. Previously, the CIA and MI6 had no sense of what the Soviet leadership actually thought. Now they had someone who could offer real insight into whether the Soviets desired a conflict and were capable of winning it.

'They are not ready,' Penkovsky explained to a relieved audience. 'Khrushchev's statements about this are all bluff ... The reasoning is simply this, to strike one sharp blow, let a little blood flow and the Americans and British will be frightened and withdraw. This is what he is banking on.' He revealed that there were those around Khrushchev who disagreed with him and might try and remove him if he failed. Penkovsky's access, thanks largely to gossip from Varentsov, was priceless and he had a brilliant ability to ingratiate himself with the Soviet elite and curry favour with his bosses (he wrote to Khrushchev complaining that Karl Marx's grave in London was in a shabby state which earned him credit in the Krelim and no doubt annoyance within the Embassy in Britain). He was even able to produce the notes of the Kennedy–Khrushchev meeting that were being distributed to the Communist Party in the USSR and internationally. Penkovsky knew this was a highly valuable document and enjoyed reading excerpts out loud.

In the Oval Office on 13 July, President Kennedy was personally briefed about Penkovsky by his CIA Director, who explained that Khrushchev was not ready for war.[51] Kennedy was a self-confessed fan of spy fiction and especially of James Bond. He had hosted Ian Fleming for dinner before he became president (during the same dinner, CIA chief Allen Dulles had been sufficiently intrigued by Fleming's ideas for destabilising Castro, including trying to persuade Cubans to shave their beards off by saying they contained radioactive particles from a nuclear test, that he tried to meet the author afterwards and would often ask the CIA if they could match the gadgets he read about in the books). Reportedly, like his assassin, Kennedy was even reading a Bond novel the day before he died.[52] Spies knew that their myths could help seduce not just agents but political leaders and it made it easier for the CIA to sell Kennedy their wares (including the Bay of Pigs). It is no surprise that the President became fascinated by Penkovsky. And the Russian's information had a real impact. On 25 July, based in part on the intelligence from the meeting in the flat in Kensington, President Kennedy addressed the American people and signalled that he would call his opponents' bluff in the showdown over Berlin. The city had now become, he said, 'the great testing place of Western courage and will, a focal point where our solemn commitments stretching back over the years since 1945 and

Soviet ambitions now meet in basic confrontation'.[53] Surprised by the firmness of the American response, Khrushchev decided to back away and opted instead for another way of preventing the human tide heading west.

Penkovsky's information was so good that it sparked a fierce debate about whether he was a plant. James Jesus Angleton, Philby's old friend and the head of counter-intelligence, thought Penkovsky might be a crank 'trying to get us in war with the Russians'.[54] Some argued for Penkovsky to be polygraphed. The British resisted, saying it would alienate him. One of those who argued strongly that he was for real was Maurice Oldfield. 'Moulders' had become the MI6 liaison officer in Washington and, when not engaging in a risky personal life involving young men, had followed the tried and tested strategy of trying to get as close as he could to the Americans. He described Penkovsky as 'the answer to a prayer' in that task.[55]

The Minox pictures Penkovsky took were so good that suspicions were aroused that perhaps the KGB were taking the pictures for him. So during one meeting a member of the team shouted 'Catch!' and threw Penkovsky a camera and asked him to take a picture of a map while they made a cup of tea (it being Britain, a tea break at four in the afternoon was mandatory).[56] Penkovsky took fifty pictures and then threw the camera back. When they were developed they were perfect. The team breathed more easily. In Moscow, he would photograph reams of classified manuals, directories, phone books and everything else he could lay his hands on, including a top-secret version of a document entitled 'Military Thought' which outlined the thinking of senior officers – MI6 and the CIA did not even know that a top-secret version had existed.[57]

Penkovsky explained to the team that his duties during his second London visit included looking after the wife and daughter of General Ivan Serov, the head of Russian military intelligence, the former head of the KGB and the man who had been in charge of crushing Hungary in 1956.[58] He took the two women to their hotel and wined and dined them – dancing to rock and roll in a nightclub. He even lent them money when they ran out. 'He did everything, except he overdid it,' recalled Kisevalter later.[59] 'He began to play footsie with Serov's daughter Svetlana, and I begged him on my knees almost, "This is not the girl for you. Let us not complicate life."'

'But she likes it,' Penkovsky said.

'There are others. Not this one,' Kisevalter pleaded.

To aid the process of winning over Svetlana's father, Kisevalter even went shopping and bought a V-neck sweater for the head of Russian military intelligence to wear while playing tennis.[60] Serov summoned Penkovsky on his return to thank him personally and said he would see about getting him sent to Washington.[61]

Penkovsky increasingly referred to the West as 'we' or 'us'. To encourage him, Shergy and Bulik brought out American and British colonels' uniforms for him to try on. Shergy later complained to the Americans that he had not been told they would be putting medals on their uniform which made it look better.[62] Penkovsky at times encouraged his new comrades to start a minor war with the Soviets, in Iran or Pakistan, in order to expose the weakness of low morale within the regime. He really did want to be a general directing armies and not just a spy providing intelligence. 'Penkovsky was the classic example of the pathology that affects the mind of the really important spy,' Dick White recalled later. 'Penkovsky thought "single-handed I can alter the balance of power".'[63]

Paris in September 1961 hosted the next set of meetings as Penkovsky led another delegation. Wynne met him off the plane and took possession of eleven films and copious notes. 'Greville, this is great, really great. Paris, here we come!' The two men enjoyed the bright lights, spent plenty of time on the Champs-Elysées watching the women (to whom Wynne was also partial). At a cinema a spy film was showing.

'Maybe we could learn something, Greville.'

'I shouldn't wonder,' replied Wynne.

'One thing you can be sure of. It will all end happily,' said Penkovsky.

'He'll get the girl, I expect,' mused Wynne.

'I was thinking more of the man himself.' Penkovsky paused. 'I don't have to go back. I could stay in the West.'

'It's up to you,' said Wynne. He had been told by MI6 not to try and pressure the Russian either way.

Penkovsky explained that the decision was troubling him. 'I'm really two people, can you understand that?' he said to Wynne.

'Yes,' said Wynne, 'I understand.'

'If we could be like all those people. If we could go back to the beginning, I wonder what would happen.'

'It would be the same over again. You know that.' Just as Wynne wondered what to say next, he realised that Penkovsky had stopped paying attention. A chic Parisian blonde had sat down at the next table.[64]

Penkovsky's eye for the ladies was hard to miss and, liberated from the watching eyes of informers in Moscow, he wanted to make the most of his ventures abroad. 'The trouble is, Greville, that I need girls, I really do,' he told Wynne once. 'Not to give my heart to, that would be too dangerous. But just to have a good time with. What I need is a permanent supply of little sugar-plums to help me forget myself.'[65] One thing the British and Americans noted about Penkovsky, though, was that while he talked about women, he never really spoke of any close male friends. He was a man who wanted to belong.

The reality of life in the British Secret Service is that rather than consuming vast quantities of loose women as James Bond does, the British officer is more likely to be taking on a less glamorous role more akin to pimp. One job for the officers was to organise women who could be trusted in London and in Paris. Wynne introduced his friend to some English girls who 'just happened' to be over. He did not reveal to Penkovsky that they had been carefully selected and approved by MI6 to avoid the risk of his meeting any local girl and talking too freely. 'But what's the use of it all?' Penkovsky complained after meeting one. 'I can't be myself with her because she knows nothing about my work. She's like all the others. There's nothing permanent, not ever, not anywhere. Why does everything have to be so difficult?'[66]

Paris was not as easy a location in which to operate as London. The French police were everywhere on the streets as the struggle over Algeria was spilling over into violence in the city. But the Americans were surprised at just how many 'assets' like safe houses and vehicles MI6 had in Paris – and how nice they were.[67] MI6 also had a former racing driver as their helper who enjoyed motoring down the Parisian streets at hair-raising speeds. Penkovsky presented the team with caviar and a 'Georgian horn of plenty' at their first meeting. He revealed that his wife was expecting a baby and had cried because she wanted to go to Paris but was not allowed.

Since their last meeting one of the defining moments of the Cold War had taken place. Just days after Penkovsky had returned to Moscow, the Soviets had decided to stem the flow of refugees by flinging up the barbed wire of the Berlin Wall to seal off the Western sectors of the city. The last chink in the Iron Curtain had been slammed brutally shut. On the Western side, a young MI6 officer, David Cornwell (also known as John le Carré) witnessed the force that met the last frantic attempts by some in the East to clamber to freedom. Across the city, on its Eastern side, a young Russian Foreign Institute student had arrived days earlier for six months' work experience just in time to watch the Wall's rise. Years later he would become MI6's most important spy inside the KGB.[68] Their failure to provide any advance warning of the Wall's erection was a serious embarrassment for both MI6 and the CIA, and so the team listened with great interest in September as Penkovsky explained that he had known about the plan four days in advance but had no way of contacting anyone urgently. Everyone agreed that a system needed to be devised to pass intelligence in an emergency.

A birthday party the previous week had provided Penkovsky's latest treasure trove of information. He had not just been invited to Marshal Varentsov's sixtieth but had organised the entertainment. All the top generals had been in attendance (no one had less than two stars), including the Soviet Minister of Defence. Penkovsky had delivered a Cognac which the label claimed had been bottled in the year of the Marshal's birth (it hadn't been – MI6 had faked the label). 'My boy,' Varentsov had called him with pride as he cracked it open. All the time Penkovsky had kept his ears open, learning about plans for Berlin including news of upcoming military manoeuvres which could be used as cover for war if needed.[69]

The claustrophobic intensity of the meetings in Paris was heightening tensions within the team. Some were simply personal. Because they were no longer on home turf, they were largely confined to a small two-bedroom apartment where they all shacked up together.[70] Kisevalter snored and was put on a couch. There was no privacy. Bulik at one point turned to Kisevalter and said: 'George, buy a hotel room and help me pick up a whore for Oleg.' Kisevalter thought

Bulik wanted to show off that the Americans could also provide the entertainment, but he felt it was a mistake since the British girls were always carefully selected and he refused.[71] For Kisevalter the strain of leading the debrief night after night was taking its toll. He had never warmed to the more grandiose Penkovsky in the way he had with the earthier Popov. Trying to restrain the Russian's urges while also dealing with his colleagues was making him 'morose, agitated, and impatient'. One night he and Stokes went to a bistro to unwind. When they got back Stokes told Shergy that Kisevalter had made a scene and had been talking too openly about the meetings. Shergy told the Americans and Bulik decided that Kisevalter would be off the team after Paris.[72]

There were also underlying professional differences between the team which began to surface. Bulik had never been keen on the Brits and he began to argue with Shergy. He did not like having to depend so much on someone else. Each would much rather have been running the show themselves and then sharing the take with their jealous partners. There were also differing styles to running agents. The Americans preferred a bit more glad-handing and a friendlier relationship, playing along with the agent's quirks and desires. The British – and Shergy especially – liked to maintain just a touch more distance, to make it clearer that this was a professional relationship rather than a personal friendship. One area where the difference was apparent was over money. Bulik was content to keep it flowing to Penkovsky to keep him happy and confident, Shergy wanted him on a tighter rein and the Americans came to think of him as stingy. Although it is tempting to see this as a microcosm of the contrast between a cash-strapped MI6 and a CIA overflowing with cash, Shergy did have his motives – if agents start splashing the cash, it tends to get noticed and people start asking questions.

Greville Wynne had, out of necessity, become a key player, but the team worried that he was also the weakest link. The CIA in particular disliked using him. 'Remember he is a simple mortal, and not an intelligence man,' Kisevalter told Penkovsky at their first meeting. Penkovsky frequently commented on their increasingly difficult relationship and Bulik became frustrated at the amount of time spent talking about Wynne.[73] 'Wynne right now feels that I have a good deal of money, that I have been rewarded,' Penkovsky told them. 'He gives me glances and hints which say I should "fix" him also.'[74] He wanted the team to tell the businessman not to ask him for money. At times he almost laughed at Wynne with his new friends, remembering how the Englishman had been so reluctant to take the documents in Moscow at first. 'He was afraid. Oh how he was afraid!'

On the evening of 27 September, Penkovsky reported that Wynne had told him he wanted out.[75] Wynne had said the time devoted to acting as a courier meant his business was collapsing. Penkovsky told the team how much he thought Wynne was being paid. Shergy replied that the figure was all wrong. Wynne had already received £15,000, far more than Penkovsky thought.[76] Tellingly, Wynne had also told Penkovsky he was annoyed that the Russian could not talk to him about his clandestine meetings with the team. Wynne's self-image was that he was a James Bond who had entered the glamorous world of espionage. Yet he knew he was not in the inner circle, not privy to the real work. He was an outsider, left on the margins imagining what was happening inside the room. The team patched up the problem, but this pivotal relationship between Wynne and Penkovsky was fracturing.[77]

Janet Chisholm joined the group to discuss meeting places in Moscow. It was agreed that from 20 October every week they would meet at a shop with a fall-back a few days later at a delicatessen after her ballet lesson. They would catch each other's eye before one would follow the other to a discreet spot where they could make the exchange. At the next meeting a technician came and showed Penkovsky a secret, battery-powered short-range-burst transmitter which could be concealed in clothing. It could send a compressed message entered on a keypad through an antenna a distance of a few hundred yards. When perfected, this gadget could be used by Penkovsky when he was near the American Embassy.[78]

What if Penkovsky had an urgent message? What if he learnt that a nuclear strike was imminent? The desperate desire for a tripwire to warn of Soviet attack had evolved from the days of questioning defecting soldiers in Vienna into a vast bureaucracy that dominated the work of the transatlantic intelligence community. In London, a Red List and an Amber List catalogued possible signs of either a surprise attack or long-term preparations right down to the increase in petrol prices as a clue that the military was stockpiling supplies for war.[79] Across the world, legions of men working for the British eavesdropping agency GCHQ and the military sat in small out-stations listening on their headphones for any sign of war in inter-cepted Soviet communications, perhaps spending their whole career relieved never to have heard anything out of the ordinary. The fear of war was real and ever present and all the elaborate systems were needed precisely because there was no spy who could tip the West off about Soviet intentions. The remarkable aspect of Cold War intelligence is that perhaps 90 per cent of the material was never directly used. It was there to warn of an attack which never came or to help fight that war if it did start.[80] That is not to say it was useless. The more understanding there was of the enemy, the less chance there was of a misjudgement about their capabilities or intentions, a misjudgement which could in turn trigger a war. During the years Penkovsky was spying, Britain was particularly concerned about being blind to a Soviet attack. A Joint Intelligence Committee meeting in September 1960 was informed that due to technical changes there might not be any warning, not even a few minutes, of a Soviet attack and this would remain the case until a new radar system came on stream in 1963.[81] For this reason Penkovsky offered something enormously valuable at a critical moment. A plan was agreed in which he would telephone an American official. If a male voice said hello, he would hang up and repeat it. He was to say nothing on the phone line since the KGB recorded all calls and would match his voice.[82] He would also place a dark smudge on a pole which would confirm the call. He could then load an assigned dead drop with a message on his way to work at 8.45 knowing that it would be clear within half an hour. This was to be the signal that war was imminent.

There was a darkening of the mood in Paris. A cloud increasingly loomed over discussions. The British and American case officers knew that they lost control of the single-minded spy when he was back in Moscow and that he would then dictate the pace. At the end of one meeting, Penkovsky asked what he should do if he was compromised. Should he run to a Western embassy? Shergy told Kisevalter to translate: 'They can't do anything for him because they can't get him out of the country.' Perhaps he could be exfiltrated by submarine through the Black Sea? Earlier he had talked about going to Riga in the Baltics where one of those fast boats that MI6 ran could perhaps extract him. Berlin might be better, Kisevalter suggested.[83] The discussions never came to a resolution.[84] At their last meeting, there was champagne and canapés. Penkovsky kissed and hugged each officer in turn. They then all sat down for a moment of silence.

A heavy fog had closed in around Paris the next morning. Penkovsky's flight was delayed four hours. He became nervous and drank coffee and brandy. The delay meant that Kisevalter and Bulik saw him in the airport waiting room, but they avoided each other. As he walked through Customs, he stopped and Wynne, who was escorting him, thought he would turn round. He put his bags down and stood without speaking. Then he picked them up again and left.

The first few meetings with Janet Chisholm in Moscow went to plan. On 20 October, they spotted each other in the shop and walked separately down the street and into a building where the exchange occurred. Through November, the pattern continued – the exchange often lasted less than half a minute. On 9 December Penkovsky was a no-show. Next week he explained it had just been bad weather.

Tensions over tradecraft were growing and the team and their bosses were beginning to argue. The British were worried that the Americans were placing too much faith in Penkovsky's signal for war – they argued that if it was received it needed to be carefully assessed by the Joint Intelligence Committee in case it was a false alarm. They were nervous of the American plan to send it immediately to the President, fearing this might trigger a war. The two sides agreed to disagree.

The real dispute came over whether to try and restrain Penkovsky. His intelligence was phenomenal and no one had ever seen anything like it before. This created pressure for him to supply more, but that brought dangers. The Americans were worried the British were taking too many risks. 'The pace set by the British was a little too hard and fast,' Bulik reckoned.[85] By January 1962, the CIA was worried by the way in which Penkovsky was whipping out his camera at every opportunity. In one case he had photographed a 420-page manual on atomic weapons which proved to be of 'only marginal interest'.[86] The CIA believed that the admonitions to be careful had not been clear enough, especially when coupled with simultaneous requests for more information. 'They are of a "stop it, I love it" nature and have clearly been interpreted by Penkovsky in this vein,' wrote one CIA officer. Just because the risks were justified at the start did not mean they were now, especially when a huge backlog of material to translate and analyse was building up. Penkovsky himself was not a good judge of what risks he could and should take, they thought. He needed to be cooled off.

Shergy agreed there was a danger, but believed that there was no way Penkovsky would respond to a call to slow down. The Russian was too driven to be the best and to change the world. It was a matter of his running himself rather than the team running him. An instruction to stop meeting might destroy him psychologically as it would be seen as a rejection. Penkovsky simply did not see himself as an agent and the team did not have that kind of control over him, Shergy argued.[87] Penkovsky 'revels in what he is doing, is determined to be the best of his kind ever (perhaps not appreciating that he has probably achieved this status already). We feel that it would be a tactical and psychological mistake on our part to renew the warning at this juncture.'[88] 'Penkovsky was an extremely difficult person to control,' Dick White said later. 'He took immense risks. He wanted to appear as the person who altered the balance of power between the two sides. His vanity was enormous.'[89]

On the streets of Moscow, events outpaced the discussions as the first signs emerged that something was going awry. On 19 January, Janet Chisholm saw Penkovsky scanning for surveillance from a phone booth. He had seen a car go the wrong way down a one-way street the previous week and saw it again this time. As she took a bus to her ballet class she had also noticed a car make a U-turn and follow behind. MI6 now agreed that street meetings looked too risky. 'It appears we will not have any trouble [with the British] on this score in the future,' a CIA officer wrote.

There were more investigations by the KGB into Penkovsky's father, including a search for his burial place.[90] An added complication came when Janet fell pregnant. She was replaced by Pamela Cowell, wife of Gervase Cowell, the new MI6 man at the Embassy who had 'pram age' children. Cowell had been recruited at Cambridge and then sent to Berlin. There he had intercepted a set of cyanide bullets, designed to kill one of his agents, that had been hidden inside a cigarette packet from which they could be fired completely silently.

For years afterwards, he would take a step back if someone offered him a cigarette. To reassure his agent that the British had better weapons (which they did not), Cowell showed him a massive sleeve gun which, he later observed, 'you could only fire if a locomotive happened to be leaving Frankfurt station at the time and then at the risk of dislocating your shoulder [as] you let off this enormous clang'.[91] He had also discovered that a large network of agents reporting on the movement of Russian matériel on the East German railways was a figment of the imagination of one man sitting in West Germany reading railway magazines. 'I'm terribly sorry but you know all those reports that you got, they are all fabricated,' he explained to officials back in London.

'Oh actually, old chap, if you could keep on sending them, because they are rather good,' came the reply.[92]

Meetings with Penkovsky continued sporadically at official functions over the summer. At cocktail parties, he would pick up a tin of Harpic bleach in the bathroom to find film and instructions stashed by Pamela Cowell or he would follow her into a room and then turn his back to indicate a cigarette packet with a message inside which she would quickly snatch. Gervase Cowell would later pay tribute to the British Ambassador for 'the tolerance and equanimity with which he allowed us to rampage around Moscow in those uncertain and potentially very dangerous circumstances, running an agent which had never been done before'.[93] Penkovsky's letters revealed his fears that events were taking a turn for the worse.

The CIA finally managed to get operational officers into the American Embassy, leading to their first direct contact in Moscow, and they began to take over. Hugh Montgomery was one of the first officers posted over. He was followed everywhere by KGB men who were happy to let him know they were there. He could even hear them clatter round and change the tape in the recorder above his flat. Carrying out operational meetings was close to impossible. There were a few tricks that the team used when they wanted to lose their tails – one involved two people in a car and one jumping out as it turned a corner. A dummy in the passenger seat would then pop up to make it look to the following car as if both passengers were still there. Exchanges of information were hard but could occur.

At a heaving Independence Day party at the American Ambassador's residence, both Khrushchev and Penkovsky made an appearance among the hundreds of guests. As hands were shaken at a receiving line there was not a hint from Penkovsky that he was anything other than another Soviet official in attendance. Benny Goodman and his jazz band had come over to play ('I like good music but not Goodman,' Krushchev joked sourly). Penkovsky drank heavily and, although he did not appear drunk, the Americans thought he looked morose. A quick exchange was made. Penkovsky deposited a packet in the bathroom and Montgomery followed after he left. But the package had fallen into the cistern rather than remaining taped to the side, and the CIA man had to climb on to the sink, which proceeded to come away from the wall (the Ambassador would later express anger at whoever had trashed his bathroom and was never told the circumstances). In the communications, Penkovsky was starting to sound hunted and desperate and as if he was looking for a way out. Trips abroad were being cancelled. The loneliness of the long-distance spy was taking its toll.

Wynne arrived in Moscow on 2 July and found a changed man. 'He looked pale and taut, there was a shocking weariness in his eyes.' With the music and taps turned on at the hotel, they talked hurriedly. Penkovsky broke down. He was frightened. At one point, he asked Wynne for a gun.[94] The next night, they were due to meet at a restaurant. Two men were skulking in the doorway. As Wynne entered, Penkovsky instead of greeting him signalled not to make contact before whispering, 'Follow behind.' He had spotted surveillance. They headed down a street and into a courtyard. 'You must get out, quickly! You are being followed,' Penkovsky said hurriedly. The same two men appeared at the end of the alley. Penkovsky moved away quickly. Wynne was left facing two men for a few heart-stopping moments. Back at his hotel, Wynne found his room key missing from reception. When it was returned, there was evidence of a search. On a bathroom shelf was a tin of Harpic bleach with a false bottom. Had it been discovered? The last communication came in late August. 'It will soon be a year since our last meetings. I am very lonely for you, and at the present time still do not know when we are fated to see each other,' Penkovsky wrote.[95] The skies were darkening over Moscow. Then they went black. From September, Penkovsky dropped off the radar entirely. At that exact moment, the Cold War threatened to turn hot.

Cuba had replaced Berlin as the flashpoint that could lead to nuclear Armageddon. In his first meetings the previous year, Penkovsky had warned vaguely of Soviet intentions there.[96] Khrushchev believed that if he moved fast enough to install missiles on the island he would be able to counterbalance his present weakness in overall missile numbers. He nearly got away with it. Few in Washington had believed that Khrushchev would take such a provocative step. Only the new CIA Director John McCone suspected that the Soviets might be so audacious and ordered the resumption of U2 spy-plane flights in October 1962 which detected missiles being installed. This time the giant machines that Graham Greene had presaged in *Our Man in Havana* were for real.

Penkovsky's technical information, including the manual for the SS-4 missile which had been passed to Janet Chisholm, helped analysts interpret the reconnaissance pictures to identify the missiles by their footprint. The Penkovsky material had 'special value', according to one of the photo-analysts who worked on the images.[97] This helped decision-makers establish that the missiles would eventually be able to reach Washington DC but were not ready yet.[98] The President and his National Security Advisor said the identification 'had fully justified all that the CIA had cost the country in its preceding years' because it allowed them to face down the Soviet Union before the missiles became operational.[99] Penkovsky's intelligence was only part of the story. It was the overhead imagery which was of crucial importance and which Penkovsky's information simply helped the Pentagon to interpret.[100] In the next few years, Penkovsky's role would often be inflated by CIA officials precisely to hide the new capabilities up above which remained top secret.[101]

A new era of satellite spying was dawning. Spotting trains could now be done by an unseen eye high in the sky rather than by a human spy on the ground. But no satellite image could explain what Soviet leaders were thinking and what their intentions were. In Washington, technology would become king. But in Britain, oddly, the advent of satellites placed an even higher premium on MI6's human spies. Satellites cost the earth. Britain could barely afford them and came to depend on the largesse of its American ally. The best way of ensuring undiminished access to the flow of American technical secrets was by staying close and by bringing human sources to the table. If they could maintain this relationship then Britain's spies knew, as in the Second World War with the breaking of the Enigma codes, that they in turn could bring to their Whitehall masters something precious which justified their existence. After Suez, staying close to the Americans and their vast intelligence machine was becoming gospel.

The Cuban drama was a moment Penkovsky – who always thirsted for recognition as someone who could dictate world events – would have savoured had it not already been too late for him. The decision to slow down had become futile. Through September and October, he was silent.

Hugh Montgomery was woken out of a deep sleep by his phone. It was two o'clock in the morning on 2 November but the remnants of his slumber were soon shaken off as the CIA's deputy station chief in Moscow heard three breaths at the end of the line. Then the click of the phone hanging up. Then the same again. He was all alone, and he uttered an expletive. It was the signal for war. He knew he had to make the drive to the Embassy to cable Washington.

He walked out into a howling blizzard. It felt like fifty below outside as he struggled to start his car. There were only three other cars on the street as he drove off – his car and three KGB Volgas, one driving alongside him, the others in front and behind. When he made it into the Embassy, he despatched a flash message of the highest priority saying that the signal for war had been received. 'While we have serious reservations about its authenticity, nonetheless we are obliged to inform you in case you have any other relevant information,' he wrote. Gervase Cowell would also later say that he had received a warning signal of three breaths but in a display of sangfroid decided simply to ignore it, not even telling his Ambassador.[102]

In the morning, Montgomery called Richard Jacob, a twenty-five-year-old CIA officer on his first overseas assignment, into the 'bubble' – the secure room in the Embassy which was suspended in the air to prevent microphones being drilled through the walls. He explained to the young officer that there had been a signal on the designated lamppost and so the dead drop needed to be cleared.

They knew it might be a trap. Jacob headed for the doorway of the apartment where the message was due to be left and pulled a matchbox from behind the radiator. At that point four men jumped him. In the confusion he managed to drop the matchbox. He was taken to an office. He was an American diplomat, he explained. That surprised his interrogators who believed they were dealing with a British operation.[103] 'I wish to say at this time that I have never in my life seen the material that you have there on the desk,' Jacob said when presented with items of 'an intelligence nature' and a confession to sign.[104] They stared at him. He stared back, locking their gaze for two minutes. 'Well, your dirty career is finished,' one of the men finally said to him.

President Kennedy was told the next morning that Penkovsky was now compromised. He had clearly talked and given away the signalling procedures. The KGB had decided to use them to smoke out Western intelligence officers and Montgomery, along with twelve other Britons and Americans, was expelled. One theory still troubles those involved in the case – had Penkovsky explained that the phone signal meant war and had the Russians tried it anyway? Or had he not told them what it meant in the hope of finally fulfilling his desire to change the world and, by starting a war, destroy those in Moscow who had thwarted him?[105] 'He knew he was doomed, he figured that he might as well take the Soviet Union down with him,' Bulik later reflected.[106]

How had their man been caught? the team wondered. Tensions surfaced across the Atlantic. We should never have used Wynne, the Americans grumbled, he was an amateur. In a memo, a CIA official blamed 'a penetration in the British government who saw Wynn [sic] and Penkovsky together'.[107] Others began to wonder if there was another mole in London or Washington – another Philby. It would have to be someone high up since the operation was such a closely guarded secret.

There was a more likely explanation. Rauri Chisholm had previously worked in Berlin. Alongside him in the MI6 station was George Blake. MI6 knew he was blown and his file was marked 'Sov Bloc Red'.[108] The discovery that the Americans had managed to run Popov in Moscow had deeply troubled the KGB and it had begun blanket surveillance of diplomats. It also realised that wives were sometimes employed in clandestine activities, so they may have begun tailing Janet. They spotted her heading into apartments in January and saw someone nervously following her in.[109] They were not yet sure who the Russian was but the frequency of those meetings in public places and the fact that they continued after the first suggestions of compromise made the KGB task easier. By the time Penkovsky had spotted the surveillance on 19 January and decided to halt the meetings it was too late. A KGB investigation had begun which led eventually to surveillance of Penkovsky's apartment and of his meetings with Wynne.[110] It took time as they had to establish that he was not running a legitimate GRU operation and they knew he was protected by his friendships within the elite. Cameras were installed to look down into his apartment. A poison was smeared on his chair to force him into hospital, allowing his flat to be searched. A Minox was found and the one-time pads used to decipher messages broadcast over the radio. He was brought in. 'When he realised what we had found and was in our possession, Penkovsky knew he didn't have a leg to stand on,' an investigator later recalled. 'He started to confess that he was an agent for the British.' He was taken in to see a top official and crumpled into a chair. 'He came in dragging his heels,' the official recalled. 'He was limp like a wet rag hanging on a hook.'[111] The use of the Chisholms had been a risk – everyone knew that – but Shergy thought there was little choice. 'Everybody in the British Embassy was under surveillance,' he later recalled. 'The name of the game was to avoid surveillance.'[112] The Penkovsky operation was success and failure all rolled into one.

The same night that the telephone rang for Hugh Montgomery in Moscow, Greville Wynne was at a trade fair in Budapest, having just arrived from Vienna.[113] In his later years, he would claim to have been on a daring rescue mission to smuggle his friend out in a false-bottomed trailer. No one else involved in the case knew anything about such a bizarre plan. As he walked down the steps from the trade pavilion in the fast-dimming light, he realised that the Hungarians he had been drinking with for the previous two hours had all melted away. Now there were four men – all wearing trilby hats at the same angle – walking towards him.

'Mr Veen?' one man asked in a thick accent.

'Yes, that is my name.'

A car pulled up. His arms were grabbed. The back door of the car was opened and he was pushed inside. He shouted for his own driver to help but it was too late as a door and then something else hard slammed against his head. He awoke a few moments later, his hands cuffed and blood on his face. He was taken to a dirty room.

'Why do you spy on us?' an unshaven, tired-looking man said.

'I don't know what you are talking about.'

Wynne was stripped naked and examined roughly. The next morning he was on a Soviet military aircraft flying to Moscow. 'I suppose that James Bond would have spat from his mouth a gas capsule (concealed in his molar) which would have overcome everyone but himself and would then have leapt to safety with a parachute concealed up his backside. But I regret to reveal that the British Intelligence Service lags behind Bond in ingenuity.'[114]

He was taken to the basement of KGB headquarters in the Lubyanka – a dark place where dark things happened. Under interrogation he maintained he was just a businessman. He might have passed some notes, he said, but he had no idea what was contained within them. They played the tape of his conversation at the hotel with Penkovsky which the two thought had been obscured by music. He realised he was in trouble.

As he was moved from his solitary cell one day, he says he was sure he saw Penkovsky through a spy-hole shutter. 'He sits motionless with his head down, like a bull after the lance-wound has weakened him.'[115]

Wynne's wife came to visit on 17 December bearing vitamin pills, English tea and cigarettes. She found Wynne's mood oscillating between dejection and excitement. Wynne said that he had seen all the evidence and he had no defence against it. He asked his wife to try and see the Prime Minister to plead for some kind of deal. 'He said that "British intelligence" had pushed him into this and it was for Her Majesty's government to get him out of it,' she told officials afterwards. Wynne's fate did lead to much soul searching within MI6 about the use of businessmen and questions about whether the risks of their work on the side had been sufficiently explained.[116]

For Wynne, the game was up. But this was no game. And in Washington and London they understood the price that Penkovsky would pay. The heads of the CIA and MI6 argued over whether to negotiate with the KGB directly and threaten to expose its secrets. Joe Bulik pressed hard for something to be done. 'I feel we owe him a tremendous debt,' he wrote in a CIA memo. 'For us not to consider ways and means of saving his life is to me a reflection of low moral level.'[117] His anger grew. 'There was no gratitude,' he said later. 'He was expendable. An abandoned hero.'[118] He also vented his anger in later years against the British. 'The big lesson on the Penkovsky case is never to enter into a joint operation with another service,' he would say. 'Joint operations, by definition, double the risks of exposure. The differences in any two services' operating styles lead to confusion, misunderstandings and raise the possibility of compromise.'[119]

The trial came in May 1963. The courtroom was stiflingly hot. Wynne and Penkovsky had been put through their rehearsals for the crowd that had gathered, bristling with anger. Penkovsky may have been a hero to the CIA and MI6 but to them he was just another shabby traitor who had sold out his country for some Western trinkets. Wynne was first in the dock and had visibly aged. The luxuriant black hair was grey and shaved, his moustache tinged white; he looked gaunt, with lines across his face. He read most of his script correctly but incurred some displeasure for the occasional deviation. Had he been deceived by his own countrymen into being an unwitting spy? he was asked. 'Exactly so,' he said to the merriment of the crowd. 'It is exactly because of that that I am here now.'[120]

Wynne, whose status as a British citizen ensured that he garnered most of the international attention, was the light relief. The real venom of the prosecutor was reserved for the Russian. What had made him do such a wicked thing? 'It was the base qualities which have brought him to the prisoner's dock,' the prosecutor suggested. 'Envy, vanity, the love of an easy life, his affairs with many women, his moral decay, brought about in part by his use of liquor. All of these blotches on his moral character undermined him; he became a degenerate and then a traitor.'[121]

Penkovsky played it by the book. His moral decay was due to alcoholism and frustration over his job. 'I lost the road, stumbled at the edge of an abyss and fell,' he explained in a dull, monotonous voice. The crowd became silent at this, its bloodlust finally sated by seeing the walking corpse in front of it. 'I deceived my comrades and said that everything was well with me, but in fact everything was criminal, in my soul, in my head, and in my actions.'[122] Wynne listened to the translation, headphones pressed to his ears.

Penkovsky talked and perhaps told the KGB everything in return for his family's safety. But the Soviets tried to cover up just how damaging he had been and how well connected he was. They also tried to sow division between the British and Americans, claiming that the Americans in Paris had tried to cut out the British. When he recounted his meeting with Janet Chisholm in the park – 'I patted the child on the cheek, stroked him on the head and said, "here is some candy for you, eat it"' – the crowd uttered 'noises of indignation' at the idea that innocent children had been dragged into the midst of this degradation.[123] He admitted he had worn the uniforms of a British and an American colonel. 'Which did you like better?' he was scornfully asked.

'I did not think about which I liked better,' he replied.[124]

By the end of the trial, Penkovsky looked a wreck. Unshaven, his eyes darted back and forth as if looking for a way out. But there could be no doubt about the verdict. 'Oleg Vladimirovich Penkovsky: guilty of treason to the Motherland, to be shot to death.' The crowed jeered and clapped. Women clambered on benches to catch sight of the traitor's reaction. Penkovsky stood silent.[125] Wynne was sentenced to eight years in prison. He was taken out of Moscow to a flat and barren land. He reached the gloomy Vladimir prison in twilight with the rain pouring. His moustache was shaved off and he was placed in a cell with an old oil drum for a toilet. Others also paid a price. General Ivan Serov was demoted and fired as head of Russian military intelligence. Marshal Varentsov – the man who thought of Penkovsky as his son – became Major General Varentsov and was expelled from the Central Committee. How he looked back on his sixtieth birthday is easy to imagine.

Penkovsky is believed to have been shot on 16 May 1963 and then cremated. His wife – who had never known he was a spy – was simply handed a death certificate.[126] Rumours – probably untrue – surfaced that he had been cremated alive in front of other officers to send a message about the fate of traitors.

Penkovsky may not quite have been 'the Spy who Saved the World' as some claimed. But he was the spy who helped save MI6 and the CIA. Both organisations were reeling when he walked through the door of Room 360. Blake had just been exposed as a traitor for the British, while the CIA had just days earlier embarked on the catastrophic Bay of Pigs intervention in Cuba which ultimately cost Allen Dulles his job as director. Penkovsky's manic, messianic spying generated 10,000 pages of intelligence reports. Within it were the first real insights into Soviet intentions and capabilities at a time when the Cold War had yet to settle into a stable pattern of mutually assured destruction and when fears of missile imbalances and crises in places like Cuba, the Congo and Berlin threatened all-out war. Penkovsky allowed the spies to show the policy-makers that what they did mattered and could make a difference.

The Penkovsky case, even though it ended tragically, represented a ray of hope for the British Secret Service. After all the disasters and betrayals of Blake and Philby, all the frustrations of Albania and the Baltics, the dead agents and the probing questions from Whitehall mandarins, it was a sign that it could – at least for a while – successfully run a valuable agent even in the hardest possible place and provide intelligence that was genuinely valued. The case did not just restore confidence, it also set a marker for a new professionalism in the service, an end to the era of Robber Barons and crazy operations. Perhaps there was a light at the end of the tunnel from the horrors that had gone before.

Dick White wanted a professional service – one that did not engage in hare-brained mini-wars and pointless bravado but quietly and skilfully acquired secrets, one that could put the past behind it. The shy but determined Shergy was the man who would help deliver it. With Penkovsky his model, Shergy would create a nucleus of staff in MI6's Sov Bloc division who over the coming decades worked their way outwards and upwards through the organisation instilling such concepts as 'need to know' and focusing on the careful collection of intelligence. These officers would become known as the 'Sov Bloc master race', a term often employed by their colleagues from other parts of the service who felt a touch put out by the arrogance of those who felt they were the elite.

Shergy's mission was to find more Penkovskys. He wanted to identify and target disaffected Soviet officials who could stay in place and spy, rather than drop agents by boat or parachute in the style of the Second World War. This required a different mind-set and skill-set. One of the young officers drawn into this sub-culture of the service was Gerry Warner. Never one of the club men and something of an outsider, his disillusionment with the quality of work in Burma had led him to decide to quit. One evening just before he planned to leave he was sitting in the small bar in the basement of the service's Broadway headquarters. He overheard a racist and offensive joke and voiced his objection. 'Who are you?' the man who had told the joke said.

Warner replied, 'Who are you?'

'The head of personnel. I've got your file on my desk. Come and see me tomorrow.'

Shergy and the Sov Bloc team were trawling through the personnel files to look for young entrants who might be suited to agent running. Their preference was for people who were 'clean' and had not worked in the region before and so were less likely to be blown to the Soviets. Warner was one. Another was a young officer just back from Laos called Colin McColl. He, like Warner, had joined after the customary interview with Admiral Woodhouse in which intelligence work had been hinted at but never openly discussed (the Admiral's attractive secretary had also provided an extra inducement for some applicants to join up). After being taught Polish by an eccentric Yugoslav on a barge in East London, Warner was sent to Warsaw under cover as cultural attaché. Here came one of the early successes for Shergy's team.

One day a rake-like young Pole with wispy, thinning hair walked into the British Embassy in Warsaw. His name was Adam Kaczmar-zyk, he explained, he was a cipher clerk in the Warsaw Pact HQ and had secrets to pass on. Agents provocateurs were commonplace, but cipher clerks were not normally planted because any ciphers they handed over could quickly be checked by the experts at GCHQ to see if they were genuine or not. Cipher clerks were also highly valued since they had access to all the secret traffic that went through an embassy. Warner took the Ambassador down to a secure room to tell him that he would come up with an operational plan to organise meetings with the potential agent. The Ambassador, whose job was to advise on whether the benefits of recruiting an agent outweighed the political risk of being discovered, was reluctant. The next morning, Warner showed him what the latter assumed to be a draft of a telegram. In it Warner indicated that the Ambassador had signed off. 'Quite right, I've changed my mind,' the Ambassador said. This was fortunate as the telegram had already been sent to Shergy. Warner always explained the risks to anyone becoming an agent. 'I was always a bit anxious about whether the person I was going to ask to work for the British government, for the Queen, was fully conscious of the risks that he or she was taking, whether they were sufficiently mature to know what they wanted to do ... And all this was a very intense business. It was as intense a sort of relationship as you could possibly get into and that led on of course to what I think is one of the basic principles of the secret service that the first responsibility of any officer of the service towards his agents is their safety and their security. That is the first basic principle and after that everything else flows.'[127] Not all agents would listen though.

Warsaw would provide a key testing ground for rising stars of the service and the team that ran the agent over a period of nearly three years included two future deputy chiefs of MI6 and one chief, Colin McColl. They supplied the clerk, codenamed 'Beneficiary', with a Minox camera and met him regularly at a heavily curtained British Embassy flat (a small Union Jack on the front door was the signal to enter).

To talk to him there, they used a strange device known as a hush-aphone. This looked like an adapted doctor's stethoscope with a speaking and listening mask at each end. The two parties to a conversation would speak through it to ensure their words could not be picked up by bugging devices. Money and a good time proved to be Beneficiary's only motivation. MI6 were somewhat surprised when they developed the film from his camera and found pictures of ciphers mixed up with those of his unclothed 'girlfriend', pictures he explained he would like back. He spent freely on drink and prostitutes and a fancy car. Empty champagne bottles accumulated outside his house. Neighbours began to notice. Making an agent aware of the risks did not always make them unwilling to take more risks. One day he explained that he thought it would be a good idea to approach a colleague to join the spy ring. The team said no, realising that if the colleague refused it would probably be game over. He said it was too late. The team had to decide whether or not to meet the agent the next time, knowing he might have been compromised. He was.

Kaczmarzyk was arrested at one of the expensive restaurants he had begun to frequent in August 1967. At the same time an MI6 officer was arrested along with his secretary. The press reported that 'spy documents and sketches' were found in her handbag. In her flat, the secret police found a hardback copy of the latest James Bond book. Unfortunately that edition included what purported to be secret maps tucked into the back cover. The secret police were convinced they were real secret maps and gave the poor secretary a particularly hard time. After a four-day trial, Kaczmarzyk was sentenced to death and was killed by firing squad at a military fort.[128]

Beneficiary burned brightly but only briefly. Shergy's protégés on the Czech desk secured a longer-running agent codenamed 'Freed', eventually a major in the Czech Security Service, the StB. Freed's real name was Miloslav Kroča. He had begun his career hunting saboteurs in industry before going to Moscow for training with the KGB. Like Penkovsky, his career had stuttered, partly for personal reasons. A new girlfriend in Moscow led to a divorce and a black mark against his name as well as financial strains. In the early 1960s he managed to secure promotion to work on operations against the British. Around the same time, he also became a spy for the British Secret Service. Recruiting an opposing intelligence officer in such a position was a huge coup in terms of classic spy-versus-spy counter-intelligence. Freed knew all the details of operations against Britain and had access to Czech records. His career prospered with the help of MI6. Poor health, perhaps due to the stress of his double life, took its toll over the years and eventually he died of a heart attack. Only then was his betrayal discovered in spring 1976. Where Beneficiary was mildly crazy and reckless, Freed was cerebral and cautious and survived much longer. Freed's sudden death meant that Czech investigators never knew the full scale of his betrayal. Their investigative files reveal that they were unsure when he started spying for the British; certainly it was by 1969, but some wondered if it was as early as 1962. They did establish, though, the identity of the MI6 officer who was handling Freed at the time of his death. Richard Dearlove was spotted arriving at a number of locations to meet Kroča before he realised he had died. The Czech investigators established that Dearlove, whom they codenamed 'David II', organised meetings both in Prague and in a forest outside the city. The StB spent much time puzzling over where Freed might have secreted payments from the British, a mystery only solved with MI6's help after the end of the Cold War.[129] The successes of Beneficiary and Freed would help launch careers. Insiders say there were other successes in those years which have remained secret, not least because unlike these two, the other agents remained alive. Together the cases would be vital for Shergy as he began to fight his own internal battles against those who saw the shadow of Philby and other moles still haunting the service.

The CIA was also learning from Penkovsky. 'Who are the people that dream of power and glory, and, not only frustrated in these dreams but perhaps even ridiculed in their daily lives, become so bitter as to turn their backs on family, friends and nation?' That question was posed to colleagues by a CIA officer soon after Penkovsky. 'The single, self-evident observation is that the enormous act of defection, of betrayal, treason, is almost invariably the act of a warped, emotionally maladjusted personality,' the officer continued. 'It is compelled by a fear, hatred, deep sense of grievance, or obsession with revenge far exceeding in intensity these emotions as experienced by normal reasonably well-integrated and well-adjusted persons ... a normal, mature, emotionally healthy person, deeply embedded in his own ethnic, national cultural, social, and family matrix just doesn't do such things.'[130]

What made someone like Penkovsky take such crazy risks? The unbalanced nature of such spies, the CIA officer argued, was reflected in his own experience of agents.

All of them have been lonely people ... [who] have manifested some serious behaviour problem – such as alcoholism, satyriasis, morbid depression, a psychopathic pattern of one type or another, an evasion of adult responsibility ... It is only mild hyperbole to say that no one can consider himself a Soviet operations officer until he has gone through the sordid experience of holding his Soviet 'friend's' head while he vomits five days of drinking into the sink.

A retired MI6 man agrees. 'Most agents were unattractive people. Half were nasty characters who you wouldn't want to spend much time with. It was a very strange relationship when you meet them in some woods and he hands you some Minox and begins telling you about his life.'

'Normal people aren't traitors,' Dick White once declared. One recommended CIA strategy was to look for the 'emotionally weak, immature and disturbed fringe elements' seeking revenge for real or imagined slights. They should be investigated using telephone taps and the gossip of wives and by watching the small signs of irritation and professional or personal jealousy at social events. These irritations could even be encouraged by an officer who got close but who would do so while avoiding polemics and political evangelism. Watching the response to a carefully planted question about how promotions work in the Soviet military might be one way. The aim of the contact is to 'awaken resentments and anxieties, to plant ideas, to make oneself a sympathetic friend . . . The process is one of pinning the blame for his intense personal dissatisfactions on the regime.' In a final aside, the officer also suggests looking for the 'unique vulnerabilities of middle age . . . The period of life from say age 37 on shows the incidences of divorce, disappearance, alcoholism, infidelity, suicide, embezzlement . . . because it's a time when men take stock' and the result is often 'traumatic in the extreme'. 'Nobody ever defected because they were happy,' a CIA psychologist decided after studying the files, including that of Penkovsky.[131]

Most of the spies Britain and the US ran in the Cold War were walk-ins, like Penkovsky, rather than the result of careful cultivation. But still the hope was that spies could be recruited through careful preparation leading to an approach. 'Ideally you should have got to know the person so you have built up some sort of trust and you are much more likely to get a yes if you have done that,' explains Colin McColl. 'The cold approach is very, very dicey. It has worked.'[132]

The CIA took an especially aggressive attitude, trying to hoover up as many sources as it could, while the British were more selective even though they understood the same dynamic. But there was a fear which haunted intelligence officers from both services when it came to targeting Soviet officials. The fear was betrayal from within. In the immediate aftermath of Penkovsky's capture no one knew how or why it had gone wrong or who was to blame. They feared the worst. The poison injected into the system by Philby and Blake was worming its way deep and inducing a delirium. The distrust was not just between Britain and America but within each service. What if a newly recruited agent was betrayed by a traitor? Or what if a new agent had in fact been planted by the KGB as part of some fiendish master plan with the connivance of someone on the inside? Such a fear could be paralysing and its chill was about to reach into the heart of the service. The era of the molehunts was dawning.

5

THE WILDERNESS OF MIRRORS

Anatoly Golitsyn broke into a cold sweat when a colleague announced that all the staff inside the KGB Residency in Helsinki would have to be searched.[1] It was Friday night in the Finnish capital and everyone wanted to get home. But a secret telegram had gone missing. Golitsyn did not have the telegram but he did have a dozen other secret documents surreptitiously stashed in his inside pocket. The missing telegram was found. Golitsyn, a short, heavy-set man with black hair and an intense look, walked calmly out into the dark and cold of a Helsinki evening with snow deep on the ground. It was the middle of December 1961.

He had arranged to meet his wife and daughter in a park. When his taxi pulled up, they were nowhere to be seen. Had she changed her mind? Three months earlier he had begun the planning for this day and he had asked Svetlana if she would join him. She was taken aback and uncertain. But she had agreed to follow him with their daughter Tanya. Golitsyn went back to his apartment and found his wife and daughter waiting there, perhaps unwilling to believe what they were about to do.

The KGB officer called a local number. A man answered and Golitsyn hung up without saying a word. He now knew that the American was at home. Golitsyn had previously met Frank Friberg at a diplomatic reception and decided he must be CIA. Finland was on the Soviet frontier and was a key northern staging ground for spies from both sides. Golitsyn took a few photos, grabbed Tanya's favourite doll and, telling his daughter they were going to a party, led his family out of the door.

The fifteen-minute taxi ride to the well-heeled suburb of Westland seemed the longest of the KGB officer's life. He, his wife and his daughter were silent, lost in their own thoughts about those left behind. If Friberg had gone out since answering the phone then Golitsyn knew he would have to try again over the weekend, the risks growing with every moment that passed. When he rang Friberg's bell, there was an agonising wait followed by relief when the door swung open.

Frank Friberg had just been having a shave and getting ready to leave for a cocktail party when his doorbell rang. There was no recognition, only surprise as he stared at the man on his doorstep.[2]

'Do you know who I am?' asked Golitsyn, who was wrapped in a thick overcoat and a fur hat.

'No,' replied Friberg.

'I am Soviet Vice-Consul Anatoly Klimov,' Golitsyn said, giving the cover name he used in Finland.

The penny dropped for the American. 'We know you're KGB,' Friberg said.

The Russian spoke little English and his accent was heavy. Golitsyn kept repeating a word which sounded to Friberg like 'asool'. It was only when the family came in and Golitsyn wrote it down that he realised the word was asylum.

Frank Friberg's hope for a peaceful evening had been shattered and on that evening in Helsinki a fast-burning fuse had been lit beneath the British and American intelligence communities. The stocky Russian was like one of Penkovsky's satchel atomic bombs – compact and primed to explode in the enemy capital. The radioactive fall-out still tumbles to the ground today. He had a story to tell that would hint at dark conspiracies behind the deaths of political leaders on both sides of the Atlantic, a story which would cascade through the corridors of MI6 and the CIA, nearly bringing both to their knees.

Back in Vienna in the early 1950s, Golitsyn had been singled out by the defector Pyotr Deriabin as a possible target for the CIA because he appeared out of sorts among fellow officers. In Golitsyn's own account, the disaffection was political and came in 1956 when Stalin's crimes were exposed by his successor Khrushchev. He believed it was too little, too late and meaningless, and felt strongly that the Party, not Stalin alone, was responsible for what had happened. The strategy he says he had decided upon to maximise his eventual usefulness to the West was clever but also proved hazardous.

He would collect as many tidbits of intelligence as he could until he was ready to make his move and then use them to enhance his value to the West. In the late 1950s he attended a training academy and took a risk in selecting as his thesis topic: 'The Prevention of Betrayals and Defections by Members of Official Organizations, Visiting Delegations and Tourist Groups Abroad'. It allowed him to learn how people got caught when they were doing exactly what he hoped to do. He also spent time working on the NATO desk of the KGB watching and listening. He understood that defectors were coldly evaluated so he mentally filed away every piece of gossip, every file he read, every rumour he heard, knowing that each would buy him a little more importance in the West.

In Friberg's house, Golitsyn was intensely nervous, fearful of discovery. He told the CIA man he wanted to be out of the country that night. There was an 8.15 p.m. flight to Stockholm and he demanded to be on it. Friberg called up one of his officers who quickly came to collect passports and organise visas and flights to New York. As they left the house, Golitsyn went to Friberg's driveway and pulled out a package of a dozen documents that he had buried in the snow just before ringing the bell.[3]

They made it to the airport less than half an hour before the plane was due to take off. 'We've made it. Now we're safe!' Golitsyn said to Svetlana. He had spoken too soon. If ever there was a journey to put fear into the heart of an already edgy defector this was it. When he arrived in Stockholm, Golitsyn said he did not want to catch the next flight out because it had originated in Helsinki and he feared being pursued. Friberg secured seats on a US air force plane but it was unpressurised and Tanya began to suffer. Next they went to Frankfurt for a flight via London. As they arrived in London, there was a bomb alert. Golitsyn says he had asked for all the baggage of passengers who had joined the flight in London to be searched in case the KGB had been following him.[4] By the time the plane departed from London, fog had enveloped New York and the plane was diverted to Bermuda. From there, Golitsyn eventually made his way to the United States. In all, it had taken four days to get to Washington. During their long and difficult journey, Friberg had found Golitsyn nervous and occasionally prone to recalling the wrong name or place. In contrast to Golitsyn's claim that his defection was ideological in

Vienna in the aftermath of the Second World War. On the city's streets, rival intelligence services first began to get the measure of each other. (Getty)

Graham Greene (seated) and film director Carol Reed. Greene's screenplay for *The Third Man*, which Reed directed, captured Vienna after the war on celluloid. (Getty)

Anthony Cavendish on his motorbike in Cairo, shortly before being recruited as the youngest ever member of the Secret Intelligence Service.

Kim Philby just after he left Cambridge in 1933 and around the time he went to Vienna. There, his intellectual commitment to communism would be reinforced by clandestine activity, and set him on a path to betrayal.

Anthony Courtney at his investiture at Buckingham Palace in 1949. Soon after, he began to organise the infiltration of agents behind the Iron Curtain. His later parliamentary career was cut short by a KGB blackmail plot. (Photoshot)

Lionel 'Buster' Crabb went missing in 1956 after diving beneath a Soviet cruiser visiting Portsmouth in a disastrous MI6 operation. The frogman's headless corpse was found a year later. (Getty)

MI6 officer and KGB spy George Blake. This picture was released by the police after his escape from Wormwood Scrubs prison in 1966. (Getty)

Kim Philby at the press conference at his mother's flat in 1955, when he denied being the so-called 'Third Man' who had assisted Guy Burgess and Donald Maclean to flee to Moscow. (Getty)

The young Daphne Park helped train the French resistance in Britain during the Second World War. Initially rejected by MI6, she went to Vienna with military intelligence before being recruited to the Secret Service. In MI6 she forged a formidable reputation with postings in Moscow and the Congo.

Daphne Park's American counterpart Larry Devlin looking out at the ferry in Leopoldville. Devlin would be described as the 'arch-puppeteer' of Congolese politics. He and Park remained lifelong friends.

Patrice Lumumba arriving for the Congo's independence day ceremony in July 1960. Daphne Park had already forged a relationship with the nationalist politician. Devlin would be involved in a plot to assassinate him. (Topfoto)

Patrice Lumumba (centre) at Leopoldville airport, 2 December 1960. He had just been arrested the previous night and would be executed soon after. (Topfoto)

The joint CIA–MI6 team that ran Oleg Penkovsky, one of the key agents of the early Cold War: (from left to right) Michael Stokes, Harold Shergold (Shergy), Joseph Bulik and George Kisevalter, pictured at the Mount Royal Hotel London in April 1961.

Harold Shergold listens as Penkovsky (with his back to the camera) makes a point.

Oleg Penkovsky wearing the uniform of a British Colonel as a sign of his desire to transfer his allegiance from the Soviet Union to the West.

British businessman Greville Wynne was a key go-between with Penkovsky in Moscow. He would later be put on trial and imprisoned for his work for MI6.

Miloslav Kroča was a major in the Czechoslovak security forces and a long-standing agent of MI6.

(Archive of Security Services, Czech Republic)

nature and had been nurtured for five years, Friberg later said he thought it had been in the works for only a year or so.[5] The CIA man said he believed it was due to a falling out with the KGB Resident in Helsinki, Golitsyn saying his defection served him right after they had clashed and after he had received a negative evaluation that might lead to demotion. But en route Golitsyn had also begun to offer up just some of the secrets he had been hoarding away. A senior Finn was a KGB agent of influence, he explained, giving away the first of his nuggets. The details he provided in those first few days would easily be enough to prove that he was a real defector and no plant. And he also provided the first elements of his biggest bombshell. He explained one of the reasons he was so nervous was that the KGB had penetrated Friberg's own organisation, the CIA. In Germany, they had an agent codenamed 'Sasha'.

In Washington the hunt would begin for a traitor. The existence of one could explain Popov and Penkovsky being caught and all the other recent disasters. It was known there had been high-level penetrations in Britain and Germany. Why not America? Golitsyn's information was tantalising but vague. The mole was someone with a Slavic background who had been in Germany. His codename was 'Sasha' and his real name began with a 'K' was all he could say.

It was clear that Golitsyn would be hard to handle. He demanded a meeting with the President or the FBI Director (eventually he met Attorney General Robert Kennedy). Penkovsky's and Popov's former handler, George Kisevalter, who was originally assigned to deal with Golitsyn, found him exhausting and their relationship soon broke down. Golitsyn had accumulated hundreds and hundreds of fragments of intelligence, some based on files, others on conversations. Sometimes they overlapped and referred to the same person, sometimes they were frustratingly vague. Sorting through it, when so much was at stake, produced chaos.

Golitsyn's relationship with his first set of CIA handlers had fractured by late 1962, but his ideas would eventually find refuge in the welcoming arms and fertile mind of James Jesus Angleton. Since his friend Kim Philby had left Washington, Angleton had grown in power within the CIA, becoming head of counter-intelligence in 1954. Counter-intelligence is a specialised discipline which aims to understand and work against an opponent's intelligence service. Part of it is classic spy-catching or counter-espionage, looking for the Blakes and Philbys who are betraying from within. But there is more to it than that. Spy versus spy, it is the world of double and triple agents and requires a peculiar mind to understand the dizzying complexities of the tricks and games a wily foe may be playing against you, spotting the false agents they may be planting carrying misleading information. This means checking out the agents that others on your side are recruiting and making sure they are legitimate, sometimes to the annoyance of their handlers who may have invested heavily in them. And it involves attacking your opponent in a careful chess game, understanding his intentions and getting inside his operations and subverting them from within and deceiving him. British intelligence had succeeded in this during the Second World War with its Double-Cross System in which German spies landing in Britain were turned to provide false information back to their masters. Philby did something similar, though on a smaller scale, as a penetration agent when it came to Anglo-American operations in Albania, Eastern Europe and the Soviet Union. By getting inside your opponent's service, you know what he knows, at a stroke destroying the value of all the secret information he has collected and allowing you to mislead him. This was Angleton's world.

For its practitioners, counter-intelligence was a complex, intricate art which involved navigating supple confusions and ambiguities, reconstructing events from tiny fragments like an historian of the dark ages. Perhaps then it was no coincidence that medieval history was the pastime of the drily sceptical Maurice Oldfield who would become MI6's counter-intelligence chief. When he was in Washington, the CIA had thought the portly, taciturn Oldfield, with his large glasses, had been invented precisely to deflate the caricature of British secret agents being like James Bond. Oldfield disliked the aggressive special operations crowd because of their impact on his carefully hatched plans to collect intelligence.[6] He was not, as some thought, the model for John le Carré's fictional, and scholarly, counter-intelligence chief George Smiley, but there were similarities (medieval history was also the passion of the Oxford academic who was the real inspiration for Smiley).[7] In the subtle world of counter-intelligence, like medieval history, the truth was often inaccessible and so arguments, occasionally vicious, would rage over what each fragment meant since entire interpretations would be built upon those tiny shards. Counter-intelligence required a suspicious mind and you could always trump your colleagues by showing that you were intellectually capable of suspecting something even more devious than they could manage. You should not work in counter-intelligence for too long, a few noted. It did something to your brain. You would see shadows everywhere.

Kim Philby's ghost haunted the corridors of the CIA and MI6. Angleton had been indelibly scarred by the experience of having a man he trusted so completely betray him. 'I think that it had a devastating effect on Angleton,' argues one former CIA colleague, 'that just drove him over the edge.'[8] Years later Angleton would always maintain that he, the man who saw everything, had suspected Philby. But this was a lie to cover the fact that the man who was supposed to watch for KGB penetration had been suckered by the greatest KGB penetration of all. If he could be fooled, then the KGB had to be *really* clever and devious, he concluded.

Word of an important new defector had quickly reached London. The Prime Minister Harold Macmillan was briefed about Golitsyn at Chequers on 18 April 1962 by the Cabinet Secretary ahead of a meeting with the Americans. 'His revulsion against the Communist regime in the Soviet Union appears to be genuine and deeply felt,' the briefing note read. 'His desire to use his knowledge to help Western countermeasures shows every sign of being sincere and unemotional. His interrogators rate him as a reliable and an accurate reporter.' But the note remarked of his knowledge: 'nowhere has it any great depth'. Golitsyn had warned that the Foreign Office, Admiralty and 'British intelligence' were all penetrated and that five unnamed MPs accepted tasks from the Russians. 'Enquiries are being made by the Security Service in collaboration with the departments concerned,' the Prime Minister was told.[9]

Two British officers were sent out to talk to Golitsyn in March and September of 1962. One was Arthur Martin, the dogged MI5 investigator and Philby's pursuer-in-chief, whose unassuming face masked a quiet ferocity. Since Golitsyn seemed to have information about penetrations in Britain and his relationship with his original case officers was breaking down, he agreed to relocate with his wife and daughter to work with British intelligence, sailing over on the

Queen Elizabeth.[10] His nerves were never far from the surface. On the boat he thought someone was looking for him. On arrival he was taken to a safe house but as he stepped out of the door he was convinced he was being followed. He could not settle easily anywhere. The next stop was Stratford-upon-Avon, where again he became convinced he had been spotted, and he sent his family back to America. His fear was not irrational – he was indeed high up the KGB target list for execution.[11] He tried remote Truro in Cornwall, where Arthur Martin would visit on a Sunday.

Those who worked with him talk of 'vintage Golitsyn' – the information he passed in the first few months which was accurate and contributed to the arrest of spies in Britain, France, Norway, Canada and NATO. But as the debriefings continued even some of his one-time supporters acknowledge he was mishandled.[12] 'Defectors are like grapes – the first pressings are the best,' Oldfield would say.[13] That first pressing produced information before a defector began to feel the pressure of what others wanted to hear and before the worries that he had nothing left to give preyed on his mind

Golitsyn received so much attention partly because sources such as himself were so rare at the time. This also meant there was little scope for cross-referencing his information. In London, there were more insecurities for Golitsyn to work on than there were in Washington. Spy mania was gripping the country courtesy of a cast including George Blake, and the intelligence services were fearful of what else might be placed on public display.

One of Golitsyn's British leads centred on a naval attaché which guided MI5 to John Vassall (see Chapter 6). But the information which really captivated Martin was the talk Golitsyn had heard in Moscow of a 'ring of five' British spies who had all become acquainted at university and who had all been providing valuable intelligence.[14] The reference to a 'ring' indicated that they all knew each other. Burgess and Maclean were long gone. Philby had long been suspected. But who else made up the five?

Soon after Philby was exposed in 1963, Arthur Martin arrived at the Courtauld Institute to interrogate Anthony Blunt, Surveyor of the Queen's Pictures. Blunt had been a young Cambridge don in the 1930s and a close friend of Guy Burgess. Burgess had helped recruit the tall, languid academic to the Communist cause, which he had faithfully served as a wartime MI5 officer providing reams of pur-loined documents to his controllers. Martin was now armed with the testimony of an American student the former Cambridge don had tried to recruit. 'I saw Mr Straight the other day and he told me about his relations with you and the Russians.' Blunt's hangdog face gave nothing away.[15] Martin offered immunity in return for a confession. Blunt walked to the grand window, looked out, poured a drink and said, 'It is true.' So began eight years of interviews for Blunt, which he dealt with through copious amounts of booze. Martin and others came to him again and again, trawling through every friendship and meeting from Cambridge and after, looking for anything that could point to more spies.

Where Philby decided to run, Blunt stayed, taking the offer of immunity. Although he had passed vast quantities of crucial infor-mation, Blunt was never a hardened, dedicated spy like Philby nor truly ever dedicated to the idea of Communism. 'I realised that I would take any risk in this country, rather than go to Russia,' he wrote later.[16] As a fellow academic said of him, Blunt liked to run with the hare and hunt with the hounds, to be part of the estab-lishment and attack it. When his treachery was finally exposed publicly in 1979, he would choose to defend himself in literary style by citing E. M. Forster's dictum: 'If I had to choose between betraying my country and betraying my friend, I hope I should have the guts to betray my country.' By confessing, he had betrayed both. But the establishment thought at the time that at least it had managed to sweep this case under the carpet without a public fuss. The same year as Blunt confessed, John Cairncross, another immensely clever intelligence officer and civil servant, was identified as a Soviet spy. But it was only much, much later and after much anguish that MI5 would conclude that Blunt and Cairncross completed the ring of five. Because they had not been recruited at Cambridge at the same time as Philby, there had been a belief that the remaining members were still at large.[17] There were indeed more spies than the Cambridge Five operating during the Second World War and after. Their KGB controller just after the war boasted that the KGB had a total of thirty agents in 1944, providing so much information that it had to prioritise by picking the best five to work with. Much of the intel-ligence produced by the rest was simply left to pile up untranslated (what would those who provided the intelligence have made of their work being ignored if they had known?).[18] Martin and other mole-hunters were now determined to find every one of the traitors that had operated then and their successors.

Golitsyn's initial debriefings by Arthur Martin provided a haul of over 150 leads relating to Britain and the Commonwealth. A few of these required the involvement of MI6 because of overseas connections. The MI6 counter-intelligence branch was tiny, effectively just one officer, so another, named Stephen de Mowbray, was called in to work on the Golitsyn leads. De Mowbray divided his colleagues into two camps – 'thinkers' and 'doers' – and he was the former. After serving in the Fleet Air Arm in the Second World War, he had made his way to New College, Oxford.[19] There he had been taught by one of the century's great thinkers, the political philosopher Isaiah Berlin. The young Berlin had witnessed the Bolshevik Revolution in Russia before coming to England. During the war, he was one of those dons brought into government service and, rather curiously, his irascible friend Guy Burgess had tried to get Berlin posted first to Washington and then to Moscow.[20] After the war he returned to Oxford and one day found de Mowbray visiting his study. The student had set his heart on the life of an academic but before his final exams decided he might not make it. 'I think you'd better be a spy,' the laconic Berlin told him. Another tutor, a former SOE man, passed on his details and, at a house on Kensington High Street, George Kennedy Young swiftly took de Mowbray through the formalities of an interview, most of their conversation revolving around a shared interest in classical music.

Fresh from a posting to South America, de Mowbray was assigned to support MI5's investigations into two Britons whom Golitsyn said had been targeted by the KGB in Vienna for their homosexuality. After a few months, his boss came into his office and told him he had something 'special' for him to work on with two MI5 officers. He was told to head over to a safe house the following day. There he was met by the two central figures of the spy-hunt. Alongside Arthur Martin was Peter Wright. The latter was the Security Service's master technician and authority on bugging. The Security Service operated outside the law during this period. It was overseen, but only in the loosest sense, by politicians and civil servants but was not governed by any statute. 'We bugged and burgled our way across London at the state's behest, while pompous bowler-hatted civil servants in Whitehall pretended to look the other way,' Wright said with relish of his work.[21] But some of Wright's beloved bugging operations had mysteriously come to nothing, he explained to de Mowbray. He and Arthur Martin had independently come to the same conclusion: 'We believe MI5 is penetrated.'

Sometimes when two people come together, the sum is greater than the parts. With Martin and Wright, their individual beliefs in a conspiracy were confirmed and compounded over long evenings spent in the pub agonising over the problem. They alone, they thought, could see the darkness at the heart of British intelligence and they would have to struggle to shine a light on it. But there was something more to their bitter struggle, a sub-text that neither man might have openly acknowledged but which lurked behind so much of British life. It was class.

Wright and Martin were not cut from the same cloth as their prey. They were not 'officer class'. Wright's father had been a radio engineer but had lost his job in the Great Depression. It had plunged Wright senior into alcoholism and forced him to take young Peter out of private school since he could not afford to educate both his sons. The trauma left Peter with a chronic stammer, just like Philby. Arthur Martin too was no public-school boy and had a chip on his shoulder about it. As the two men began to investigate the lives of the gilded elite who had walked through the manicured courts of Trinity Cambridge, they burned with resentment of those who had been given everything and yet had still betrayed their country. As they visited country piles in Britain and farmhouses in France bought with family money, they struggled to grasp what had driven these people to betray. 'They had enjoyed to the full the privileged background and education denied to me, while my family had suffered at the capricious hand of capitalism,' Wright said later. 'I experienced at first hand the effects of slump and depression, yet it was they who turned to espionage. I became the hunter, and they the hunted.'[22] The two men rooted through the dirty laundry of the British establishment, and how the establishment despised them for it. 'I had seen into the secret heart of the present Establishment at a time when they had been young and careless. I knew their scandals and their intrigues. I knew too much, and they knew it.'[23] At one meeting, Anthony Blunt lectured Wright on the atmosphere of the thirties. 'Unless you lived through it, Peter, you can't understand.' Wright lost his temper. 'Oh I lived through it, Anthony. I know more about the thirties probably than you will ever know. I remember my father driving himself mad with drink, because he couldn't get a job. I remember losing my education, my world, everything. I know all about the thirties.'[24] As they investigated an Oxford ring of spies, one MP whom they confronted killed himself. Even Graham Greene was called in for questioning about his former boss. He knew more than he was letting on, it was thought, but was cleared of any involvement.[25] But it was the thought of a traitor within their own ranks that really drove the two men.

Martin had already gone to C, Dick White, with his concerns. White, a former head of MI5, had high regard for Martin from their time working together. Like Angleton, he had been involved in the Double-Cross System in the Second World War and so was fascinated by the possibilities of deception, and for a while bought into the idea of a high-level penetration. White had also always had a fixation with Philby. It was Martin's theory that his old foe had been tipped off that most intrigued the MI6 chief. There was one piece of evidence which was puzzled over endlessly. When he had been invited to see Peter Lunn in Beirut and found his old friend Nicholas Elliott waiting, what had Philby meant when he said, 'I rather thought it would be you'?[26] This remark sent shivers down the spine of Martin and White. Had Philby been tipped off that he was blown and known that someone was coming out for him? There were other explanations for Philby's curious phrase, but Martin was convinced it signposted a tip-off, and White agreed. If true, it would suggest a mole at the highest levels. Only five men in MI5 had known of the plan to tackle Philby in Beirut. Only two of them had been around long enough to fit the profile of a long-term penetration agent. The problem was that the two men were the head of MI5, Roger Hollis, and his deputy, Graham Mitchell.

The certainty of Wright and Martin grew out of a number of events which they felt brooked no other explanation. Both had seen their operations go awry. Wright had been planting bugs in buildings due to be occupied by the KGB who then suddenly appeared to change their plans and move elsewhere. Wright also said there had been a rise in radio transmissions when a Soviet spy, Gordon Lonsdale, had been arrested, suggesting that a warning was being passed back to Moscow. The fact that Lonsdale had not been warned himself was a sign that he must have been sacrificed for an even more important spy. When Soviets were not caught it meant there was a spy; when they were found, it also meant there was a spy but he was being protected. This logic was hard to disprove. A Soviet defector at the start of the Cold War in Canada had talked of two agents called Elli. One had been identified, but who was the second?

And now there was Golitsyn. 'In the tense and almost hysterical months of 1963, as the scent of treachery lingered in every corridor, it is easy to see how our fears fed on his theories,' recalled Wright. Golitsyn's talk of penetrations and the fact that he appeared to have seen recent material from the Security Service, including one of Wright's technical papers, reinforced the growing convictions of Martin and Wright. Golitsyn had nothing on Hollis or Mitchell specifically. 'The vast majority of Golitsyn's material was tantalizingly imprecise,' Wright wrote in retrospect. 'It often appeared true as far as it went, but then faded into ambiguity, and part of the problem was Golitsyn's clear propensity for feeding his information out in dribs and drabs. He saw it as his livelihood.'[27]

Dick White had told Martin to go and see Hollis and explain his doubts about Mitchell, but not about the MI5 chief himself. Martin spent half an hour explaining his theory. Hollis, the son of a bishop and a dour and dry man, had listened quietly, barely saying a word. Martin described how 'his face drained of colour and with a strange half-smile playing on his lips'.[28] Hollis did not demur but said he would think it over. He knew he had little choice but to countenance an investigation. His former boss Dick White, the senior figure in British intelligence, had already called him.[29] Why did the two chiefs go along with it? For White and Hollis, the fear of penetration was real but so was the fear of missing it and, even more important, of being accused of having missed it deliberately. A few days later Martin had been summoned to see Hollis again and told to begin. Soon afterwards he had met Wright and they began to compare notes.

Who watches the watchers? How could MI5 investigate its own top men? It could not, since Graham Mitchell had oversight over all operations. So Wright and Martin explained to de Mowbray that it had been agreed with Dick White that MI6 would instead undertake the surveillance and that he was to be in charge. Thus began one of the stranger episodes in the history of British intelligence which occasionally edged into farce. In all, forty members of MI6 staff were engaged in spying on the number two of their sister organisation. These were not trained 'watchers' of the type MI5 employed to carry out surveillance on the streets of Britain. These were officers, technicians and mainly secretaries who had either not been tutored in the arts of surveillance at all or had only the most rudimentary education. They were run out of an MI6 safe house near Sloane Square. Time was short since Mitchell was due to retire in six months. He would be tracked from MI5 headquarters to Waterloo station, where two women would follow him on to his train. One summer's evening the women followed him in the hope that he was leaving something incriminating in a dead drop. There was nothing. De Mowbray frequently did the tailing himself as the two men had never met. One evening, de Mowbray was remaining close behind for fear of losing his man in the rush-hour mêlée. Mitchell suddenly stopped, turned and faced de Mowbray. He stared directly at him. Seconds ticked by. Then he turned again and walked off. He knew what was going on. Mitchell was old-school establishment, Winchester and Oxford, and his hobbies included yachting and chess. On one occasion, de Mowbray raced down to the south coast in a fast car driven by an MI6 colleague to where Mitchell was taking part in a chess tournament also attended by some Russians. All of the surveillance drew a blank. A hole was drilled in Mitchell's office wall to allow a small camera to capture him at work. Three women from MI6 took it in turns to watch him. It was a surreal experience, as Mitchell often sat in front of the camera picking his teeth. The strain of knowing that he was under suspicion began to take its toll on him. He would mumble in a way which made it hard to make out his words.[30] The women watched as his eyes became dark and sunken. When people were in the room he carried on as usual, but when he was alone a tortured look came over his face. His phone was tapped and de Mowbray would listen in to the calls of senior MI5 officers and despair of what he saw as the poor quality of those leading the organisation. 'Are we on the right man?' the team wondered.

There was an awkward problem for those who believed that British intelligence had been penetrated at the highest level. Its name was Oleg Penkovsky. Mitchell and Hollis were among the few to have known about Penkovsky's betrayal. If either was a Soviet plant, then surely they would have told their masters and Penkovsky would never have been able to spy for so long and hand over so much material. There was only one way around this conundrum for the molehunters. Penkovsky himself must have been a plant by the Soviets. Some reasoned he was planted from the beginning. Others believed that he had genuinely betrayed his country before being turned as a double agent towards the end after being betrayed by the British mole. Wright began to bury himself in the files; forwards and backwards he went, poring over the fragments of this and every other case, convinced there was a dark secret.

Golitsyn first heard of the Penkovsky case in early 1963 when an MI6 officer in Washington said the service had just lost a valuable agent in Moscow.[31] He was in England when the show-trial in Moscow took place. How could Penkovsky be genuine? Golitsyn wondered. He told Martin he wanted to see Dick White. At the meeting, Golitsyn asked to see the Penkovsky file. A few weeks later he was taken to the MI6 annexe office at Carlton Gardens and ushered into a grand chandeliered room. Two precious volumes were laid before him. For days he devoured them, taking notes watched by an MI6 officer and a security guard. Golitsyn then asked to take the files out. The request was granted. By his own account, he would sit in London's public parks and squares reading one of the most sensitive files held by British intelligence until they were handed back at the end of the afternoon. Golitsyn became convinced that Penkovsky was a plant sent as part of a 'master plot'. Among the reasons was that Penkovsky had proposed a particular woman as a courier. Golitsyn said that he knew her as the wife of a colleague and that he had been told she was involved in a KGB operation by General Oleg Gribanov, the chief of the Second Directorate. Golitsyn told Peter Wright what he had found. Wright at first strongly disagreed (although he later changed his mind) and told him there were people in MI6 who had made their careers on Penkovsky. He mentioned Harry Shergold and warned that he would be furious.

In the summer of 1963, the presence of a Soviet defector, wrongly named as Dolitsyn, found its way into the British press. Golitsyn believed the story came from the Russians but many others thought that it was Angleton determined to get his man back on his side of the Atlantic. By the time Golitsyn returned to Washington, he had been bled dry of his original intelligence, but he had come up with a new way of making himself useful. He said that if he was allowed to study the actual in-house intelligence files, it would trigger associations in his mind and allow him to recollect and piece together new leads based on the fragments in his memory. Angleton and others were convinced of the possibilities of what Golitsyn grandly described as his 'methodology'. Angleton had backed Penkovsky's bona fides but, fascinated by Golitsyn, he agreed for select aspects of the case to be shared, though never the whole file – the Americans were not as trusting as the British. Golitsyn still found aspects of Penkovsky's career and his access to secrets that he considered suspicious. Penkovsky's offer to blow up buildings in Moscow, Golitsyn thought, was simply to gauge whether there was any interest in the West in such schemes and then control any resulting plans. Golitsyn surmised that the Cuban crisis had been 'deliberately provoked by the Soviets to get the deal they wanted' and they had used Penkovsky to pass accurate information to the Americans to ensure that a bargain could be done. The theory may have been aided by the Soviet Ambassador to the UN who, probably hoping to minimise the embarrassment of the betrayal, told a Western diplomat that Penkovsky 'is very much alive and was a double agent against the Americans'.[32] The officers who handled Penkovsky were furious with the aspersions cast on someone they saw as a good man who had paid the ultimate price. Joe Bulik was called into Angleton's office to have the theory presented to him that not just Penkovsky but all his other agents from 1960 were plants. 'I was so angry I just turned and left and we never spoke again,' he recalled later.[33]

When Peter Wright in London produced a paper claiming that Penkovsky was a plant, he showed it to Maurice Oldfield. 'You've got a long row to hoe with this one, Peter, there's a lot of K's and Gongs riding high on the back of Penkovsky,' referring to the knighthoods and honours the celebrated operation had produced. Shergy was, as predicted, furious. 'Harry Shergold ... practically went for me at a meeting in MI6 one day,' Wright wrote. 'What the hell do you know about running agents?' he snarled. 'You come in here and insult a brave man's memory and expect us to believe this?'[34] The fury was so intense that it stuck in the mind of one conspiratorially minded molehunter. Surely Shergy couldn't be bad as well? But Shergy understood what was taking place and was playing his own game.

After Golitsyn had returned to Washington, he began to pursue the idea that the Soviet Union was undertaking a 'master plan' of 'strategic deception' to fool the West and its intelligence agencies. Just before he left Moscow, Golitsyn said he had heard talk of a massive deception and disinformation campaign. He says another officer told him of plans to finish with the United States once and for all.[35] The plot included fooling the West that there was greater disunity in the East than was really the case. For instance, Golitsyn maintained that the split between the Soviet Union and China was in fact a charade, as was that between the Soviets and Tito's Yugoslavia.[36] The master plan would be perpetuated by the agents placed everywhere in Western governments and especially their intelligence services whose careers and whose judgements would be bolstered by defectors. The whole operation was being controlled by an inner core of the KGB. The rest of the KGB knew nothing about it and everything they did could be compromised as part of the plot. Anything that fitted this theory was true, anything that did not support it had been planted as part of the master plot and therefore provided proof of its existence. This was a worldview which, once accepted, was internally coherent and explained everything. It was a faith and one that Angleton placed his trust in.

Western intelligence was, Angleton said, trapped in a 'wilderness of mirrors' designed like a fairground trick to bend and shape the truth so that the observer would become disoriented and lose any sense of proportion. Angleton had borrowed the phrase from a friend of his, the Anglo-American poet T. S. Eliot, whose words, like an intelligence puzzle, required deciphering by the knowledgeable and were open to many interpretations. Only a truly sharp counter-intelligence mind could see the truth of the KGB's intentions, Angleton thought, and Dick White agreed. In their eyes the KGB was all-powerful, ever cunning and infallible, the stuff of nightmares. It had fooled MI6 in the 1920s with its fake émigré group, the Trust, and in the late 1940s in Albania. There were no coincidences, no room for missteps from the other side.

As with buses, the CIA found that having waited ages for a defector, two came at once. Yuri Nosenko would pay a heavy price for arriving just after Anatoly Golitsyn. In early summer 1962, he approached an American delegate at an arms-control meeting in Geneva. He shook hands and checked that no one else was in earshot. 'I would like you to help me with contact with CIA people. You see I have some problems. It's a private matter.'[37] At an apartment the well-built man in his mid-thirties with a slight hunch asked for a scotch and then told the first officer he met, Pete Bagley, that he was a KGB officer who had got into money problems. Bagley spoke little Russian and Nosenko little English, but the KGB man explained that he had no desire to defect since he still had family in the Soviet Union (his father was at one point minister for shipbuilding). But he needed 250 dollars in Swiss francs, a pathetically small sum, and would be willing to meet CIA officers on later trips anywhere but Moscow. The truth, which Nosenko did not reveal at the time, was that he had been over-excited by his first taste of freedom outside the USSR and had taken a prostitute back to his hotel room. He had woken up the next morning to find his wallet missing. Inside were his 250 dollars' worth of KGB expenses which he needed to account for.[38]

Kisevalter came out and joined Bagley for a second meeting at which Nosenko, having had one drink before and another during the meeting, explained how Kisevalter's former agent Pyotr Popov, first recruited in Vienna, had been caught. It had not been through a traitor as some suspected but through surveillance of an American Embassy official in Moscow posting a letter. He also said he knew a little about a spy in the British Naval Attaché's office in Moscow who had been blackmailed over his sexuality (another reference to John Vassall).[39] Nosenko had worked on targeting American officials, journalists and tourists in Moscow and said he also knew about the first CIA man in Moscow in the 1950s who had been targeted over his affair with a KGB maid. Bagley kept asking for more, Nosenko remembered, hungry for every scrap of intelligence. He said he also knew that the KGB had recruited an American officer in Germany – codenamed 'Sasha'.[40] They agreed that if he made it out again he would send a telegram to a US address signed 'George'. Two days after sending it, he would meet his contact in front of the first cinema listed in the local phone book in the city from which the telegram was sent.[41] The two CIA officers returned on separate planes, one carrying the tapes, the other their notes. Just in case.[42]

When Bagley got back to Washington, he talked to Angleton about Nosenko. The counter-intelligence chief then inducted him into the secret of Golitsyn's defection six months earlier. Two defectors one after another was a little odd. What was interesting was the overlap between the two, for instance on the spy in the British Naval Attaché's office. They also both talked of a senior KGB officer coming to the US on an unexplained visit. Nosenko's account seemed to explain it away as the targeting of a low-level official, while Golitsyn believed it might have been linked to the mole within the CIA. Golitsyn also differed in other areas, for instance over how Popov was caught. Golitsyn thought there was a high-ranking spy in the CIA, Nosenko thought Sasha was just an army captain. Angleton and Bagley agreed there was something suspicious going on. Golitsyn himself had warned that the KGB would send others after him to try and muddy the waters. Could this be what was happening? Was Nosenko part of the KGB's grand deception strategy unfolding and an attempt to protect its mole within the agency itself? 'Nosenko will mutilate the Golitsyn leads,' Angleton told Bagley, as if talking about a weed corrupting the purity of one of the orchids that he bred in his spare time.[43] Anyone who followed Golitsyn and who did not back his case would be seen by Angleton as a false defector sent to confuse. That was the case with Nosenko, it was decided.

Nosenko resurfaced in Geneva in January 1964. It was a cold night and the first cinema in the phone book was closed. Bagley, in disguise, brushed past the Russian who was waiting outside and handed a note with the location for their meeting.[44] 'Yuri has a bit of a surprise for us,' Kisevalter told Bagley when he arrived. In a strangely emotionless and mechanical voice, Nosenko declared he was now ready to defect.[45] 'I don't want to go back,' he said.[46] Bagley and Kisevalter were not keen on the idea. Nosenko said the KGB was on to him, although it seemed strange that he had been let out of the country if it was. At a second meeting, he claimed to have received a telegram recalling him home. 'I just defected now; this day, this hour, this minute, I just defected,' he told them.[47] He provided details of microphones hidden in the US Embassy in Moscow and also dropped a sensational bomb-shell. He said that in his job working on Americans in Moscow he had personally been responsible for the file on Lee Harvey Oswald, the man who had assassinated President John F. Kennedy just two months earlier. Oswald was a former marine and radar operator who had tried to defect in the USSR before returning to the US and who had more recently been in touch with the Soviet Embassy in Mexico City. When he was named as the assassin, Nosenko explained, the Soviet leadership demanded all files relating to him to be flown to Moscow immediately by military plane.[48] The KGB had thought Oswald a nuisance – he had even tried to slash his wrists to get attention – and so it had decided he was mentally unstable and not even worth debriefing. The KGB had had nothing to do with the assassination, Nosenko now explained.[49] This revelation meant that debriefing Nosenko was vital. The timing was remarkable. And suspicious, some thought. Was it really plausible that the KGB had not been interested in Oswald? Had Nosenko now been sent by the KGB to divert attention from the truth that it had assassinated an American president?

Nosenko was brought to the US by the CIA in February 1964 and taken to the attic of a house in the suburbs of Washington DC. Word went out that he must be broken. He was grilled by CIA officers after being denied sleep for up to forty-eight hours. 'At times the interrogation descended into a shouting match,' recalled Bagley.[50] One tape recording is said by a former CIA officer to include Nosenko mumbling 'From my soul, I beg you to believe me' and a voice screaming 'That's bullshit' again and again.[51] The hope was to secure a confession that he was a plant and then send him back to the Soviet Union. Nosenko said he believes he was administered drugs, possibly LSD, an indication that Sidney Gottlieb's methods might have been in play. Others have disputed the idea that drugs were used. His treatment foreshadowed the way in which the CIA treated suspects of a different time after 11 September 2011. He never had access to a lawyer or any legal process. He was shackled and blindfolded and taken on a plane. He thought he was being sent back to Moscow but was in fact taken to a specially built facility at the Farm, the CIA's training establishment in rural Virginia. He was kept in a concrete cell watched by a camera, with no pillows, blankets, air conditioning or heating. 'To say it was a nightmare is not enough. It was a hell,' he would later recall.[52] To occupy his mind, he would fantasise that he was a submariner or a pilot or a fireman carrying out heroic deeds. At night he would talk in his sleep in character, confusing the guards.[53] In his interrogation and polygraph, Nosenko was not helped by the fact that he was a drinker and that he had lied about his rank and exaggerated his importance. Among his falsehoods was the claim that a telegram had forced him to defect. None of this helped his case within the CIA.[54] His knowledge was patchy in some areas where it should have been stronger. He had come from a very privileged background but had consistently under-achieved, flunking various exams, and had tried to hide this from the CIA.[55] Was he a loser or a cunning double agent? Some officers invested their career in arguing that Nosenko was a plant and that there was a high-level penetration. Golitsyn was also allowed to review Nosenko's file and, perhaps unsurprisingly, concluded that his rival was indeed a plant. The head of the CIA was originally convinced that Nonsenko was a plant, but by 1966 doubts were beginning to creep in and further reviews were ordered.[56]

There was a growing and disturbing suspicion in some parts of the CIA that Nosenko might be innocent. There were also concerns over the legality of his detention.[57] Some of his guards even found his treatment troubling, telling Kisevalter of their concerns when he went down to the camp to work as an instructor.[58] But what should be done? The way he had been treated could cause a scandal. Pete Bagley wrote some notes which included the options of 'liquidating the man' or 'render[ing] him incapable of giving a coherent story'. He always maintained that these were his private scribbling, in which he was venting his frustration and that there was never any serious intent to kill Nosenko.[59] Eventually, Nosenko would be released and rehabilitated. In all he had been held for a total of 1,277 days. Years later he called up Angleton on the phone. 'I have nothing more to say to you,' Angleton said. 'And Mr Angleton, I have nothing further to say to you,' Nosenko replied.[60]

The molehunts on either side of the Atlantic moved largely in parallel, but their paths sometimes crossed. The British molehunters understood they had allies in the CIA and would occasionally use this as a bargaining chip. On one occasion, they issued an ultimatum to Hollis saying they would resign unless he told the Americans about the investigation into Mitchell. Hollis performed the drearily familiar ritual of flying over to Washington to tell the Americans that there might be yet another leak, this time no less than his number two. The President was informed.[61] The CIA was getting worried about the British. Teams were sent over – sometimes with the knowledge of British intelligence but sometimes without – to look into their cousins and see how bad things were. One report in 1965 said MI5 was suffering from poor organisation and leadership.

Arthur Martin began to drink heavily and put on weight under the strain of his hunt for the spy. His hair turned grey and anger flared. Even his friends acknowledged that he lacked tact, but he became increasingly reckless, even self-destructive, in his single-minded pursuit. As promotion passed him by, a sense of victimhood increased. At meetings, the tension between Martin and Hollis crack-led like electricity in the air. Hollis decided that enough was enough. He confronted Martin and in late 1964 suspended him. But this was not the end for Martin. His old mentor Dick White immediately took him on at MI6. White's MI6 was becoming almost a safe haven from which the hunters could operate against his old service.

There could be only one reason why Hollis had been so reluctant to brief the Americans and to sign off on more intrusive investigative techniques, the hunters decided. And so they trained their guns on him. The MI5 chief was by most accounts a mediocrity with many unable to see how he had risen to the top. He was codenamed 'Drat'. There were a few mysteries to his past and Peter Wright travelled to Oxford to go through university records. Why had he dropped out of university in the 1930s before finishing his degree? Why was he shy about admitting to friendships with a few Communists at the time? And was it entirely clear what he had been doing in China before the war? Even Hollis's friend Anthony Courtney, the naval commander of the Baltic operation, had been startled when Hollis visited him in Germany and said, 'My experience is that every man, without exception, has his price – but mine is a very high one.'[62] Nothing was conclusive. But it was suggestive to those of a certain bent of mind. The Americans were told of the new investigation, and Angleton plotted to have Hollis removed.[63] CIA Director Richard Helms was briefed on 'what could have been a scandal far outstripping even the

Philby disaster'.[64] But while the Americans were briefed, the British Prime Minister was not informed at the time. As his stint as head of MI5 drew to a close, Hollis confronted Wright at headquarters. 'There is just one thing I wanted to ask you before I go,' Hollis said. 'I wanted to know why you think I'm a spy.' Wright went through his reasoning. 'All I can say is that I'm not a spy,' Hollis said and exited, he thought, stage left.[65]

The hunt was not over. De Mowbray was sent to the US as the counter-intelligence officer under Christopher Phillpotts, a high-flyer who believed he was heading for the top and who had bought into the idea of penetration. De Mowbray's brief was to stay close to Angleton, whom he found fascinating. All the molehunters would visit Angleton's curtain-shrouded, dimly lit office to hear from the master. Files would be scattered on the desk and the cigarette smoke generated a haze which was enhanced by his furtive pronouncements.

A few months into his tour, de Mowbray went up to New York with Arthur Martin to meet Golitsyn in person for the first time. It was the beginning of a long and complicated friendship. He found Golitsyn strong willed. 'He is a very fierce man. At times I used to have hell from him,' de Mowbray recalls. The molehunt looked to have run out of steam, but then in 1968 a new chief of MI6 arrived. Sir John Rennie was an outsider, a Foreign Office man. As such he was distrusted and disliked by most of the service. Among the only people who liked him were the molehunters. Rennie went over to Washington soon after starting and met Golitsyn. He then had dinner with Phillpotts, who like others was frustrated that MI5's leadership had failed to pursue the penetration theory. Phillpotts explained his concerns to Rennie. 'Let's do something,' the new Chief said to him. Phillpotts returned to London as head of counter-intelligence and began an aggressive investigation, which included scrutiny of the service itself.

There were many Communists, some former and some current, littered around the establishment, including MI6. The molehunt led by Phillpotts in the late 1960s never found another Philby in the service. But ten officers, some very senior, were forced to retire early because of 'irregularities' in their past, often relating to Communism. None was proved to have been a traitor. The purge had been restrained by the ever cautious and calculating Oldfield, but once he moved post it drove forward. Andrew King, the Pekingese-owning former station chief in Vienna, was among those to fall foul of it. As well as engaging in what were seen as 'unnatural vices', King had joined the Communist Party in the 1930s (he had noted at the time that giving 20 per cent of his income to the party seemed a 'jolly high' proportion). He said he had declared this at the time and also when he had first been interrogated soon after the war. After that interrogation, he told the molehunters his then boss had asked the Chief whether more security checks were required. 'C says that since spies are only people of foreign origin, don't bother.'[66] This was the type of culture the hunters believed had allowed the service to rot from within. Most damning of all, even though there was no evidence he was a traitor, King admitted he had always known that Philby and Burgess had been Communists.[67] Another senior MI6 officer, Donald Prater, was summoned back from Stockholm and dismissed in 1968 for pre-war Communism in Oxford.[68] Another officer left because he had been a schoolfriend of Philby and had been recommended for the service by him. Nicholas Elliott was also interviewed – his friendship with Philby inevitably bringing him under suspicion. This was a bitter and miserable period. One of the ten who resigned quit simply because he did not like what was being done to his colleagues. A chilled delirium overcame the service. It was a McCarthyite witch-hunt, a few whispered privately to each other. Antipathy against the molehunters spread, but few dared speak openly for fear of the consequences. At MI5, younger officers avoided Peter Wright in the canteen, whispering of the Gestapo and referring to him as the 'KGB illegal'. Within the claustrophobic confines of MI5 and MI6 headquarters, an atmosphere of mistrust developed. In the highly compartmentalised world of British intelligence, new recruits were never informed of what was happening or about the suspicions, but they could sense that something bad was afoot.

Shergy was worried. The core of professionalism he had built up in Sov Bloc operations was under threat from the hunt. Success was the key to winning the argument, but he also knew that he had to tread carefully. Just after he returned from Warsaw, Gerry Warner was asked by Shergy to speak at the Fort, the service's training establishment. What would you like to speak on? Shergy asked. How about the desirability of officers working on Eastern Europe in London visiting the region so they could understand the conditions better? 'You can't have that,' Shergy told him. 'But it is terribly important,' protested Warner. 'If you insist on this, I'll have to send you back to London straight away.' Shergy understood that the molehunters believed that anyone who spent time behind the Iron Curtain would be subverted and if they discovered he had allowed such a talk to be given, it would not just be Warner who would pay the price.

Out in the field, officers learnt to fear the dread hand of suspicion reaching out to them. Following Poland, Gerry Warner was based in Geneva. His wife was a mathematician who had worked on a doctorate during their time in Warsaw and had to go back to defend it. The week before she went, one of the molehunters came out to see the station chief who was frequently heading down to a neighbouring European capital to carry out surveillance on the MI6 head of station, whom Phillpotts suspected. Warner and the visiting officer had dinner one night out on the shores of the lake and Warner mentioned that his wife was going to Warsaw. After dinner was over, the officer raced to see the station chief to tell him. A few months later, Shergy appeared in Geneva. 'You won't be pleased to see me when I tell you that you have to leave Geneva in a fortnight,' he told Warner. They went for a walk out on the streets, unwilling to talk openly in the office. 'You've got to know too many Russians.' But that was the job, Warner protested. Shergy explained that the real problem had begun months earlier when the hunters had learnt that Warner's wife was planning to visit Warsaw. Since then they had been trying to have him removed, and Shergy had held them off by saying he would have to see Warner in person and had only been able to do that now. Warner was given a few extra months' leeway, but moved out of Sov Bloc work. The sudden shift had damaged his personal life though not his career. He was moved off into the Far East controllerate where he began to rise.

De Mowbray returned to London just after Phillpotts to work with him and join the Fluency Committee, the joint MI5–MI6 team set up to review the issue of penetration. Its 1967 report concluded there were twenty-eight anomalies that could not be attributed to any spy who had yet been identified.[69] Golitsyn returned to Britain, again fearing that the KGB was on his tail as he headed for the south coast. He visited four times, on each occasion for a month. De Mowbray was one of those assigned to look after him. Golitsyn was now given the freedom to range over the MI5 files on individuals. Whatever he asked for he received so long as it predated his defection. He was paid £10,000 a month for his work (having asked for more).

Even de Mowbray's former tutor came into the sights. Golitsyn thought Isaiah Berlin's familial links to Russia were suspicious and constituted a vulnerability. This was too much for de Mowbray who argued it out with Golitsyn. Hollis was brought back from retirement for interrogation (he had found a strange refuge by occasionally sitting in John le Carré's house).[70] He admitted nothing and there was no hard evidence, just belief. 'Dear old Roger; to do this successfully would have required intelligence and skill of a very high order,' one colleague later said of the idea that Hollis could have been a spy.[71] Rumours swirled through the secret world and began to filter out. The investigations provided plenty of ammunition for reputations to be smeared (Wilson himself claimed – perhaps wrongly – that Judith Hart, a Labour minister, was deemed a security risk because MI5 had muddled her up with Edith Tudor-Hart who had recruited Philby).[72]

Golitsyn said that a KGB chief of operations in Northern Europe had talked of killing an opposition leader in the West. The leader of the Labour Party Hugh Gaitskell had died in January 1963. Was he the victim of an assassination plot designed by the KGB to get 'their man' into Downing Street? Arthur Martin spoke to Gaitskell's doctor, who said it was mysterious how the Labour leader could have contracted the unusual disease which killed him. Harold Wilson had taken over as leader. Perhaps he was a KGB man? they speculated. After all, he had conducted some business dealings in the Soviet Union and had some friends with suspicious connections. From 1964 when Wilson won the general election, some in Washington, and even a few in London, believed that the Prime Minister worked for the KGB. Golitsyn never said he was definitely a spy but trusted that the bits and pieces he had seen 'fitted' with Wilson. Angleton once even flew over to London saying he had new information to back up the claim but could not pass on the details.[73] In fact, the KGB had once opened a file on Wilson in order to target him but had never had any success. For Wright and one or two others, a sense had grown up that they were the ultimate guardians of the sanctity of the state against some terrible plot which everyone else was blind to. The idea that the spies were manning the 'last watchtower' while the citizens slept blissfully unaware of the dangers is a notion that occasionally arises within secret services, particularly when there is a deep-seated belief in subversion from within, and it could occasionally edge into something dangerous and itself subversive.[74] Wright dwelt on the idea of plotting to remove the government. He would later admit that almost no one else within the secret world was ready to follow him in that direction, although there were some of its former members who were also thinking along the same lines, not least George Kennedy Young, the former MI6 deputy chief who created an 'action' committee called Unison dedicated to the 'security of the realm', which, he claimed, even had police chief constables on its books. These murmurings (including one discussion in the late 1960s in which Lord Mountbatten was invited and declined to take part in a prospective coup) never really came close to actually toppling the government but they helped heighten an increasingly febrile atmosphere.[75]

The American molehunt had been nearly as savage as the British. Officers whose name began with a K had their careers wrecked. Then it spread wider as Golitsyn scoured the personnel files. In all, around fifty officers came under suspicion at one time or another, a dozen and a half investigated heavily. After he retired Richard Helms had a conversation with the editor of the *Washington Post*. 'Do you know what I worried about most as Director of CIA?' he asked rhetorically. 'The CIA is the only intelligence service in the Western world that has never been penetrated by the KGB.'[76] The pursuit paralysed operations against the Soviet Union. It was simply too dangerous to recruit anyone in case they were either betrayed or had been planted as part of the master plot. Perhaps the only thing worse than having a mole is the fear of having a mole. The CIA was left emasculated, governed by a fear that the enemy was inside its walls, watching its every move and pulling the strings behind its every move. 'Angleton devastated us,' explained one official from the Soviet division. 'He took us out of the Soviet business.'[77] One defector was sent back to the Soviet Union on the basis that he was a plant. He was almost certainly not and was most likely killed.

By the 1970s the CIA had entered into a dark place. When one CIA officer was posted to Paris as station chief, Angleton actually warned the French that his colleague might be a Soviet agent.[78] Angleton became an insomniac. When Peter Wright visited he would stay up drinking and comparing notes with the MI5 officer until 4 a.m. At one point, he turned to Wright and said, 'This is Kim's work.'[79] Perhaps he meant that Philby was behind the plots. He was certainly behind Angleton's fear. It was Angleton who was to become lost in his wilderness of mirrors, watching Philby's disjointed reflection darting around his own angular self.

Eventually, and with a grim inevitability, the revolution began to devour its children. Someone asked who had damaged CIA activity most. That old friend of Philby, James Jesus Angleton. One officer said there was an 80 to 85 per cent chance that Angleton was himself the spy, the attachment of a percentage to such an issue, a sign of the absurdity to which it had all descended.[80] Or perhaps Golitsyn, not Nosenko, was the plant, sent by a cunning KGB to manipulate the growing paranoia of Philby's old friend and lead him down the garden path? (He was not, as was evidenced by the KGB's reaction to his defection and its plans to assassinate him.)[81] Angleton was not a spy, but his time had passed. A new CIA director began to break up the sprawling Angleton empire, removing his power of veto over operations. One officer was tasked with investigating his work. He went down to Angleton's private vault at the end of his office. Past a combination-locked door was a private library of files, inaccessible to the rest of the CIA. In all there were 40,000 files on individuals in ten racks eight feet high, kept in brown envelopes.[82] There were forty-nine volumes on Kim Philby alone. One safe had the Hollis and Mitchell files, as well as those on Harold Wilson, Henry Kissinger and other top Western officials. Inside this vast storehouse was another smaller vault beyond push-button locks where even more secret material was housed. It took the officer six years to complete his study, which ran to 4,000 pages.[83] The sum was far less than the parts, a collection of leads which went down winding paths but never quite reached a destination. Sasha was eventually agreed to be not a CIA officer but a head agent in Germany called Orlov.

In 1975 Angleton was finally forced out on the pretext of his involvement in domestic surveillance in which he had been opening American citizens' mail. At the same time, the Watergate scandal had damaged the CIA, as had the exposure before Congress of the role of Larry Devlin and other officers in proposed assassinations abroad. In the tussle between believers and critics of deception and mole-hunts, the pendulum swung the other way. The revulsion against Angleton was so strong that counter-intelligence became a dirty word, the last division any aspiring young officer would want to serve in. The memories of the hunt were so piercing that for years no one wanted to revisit its dark hallway.[84] The CIA began aggressively to recruit agents in the Soviet bloc. These efforts would later be met with catastrophe because, after Angleton had left, the KGB really did manage to get inside the castle walls just when everyone had stopped looking.

The struggle within MI6 ebbed and flowed. The rising star of the service was Maurice Oldfield. He played a complex, ambiguous role in the molehunt. When he was the liaison in Washington before Phillpotts, he had been close to Angleton and, as an instinctively cautious, counter-intelligence expert, had at least in part backed the theories. When Oldfield came back to London as head of counter-intelligence just before Phillpotts took the job, he walked a more ambivalent line, ever mindful of the politics. He voiced the need for care and for a more passive stance rather than for an aggressive recruitment of Soviets. Another scandal had to be avoided. When Rennie was appointed chief, Oldfield was angry about being passed over for an outsider. He became number two, controlling as much as he could and repositioning himself as the voice of reason against the molehunters. Phillpotts, once a con-tender for the throne, was outmanoeuvred and gave up the fight in 1970, a stellar career lost in the contrived corridors of suspicion. Oldfield then had de Mowbray moved away from the molehunting team. Against his protests de Mowbray was sent to work on the Southern Mediterranean. De Mowbray was indignant about his treatment but made sure he kept in touch with his fellow believers in MI5. Their numbers began to dwindle, but de Mowbray had decided he would not give up. 'I could not reconcile myself to doing nothing: I had made so many commitments to myself and to others to pursue the problem to the end that I could not wash my hands and forget about it.'

In the early 1970s, de Mowbray heard from his friends at MI5 that the CIA Director had been over to London and had been told that the case against Hollis had been closed. De Mowbray went to complain to Rennie. 'You know if I were to do something and make a fuss, one or other of us [meaning himself or the head of MI5] would have to go,' Rennie said. De Mowbray realised he would no longer get any support from within MI6. He used the connection of having gone to New College, Oxford, to approach a former private secretary to the Prime Minister now working in the City. He asked him whether he would have accepted a closed envelope to pass directly to the Prime Minister. The ex-official said he would have done. A few days later, in June 1974, de Mowbray approached a serving official at 10 Downing Street where Harold Wilson had just returned as prime minister. He was taken to one of the grand upstairs rooms, but he was told that no private message could be passed to the Prime Minister without an official reading it first. A day later, he received a message summoning him to see the Cabinet Secretary, Sir John Hunt. De Mowbray took Hunt through the investigation and said he believed that MI5 was incapable and unwilling to investigate itself. He thought Hunt had listened intently. But Hunt told a colleague, 'As de Mowbray's eyes glazed over, I had the feeling of a dangerous obsession.'[85] Hunt told the Prime Minister who then said to his secretary and confidante, 'Now I've heard everything. I've just been told that the head of MI5 itself may have been a double agent!'[86] Hunt also called Sir Dick White in from retirement.

'Is de Mowbray a screwball?' the Cabinet Secretary asked.

'No, he's not mad,' replied White. 'He's patriotic, hard-working but obsessed.'

'Was Hollis a spy?' asked Hunt. Hollis had died in 1973.

'I'd be surprised,' said White. It was a strange form of words and was delivered with little conviction. Hunt was left with the impression that it might be surprising but not impossible for it to be true.

'But how did we get to this?' asked Hunt. He decided to try and find out.[87]

A couple of weeks later another message came asking de Mowbray to see former Cabinet Secretary Lord Trend in Oxford. For two hours they talked, first inside, then over lunch out in deckchairs on a perfect summer's afternoon. Trend had been asked to conduct his own investigation into the issue and listened carefully. But at the end as he stepped out of his door on to the cobbled Oxford street, Trend turned to him 'Don't expect me to tear Whitehall apart about all this,' he said.

Trend was given an office, a safe and a secretary in MI5 head-quarters and spent a year poring over the papers and interviewing those involved. 'How did it all begin?' he asked Peter Wright. It was a question Wright had often asked himself.[88] Trend's final report remains secret. It was used to exonerate Hollis when accusations against him became public, although there are some who doubt that it was as conclusive as it was made out to be. When the investigation was complete, Oldfield summoned de Mowbray to meet with Trend and Hunt in the Cabinet Office. De Mowbray met Oldfield down in the car park of MI6's new headquarters, Century House, and they drove over to Whitehall together. De Mowbray began to talk about Russian deception. Oldfield cut across him and said someone was dealing with these problems. Hunt told de Mowbray that he had to reconcile himself to not getting his old job back in counter-intelligence. De Mowbray tried again to pass a note to the Prime Minister. By now the 1970s were fading and James Callaghan had succeeded Wilson after his surprise resignation from Downing Street. Hunt called de Mowbray back and said that the Prime Minister had spoken to the heads of MI5 and MI6, but it was over. End of story. It certainly was for de Mowbray, who asked for early retirement. He walked out of Century House never to set foot inside again. He went off to the US where he joined up with Golitsyn, now out of favour at the CIA, and began helping the Russian with a book.

The aftershocks of the molehunts and investigations continued to reverberate around the secret and the political worlds. In May 1976, a BBC TV reporter received an unusual summons from Harold Wilson who had stepped down as Prime Minister two months earlier. At his home around the corner from the House of Commons, Wilson opened a window into a world of conspiracy and fear for the journalist and a colleague he had brought along. 'I am not certain that for the last eight months when I was Prime Minister I knew what was happening, fully, in security,' he told the astonished reporters.[89] Over sherry and whisky, he said some people in MI5 were 'very right wing' and that he could not rule out individuals in MI5 and MI6 being involved in smearing him with talk of a 'communist cell' in Number 10.[90] Wilson said he had summoned Oldfield to ask about the problem and that Oldfield had confirmed that there was an 'unreliable' section in his sister service and promised to help deal with it but he had never reported back. Wilson explained that he had even gone so far as to send a friend to Washington to ask a former vice-president to find out what the CIA knew. The then-CIA Director and future President George Bush then visited Wilson in Downing Street to discuss the issue. He was convinced that a series of burglaries at his office and home, and those of his colleagues, was part of a wider conspiracy, possibly involving South African intelligence.

Spy-fever washed over British shores again in 1979. A book by a BBC journalist pointed towards Anthony Blunt as a spy. His secret was out and he was stripped of his knighthood. The Prime Minister Margaret Thatcher was forced to make a statement in parliament. In November of that year an adaptation of John le Carré's *Tinker, Tailor, Soldier, Spy* hit television screens. 'I've got a story to tell you. It's all about spies. And if it's true, which I think it is, you boys are going to need a whole new organisation,' a character tells George Smiley. Alec Guinness played George Smiley, the spymaster who hunted for a 'mole' within MI6 and found it to be one of his closest friends. To prepare for his role, Guinness had been introduced to the now retired Maurice Oldfield by le Carré in a restaurant. Oldfield had been a fan of Guinness and rather enjoyed the lunch.[91] But, like many other officers, he wanted to warn against accepting the bleak world of Smiley as the truth. 'We are definitely not as our host here describes us,' he told the actor.[92] Guinness hurried to watch Oldfield as he walked away. 'The quaintly didactic waddle, the clumsy cufflinks, the poorly rolled umbrella were added to Smiley's properties chest from then on,' remarked le Carré.[93] Although not the template for the original Smiley, the similarities were there in the glasses, the odd walk and the fascination with medieval history. 'I still don't recognise myself,' the spy chief wrote to the actor after seeing the programme. Almost everyone else could. Oldfield had risen to the top, but even the foreign secretaries he served detected a loneliness in him. He died a few years later, an unhappy obituary arriving later when his homosexuality was exposed amid questions about whether it had posed a security risk. Oldfield had been a sincere churchman from a humble background in Derbyshire surrounded by the upper crust and living out a double life. 'He must have had an awful, awful inner struggle,' a colleague reckons.[94]

The British public had become obsessed with traitors, fuelled by le Carré's fiction. Traitors provided one explanation for why everything had gone wrong in Britain after the war, why the Empire had disappeared and things were not as they used to be. Where Fleming's Bond provided escape from that reality, Smiley offered an alternative, bleaker and self-flagellating, narrative. Thrillers reflect the anxieties of their age. Early spy fiction at the turn of the century had been designed to warn people of the threats and vulnerabilities to Britain and its Empire sitting astride the world.[95] By the time of le Carré, the anxieties were much more about moral decay and what lay within. In London and Washington they disliked his work, especially *The Spy Who Came in from the Cold*. Over dinner in Washington, CIA Director John McCone complained to Dick White that the negative portrayal was undermining their work. 'He hasn't done us any good ... He's presenting a service without trust or loyalty, where agents are sacrificed and deceived without compunction.'[96]

The change in spy fiction – from the gung-ho imperial fiction of the early century to the more interior literature of traitors – mirrored Britain's changing position in the world and its perception of itself. The spies had also begun to look inward as much as outward. In Vienna at the start of the Cold War, the first question defectors from the East would be asked was whether they knew of any sign of impending war. By the latter stages of the conflict, the first question they would be asked was whether they knew of any sign that Western intelligence services had been penetrated. The spy world had become more introverted and more self-referential, inhabiting its own subculture with its own strange customs.

On both sides of the Atlantic, a fire had been lit by Philby's betrayal which was fanned by Golitsyn. It blazed with fierce intensity, nearly consuming both the CIA and MI6 until it burnt itself out. Trust is the glue which holds organisations and people together. In the world of spy versus spy, being too trusting, as MI6 had been in the past, can be destructive, opening the way for treachery. But trusting too little can also corrode an organisation from within, shattering its self-confidence, making it impossible for colleagues to work with each other and to work with partners. A poison entered the system.

The molehunters did not begin from a position of paranoia. Belief that the services could have been penetrated was not simply rational, it was true given what had come before in the form of Philby and Blake and others. Not to have carried out investigations would have been dangerously irresponsible. But the trouble came from the quasi-religious acceptance of a theory which could not be disproved by the facts, a problem that recurs from time to time in intelligence. The problem with being convinced that your enemy is practising deception is that 'the absence of evidence is not evidence of absence'.[97] 'Simply because you do not have evidence that something exists does not mean that you have evidence that it doesn't exist.' In other words, if you can't find what you are looking for, it just means that your opponent is very good at deceiving you.[98]

Peter Wright was sidelined. 'When you join the service each case looks different. When you leave they all seem the same,' he later reflected.[99] When he walked out of the old offices in 1976 to a new building, he sensed the ghosts that had still not been laid to rest. 'Walking the corridors of Leconfield House I could still feel the physical sense of treachery, of pursuit, and the scent of the kill,' he wrote.[100] The trauma of the molehunts remained hidden from public view for many years. This did not help. The closet into which skeletons were hurriedly stuffed became increasingly fit to burst. In Britain, there were no American-style Congressional committees to help ease the tension and deflate the pressure. Those who felt their country had been betrayed and their own fears ignored became increasingly agitated. Some began to do something that those in the secret world had not done before. They began to talk, first to a few journalists and writers. Then, emboldened, Peter Wright, angry at having been denied a proper pension, decided to publish his own tell-all in his book *Spycatcher*. Fear traversed Whitehall and the secret world and everything was done to try and stop it, including an absurd court case in Australia which made the Cabinet Secretary and government look foolish. But their efforts were futile and out tumbled all the skeletons and the dirty laundry in one messy pile in front of a rapt British public who had not seen anything like it before. Arthur Martin too broke cover to defend Wright, even though he was less sure about Hollis. 'If it was not Hollis, who was it?' he asked in a letter to *The Times*, warning that the failure to follow through on the investigation into this had led to 'a decade of unease'. 'It is inconceivable that the security service would have allowed an investigation to lapse if similar evidence of penetration had been discovered in any other department of government,' he wrote, beginning a public exchange with other former officers on the letters page of the newspaper. Despite the best efforts of a few, the door to the secret world could never be quite so firmly shut again. Who are all these strange people? the public began to ask.[101]

In the late 1980s, Gerry Warner was appointed MI6's director of counter-intelligence and security, the post that had previously been the power base of the molehunters. He found the staff still living a hermetically sealed existence, locked into the position of accumulating files and information as they watched for trouble rather than aggressively targeting the other side. In his new role he should have had access to all the files. As he opened the safe, he found that fifteen of them were on Maurice Oldfield and his personal life. Chris Curwen was then C and had been among the hunters. When Curwen retired three years later, he walked into Warner's office. 'You better have these,' he said and deposited a further handful of files from his own personal Chief's safe. They were files of counter-intelligence investigations that Warner had never been shown before. Perhaps it was something of an apology. Among the files was one on Warner himself. Everyone who had run the Warsaw station up to a certain date had been investigated by the molehunters based on the Angletonian thesis that anyone who had successfully run agents in the Soviet bloc, like Beneficiary the Polish cipher clerk, must have been working for the other side. The molehunters had been looking for the officer who was being groomed by their Soviet controllers for the top of the service, the new Philby. Warner read on, angry and amazed. His relatively humble background, his early reputation as a troublemaker, his wife's mathematical skills (useful for encrypting perhaps), all pointed in one direction, the file argued. The conclusion, at one point, was that he was the spy. Shergy's role in protecting him in Geneva and at the Fort, and in protecting the core of his own operations, became clearer. There was a note on the file. It asked, despairingly, why when we have all this proof has nothing happened and why does Warner continue to be promoted? Warner leant back in his chair. He did not know whether to laugh or cry.

De Mowbray went into a self-imposed silence for three decades after leaving MI6.[102] Hollis and Mitchell were not spies, he came to believe (although a few persist in their belief about Hollis).[103] 'There were suspicions with both of them. There are not suspicions now. But somebody was doing it,' he argues. 'I vowed to myself I would never let go of the case.' It would be hard, although not quite impossible, for the identity of a high-level British traitor to have been kept secret for so long on the Soviet side with all the defectors who had come over, especially in the last three decades. 'Maybe I was wrong. But I don't think I was,' says de Mowbray. 'I cannot leave this. Ever.' Anatoly Golitsyn, the man who walked out of the KGB Residency that cold Friday night in Helsinki in 1961, died in the sweltering heat of the American South on 29 December 2008. Not a single obituary marked his passing. It was as if the pain of that chapter was so great that no one wanted to remember.

6

COMPROMISING SITUATIONS

The early 1960s were a golden age for the small army of Soviet spies plying their trade in Britain. The liberalism of the Swinging Sixties had yet to take hold and the spies knew how to exploit the yawning gap between the stuffy external world of the bowler-hatted establishment and its seedy underbelly of sex and greed. Their tools were the dark arts of provocation and blackmail. It was into the strange but exhilarating surroundings of London that Mikhail Lyubimov, a twenty-six-year-old Russian intelligence officer, was plunged when he arrived in 1961. The Beatles were still waiting to release their first album and London was still shrouded in a dense, filthy smog on winter mornings. The only reason for his assignment was the shape of his face. 'I had a very British look,' he explains. 'Long faced, a little bit like a good horse. And the chief of the KGB department said, "You are very good for England." My fate was decided like this.'[1] The arbitrariness of the decision was typical of the peculiar bureaucracy of the KGB's Moscow Centre.

Lyubimov was garrulous, erudite and talented, although some of his KGB contemporaries considered him a touch over-ambitious. The Soviet Union was relaxing somewhat after the death of Stalin in 1953, but it was still a society largely closed off to foreign influences and his initial understanding of Britain had come from reading the carefully approved literature kept on a special shelf at the Moscow Institute for International Relations. It portrayed Britain as a decadent, decaying empire in which the poor were exploited by capitalist overlords. Victory was inevitable and Lyubimov's mission was to hasten the overthrow of this system, specifically by burrowing into the heart of the establishment and recruiting members of the Conservative Party to become agents of the Soviet state. 'I came full of enthusiasm and because of this horse-like look I was just directed at the Conservative Party,' he remembers. For Lyubimov, who had been expecting to go to the rather quieter venue of Finland, the bright lights of London offered their own delights. It was a plum posting – a chance to enjoy life in the West – and it began an enduring fascination for all things British, leaving him an Anglophile with a twist, a man who with some guilt enjoyed English literature and Scotch whisky but who also revelled in subverting the country that produced them.

The posting to London also presented the opportunity to work against the KGB's oldest foe, to take part in the latest chapter of that long intelligence duel dating back even before the 1917 Revolution and do battle with the enemy which had been trying to destroy the great socialist experiment through its plots. The KGB knew the British were cunning and dangerous. But Russians also believed themselves to be just a little bit smarter, and the London Residency of the KGB was its glittering prize, the place out of which Philby and the others had been run in the glory days. 'Like a banquet table laden with caviar, sturgeon and bottles of vodka, it was overflowing with valuable agents, who had, at various times, permeated every pore of the British establishment,' Lyubimov recalls.[2]

Lyubimov's cover was as a press attaché at the Embassy. On arrival, his first task was to buy a pinstriped suit. It was a stretch on his meagre KGB salary, but looking the part was important. Money was tight. He walked everywhere in London not just as part of a 'dry cleaning' procedure to rid himself of any surveillance but because London taxicabs were so shockingly expensive. He was at the bottom of the pile in the Embassy, so he shared a flat just off Kensington High Street. Though he liked Britain, he retained his socialist beliefs and quietly fumed at the stratified divisions of the British class system which were everywhere. When his wife was due to give birth, he chose a hospital in the East End because he had more faith in the obstetricians there than in those who served the bourgeoisie. He preferred Marks and Spencer to Harrods, although he found the latter a useful place to slip his tail using the lifts, side exits and crowds. He would enjoy seeing the flushed, panting faces of his pursuers. He would then put on his best 'arrogant' English expression on the bus to blend in.[3]

Next, Lyubimov began frequenting London's smoke-filled clubs to start meeting the right kind of people. As if he were a child with his face pressed against the glass of a sweet shop, every Tory, every toff, every member of the establishment was a potential target. The annual Conservative Party Conference was, to him, a veritable nirvana. In 1962 it was hosted in the sleepy North Wales seaside town of Llandudno. Amid the fading Victorian bed-and-breakfast guesthouses, Lyubimov cut a swathe through the twinset-and-pearl Conservative ladies and the moustached Conservative gentlemen enjoying their time away from home. 'I went to the parties. I even danced with the Conservative members,' he recalls. 'Females. Not males.' At night, though, he locked his room, fearing that a British 'provocation' might try and hop into his bed.

Lyubimov was something of a curiosity to those he met. Just as he arrived, Yuri Gagarin had made it into space, boosting Russia's image, so invitations to attend receptions and parties landed at a healthy rate in his in-tray. At that time it was very much in vogue to lecture about the Soviet Union, and Lyubimov would give long talks over cups of tea extolling the virtues of Communism and hoping that someone interesting might perhaps introduce themselves at the end. Among those he got to know (but whom he did not recruit and who did not spill any secrets) were Nicholas Scott, then leading the Young Conservatives, the future *Sunday Telegraph* editor Peregrine Worsthorne and Peter Walker, a newly elected MP.

His real task was to seek out, befriend and then recruit individuals who might be persuaded to provide information to the KGB. From the Conservative Party, he soon broadened out his targets to Labour and to pretty much anyone else. There was lunch with the odd Labour luminary like Dick Crossman who provided good conversation but nothing more. The Marxist intellectual Ralph Miliband was regarded as unfit to be approached by the KGB due to his independent thinking. One woman thought about handing over secret documents but gave him nothing. There was a diplomat who promised gold but provided only dross. He followed one Foreign Office official into a pub and tried to strike up a conversation as he munched on a sandwich but with no success. And a girl in Conservative Central Office nearly fainted when he explained that he was a Russian.[4] Sometimes on a long drive he would become aware of a car on his tail. Special Branch or MI5, he assumed. Sometimes his tail would appear in the same pub as him. A man in a beige mac would sit nursing a pint of warm bitter in the lounge bar of a dingy pub. Normally, the watcher and the watched would keep half an eye on one another but avoid direct contact, although on one occasion he got so lost trying to find a hotel that he turned round and asked his watchers for directions. They dutifully obliged. But such contact was the exception. Often he saw nothing. He had shaken off his tail. Or perhaps it had never been there.

The truth was that the watchers of MI5's A4 surveillance branch were struggling to contain the massive espionage operation being run out of the Soviet Embassy. In an observation post in a house opposite the main gates of the Embassy, a pair of watchers sat surrounded by overflowing ashtrays and empty coffee cups and undertook the mind-numbingly dull task of training their binoculars and cameras on Lyubimov and his colleagues as they walked or drove in and out. These officers spent years of their lives in the tiny room and knew many of the faces instantly but had a three-volume folder of photos to consult if needed. Once they had identified a target, they would radio colleagues who would then pick up the Soviet officials as they headed out into town and follow them on foot or by car. The watchers' movements were co-ordinated from a control room off Regent's Park with a huge street map of London on one wall and a constantly crackling radio. But the watchers simply did not have the numbers to cope with their wily opponents. At least sixty members of the KGB were operating, like Lyubimov, under cover in the Embassy. Dozens more worked for military intelligence, with another contingent based at the Soviet Trade Delegation. More still worked as journalists and members of the press. In all there were around 500 Soviet officials operating in Britain of whom 120 were identified as intelligence officers (the suspected figure was closer to 200). This was more than were based in the US if the United Nations was excluded. The Soviet spies had also learnt, from their agents, every trick and technique the watchers employed and devised their own counter-surveillance routes to evade them. With only minimal surveillance, the Russians were almost entirely free to engage in their pursuit of the powerful and the vulnerable with little impediment. MI5 was swamped.[5]

But Lyubimov's ambition meant that his cover did not remain

intact for long. 'Very soon I became well known as a spy in the Conservative Party,' he recalls. 'I worked very intensively and I was foolish enough at that time to be very active.' At parties he would often be introduced to other guests as 'the Russian spy, Mr Lyubimov'. He would remain silent or perhaps laugh off the remark. Spying in the early 1960s was taking on a different hue from its past connotations. The association with the Second World War was fading and being replaced not just by a sense of seriousness about the mission when it came to the Cold War, especially during the dark days of the Cuban Missile Crisis in autumn 1962 when the world prepared itself for a nuclear exchange, but also by a touch of glamour and even playfulness. Nothing epitomised this more than the arrival that same year on cinema screens of James Bond in the form of *Dr No*. Ian Fleming's creation was taking on a life of its own with President Kennedy citing Bond in his top ten books. Lyubimov met Bond's creator Ian Fleming just after *Dr No* had been finished at a party hosted by Lady Antonia Fraser. 'We were drinking and discussing world problems. He was a good drinker and we drank a lot of whisky,' Lyubimov recalls. 'I didn't know that he would be so famous. But actually Bond was never considered to be a serious film in the KGB.' That was only half true since the KGB would later encourage the creation of a Communist answer to Bond to challenge the cultural pre-eminence of 007, but without much success. From 1962 onwards, Bondmania would spread globally and become associated with the new Britain of the 1960s, a very different Britain from the author Ian Fleming's world, taking on an increasingly fantastical air, distant from the realities of both the Cold War and Britain's place in it.

Lyubimov's successes in recruiting actual agents, rather than just making friends with Conservative MPs, was limited. But one Conservative MP did fall foul of the dark side of the KGB's work in Lyubimov's time although not by his hand. The bluff naval commander Anthony Courtney, who had helped drop Anthony Cavendish's doomed agents off the Baltic coast in the late 1940s, had enjoyed another twist in an eventful career. During his time in Naval Intelligence he had worked closely with MI6, suggesting ideas for using Royal Navy surface craft and submarines for intelligence operations in the Black Sea. Kim Philby had listened with interest.

Courtney would later wonder if that was the moment he first came to the attention of the KGB. But he would almost certainly have been known to them well before that, not least from his time in Moscow during the war and his affair with a dancer.[6]

Courtney had pressed officials to post him to Moscow but without luck. He had also hoped to join MI6, but a half-offer from the Chief evaporated after others in the service and Foreign Office said they were unsure about him.[7] He had retired from the navy short of money and decided to run a consultancy for businesses trading with the Soviet bloc, much like Greville Wynne. He met with the Soviet Trade Delegation in London and threw parties for visiting Russians. He asked to visit Portsmouth with some Russian captains to look at buying old ships and he visited Moscow, dropping in on the State Scientific and Technical Commission that housed Penkovsky. In early 1959, the chance to fulfil a long-standing ambition emerged when the sitting Conservative MP for Harrow East was forced to resign after he was caught engaged in a homosexual act (still illegal at the time) with a member of the Coldstream Guards in St James's Park. The good men and women of Harrow East needed a new representative. 'An air of horrified prudishness pervaded the atmosphere in the constituency,' Courtney remembered. So the local Conservatives picked a former navy commander who could not possibly let them down.

But Courtney fell for the classic honey trap. During his visits to Moscow he had got to know Zina Volkova, a forty-something beauty with fair hair and hazel eyes, who ran a car service for visiting foreigners. Courtney kept up his business links after entering parliament and in June 1961 he arrived in Moscow for a trade fair. At the airport arriving for the same fair, Greville Wynne was picking up film from Oleg Penkovsky and then heading for his hotel, the Metropol, before going to the Embassy to hand it over to Rauri Chisholm. Courtney meanwhile was having dinner at the National with Zina. His wife had died in March of that year, and after dinner he and Zina retired to his bedroom for a few hours. What Courtney did not realise was that hidden cameras in a hotel room recorded their every embrace. 'The affair was not a success,' Courtney later remarked of that night with characteristic British understatement. It was to be his downfall.

Courtney had been speaking out in parliament from 1962 about the free rein given to the likes of Lyubimov in London compared to the harassment of British Embassy staff in Moscow. Why was the Soviet Embassy in London allowed to have Russian chauffeurs while British diplomats in Moscow were forced to employ local drivers and staff, all recruited through an agency clearly under control of the Russian intelligence services? Courtney was drawing attention to a very real vulnerability which would be used to entrap a number of Embassy staff. The relationship between the two countries, he said, 'called to mind a pair of dancers, a self-satisfied elderly gentleman performing an elegant minuet, oblivious of the fact that his partner was doing the twist'. He was thus a prime target for the KGB. According to Lyubimov, there was an attempt at blackmailing the MP into becoming an agent, something Courtney himself denied.[8] Courtney's problem was that the very summer he had dined with Zina in the hotel he had met Elizabeth Trefgarne, the widow of a peer who was to be his new wife. Courtney had told her of the affair, but it still looked rather awkward. At the same time, molehunters decided there was something suspicious about Courtney, particularly the fact that he flew his private aeroplane behind the Iron Curtain. They thought he had lied about the timing of his affair and had been turned.

Courtney's refusal to work for the KGB may explain his increasingly vociferous parliamentary outbursts against its work in London. Why had 200 British Foreign Service personnel serving in the Communist world since 1949 left their posts early, seventy-eight of them on grounds of misconduct or unsuitability? When will the government stop behaving 'like a lot of hypnotised rabbits in the face of an efficient Soviet espionage organisation?' he asked.[9] The first sign of trouble came early in 1965 when anonymous letters concerning his private life were sent to him and to his stepson – who happened to be Sir Alec Douglas-Home, the then leader of the Conservative Party. Courtney continued to press his case, calling on the new Prime Minister Harold Wilson in June that year to complain about Soviet actions in London. The confidential briefing note for the Prime Minister said that Courtney's 'suggestions have generally been impracticable and unhelpful'.[10] In July he tabled an Early Day Motion in the House of Commons on security.[11] Within weeks came the bombshell. Courtney received a phone call from a fellow MP telling him to come to the House. In the rarefied confines of Westminster

Hall with MPs scurrying about preparing for the summer break, he was handed a buff-coloured envelope. Inside was a letter and six photos, five of him with two featuring a woman. He could be seen seated on a bed unbuttoning a woman's blouse. It certainly looked like Zina. Another photograph was more compromising but showed some signs of having been touched up. They were, he conceded, 'dynamite'. To round things off was the line 'to be continued ... '. Other copies were sent to the Labour and Conservative chief whips and worst of all to his prudish Constituency Association. When he got home another buff-coloured envelope came through the letter-box. Two more copies went to his wife. The KGB called this Operation Proba and it was rather pleased with the outcome.[12]

Courtney went to see Roger Hollis, an old friend, with a copy of the letter to ask for advice. An MI5 officer was sent to see him. Courtney was slightly alarmed to find that the man did not speak Russian and did not know as much about the Russian Secret Service as he did. Courtney became irritable and could not sleep at night. Shortly after receiving copies, his wife informed him that she would be filing for divorce. Courtney moved out of their house and into a London flat, becoming increasingly lonely and isolated. The rot exposed by Philby, Burgess and Maclean had gone deep, he believed, and a taint of treachery remained, perhaps at a high level in the Foreign Office. It was clear, though, that the Conservative Party leadership were determined to avoid 'another' scandal and would not be willing to offer him much support. He kept a loaded .38 revolver at his bedside. One day he would think of suicide, another of shooting a Russian.

Slowly, word got round Fleet Street. Reporters turned up on his doorstep. *Private Eye* magazine published the story followed by what Courtney described as 'a short piece of cheap nastiness on BBC Television'. His constituency party, unable to believe that they had been caught up in another scandal, tried to deselect him. Courtney did his best to rally support among the ladies of Stanmore but at the general election in March 1966 he lost his seat by 378 votes. Ten weeks later, his divorce came through. Courtney remained a campaigner on the issue of Russian intelligence for years afterwards, recounting stories of a young acquaintance who awoke from being drugged to find himself in a homosexual embrace, with pictures being taken by old-fashioned photographers, 'black velvet hoods and all', and of a commercial counsellor in Moscow who later became a Conservative MP who had been compromised by a girl but who, to Courtney's annoyance, had never paid for it with his career.[13] More than a decade after being ejected from parliament he offered his own advice to British businessmen travelling to Moscow. Beware Russian women knocking at your hotel door 'who will be only too anxious . . . to give you a real socialist "good time"', he would tell them. 'I have spoken on many occasions round the country on these matters of which I have had some experience and perhaps inevitably I have been accused of seeing "Reds under the Bed". Well, I had one *in* mine, and the repercussions ever since have taught me that it simply isn't worth it. I hope you will agree.'[14]

A compromising situation was most easily engineered on the KGB's home turf, as happened with Courtney. An official UK government study warned of the dangers:

> The Embassy in Moscow and our other Embassies behind the Iron Curtain can only be seen therefore as, in some sort, beleaguered forces under a constant and insidious attack, carried out not only by the skilful development of seemingly innocent contacts with Russian citizens but also by the insertion within the Embassy premises of the most ingenious listening and, sometimes, photographic devices and the conscription as regular informers and reporters of the locally engaged staff working for the Embassy – for example, cooks, house-maids and chauffeurs.[15]

One British Ambassador to Moscow had an affair with his Russian maid. She was a KGB agent and photos were taken of them, forcing his departure. Another British diplomat got his maid pregnant and she asked for help with an abortion, obliging him to identify the MI6 station chief.[16] A Greek ambassador, confronted with pictures of himself *in flagrante* with his housekeeper, grabbed the pictures and gleefully showed them around the diplomatic circuit as a sign of his virility until other diplomats became rather bored. Honey traps were a speciality of the KGB, while the East German Stasi specialised in using men (known as 'Romeos') to target single female secretaries working for officials who would have plenty of access to classified material. The latter tactic, which involved manipulating someone's emotions, was often far more productive than blackmailing an unwilling individual.

Working in Moscow as a diplomat was guaranteed to put even the steeliest soul on edge. The British and American embassies were wired for sound. The US Ambassador's house had a listening device within the Great Seal of the United States in the Ambassador's office. Around fifty bugs were secreted elsewhere in the walls (the KGB even managed to bug Peter Lunn's office in Beirut when he was MI6 station chief, a particularly ironic achievement given that Lunn and Elliott had failed to record their own meeting with Kim Philby in decent quality).[17] Knowing that you were always being listened to played with some people's heads. Some cracked.

The Russians' most spectacular success in engineering a compromising situation came with an Admiralty clerk at the British Embassy in Moscow named John Vassall. The son of a clergyman, Vassall was a loner whom acquaintances thought a bit of a snob. Most of the Britons in Moscow avoided contact with Russians, finding the atmosphere in the city menacing, and chose instead to socialise among themselves. As a junior official in Moscow Vassall felt locked out of the whirlwind of Embassy parties enjoyed by the top diplomats. The well-dressed young man still managed his own busy diary of bridge games, drinks and theatre amid his official duties but also showed an openness towards Russians. One or two colleagues would later say they considered him 'a bit of a pansy' and even called him 'Vera' behind his back. But they also claimed that they had never dreamed he was what was known at the time as an *active* homosexual engaged in acts which were still illegal. Only years later would an official tribunal explain that Vassall had been 'addicted to homosexual practice from youth', language which illustrated why so many like him chose a clandestine life which in turn made them vulnerable. But in Moscow, while Vassall's colleagues may have professed not to notice his preferences, this secret could not be kept from the watching eyes of the KGB. They had their own man inside the Embassy whose job was to seek out the vulnerable.[18]

The handsome Russian interpreter had joined the Embassy before Vassall and proved all too adept at securing theatre and travel tickets and the best food from the markets which, in turn, helped ensure that he was invited to staff parties. He had already attempted to lure a member of another Embassy into a homosexual relationship and tried to involve a member of the British Embassy in the black market to open up a vulnerability.[19] He carefully cultivated Vassall, who had his 'vanity flattered' as he was taken out to restaurants and introduced to other Russians who would eventually do the dirty work. After three months, the trap was set. Vassall was invited to dinner at a restaurant near the Bolshoi Theatre. 'We were taken to the first floor where I first thought was a dining room, but they invited me into a private room,' he later confessed.

> We had drinks, a large dinner and I was plied with very strong brandy and after half an hour I remember everybody taking off their jackets and somebody assisted me to take off mine. I remember the lighting was very strong and gradually most of my clothes were removed. There was a divan in the corner. I remember two or three people getting on the bed with me, all in a state of undress. There certain compromising sexual actions took place. I remember someone in the party taking photographs.[20]

Soon afterwards, he went with another Russian to a flat in central Moscow. The man disappeared and two officials in plain clothes confronted him. One of the officials produced photographs from the party. 'After about three photographs, I could not stomach any more. They made one feel ill,' he later recalled. 'They asked me if this was myself and I replied that it was.' They told him he could be jailed in Russia for that kind of activity and then threatened to show the photos to senior Embassy staff including, rather strangely, the Ambassador's wife, who perhaps was not the type to approve. If he did not do as he was told, he would not be allowed to leave Russia. He was then driven back to his flat. That evening, the KGB man in the Embassy told him he should meet some Russian officials in a hotel. One of the men threw the photos in his face and told him he risked an international incident. Slowly, over weeks, the Russians turned up the heat until he agreed to hand over documents. Vassall was not their only target at that time. Soon after he had begun his work, a woman employee of the Embassy was compromised and she was sent back home immediately.[21]

For seven long and damaging years, first in Moscow and then in London after his return, Vassall passed reams of secret documents – first hidden in the folds of a newspaper, later camera film of reports he had photographed in the office. Back in London, where he had access to atomic secrets, he even sailed through newly introduced 'Positive Vetting' security checks, instituted after Burgess and Maclean to look for potential spies. The KGB made him dependent on it by slowly increasing payments, allowing him to move out of his parents' house and into a flat in the exclusive Dolphin Square apartment block near Westminster inhabited by members of parliament and of the establishment (Vassall would later claim that two Conservative MPs had slept with him at his flat).[22] He lived a lavish lifestyle thanks to the pay he received from the Russians of between £500 and £700 a year, usually delivered in bundles of five-pound notes. About half the money went on clothes, partying and holidays; the other half went into savings accounts and to buy Premium Bonds (the KGB managing to support the British Treasury). His treachery went undiscovered until Anatoly Golitsyn and then Yuri Nosenko provided enough clues to identify him. But evidence was still needed that could stand up in court. MI5 began eavesdropping on his Dolphin Square flat and members of its A4 surveillance team followed him to and from work on the Number 24 bus. MI5's technical wizard Peter Wright said he tried marking some documents with minute amounts of radioactive material which would be picked up by a Geiger counter at exits to the Admiralty, but the plan never worked as wristwatches seemed to set off the detector and management raised concerns about exposing staff to radiation.[23] MI5 then secretly burgled his flat while he was at work. Once it knew there were documents there the Security Service told the police to arrest him and 'find' the documents themselves.

Vassall was approached on a London street by two policemen. 'I think I know what you are after,' he told them. During the car journey to Scotland Yard, one of the Special Branch officers recalled Vassall 'panting with fear'. He began to confess. When they asked if he had any cameras in his flat at Dolphin Square, he said he had two and one of them had a film inside. 'I think you will find what you are looking for on it.' Once he had been taken to New Scotland Yard, the secrets tumbled out. 'By the way, Superintendent,' he told one of the policemen. 'You will find standing in the wardrobe in the bedroom a small corner piece. This has a concealed aperture at its base.' He explained that a secret key was hidden in an oblong box which had to be inserted into the bottom shelf to release a hidden catch, causing a shelf to emerge in which more films were stored. In 1962, Vassall, who over seven years had done enormous damage, pleaded guilty and was sentenced to eighteen years in prison. The case, more than almost any other, damaged the government by creating a widespread public belief that it had failed to get a grip on the issue of security.[24]

Blackmail had always been part of Soviet espionage, but by the late 1960s it had become even more important. The great Soviet agents of the 1930s like the Cambridge spies had been willing recruits, driven by a fear of fascism at that time and still able to see hope in Communism. Three decades later, the idealistic were harder to find, much to the KGB's frustration. And so blackmail and the offer of money were employed more regularly. Many intelligence officers feel uncomfortable anyway with ideological recruits since they are less likely to do what they are told. Once someone has received money, they will also find it harder to walk away.

Did the British employ blackmail as well? There was a debate within the service about whether or not to follow Soviet methods. One of those opposed to its use was Gerry Warner. 'I don't believe in blackmail for both moral and practical reasons. An agent who is working because he is being blackmailed, because he is being coerced into it, he – or she – is never going to be reliable. He has every good reason to betray you if he thinks he can get away with it ... An agent who is being blackmailed has no reason to tell you the truth – he may make things up. He has no loyalty to either himself or to you so it is not a practical business and quite clearly it is not a moral business. If we had descended to the kind of practices that the KGB and GRU routinely practised there was no point in doing the job.'[25] But there is evidence that blackmail was occasionally attempted. MI5 was said to have tried to ensnare a KGB officer in London by introducing him at a party to a high-class call girl who was on its books and then photographing him in the act and entering the room. But when the MI5 man confronted the naked Russian, he simply demanded to talk to his Embassy and refused to co-operate.[26] 'Obviously a new recruit is always going to ask the question "Do we blackmail people, do we seek to compromise them, do we seek to put pressure on them?" a chief of MI6 later claimed. 'No is the answer ... in 1923 an internal study of the service and the methods used by the service wrote, "an individual's vices are not played upon in order to obtain a hold upon him". There you have it in one sentence. Do we use pressure? No we don't.'[27]

Vassall had been sufficiently important to be run by the KGB chief in London, the domineering Nikolai Rodin. But the Soviet Embassy was not the only home for spies. There was another elite breed of KGB officer who truly operated out of sight. These were the famed Russian 'illegals'. On 3 March 1955, the liner *America* docked at Southampton. One of those to disembark was a Canadian named Gordon Lonsdale. Well spoken, handsome and replete with cash, he used his connections as a member of a St James's club, the Royal Overseas League (patron: the Queen), to rent a top-end apartment just off Regent's Park. He then enrolled to take a course learning Mandarin at the School of Oriental and African Studies. But while other students spent their time struggling with the new language, Lonsdale found it all too easy. The reason was that he could already speak the language fluently. The course was simply cover, an excuse to find his feet in London and meet the many government officials also taking it. And Lonsdale was not really Lonsdale.

The real Gordon Lonsdale was most likely dead. He had been a Canadian whose Finnish mother had taken him to the Soviet Union. He probably died around the age of thirty. His death had been covered up by the KGB who had stolen his identity and given it to one of their most prized assets – a man called Konon Molody. Molody was born in Moscow and had been chosen for the life of an illegal. How early no one knows, but he was sent to California to learn English with an aunt when he was aged just ten. After returning to the USSR, he then went to Canada to familiarise himself with his new identity. He had holes drilled in his teeth and went to a specific dentist in Vancouver who would recognise the cavities. That he was a patient named Molody reciting a line from Heinrich Heine would confirm that he was the right person. The dentist then helped him use Lonsdale's birth certificate to get hold of a Canadian passport, allowing him to build a credible back-story – or legend.[28] This had to be watertight. The illegals operate under deep cover. There is no pretence of being a Soviet diplomat and these men and women have no diplomatic immunity if they are caught. Even more remarkably, they give no sign of being Russian but take on a totally different nationality. These were the spies used to meet the truly important agents in the West.

Once in London, Lonsdale moved into business. He had spotted a gap in the market from his time in North America – Britain had yet to develop the American love affair with the jukebox. So he began selling the machines carrying the latest rock-and-roll songs. It was a job that allowed him to travel widely. He had a natural aptitude for business and next became director of a company selling bubblegum machines. At one point he was making so much money that he was able to pay his profits back to the KGB like the good Communist that he was. All the time, he was waiting for instructions to be activated. Every day he visited one of the red London telephone boxes near the back entrance to the Savoy Hotel on the Strand. He would pretend to use the phone but actually feel underneath the wooden shelf holding the telephone directories for a map pin. When he eventually found the pin, he knew it was a sign to head for a dead-letter box. There he found a small wedding-ring case with instructions inside on where to meet a senior KGB officer to receive his marching orders. It was time to get down to his real work. He had an agent to run.

Harry Houghton enjoyed the seedier side of life. When he was posted as a clerk to Warsaw in 1951 he had begun to dabble in the black market, travelling with a gun to seal deals in the back streets of the city involving illicit penicillin supplies (not dissimilar to Harry Lime in Vienna). Booze and women flowed freely and his marriage came under strain. This had all been noticed by his bosses and after being spotted drunk at a reception he was sent back to Britain to work at the Admiralty Underwater Weapons Establishment at Portland, joined to the mainland by a causeway at Chesil Beach.[29] Houghton would later allege that his treachery began one afternoon when his office phone rang and the caller said he had come from Poland with a message from an old girlfriend. Houghton claimed they had met at Dulwich Picture Gallery and the man told him the girl would like to leave but would be allowed to do so only if Houghton could provide some information. 'Putting it bluntly, all the later mistakes stemmed from that one mistake – chasing a bit of skirt behind the Iron Curtain,' he would later say, explaining that it all started gently with a few innocuous documents before the temperature was raised.[30] These were lies. Houghton had unilaterally offered secrets to the other side in Warsaw in exchange for cold hard cash.[31] He had provided thick bundles of documents including the Naval Attaché's codebooks. Back in Britain, his work then accelerated. He was given a Minox camera which could pass as a cigarette lighter and copied thousands of files from a safe room where security was lax. In London, amid concerns for the security of their valuable agent, the KGB – which had taken control of him from the Poles – switched to running him through Lonsdale rather than through an Embassy-based KGB officer (although initially Houghton was led to believe he was still meeting Poles in case it scared him off, a so-called 'False Flag' operation).[32] Houghton would carry a newspaper in his left hand as he entered the Bunch of Grapes pub on Brompton Road. 'Is that the evening paper you've got there?' a man would ask.

'No, I'm afraid it's the daily,' Houghton would reply.

'I wanted the racing results,' the man would say and walk into the gentlemen's lavatory. A few minutes later Houghton would follow to pick up a package. As their marriage fell apart, his wife noticed his strange trips to London on the first Saturday of each month and even spotted secret documents at home. She told a number of officials that she thought her husband was in touch with Communist agents. This information was sent to MI5, but everyone agreed she was simply being spiteful and making it up. Her accusations were 'nothing more than the outpourings of a jealous and disgruntled wife', it was said. She and Houghton soon separated.[33]

Houghton, even though he was street-smart, proved easy prey for a skilled agent handler like Lonsdale. Lonsdale convinced him that the two men were friends. 'I came to enjoy the company of the people I worked with, and the challenges they set,' recalled Houghton. 'We were a team.'[34] There was also the sheer exhilaration of being a spy. The feelings were never reciprocated. 'He was vain as well as shifty,' Lonsdale said contemptuously of Houghton. 'Once he has his claws into the agent, there's no getting away,' he added, describing how a good officer traps his target. Lonsdale always agreed the next meeting place and time so that there would be no need for phone calls or a trail for MI5 to follow.

Houghton's access to secrets was limited after it had been noticed that some documents had been misplaced overnight, but he then found a new route through a girlfriend, Ethel 'Bunty' Gee. When he first told her what he was doing she refused to believe it and then began to cry. But she quickly changed her mind and began to co-operate ('She's very friendly and talkative. But an awful cook,' Lonsdale told the KGB in one message after dinner at their house).[35] At one of many meetings a bundle of 150 five-pound notes was handed over in a brown carrier bag. Lonsdale would receive messages from Moscow on a standard short-wave radio receiver at prearranged frequencies usually at three or four in the morning.

A Polish defector – codenamed 'Sniper' – revealed in April 1960 that the Poles had recruited an agent in Warsaw, and Houghton was soon put under surveillance by MI5, whose spycatchers had been embarrassed when they realised they already had a trace on him thanks to his ex-wife's suspicions.[36] Houghton was watched meeting a man on a park bench and then in a café at Waterloo where an envelope was handed over. The man was then identified as Gordon Lonsdale. MI5 broke into Lonsdale's flat and installed a listening device. Lonsdale was seen delivering items to a safety deposit box at the Midland Bank on Great Portland Street. As the MI5 officer who opened the box flicked through a set of photographs, he saw something which halted him in his tracks. One of the pictures was of himself.[37] He had some explaining to do, but realised that he and Lonsdale had both been at a party thrown by a Canadian diplomat and Lonsdale had been taking clandestine photos. The box also contained a cigarette lighter set in a bowl. Peter Wright X-rayed these back at MI5, which revealed a hollow base acting as a secret compartment. Using a rubber suction cup and tweezers he carefully pulled out a set of tiny one-time cipher pads and London map references. Everything was carefully copied and then returned to the safety deposit box in the early hours of a Sunday morning. Did Lonsdale realise he was being watched? Wright would later believe that signs of increased radio traffic at the Soviet Embassy at the time the safety deposit box was removed was an indication that a mole in MI5 had tipped off the KGB.[38]

Small groups of watchers would tail Lonsdale from his office and then peel off to be replaced by others. This went on for weeks, MI5 officers privately wondering at the quantity and quality of women with whom Lonsdale seemed to consort. They also learnt that he used the cistern in a toilet at the Classic Cinema at Baker Street as a drop point, hiding notes and radio spare parts in a condom deposited in the lavatory. He was also spotted heading to a bungalow in the bucolic London suburb of Ruislip. It was the home of a sociable, elderly couple who ran an antiquarian booksellers on the Strand, Peter and Helen Kroger. What MI5 call a 'static observation post' – in other words a camera in a neighbour's house – was set up to watch the comings and goings of this innocent-looking couple. Peter Wright began reading some of Lonsdale's messages from Moscow which included not only professional information about how to run Houghton, but also news of his wife and children back home. They were missing him and wanted him back.

In January 1961, the CIA informed MI5 that Sniper was defecting and so the net had to be drawn in. On a Friday night, Arthur Martin and Peter Wright from MI5 sat in a brown cell-like room in their headquarters and listened in to the sounds from Lonsdale's flat which they had bugged. Listening to targets like Lonsdale sometimes generated a strange affinity among the buggers as the intimate details of a person's life were revealed. 'It's not as if he's a traitor ... not like Houghton. He's just doing his job like us,' Wright reflected.[39] They heard him make love to a girl and then in the morning persuade her to leave, saying he had urgent business. Lonsdale, Houghton and Gee were all meeting at Waterloo Bridge Road. Houghton thought he had seen someone running behind him to catch his bus but thought nothing much of it. As Gee handed over a shopping bag containing secret films, three cars drew up on the kerb and a dozen men in regulation beige mackintoshes seized the group. Special Branch went to visit the Kroger house. The Krogers were not who they appeared to be. They were two more Russian illegals – real names Morris and Lona Cohen. They had operated in the United States in the 1940s until Philby had tipped the KGB off that they might be discovered. In the London suburbs, their job was to support Lonsdale and act as the link between him and Moscow. The Special Branch officer told Lona she would be taken away for questioning. Could she just stoke the boiler before she went? she asked. The officer was sharp enough to say, 'First let me see what's in your handbag.' She refused. There was a struggle. Inside the bag, the officer found a glass slide with three microdots and a typed sheet of code. When the home was searched a microdot reader was found in a box of face powder. Microdots allowed documents to be reduced to a size sometimes of less than a millimetre and then concealed, even in a bottle of orange juice. Also discovered were seven passports and the crucial piece of equipment – a powerful radio transmitter in a grey suitcase-sized case which could compress a long message and then send it as a burst transmission all the way to Moscow in a few seconds.

Lonsdale would not talk. No one understood yet that he was an illegal. It took a strange bit of detective work to understand that he was not really Lonsdale after all. The doctor in Canada who had been present at the real Lonsdale's birth was tracked down. He remembered the birth because he had had to travel miles into the country-side down dark lanes. He checked his records which showed that the real Lonsdale had been circumcised as a baby.[40] The man who had been arrested had not been. The revelations of illegals, radio sets in the suburbs and treacherous Britons were sensational and captivated the nation, leading to much despair on the part of Prime Minister Harold Macmillan.[41] So important was the trial that Lonsdale/Molody was prosecuted by the Attorney General himself, the for-midable Reginald Manningham-Buller. The sentence was twenty-five years' imprisonment. Manningham-Buller had also dealt with the Blake case personally. He had proposed to the Prime Minister that Blake should be charged on five counts for each posting and he made sure the judge knew that at least forty agents had been betrayed.[42] The high-profile spy trials meant that reporters were frequently camped out on the doorstep of Manningham-Buller's home. He developed a distaste for the world of spies which he regarded as somewhat seedy. The Attorney General's daughter Eliza, barely into her teens, watched with curiosity, an introduction into a world into which she would later plunge.

In prison, Lonsdale briefly met George Blake. 'Of one thing I am certain,' Lonsdale told Blake. 'You and I are going to be on Red Square for the big parade on the 50th Anniversary of the October Revolution.'[43] Lonsdale was out not long afterwards. An RAF plane flew him to West Berlin. Then at 5.30 a.m. on 22 April 1964 he was taken in a black Mercedes to the checkpoint at Heerstrasse.[44] It had rained through the night and there was a thin drizzle as dawn broke. His car was joined by another yellow Mercedes with an escort of black limos coming from East Berlin. Concrete blocks laid out in a zig-zag slowed the cars as they approached. The two vehicles edged into no man's land and stopped. Lonsdale stepped out on his side as did a man from the other vehicle. They stood a few yards apart. Their identities were checked by officials from the opposing side with a nod. There were some muted hand signals and then a Soviet official shouted 'Exchange' and the two men passed each other. 'He looks sleek, well fed,' Greville Wynne thought as he passed Lonsdale. 'But then he has not been in the Soviet Union for a long time.' Wynne was taken into a black limo with a Union Jack on the bonnet. The previous day, he had realised he was heading west as his plane flew into the sunset. 'If you speak or misbehave you will be shot,' a Soviet consul had told him as they stepped into the car early the next morning.[45]

After more than a year in detention in the USSR, Wynne was now a free man but damaged. Within a few days of being back home, he had a nervous breakdown sitting in his armchair. His wife called MI6, who sent its own doctors. His business was finished and life never quite matched up afterwards to the excitement and danger he had experienced. He lost touch with his wife and son and began to spin fantasies about his role in the Penkovsky case, deceiving himself perhaps above all. Afterwards, MI6 laid down new rules for the use of businessmen, aware of the cost that it had exacted from a man who had just wanted to be part of the club. Konon Molody, Gordon Lonsdale, returned to the Soviet Union a hero but also struggled to adjust. His life in the West had left him impatient with the reality of Communism and he was particularly critical of the way in which Soviet industry was run and international trade conducted. This did not make him popular. He died of a heart attack while picking mushrooms in the woods aged forty-eight.[46]

Blake, Vassall, Portland, Lonsdale – the density of spy cases contributed to the heady atmosphere of the early 1960s as one of Britain's periodic bouts of spy mania consumed the nation. The politicians were not happy with having to answer questions time and time again about 'lax' security. When Vassall was arrested, Prime Minister Macmillan vented his fury against the spies. 'I am not at all pleased,' he told Roger Hollis, head of MI5. 'When my gamekeeper shoots a fox, he doesn't go and hang it up outside the Master of Foxhounds' drawing room: he buries it out of sight.'[47] He would refer, with some displeasure, to the 'so-called Security Service'. Often the politicians seemed to want the scandals brushed under the carpet rather than exposed in the courts, hence the offers of immunity to Philby and Blunt.

A climax was reached with the pitch-perfect Profumo Affair. This ticked every box for the hungry press pack. Politicians. Country houses. Showgirls. Russian spies. It was all there, above all the cream of the establishment mixing with the seedy underworld which it could never quite resist. On one night in July 1961, Cliveden, the glorious country house of Lord Astor, played host to the Secretary of State for War, John Profumo, Lord Mountbatten and the President of Pakistan as well as nineteen-year-old Christine Keeler and Evgeni Ivanov, an assistant Soviet naval attaché and – of course – a spy. MI5 had itself been trying to get close to Ivanov, adding another layer of complication. When the guests decided they would dive in the pool, Profumo and Keeler met for the first time. As their affair continued, no secrets were ever passed, but for the Secretary of State for War to be having an affair with the same woman as a Russian spy was quite enough once the papers got hold of it. 'This was all dirt,' a despondent Harold Macmillan wrote in his diary as his government was rocked by crisis.[48] The scandal cost Profumo his career. It also made life harder for the Russians. 'It changed the good face of Soviet citizens. After Profumo, we were considered as all spies,' says Lyubimov with just a hint of irony.[49] The British press published pictures of Soviet diplomats, warning the public that these were the people they would be rubbing shoulders with on buses and to beware.

A small purple-covered booklet became Britain's last line of defence against Communist subversion and the work of Lyubimov and his colleagues ('he may be closer than you think'). *Their Trade is Treachery* was distributed to government officials to warn them of what lay in wait. 'Spies are with us all the time. They are interested in everything ... This booklet tells you about the great hostile spy machine that tries to suborn our citizens and turn them into traitors

... This booklet tells you how to recognise at once certain espionage techniques, and how to avoid pitfalls which could lead to a national catastrophe or a personal disaster – or both.' The booklet recounted recent cases and explained how Russians might target and cultivate someone. One piece of advice offered to officials to help them avoid haemorrhaging national secrets was that great Civil Service injunction: 'Keep the office tidy.'[50]

And soon the tables were turned on Mikhail Lyubimov. After attending a public lecture he bumped into an individual whom he knew and whom he thought would make a prize agent – a Foreign Office man with links to GCHQ. After all the setbacks experienced with Lonsdale and Blake, the KGB had been keen for Lyubimov to pursue him vigorously. The two set off for a pub and ordered whisky. After the second whisky, the Foreign Office man suddenly stood up and announced that he had to go to the lavatory. Two 'rough-looking men' came and seated themselves next to Lyubimov. One seemed a bit unshaven; the other, red faced and plump, sat slumped next to him. 'Mr Lyubimov, you are a complete failure,' one of them said. They then revealed that they knew something about him, which Lyubimov will only describe as 'compromising'. They had the photographs to prove it, they explained. They then uttered the words that send chills down the spine of any diplomat. 'Mr Lyubimov. Either your career is over or you work for us.' The men were from MI5.

'Excuse me,' he said in shock and stood up. He virtually ran to his car and drove straight to the Embassy to report the incident. A formal protest was soon made to the Foreign Office about the 'barbarous provocation' against an innocent Soviet diplomat. The reply came that he had been involved in activities incompatible with his diplomatic status. MI5 had recently decided to try and throw their opponents off balance with a new aggressive strategy.[51] Lyubimov and his family were at least allowed to slip quietly away, avoiding the blaze of publicity that accompanies many an expelled spy's departure. His time as a spy in London was over. But his involvement with Britain was not. The mischievous desire to subvert remained. Lyubimov returned to Moscow to work on the KGB's British desk planning future operations against British nationals in the UK and around the world. 'I remember meeting a British trade unionist in Moscow,' he wrote later. 'He was so far to the left it should actually have been him who was recruiting me! When I mentioned that I was connected with the KGB and asked him about the political co-operation he was almost overwhelmed. "At last!" he exclaimed.[52] By the early 1970s Lyubimov had written a thesis entitled 'Special Traits of the British National Character and their Use in Operational Work'. This paper, which he wrote partly for the guarantee of a 10 per cent salary increase, became the textbook for training a generation of young KGB agents sent to Britain. Among the characteristics for the KGB man to understand and exploit were aggression, self-control, hypocrisy and understatement. It advised them not to start conversations with strangers on the tube and how to buy a round in the pub.[53]

When he was made deputy chief of the Third Department which dealt with the UK and Scandinavia in 1974, Lyubimov was faced with a challenge. The KGB's operations against Britain had been decimated. After a torrid decade of spy scandals, MI5 finally got a grip on the Soviet operation in 1971 with the mass expulsion of Soviet 'diplomats' in Operation Foot. Patience had finally run out at the top of government and concerns about diplomatic repercussions were brushed aside after the Prime Minister was briefed on the scale of a KGB operation which had led to twelve British subjects being convicted of passing secrets in the previous ten years. The defection of a KGB officer Oleg Lyalin provided the perfect pretext. In April 1971, Lyalin, ostensibly and rather bizarrely the knitwear representative with the Soviet Trade Delegation, walked into Hampstead police station asking to see Special Branch officers. Rather than sweaters and cardigans, Lyalin was in fact an expert in hand-to-hand combat and part of the ultra-secret Department V that dealt with sabotage in the event of war, the latest incarnation of the stay-behind networks of old. No one had ever defected from it before.[54] He revealed plans to land teams of special forces, flood the London Underground, blow up Fylingdales military base in North Yorkshire and assassinate key figures at the outbreak of war with the aim of demoralising the British population. Among the disclosures was that the KGB had managed to recruit a clerk in the Greater London Council's motor-licensing pool which helped them identify the MI5 and police vehicles being used to tail its officers. He was briefly run as an agent by MI5 and MI6 but his complicated personal life (involving large quantities of drink, a Russian wife, a Russian mistress, the wives of Embassy colleagues and a British mistress) soon brought an end to that.

Late one evening Lyalin was careering down Tottenham Court Road drunk. His lights were off and the mysterious blonde at his side scarpered immediately when police pulled him over. Lyalin was placed in the back of their panda car and put his feet up on the seat. 'What are you playing at?' the policeman in front asked. 'You cannot talk to me, you cannot beat me, I am a KGB officer,' Lyalin replied.[55] By the time he appeared in court the next morning, there was no choice but for him to defect straight away. Using Lyalin's information as the official justification, an existing plan was accelerated and more than a hundred Soviet diplomats were sent packing to Moscow.[56] It was the largest single diplomatic expulsion in history (although the Prime Minister was warned that even after the expulsion there were still 137 intelligence officers from Eastern Europe at work, including fifty-five Poles and forty-six from Czechoslovakia).[57] The drinks were cracked open in MI5 headquarters to celebrate, pulled out of a large safe where they were kept. Staff knew that for the first time they had cleared the nest of vipers that had been running rings around them through the 1960s. The KGB in London never recovered.

So how could Lyubimov revitalise the operations in the mid-1970s, especially when new recruits would have little chance of experiencing the realities of life in Britain?[58] And why were so many Sov Bloc officials defecting one way and so few Westerners going the other way? Who could help?

It was New Year's Day 1975 and, in a private room of an upmarket restaurant in Moscow, KGB bigwigs clinked vodka glasses and offered lengthy toasts to the health of their guest of honour who was celebrating his birthday. The guest stood for each toast and politely raised his glass, but Kim Philby looked increasingly bored. To Lyubimov's eyes, he resembled a 'run of the mill, semi-unemployed pensioner, who was dying to get stuck into some real work'.[59]

Philby's existence in Moscow had embodied the strange afterlife of the spy – once so highly prized but increasingly redundant as the store of valuable knowledge is eroded by time. Philby saw himself as a Soviet intelligence officer and had expected to be masterminding operations against Britain, just as the press back home assumed he was. But the KGB never quite trusted him, a few wondering even if he was really a double agent who had been working for British intelligence all along. 'It is very much in line with a myth about the subtlety of the British intelligence,' recalls Lyubimov with a touch of sadness for his old comrade, with whom he became close friends. 'Philby could not grasp he was no longer a valued agent but a problem.'[60] 'He was a strong romantic. And he remained a believer in Communism – not in the Communism like the Soviet one but that Communism of Marx and Engels and he had to adapt himself to the situation in the Soviet Union because there was no democracy here at all. He knew perfectly well that he was bugged.' There were concerns he might flee, especially since he never quite lost his independent, anti-establishment streak. There was also an intrinsic wariness of someone who might profess to be a Communist but who was still as British as they came, a Cambridge graduate from an upper-middle-class family. Later, Lyubimov would deliver pots of Oxford Coarse-Cut Marmalade and Scotch sent over from England as well as corduroy trousers and Jaeger pullovers. 'I am convinced that Kim missed England, even though he was at pains to hide this even from those close to him. He was an Englishman to his fingertips, and he needed those now-vanished relics of his former life.' Philby would cook bacon and eggs and fried bread for breakfast and then eat while listening to the cricket scores on the BBC World Service, reading the odd John le Carré novel.

The drinking had got worse in the early Moscow years. Hair of the dog at noon. Maybe a nasty fall later in the day, disturbed dreams at night followed by a morning hangover before it began again. His relationship with Eleanor, who had followed him to Moscow in September 1963, never recovered from his betrayal. It was not so much his being a spy as his leaving one day without so much as a word. They lived for a while in a 'huge grim block' which reminded her of the Lubyanka prison.[61] On a long walk one day she asked, 'What is more important in your life – me and the children or the Communist Party?' He answered without hesitation: 'The party, of course.' Philby never saw Guy Burgess again after their dinner in Washington in 1951. By the time Philby arrived in Moscow, Burgess had drunk himself to oblivion and was already on his deathbed. Philby, unforgiving of Burgess's 'betrayal' in running and pointing the finger at him, never visited as his former friend's overworked liver finally gave out. He barely knew Donald Maclean. They had kept their distance since the 1930s, but they began to meet, play bridge and joke about how 'when the revolution comes' they would visit Italy and Paris. Eleanor thought their reminiscing about those they had known felt stale and forced. When she returned from a brief visit to America, she found the Macleans' marriage had broken down and she realised that Philby had moved in on his fellow spy's wife. She left soon afterwards.

A fellow spy would fortuitously provide Philby an escape raft from alcoholic self-destruction. Philby had not known George Blake when they both worked for MI6, but the two former officers briefly became friends. Blake had engineered a daring escape through a window in Wormwood Scrubs prison in 1966 with the help of sympathetic peace activists who then sheltered him and drove him to Berlin in a camper van. It meant he was able to meet Lonsdale/Molody on Red Square for that anniversary after all. In Moscow one day, a colleague of Blake's wife called Rufina was introduced to Philby. He quickly made his intentions clear. She thought he looked a 'middle-aged man with a puffy face' but while the looks had gone, the charm had not, nor the determination. 'You're a lucky bloke,' Blake remarked to him.[62] Rufina found it hard to reconcile the gentle, sometimes helpless man she knew with the master spy. He told her he never enjoyed the deception. They married and she had placed him on an even keel by the time he met Lyubimov.

After that night at the restaurant, Lyubimov and Philby became close friends, meeting regularly and drinking late into the night in Philby's book-lined apartment. Lyubimov found Philby's ideas for revitalising the London Residency useful although not enormously original. His most valuable role came in running a training class for new recruits. The fresh young KGB men would arrive at a safe flat on Gorky Street to be told what to wear and how to start a conversation when in England. Philby would role-play being a civil servant and then ask them to approach him and talk to him as a potential recruit.

Only once was Philby allowed to enter the headquarters of the service he had sworn loyalty to so many years earlier. 'I have held official passes to seven major intelligence headquarters,' he told an audience in 1977. 'So I claim that this is the eighth major intelligence organisation which I have succeeded in penetrating.'[63] 'There was a terrible silence,' remembers Lyubimov and then a few angry whispers before Philby added that where before he had been surrounded by wolves, this time it was by comrades. There was relieved and enthusiastic applause.

He took the gathered officers through his recruitment, explaining what had made his first case officer so appealing and how important his controller's patience had been in waiting for him slowly to establish his credentials so that he could eventually join the Secret Service. He also gave them a piece of advice: never confess if confronted – an interesting remark given that he had provided half a confession to Elliott in Beirut. KGB officers found Philby very different from Blake. Blake clung to the belief that his work had not led to the death of any agents. Philby knew it had 'and it didn't seem to bother him'. It was a war, a Cold one perhaps, but a war nevertheless.[64]

There was only one Englishman and one former member of MI6 who truly understood Philby. Some friendships could survive betrayal. When Graham Greene came out to visit, it had been thirty-five years since the two had last met. Both were nervous. Greene sat silent in the car as it approached Philby's Moscow apartment.[65] When he walked in, they hugged each other and clapped each other on the back. The vodka came out and two greying old men talked about what they had done in the war. Greene had written an introduction to Philby's 1968 memoir, *My Silent War*, which was remarkable in its defence of his old colleague. Greene wrote of how he had been dismayed by Philby's brutal manoeuvring against a colleague and how he had seen it as pure ambition. 'I am glad now that I was wrong. He was serving a cause and not himself and so my old liking for him comes back.' Greene offered a strange defence of Philby. It was like English Catholics who had helped Spain, he wrote, and who would have had to live through the Inquisition. What mattered to Greene was that Philby had acted out of belief and not self-interest. He even later defended his role in the deaths of the agents sent by boat to Albania. 'They were going into their country armed to do damage to that country. They were killed instead of killing.'[66] The introduction was a very public message – you are still my friend.

Greene had also sent Philby a draft of a novel he had waited many years to write. *The Human Factor* was the story of an MI6 officer who betrays his service to the Soviets, but for love not ideology. The hero-of-sorts falls for the girl in Africa not Austria, but, as with Philby, the die had been cast from that moment. Philby said the one thing he disliked was the portrayal of the drab life in Moscow for the man after he is forced to flee Britain. Greene did not change anything.[67] The same year the book came out, he had been asked what he would have done if he had known of Philby's treason in the 1940s. 'I think perhaps, if in a drunken moment he had let slip a hint, I would have given him twenty-four hours to get clear and then reported it,' he replied.[68] For Greene, there was always the fascination with intelligence as a game in which human motivations were played out.

> The 'turning' of a KGB man, for instance, would never surprise me, because the profession can become a sort of game as abstract as chess: the spy takes more interest in the mechanics of his calling than its ultimate goal – the defence of his country. The 'game' (a serious game) achieves such a degree of sophistication that the player loses sight of his moral values. I can understand a man's temptation to turn double agent, for the game becomes more interesting.

When it came to Philby, Greene added that he still admired the way his friend had played the game and especially his constancy. 'I myself would not be capable of such courage, of such a force of conviction.'[69]

That day in Moscow, the two men realised that a deep bond lay between them. Yet it was not faith but doubt. 'He is burdened by doubt as well,' Philby told Rufina afterwards.[70] Greene had cited one of his heroes Monsignor Quixote: 'Sharing a sense of doubt can bring men together perhaps even more than sharing a faith.' Greene was never a Communist, Philby never a Christian. But both men understood the other's faith and with it the awareness of a chasm of doubt which, if fallen into, would render their lives as lived meaningless. 'For the first time, we were able to speak frankly with each other.' Philby had been used by the KGB in the first years after arriving, including not just writing his own book but also ghosting Gordon Lonsdale's, 'but when they didn't use me, the doubt crept in,' he later said.[71] Greene was excoriated in the British press for his dinner ('morally on a par with having a holiday with Dr Goebbels while this country was at war with Nazi Germany', said the *Daily Mail*) but he went back three more times.[72] For others the treachery remained too much. In the late 1980s, John le Carré was allowed into Russia and received a message at a party saying that a 'great admirer' Kim Philby wanted to meet him. 'It was a horrific suggestion,' le Carré later explained. 'I couldn't possibly have shook his hand. It was drenched in blood. It would have been repulsive.'[73]

Was friendship Greene's only motivation? He kept in touch with MI6 long after leaving and did the occasional job for them.[74] He passed on to the service the letters and postcards he received from Philby, once saying, 'Well, if there was anything political in it, I knew that Kim would know that I would pass it on to Maurice Oldfield, so it was either information or disinformation.'[75] The friendship may have been real between the two men but it also might have been useful for the service to know what the old boy was thinking and also to keep a channel open in case he ever wanted to change sides again and get out. The Soviets certainly worried about the latter possibility. They sometimes wondered if he had fooled them all along, like he had fooled everyone else. Yet until his death in 1988 Philby always remained an Englishman in his manners but a Communist in his beliefs, willing to criticise both worlds but ultimately loyal to the latter. Even his former KGB controller was never quite sure about Philby. 'In the end I suspect that Philby made a mockery of everyone, particularly ourselves.'[76] When Philby died, Lyubimov would mourn the departure of a friend. But he would also be living with his own experience of the bitterness of betrayal as another of his friends had become the man who gave MI6 their opportunity to avenge the past.

7

ESCAPE FROM MOSCOW

It was June 1985. As he opened the door of his Moscow apartment, Mikhail Lyubimov did not need to draw on his largely redundant spy skills to realise that something was wrong. Tension was etched on to the face of the old friend who stood on his doorstep. There were too many beads of sweat even for the stifling city heat of a Moscow summer.[1] Lyubimov was an outsider now. A second divorce and an independent streak was enough to draw the ire of the hard-liners in the KGB who had forced his departure a few years earlier. He had embarked on a new career as a writer.[2] But his visitor was still an insider and he was not supposed to be in Moscow. He was supposed to be in London.

The lean KGB officer stepped into the kitchen and turned on the tap. 'What are you doing?' Lyubimov asked, thinking that he was trying to drown out any conversation if anyone was listening in. He just needed a drink, the man explained. He was in a bad way. His throat was dry. The vodka came out.

Memories had begun to pierce the fog that enveloped Oleg Gordievsky's mind and that shrouded events of a few days earlier. The journey to a small guesthouse on the outskirts of Moscow and the offer of some Armenian brandy was clear. But after that there were only brief, malevolent flashes like a dark forest lit up by lightning strikes. There were the faces of the men staring at him and the words 'confess' repeated again and again. He had been drugged, he knew. But what had he said? He remembered a kind of euphoria that had come over him after the brandy which left him laughing and arguing and talking expansively with no nervousness or fear. He knew he had been close to breaking. He knew they were on to him.

As the memories slowly fought their way to the surface, Gordievsky had begun to recall more of what had been said.

'Why do you have all those anti-Soviet volumes – Solzhenitsyn, Orwell, Maximov and the rest?' the voice asked him.

'But of course,' he heard himself say, 'as a PR [Political Reporting] Line officer I was supposed to read books like that.'

'You used your diplomatic status to import things you knew were illegal in this country.'[3]

There were other accusations that had also seeped into his consciousness before he arrived at Lyubimov's apartment which he did not now mention to his friend.

'We know very well that you have been deceiving us for years,' they had said. 'We know you were a British agent. You'd better confess.' Confess, the man said again and again. You've already done it, just do it again, they said, talking slowly as if to a child.

'No, I've nothing to confess,' Gordievsky could recall replying. He did not mention these exchanges, only the books, to his friend. Gordievsky and Lyubimov had bought the banned books together years earlier when their friendship had been forged serving overseas, happier times when both men were rising through the ranks of the KGB. Those were days when Gordievsky had knocked on Lyubimov's door and walked in with a batch of telegrams from Moscow Centre and the latest gossip, not with a bottle of vodka and talk of interrogation. Lyubimov, unaware of how serious events were, tried to reassure his friend that even if he was fired it was not the end of the world. 'I had to leave the KGB,' he explained. 'Find something interesting to do. It may be a blessing.' Once Gordievsky had left, Lyubimov hurried to find his copies of Solzhenitsyn, wrapped them in plastic and buried them in the garden. Just in case.[4]

The KGB was family to Gordievsky, but not everyone loves or is loyal to their kin. His father and brother had both served in its ranks. But within his home lay the seeds of mistrust which would lead to betrayal. His father was a committed Communist who never spoke to his son of his work. But the young Gordievsky could sometimes glimpse the fear that lay hidden beneath the loyalty. In the late 1930s his father had watched friends and colleagues in the NKVD, the KGB's forerunner, being arrested as part of the great purges that engulfed the Soviet state. Some had been executed, others exiled to Siberia. The father would repeat the mantra 'The NKVD is always right,' but the son would remember the dread that lay beneath the profession of faith. Sometimes the young Oleg would overhear his parents arguing in their bedroom about politics, the only place they could talk freely.[5] His mother was not a true believer in the cause; she was more willing to question and criticise. She could see the intrigues and the brutality that her husband, perhaps for self-protection, chose not to speak of. For Oleg the combination of fascination and fear of the secret state came young.

The interwoven strands of loyalty and mistrust coexisted in the young man as he grew up and went to college, planning on a career in the Foreign Ministry. On the surface he was a normal *Homo Sovieticus*, able to live under the doublethink that George Orwell described in *Nineteen Eighty-Four*, toeing the party line in public, thinking more freely in private. Parents would warn children what to joke about, especially outside the home. When he studied languages at college, Gordievsky noticed that many other students chose not to read Western newspapers even when they were finally allowed to for fear of being seen as overly interested in 'subversive' views. Gordievsky was curious enough to read them and began to open his mind.

The unusual opportunity of six months' work experience abroad bought Gordievsky's ticket on a train that arrived in Berlin late on the evening of 11 August 1961. The talk in the city was of refugees heading west by the thousand. 'Don't go out anywhere,' he was warned by an Embassy official the next evening. By morning, barbed wire was rising across the city, marking the ugly, painful birth of the Berlin Wall. He watched the violence which met those who tried to escape its rise. The reality that coercion rather than consent underpinned Communism was being laid bare before his eyes and yet he was still enough of his father's son to take up the offer to work with the instrument of repression, the KGB. The lure of foreign travel, the excitement of emptying dead-letter boxes and the thrill of meeting deep-cover illegal agents was too strong a pull for the adventurous young man, even if the first doubts had taken root.

Next came marriage to Yelena and a first foreign posting to Copenhagen, a taste of the West. The small liberties were what struck him – the opportunity to listen to church music, or to borrow whatever books you wanted from a library. Gordievsky's cover was in the consular department but his real task was supporting the illegals in the country, checking dead-letter boxes and signal sites. It was also here that his friendship with Mikhail Lyubimov began. After Her Majesty's Government had declared him persona non grata, Lyubimov had found his way to Copenhagen and the position of deputy resident. He had initially missed the bright lights and glamour of London's streets and parties but slowly began to find some compensation in the bracing walks, fresh fish and unstuffiness of Danish life. The two men, both educated at the Institute of International Relations, recognised an independent, free-thinking streak in each other – although Gordievsky's would take him to a place Lyubimov would not follow. They considered themselves to be different from some of the more thuggish zealots of the KGB. In the evening, the Embassy club showed Russian films and served cheap vodka, but the two men often opted out in favour of classical music and conversation.[6] Both agreed that banning the dissident writer Solzhenitsyn had been a mistake. That the two men felt comfortable enough in each other's company to talk politics was a sign of genuine trust, since a report to superiors about an indiscretion could be terminal for a career.

The two KGB officers had watched in curious trepidation in 1968 as liberal reformers in Czechoslovakia first began to open the country up. This had turned to horror as the Soviet tanks went in to crush the 'Prague Spring' and with it hopes of socialism with a human face. For Gordievsky, the feeling of alienation from the system he served went deeper as he watched crowds gather and hurl missiles at the Embassy in Copenhagen. The seeds of dissent planted earlier in life and nurtured by the sight of the Wall going up in 1961 had grown into a deep-seated but clandestine conviction that he no longer wanted to work for a 'criminal' regime. He needed to cleanse his conscience. But rather than resign he wanted to subvert from within and started to think about how to offer himself up to his enemies. 'They've done it! It's unbelievable,' he told his wife over the phone as the tanks made their way through Prague. 'I just don't know what to do.' He knew the phone would be tapped and hoped that someone would pick up on his comments. But before anyone acted, his time in Denmark was up and by January 1970 he was back in Moscow. Events in London then intervened. In the wake of Oleg Lyalin's 1971 defection in London and the expulsion of 105 Soviet intelligence officers, Gordievsky's department, which covered Scandinavia as well as Britain, was shaken up. The Danes expelled three 'diplomats' and suddenly in October 1972 he had an opportunity to return to Copenhagen.

For his second Danish tour, Gordievsky switched to Line PR of the KGB – reporting on politics. Lyubimov returned a year or two later as resident, allowing the two men to resume their conversations over long walks in the Danish woods. Copenhagen may have lacked London's pizzazz but at least now Lyubimov was the boss, he reflected. A black Mercedes ferried him to the set of white villas surrounded by gardens which made up the Soviet Embassy just to the north of the city centre. The KGB offices were on the first floor (to prevent tunnelling). A concealed bell had to be rung to gain entry. Lyubimov had his own office in which he hung portraits of his twin heroes, Lenin and Philby, the latter with an inscription from the British spy wishing him luck. 'Your silver-framed portrait hangs directly above our officer counter near the portrait of the Gods. If my office were raided it would be evidence enough to have me declared persona non grata,' Lyubimov wrote to Philby, also sending the odd jar of marmalade, some whisky, once even a book of nine-teenth-century erotic pictures.[7] Lyubimov spent his days con-templating what pitches and dangles to play on the Americans, whose Embassy was separated from his own by only a few hundred yards and a graveyard. His thoughts would be interrupted by the occasional knock on the door and his lean, strong-jawed deputy would enter.

Gordievsky was Lyubimov's right-hand man. There was no reason to doubt his loyalty. He was always respectful and kept Lyubimov informed of what he was doing, even down to when he was setting off to play badminton. But his loyalty was a lie. Beneath the calm surface, a profound conversion had taken him down a path he had long contemplated. The human factor had also worked along the grain of ideology. Gordievsky's marriage was breaking down. His wife had embraced feminism and said she did not want children. He had become privately convinced of his decision to work for the other side but had been unsure how to make the approach. A brazen walk into an embassy might be rebuffed, he feared. Then the other side made its move.

On the evening of 2 November 1973 there was a knock on the door of his flat. A Hungarian he had known from Moscow was at the door. Over a whisky, he gave a roundabout story to explain why he happened to be in Denmark and had chosen to drop by. Gordievsky sensed something was up, especially when the man said he had defected from Hungary in 1970. There were nerves on both sides, but they agreed to have lunch the next day. At the lunch, Gordievsky was careful not to show his hand too much, remaining non-committal. Then there was nothing for three weeks. MI6 finally took the plunge at one of Gordievsky's regular badminton games. In the middle of the game, a man appeared in an overcoat. Gordievsky immediately recognised him as Rob, a forty-something self-confident British diplomat. Gordievsky was surprised by the brazenness of the gambit and broke away from his game to ask what the man wanted. Rob said it would be good to meet and they planned lunch in three days. Gordievsky understood that he had to play it carefully with his own Embassy and informed them of the approach. He was given official permission to meet. Over lunch, the two men chatted warily but amiably.

'Of course you will write a report about our meeting,' Rob said at the end.

'Yes I will, but I will write it in such a way that nothing serious will be said in it,' Gordievsky replied.[8] It was a hint. But then there was nothing. For nearly a year British intelligence failed to reel in the fish that had taken their bait. They were 'quite timid', Gordievsky would later say.[9] The reason was that they thought he was literally too good to be true. The KGB man had to be a dangle, a plant, luring them into a trap. Gordievsky had deliberately tried to provoke an approach and that seemed suspicious to an intelligence service still saturated by a fear of moles, double agents and deception. But after a year Rob appeared again at the badminton court and suggested a meeting. Finally, in a bar at an upmarket hotel, the two men began to open up. 'Now, Mr Gordievsky. It is dangerous to meet here,' he said. Gordievsky understood that the opening up of a clandestine path was also the offer of betrayal. 'The Russians do not come here,' Gordievsky replied, crossing an invisible line that both spies understood. An agreement was made to meet at a more secure venue on the outskirts of Copenhagen. This was to be the point of no return.

But at the meeting the limits of British knowledge were still clear.

'You're KGB,' Rob said.

'Of course.'

'Tell me, then. Who is the PR Line Deputy in your station?'

Gordievsky stared and smiled before saying, 'I am.' But behind the smiles he was nervous.

At their next meeting, Rob introduced a tall, well-built MI6 officer and explained that he would be Gordievsky's case officer. It is common practice to use one officer to carry out the recruitment of an agent and then another to run them. While a few individuals can manage to be both 'hunters' and 'farmers', MI6 officers are carefully assessed to see if they are more suited to either recruiting or running and to doing so in a particular environment. In the Middle East a brazen, confident pitch might be expected by the recipient while with Soviet officials even an invitation to dinner might be considered far too forward. The emphasis with them was instead on being perceptive about the small signs that someone might be just that bit different and willing to take risks, perhaps by having a local girlfriend. It was more about being receptive so that a Soviet official understood they could talk to you if they wanted to. Many MI6 officers wondered how Rob had managed to recruit the service's most important agent as they considered him rather unimpressive, but his sensitive manner had ensured that Gordievsky found him easy to talk to. In Gordievsky's case there was an added factor. It was not the British who had spotted him first but the Danes. They had decided that Gordievsky looked interesting and had studied him for some time, but they realised they were not in a position to recruit him and run him properly. That would require Russian-speakers, resources and an established infrastructure. They worked closely and had a good relationship with the British (closer than with the Americans, who sometimes exhibited a tendency to ride roughshod over local services) and so had reached out. Running Gordievsky in Denmark would be much easier for MI6 with local help.

The tall new officer was the man who would run Gordievsky, but their opening meeting was a disaster. Gordievsky did not take to the unsmiling figure and found him vain and pushy. Gordievsky's English was poor, so the two men spoke German. The MI6 officer nearly blew the whole affair with an aggressive, hostile approach, pounding Gordievsky verbally with question after question about KGB operations. 'Why is he so aggressive? I came with an open soul,' Gordievsky thought. He was unsure what to do but told himself to calm down and suppress the feelings of disappointment. This man cannot be typical of the British, he thought.[10]

It was only decades later that Gordievsky learnt the reason for his aggression. When they finally met again, Rob, who had recruited him, would confess that he had been convinced Gordievsky was a double agent and had filed reports strongly expressing that view. 'From the start to the finish, I thought you were an agent provocateur,' he later told Gordievsky, explaining that he simply could not believe that any KGB officer could be so willing to provide so much and be so open (although the KGB almost never used its own officers as agents provocateurs since they knew too much and might decide to turn for real).[11] But once MI6 officers saw the volume and quality of Gordievsky's reporting, they soon changed their mind.

Gordievsky was discomfited by the British aggression but he had made his choice. He said he did not want to do anything to hurt his colleagues in Copenhagen and he did not want any money. He wanted to do it for belief.[12] The British failed to appreciate the depth of his ideological conversion, and his case officer occasionally brought newspaper cuttings designed to show the Soviets in a bad light. Back at the Embassy, Lyubimov never suspected a thing. 'He was very tactful. He showed his loyalty from time to time,' he says of his friend. 'He was very attentive.'

And so it began. The rushed meetings in Danish flats. The gradual softening of the relationship with his case officer until, after two years, he was replaced with a more amenable officer. The relief, bordering on euphoria, of having finally embarked on the path he wanted to walk coupled with the perpetual fear of being discovered with a camera in hand and secrets on film. The fear ratcheted up a level when a KGB agent in Norway was arrested thanks to his assistance and word got round that there might be a leak. Eventually his tour was up and it was time to return to Moscow. One problem was a divorce from his wife and a new relationship. This was awkward in KGB circles. Fortunately, Gordievsky's boss and friend helped him out. Lyubimov warned him of trouble and promised to help by sending favourable reports to Moscow on his work, saying that he was a good candidate for promotion and particularly for the job of deputy head of the Third Department of the First Chief Directorate.[13] There would be no hushed meetings and clandestine contacts between Gordievsky and the British in Moscow. Even with the strictest Moscow Rules, it would have been suicidal. Everyone who had tried it had been captured. Two decades on, the lesson of Penkovsky – that the KGB was dominant on its home turf – was still keenly felt.

Then came one of those strokes of luck which a good intelligence operation needs. In late 1981, a job came up in London. Slots were precious and hard to come by following the 1971 expulsion. The arrival of a visa application for an Oleg Gordievsky was met with intense excitement at Century House, MI6's grey tower-block headquarters south of the river where it had moved from Broadway in the mid-1960s (and which looked more like something out of the Soviet Union than most of its denizens would care to admit). Having been too cautious early on, MI6 was now nearly too eager, the visa being granted a few days more quickly than normal. In preparation for his arrival, Gordievsky was allowed to study the existing KGB files on its past operations in Britain, heroic accounts of the 'Magnificent' Cambridge Five and the other moles and spies that had riddled the British establishment. He paid very close attention.

The city that Gordievsky watched out of the window of the Embassy car that crawled through the traffic from Heathrow in June 1982 was a world away from the clean, compact openness of Copenhagen. It was big, smelly, sprawling and dirty. Where Lyubimov had been enthralled by his London of the 1960s, Gordievsky was initially shocked by the country to which he had offered his loyalty but in which he had never set foot. That year unemployment had topped three million for the first time since the 1930s as Thatcherism began to bite. But the Iron Lady's popularity had skyrocketed thanks to victory against Argentina in the Falklands War that spring.

Gordievsky never had any doubts he was following the right path ideologically. But it was his personal ties that introduced the only moments of intensely private questioning. He was arriving in London with his second wife and two daughters. He had embarked on his clandestine life as a British agent when his first marriage was on the rocks. Now, he sometimes looked at his wife and daughters and occasionally wondered where his path would lead. 'What have I done? How do I get out of this?' he thought to himself. He knew there was no way out. Sometimes he felt the urge to tell his wife. One time he was bitterly criticising some decision in Moscow and she told him to stop. 'You cannot do something about it,' she said. 'Maybe I can do something. Maybe one day you will see that I was able to do something about it,' he replied. He nearly went further but stopped himself. Her mother and father worked for the KGB. What if she betrayed him? Even if she would not do that, would it not be safer for her not to know in case she was ever questioned? He never shared these moments of doubt with his MI6 case officers and they never suspected.[14]

On his second night in London, he went to a phone box and called a number. A tape recording was waiting on the other end. If an agent surfaces anywhere in the world there is usually an attempt initially to reconnect him with his old case officer even if he has moved on. The next time Gordievsky called, his last handler from Denmark answered and they met in Sloane Street. He was to meet in the lobby of a hotel and then follow him to his car. They then drove to a safe flat in Bayswater. The man explained that he was now posted abroad but had come back to pass Gordievsky over to his new case officer.

Like handing over a priceless vase, the process of passing an agent from one officer to another is a delicate procedure. Agents rely on their handlers as the only person they can confide in, and so poor chemistry, as Gordievsky had encountered at the start, can lead to a stumble and perhaps a fall. Gordievsky's new case officer was only in his mid-thirties but with the first hint that the dark hair was receding. He was a details man who had a natural empathy and an understanding of Russian which meant Gordievsky took to him straight away.

John Scarlett has never publicly confirmed that he was the officer assigned to Gordievsky. MI6 has never even formally acknowledged that Gordievsky was its agent. It never publicly confirms or denies the identity of anyone who has spied for it for a simple, utilitarian reason. While the CIA will always be able to offer more cash to lure potential spies motivated by money, the British argue that they maintain their own competitive niche in the spies' marketplace by offering something that some spies may treasure even more highly than money – the promise of secrecy and of never revealing their identity. This, oddly, applies even when an agent identifies themselves publicly and, in Gordievsky's case, even after they receive an honour from the Queen, a CMG for 'services to the security of the United Kingdom', the same honour, it was noted at the time, that James Bond received in fiction.[15]

Scarlett, a doctor's son, had grown up in South London and read history at Oxford before joining MI6 in 1971. His first posting was to Nairobi where a letter from Shergy, then head of personnel, informed him that he had been chosen to learn Russian before being sent to the Soviet Union, a sign that he was being fast-tracked and that those above him thought he had what it took to play by Moscow Rules. 'Running agents in the old Soviet Union was an extremely difficult thing to do and it was very stressful and it could be very exciting,' Scarlett explained in a BBC interview.[16] 'There was huge attention to detail, very careful case management, very careful tradecraft, very careful planning. So it was not easy.'

Moscow and the Soviet Union lay at the heart of Scarlett's career and eventually provided his path to the top of the service. But his cover was blown early, according to Russian reports.[17] On his arrival in Moscow he inherited an agent in the Soviet navy. Unfortunately, the officer was a plant under Soviet control being used to identify members of the MI6 station. Having your cover as an MI6 officer blown when still in your twenties is normally a minor disaster, restricting your ability to carry out undercover assignments. When Scarlett had to go back behind the Iron Curtain to meet an agent he had to go in disguise and under so-called natural cover, posing as someone else rather than working as a diplomat. On one occasion, he went in disguise to meet an agent in a claustrophobically small safe flat. 'The agent arrived. He was very nervous, understandably, so my job was to make him less nervous,' Scarlett recounted later. 'I explained that in order to be doubly, doubly sure that we weren't under any observation – which in itself was a bit disconcerting for him to think that we might be – we went into the bathroom and then to make doubly, doubly sure that the bathroom was covered as well

I turned on the taps and had the running water going on in the background. And after about three minutes I realised that he was sweating profusely and I was beginning to too and I thought, "I knew he was nervous, I didn't realise he was going to be that nervous." Then of course I noticed that I had boiling hot water coming out of the taps and the place was absolutely sweltering.' With a turn of the hand, Scarlett became the spy who turned on the cold and finished the meeting.

The problem of being a Russian specialist already identified by the enemy ended up working to the advantage of Scarlett in the early 1980s. It had made him the ideal officer working out of the London station to deal with a Russian-speaking KGB officer who was arriving in the capital. It was the kind of assignment that could make a career. Dealing with Penkovsky had required quick-footed improvisation by MI6. That operation had been mounted in a rush at a time when the amateurism of the past had yet to be fully excised. Shergy's legacy was that by the late 1970s and early 1980s, the professionalism he had engendered had been institutionalised and MI6 was able to run a valuable agent like Gordievsky for close to a decade. For those engaged in the task there was also a clandestine thrill beyond the ins and outs of the intelligence produced. This, they felt, was payback for Philby.

For Scarlett and every other officer who sat in a room with him listening to secrets pouring out, Gordievsky was the best agent they ever dealt with. 'It is quite likely the agent is taking a great risk and a great chance and he's placing a great deal in the hands of the case officer so he has to trust him,' Scarlett later noted when discussing such relationships. 'He has to have confidence in his judgement; he has to have confidence in his ability to run the matter securely ... the case officer has to have an adequate degree of expertise in the subject with which he is dealing and of course he has to be backed up – as he is – by teamwork ... All successful operations are the result of teamwork, although of course when it comes to it, it may well be that the meeting itself takes place between the individual case officer and the individual agent.'[18] Running Gordievsky was a full-time job but one carried out with back-up.

The meetings with Gordievsky largely took place in a safe flat in Bayswater, West London. Gordievsky would arrive by car during his lunch-hour bearing whatever documents he had removed from the Embassy in nearby Kensington. A few sandwiches and a bottle of beer would be waiting on the table alongside a tape recorder. They only had an hour, so a support officer, known to Gordievsky as Joan, would photograph and copy the documents while Scarlett and Gordievsky talked in Russian. The support officer was a crucial member of the team and offered a subsidiary relationship so that an agent was not overly dependent on one person. Joan was in the Daphne Park mould. She had joined as a secretary before becoming a general officer. A genteel, Home Counties exterior masked a steely determination and a deep expertise in tradecraft. Scarlett, and others later, would defer to her on the details as she organised the timings, transport and logistics. She remained when Scarlett moved on after two years, and Gordievsky would eventually owe much to her.

The nerves always came for Gordievsky as the meeting approached its end and he knew it was time to return to the Embassy. Security was the primary concern. 'John would ask me, "Where's the car? Is it in the basement underneath or did you leave it in the street?"' he later recalled. Gordievsky would sometimes have to admit sheepishly he had left it in the street. The security worries were real even in London. One day as he left, he saw the big black car of his KGB Resident drive past. Gordievsky returned to the Embassy fearing that he would be questioned, but he had not been spotted. Scarlett and Gordievsky would meet once a week, although there was much debate in Century House over whether that was too often. As with Penkovsky, there was a tension between the desire to extract as much as possible from such a unique source and the awareness that every meeting – even in London – carried a risk.

Almost everything Gordievsky said during those meetings met the standard of being classed intelligence 'product'. Scarlett would work through the transcript straight away, often issuing ten reports from each meeting within a day or two, the most urgent ones first which would arrive in Whitehall in-trays. It was as if MI6 had tapped into a rich seam and a gush of intelligence was pouring out which needed to be captured. There had been nothing like it since Penkovsky, but with two crucial differences. Gordievsky lasted much, much longer and was far more emotionally stable, easier to work with and better disciplined. The circle who knew about Gordievsky even within MI6 was tiny as they worked within a secret unit, even under cover within their own organisation. The reports officer who processed the incoming intelligence and distributed it to others in government was believed by most colleagues to be working on material from Russia.

Gordievsky's insights were in two main areas. One was on the work of the KGB in London, classic counter-intelligence information about the operations of the enemy. The other was politics and strategy in Moscow. When it came to the former, the KGB station in London lacked the scale and swagger it had had in Lyubimov's time, but it still kept itself busy trying to recruit agents and maintain a network of illegals. Before Gordievsky arrived, Lukasevics, the man who had lured Anthony Cavendish's Latvians to their doom after the Second World War, had just left as resident and been replaced by the hulking form of Arkadi Guk. In Gordievsky's eyes he was 'a huge, bloated lump of a man, with a mediocre brain but a large reserve of low cunning' who plotted against his own Ambassador while drinking neat vodka.[19] Guk ordered his staff not to use the Underground – because, he said, behind the adverts were secret spying booths for MI5. Some officers were even convinced that a tunnel had been dug below to target the Embassy. The obsession with being watched and listened to created the type of deeply paranoid atmosphere that pervaded the CIA in Moscow in the 1950s and 1960s. Guk's office had special windows and jamming devices with radio loudspeakers installed in the space between the double glazing. Now and again, KGB technicians from Moscow would come in and strip the offices and then line them again with new substances to repel the bugs. A metal-lined conference room would become unbearably hot when crammed with staff for a meeting. In this environment, seeking out agents in British public life continued with only mixed success and a large degree of healthy exaggeration in reports back to Moscow.

The reality of life and work for the KGB in London was passed on by Gordievsky. 'The amount of information about the Soviet intrigues of different character was piling on my desk. So I had to select the most important and the most dangerous points and tell them about them orally. Tape recorder was on the table and John Scarlett was ... listening.'[20] Scarlett would absorb every detail of life within the protected walls of the Residency. 'You are an extra member of the KGB Residency,' Gordievsky would joke with Scarlett, a remark that would no doubt have excited the molehunters of the past if they had heard it.

Gordievsky was able to identify a number of agents who were talking to the KGB, although the truth was that the cupboard was pretty bare and the successes were greatly exaggerated in order to enhance officers' careers. Most of the KGB's real spies now focused on technical and scientific intelligence, received in exchange for money. There were also many 'paper agents' who were kept on the books in order to make officers look busy to Moscow. Additionally, many individuals were listed as 'confidential contacts', a level below 'recruited agents'. With a confidential contact, a KGB officer might take someone to lunch and then write up a report on the gossip and information produced, the kind of work diplomats and journalists do all the time. The informant might have no idea the Russian was a KGB officer or that anything they said was being written up. Some might also receive a nice fat envelope now and again, which should perhaps have raised their suspicions. Moscow Centre might also be told that such an agent was being carefully cultivated and was close to being recruited as a proper spy (that point coming when they agreed to secret collaboration with the KGB).[21] KGB officers had to fill in immensely long questionnaires on their targets and it could always be claimed that a few more good lunches on expenses were needed before making the final pitch. Gordievsky had learnt from Lyubimov how in London in the 1960s he had recruited contacts and treated them as secret agents, using the 'paraphernalia' of espionage. 'Why did you bother with all that cover stuff?' Gordievsky once asked Lyubimov. 'Why didn't you just have overt relationships with them?' Lyubimov had explained that Moscow expected agents to be treated like that and also that using dead-letter drops made the agent feel that they were important, drawing them into the excitement of being a spy.

But even though there were few high-level agents, Gordievsky was able to lay to rest some of the fears that had warped the life of British intelligence since the days of Philby and his friends. He confirmed that John Cairncross, the Cambridge-educated former civil servant, had indeed been the fifth man and that there were no further high-level penetrations. This included Roger Hollis, just as word of the investigation into him was emerging into public view. In Moscow the media reports that he was one of their spies were met with bemusement. 'The story is ridiculous. There's some mysterious, internal British intrigue at the bottom of all this!' a KGB colleague told Gordievsky when they saw the British stories.[22]

Gordievsky's most important success in counter-intelligence was preventing the Soviets acquiring a new mole deep within MI5 and wreaking the same kind of damage they had managed in their golden age. In June 1983, Guk turned to Gordievsky. 'Would you like to see something exceptional?' the KGB boss asked him. He showed Gordievsky a British document outlining the 'order of battle' of the KGB and GRU in London. It was clear that it came from MI5 and from K branch – the team dedicated to working against Soviet spies. Guk revealed it had been pushed through the letterbox of his home in Holland Park, West London. It was the second packet to arrive, the first having come on Easter Sunday. The letter that accompanied the intelligence suggested a dead drop at the cistern of a cinema toilet on Oxford Street and was signed 'Koba', the name Stalin had used before the revolution.[23] Guk was faced with a once-in-a-lifetime opportunity to recruit a serving intelligence officer, to restore the station to its former glory. But he was convinced it was a trap. The traitor had thought he was being clever by passing on a staff list because he believed that Guk would be able to verify that it was true. But instead the Resident concluded that, precisely because it was something he already knew rather than fresh intelligence, it was the sign of a plant. Part of the problem was that, compared with those carefree days in the 1960s that Lyubimov had revelled in, the KGB had now become smaller and more cautious in London, less willing to take risks, more worried about what the other side knew.

Gordievsky called for a meeting with the British when he heard the news. He told MI6 he realised this must be a game – a double agent or a plant by them to lure Guk into a trap. Scarlett and the team knew it was not and broke the news calmly to him. They had a problem. The revelation of an aspiring traitor inside MI5 meant that a spy-hunt was needed. But the old question once again arose – how could MI5 investigate itself? In this case there was an answer. The person offering the information had clearly not known that Gordievsky was spying for Britain or else they would never have risked an approach to the Residency. A very small number of MI5 officers who worked on the KGB desk had been indoctrinated into the secret of Gordievsky's true loyalty. The traitor could not possibly be one of them, because if they had been they would have tipped off Guk to Gordievsky or avoided approaching the KGB in London knowing there was a British agent in place who would betray the move. So a team was formed out of this small group of officers. If ever there was an example of why the identities of agents have to be restricted to a 'need to know' basis, this was it. If Gordievsky's identity and activities had become common currency in MI5, he would have been betrayed and on a plane back to Moscow with a firing squad waiting for him. Gordievsky did return to Moscow during the investigation for a holiday. He did so knowing that British intelligence was leaking somewhere, a display of remarkable confidence.

One of those assigned to work on the case was a female MI5 officer who had experienced an early introduction to the world of the molehunt. Eliza Manningham-Buller had seen her father as attorney general prosecute a previous generation of traitors, including George Blake. After Benenden School and then Oxford (playing the Fairy Godmother in a drama production), she had taught English until talent-spotted at a party. Her father had tried to dissuade his daughter from joining MI5. 'He thought it was a bit murky,' she later recalled. 'He thought the whole espionage and counter-espionage business was slightly sordid which, to a degree, he was right about.'[24] Her decision to ignore his entreaties may have had something to do with her mother having had a small taste of the secret life in the Second World War when she had trained carrier pigeons which would be dropped in France and then return to her Gloucestershire cottage carrying secret messages which would be quickly picked up by a despatch rider.[25] In 1974, Eliza had joined an organisation she found to be strangely inward looking. Despite her pedigree, she had been unsure quite what to expect. 'I hardly knew what I was joining because in those days it was much more secret,' she recalled later. 'When I arrived I was astonished – I was very naive I think – that this was an organisation that listened to people's telephone calls and opened their mail.'[26] MI5 was still stuck in the past. Former members of the Colonial Service who had once kept an eye on subversives in places like Malaya and India until independence and then needed a new job still dominated the organisation. The gloomy Leconfield House headquarters with its dirty windows suffered from the lethargy of some far-flung outpost. 'They would quite often go off at lunch-time for a drink and not come back till four o'clock,' recalls Stephen Lander, who joined in 1975. 'I remember one colleague used to shut his door at lunchtime, put on his bedroom slippers, put the phone in the drawer and have an hour's sleep ... I nearly left in my first year. I thought they were all mad.'[27]

Attitudes to women were also a throwback. 'When I joined, women were definitely lesser citizens,' recalls Manningham-Buller. 'We weren't allowed to do the full range of intelligence work. We weren't allowed, for example, to mount an eavesdropping operation. We weren't allowed to approach and try and recruit people because who would want to work for a woman? And there was a paternalistic attitude that we mustn't do anything to put the little dears in danger.'[28] With the arrival of a new generation of university graduates through the 1970s, attitudes began to change. 'These young men were indis-tinguishable from us women with degrees so after a time we bundled together and we had a quiet female revolution,' recalls Stella Rim-ington, who was one of the first women allowed to run agents and later became director general. 'We wrote a letter to the bosses. And the bosses scratched their heads at this ... a few women started to be promoted, barriers began to break down.'[29] Attitudes to MI6 had also begun to evolve. For many years, the foreign spies had enjoyed the touch of glamour, looking askance at the Security Service as super-annuated policemen in grubby macs who rooted around files. Mean-while, the MI5 officers viewed their cousins somewhat despairingly, perceiving a macho, individualistic and amateurish culture. But, slowly, joint working began to evolve, particularly on a case like Gordievsky and particularly when the evidence of a traitor arrived, sending a shockwave through both organisations.

Manningham-Buller had worked on the KGB desk analysing Gordievsky's output on Soviet activities in the UK, and so she was informed that close to her was a traitor. 'I felt very shaken by it. Because you have to work on the assumption – and most of the time it's entirely justified – that your colleagues are trustworthy people of integrity. And when you discover that you have somebody who doesn't fall into this category, it is a shock ... And it was one of the nastiest times in my career, particularly in the early days when you didn't know who it was, because you would get in the lift and look round and wonder.'[30]

There was a sense of intensity and urgency for the small team. This molehunt was the mirror image of that of the 1960s. Then Peter Wright and Arthur Martin had their suspects but were looking for evidence to back up their theories. This time, the evidence of betrayal was clear but the suspect was unknown. Meetings could not be held in MI5 headquarters in case the spy was alerted. So the London flat in Inner Temple of Eliza Manningham-Buller's now widowed mother was used as a place where MI6 and MI5 officers could gather. Her mother was never told why people were meeting there but guessed it was sensitive. When her other daughter asked to come round, she was told that she could not because of church meetings. 'One of my sisters complained that my mother had become obsessively religious with meetings apparently every other night,' Eliza recalled.[31]

Suspicions based on who had access to the documents Gordievsky had seen began to centre on Michael Bettaney. His behaviour was odd, he drank too much and he was a little too interested in certain files. Bettaney told one officer that even if the KGB were offered a 'golden apple' or 'peach' of a source, they would not take it. He speculated openly about Philby's and Blake's motives. The team followed him and had his house broken into in a desperate search for hard evidence. Signs emerged that he was planning to go to Vienna, possibly to approach a KGB officer there who had been expelled from London in 1971. The decision was taken to interrogate him before he left. It had to be done carefully to avoid in any way exposing the fact that Gordievsky had tipped off the British. Bettaney was on a training course run by MI6 when he was summoned for a meeting. He was taken to a flat in Gower Street. The evidence – such as it was – was laid out before him, including a photograph of Guk's door to suggest that Bettaney might have been photographed in the act (which he hadn't been). As in the days of Blake, the idea was to talk him into a confession at which point the police would be called in to hear it again formally (in the time of Blake and Vassall, Manningham-Buller's father was waiting literally next door for the formal process). Bettaney was not arrested, which would have led to his being offered a lawyer who no doubt would have told him to say nothing. He was kept overnight and the next morning Eliza Manningham-Buller cooked him a breakfast which he did not eat. Bettaney began to crack, first referring to a hypothetical spy who might have done these things and then moving into the first person in discussing events. He expressed some sympathy for 'Kim' and 'George', as he called Philby and Blake. Exhausted, he eventually said, 'I think I ought to make a clean breast of it,' and confessed all.[32]

Gordievsky, unlike Penkovsky, could offer relatively little on the Soviet military and its operations. But his reporting on the political and strategic thinking in Moscow proved highly influential and, like Penkovsky, extremely well timed. It took a while for MI6 to realise how acute Gordievsky's political observations were and how much he had to offer on the mindset of the Soviet leadership. By the 1970s, the 'train-spotters' of old who had counted tanks and the like had been replaced by highly effective signals and satellite intelligence. But that only told you so much. What did the Soviet leaders want to do with the tanks and missiles? The answer to that lay within their heads. While intercepted communications could tell you something of this, the real answers could come only from a spy to whom you could put questions. This had been a weakness. 'What we were less successful at is getting into the mindset of the leadership,' Scarlett explained. 'I remember when I was a young officer in Moscow in the 1970s reading this and that, trying to understand Soviet policy in various parts of the world, and thinking and saying "If only we knew what it was they were saying to each other when they discussed these issues and these policies in the politburo. If only we knew how they were developing policy towards Afghanistan." And it was very difficult to get into that mindset because there was so much propaganda and jargon around.' Gordievsky offered answers.

Early on in his time in London Gordievsky produced a report on Operation Ryan. It was very short and attracted only limited attention from both Gordievsky and the service. Scarlett was told by his predecessor to keep an eye on it when he took over. It was close to a year and a half before it became clear just how important it was. Ryan was a sign that the Cold War was once again going through one of its dangerous phases, not quite on the scale of the Cuban Missile Crisis when Penkovsky had operated, but not too far off either. Yuri Andropov, the former KGB chief turned Soviet leader, was convinced that the West was preparing a 'first strike' using nuclear weapons.[33] 'Reactionary imperialist groups in the USA have openly embarked on a course of confrontation,' read one top-secret KGB memo sent out to embassies; 'the threat of outbreak of a nuclear war has reached dangerous proportions.'[34] Moscow believed that President Reagan's rhetoric was designed to prepare the population for a nuclear war that the Americans hoped somehow to survive and win. As a result Andropov launched Ryan, the largest Soviet peacetime intelligence operation in history, run jointly by the KGB and the GRU. Its goal was to look for the warning signs that war was imminent. It was the same low-tech intelligence tripwire that MI6 had been building with its train-spotters in Vienna and that the JIC later developed into its Amber and Red Lists. The deployment to Germany of Pershing missiles which could reach Moscow in four to six minutes meant that Moscow was desperate for any sign of impending preparations for conflict.[35]

Gordievsky, like officers in embassies across the West, received a list of signs to look for. The indicators ranged from the substantive involving troop movements to the odd such as checking if there was a rise in the price of blood from donors because of the authorities buying up supplies for wartime to treat burns from nuclear fall-out. No one had noticed that in the West blood was not paid for but donated free of charge. Another idea was to count how many lights were left on at the Ministry of Defence at night. An increase in the number would show that civil servants were planning something. Many staff in residencies abroad, including Gordievsky, treated this as just another stupid order from headquarters which they had to comply with rather than argue about. So they all duly reported even the smallest hint of preparations for war in order to keep their superiors happy. One problem was that their superiors then believed every sign, an indication of a frequent problem in which those living insulated lives at the top understand less than those seeing reality on the ground.

The West had thought that the alarmist language coming out of the Soviet Union was just that. Now, thanks to Gordievsky, they realised that it reflected a real underlying fear which their assessments had not picked up. Part of the problem was that the Soviets were listening to the American rhetoric and watching US actions with increasing alarm, as President Reagan talked in 1983 of an 'evil empire' and of the Soviet leadership being the 'focus of evil in the modern world'. A few weeks after that statement he announced his ambitious Star Wars Strategic Defense Initiative, which threatened to undermine the notion of mutually assured destruction that had kept the balance of fear in place. Reagan's strategy of putting pressure on the Soviets through an arms race (in addition to psychological tactics like probing gaps in air defence) was working, but it also carried risks if pushed too far. The combination of fear and ignorance was potentially catastrophic. A top-secret Soviet plan outlining KGB priorities for 1984 talked of imperialist intrigues in Poland and Afghanistan, arguing that 'the threat of an outbreak of nuclear war is reaching an extremely dangerous point' and warning of an 'unprecedented sharpening of the struggle'.[36] It was a surprise attack the Soviets feared most.

The realisation of just how catastrophic this misunderstanding could be came in November 1983. NATO was running a high-level command exercise codenamed 'Able Archer'. Gordievsky and others across Europe received 'Most Urgent' flash telegrams from Moscow. The Soviets feared that the exercise might be a prelude to a real attack with the exercise used to mask the preparations (a tactic the Soviets themselves had contemplated). When Gordievsky passed on the reporting, the reaction in London was one of alarm, particularly as officials saw signals intelligence which dovetailed with and was explained by Gordievsky's reports. Part of the Soviet land-based missile force went on to its own heightened alert. The world was not on the brink of war but there was a danger that, as in the First World War, mobilisations and preparations could be embarked on from which no one could back down. No one had realised just how scared the Soviets were about an imminent attack or just how blind they were in terms of intelligence about the real thinking and plans of the West, a mirror image of Western blindness in Vienna at the dangerous start of the Cold War.[37] 'There was a degree of misunderstanding and fear among the Soviet leadership which we had underestimated,' argues Scarlett. 'And that was a bit of a wake-up call – [you have] got to be careful how you manage tension, you mustn't let it get too acute. We didn't understand the extent to which the Soviet leadership didn't understand us.'[38]

Prime Minister Margaret Thatcher was one of only a handful of people outside MI6 to know that a senior KGB officer in London was offering up secrets. A fan of Frederick Forsyth novels, she took a close interest in intelligence (preferring the hardliners of MI6 to the 'wimps' at the Foreign Office) and in the Gordievsky reporting specifically. It was among the only raw intelligence, known as red-jackets because of the folders in which it came, that found its way on to her desk, courtesy of her Foreign Affairs Adviser Charles Powell, who acted as a filter. The papers would be put into a blue box for which only the Prime Minister, Powell and Robin Butler, her Civil Service private secretary, had the key. The reports around the time of Able Archer led to a recognition that some of the rhetoric had to be toned down. MI6 knew it was on to a winner with the reporting and made the most of it. 'It was like a cat which had swallowed gallons of cream,' a Whitehall official recalled. One of the intelligence officers put it another way. 'At that time, on this target and on these issues, it was the apogee of what the business was all about.'[39] The reporting fed into a seminar at Chequers, the Prime Minister's country retreat, in which the decision was made to reach out to reformists in the USSR by inviting some of them to Britain. The hardline language was toned down.[40]

Another importance of Gordievsky was not what he produced but the fact that he produced anything and that he produced it for so long. It meant the days of paralysing fears of penetration were past and that the service could successfully run an agent over an extended period. This built confidence not just within the Secret Service but also in its relations with allies and especially the Americans. MI6 always knew how to play its cards cannily at home and abroad and made sure the Americans saw the material. Whereas signals intelligence from GCHQ and America's NSA is almost all shared under an agreement, human intelligence was subject to more of a barter process between the allies. Gordievsky's material was gratefully received. It was treated as the holy of holies in the CIA, seen only by a small group who read it in hard copy under strict conditions. The CIA had plenty of agents who could count tanks but none who could offer the same insight into the Soviet Union's thinking (one Polish agent would provide vital information on the Warsaw Pact, but there was no one in Moscow at the level of Gordievsky).[41] Gordievsky revealed just how skewed the Soviet perception of Western motives had become – wars can follow on from such misunderstandings, the CIA analysts understood, and these had become dangerous times. Gordievsky's warnings of Soviet fears began to have an impact in Washington, and also helped 'reinforce Reagan's conviction that a great effort had to be made not just to reduce tension but to end the Cold War', according to the then Deputy Director of the CIA, Robert Gates.[42]

Gordievsky's intelligence highlighted one of the central debates within MI6. Should intelligence be protected cautiously in order not to reveal the source, as traditionalists argued or, as modernisers contended, was such intelligence useless if it was locked away in a box preventing it having any impact? No one took a position at the extremes, but every day there would be decisions about where on the spectrum to reside. Gordievsky showed the benefits of distributing intelligence widely – it certainly had an impact in London and Washington. But it would also show the risks, not least to the agent.

Trust only goes so far even among the most intimate of allies, and it was never quite the same between Britain and America after Philby. Britain had passed the intelligence from Gordievsky to the CIA but with the identity of the source disguised. This was not good enough for the CIA, which occasionally experienced a touch of jealousy over its smaller cousin's success in recruiting human sources (MI6 liked to think it was more subtle in its approaches, relying less on cash and more on understanding an agent's motivation). The CIA tasked the head of counter-intelligence in the Soviet division with discovering the spy's identity. By March 1985 the counter-intelligence chief concluded that Gordievsky was a likely candidate and sent a cable to the CIA's London station asking if he fitted the profile. The London station said yes. The CIA never told the British it had guessed who its spy was. When they later found out what had happened – and what the consequences of this action had been – British officers were furious. 'It wasn't a game. If we had wanted to tell them, we would have done,' one person involved fumed.[43]

The conviction of Bettaney in 1984 had provided a unique opportunity, British intelligence realised. The British had already expelled one official, which enabled Gordievsky to become head of political reporting. Now they had a pretext to expel Guk. Summoned back to

Moscow, Gordievsky was told he was a candidate for resident. Within sight lay a unique opportunity to subvert pretty much all of the KGB's operations against Britain. As the battle raged in Moscow over who should get the job, Gordievsky in London had an important visitor to deal with. One reformist who had accepted an invitation from the British government was the rising star Mikhail Gorbachev. Gordievsky was asked to prepare the briefings for him. Reports were written on the miners' strike, CND, Margaret Thatcher and the Labour Party to prepare him for his meetings. When he spoke at the Embassy on his arrival, Gordievsky thought him strangely disappointing, talking for far too long. 'Just another Soviet apparatchik,' Gordievsky concluded with his jaded eye.[44] It was obvious, though, that Gorbachev was different from the old guard – he was saying that American foreign policy was not shaped by a secret cabal – but he was not yet ready to call for openness and a new policy of glasnost.

The visit was remarkable because Gordievsky was able to brief both Gorbachev and the British government (through MI6). MI6 even showed Gordievsky a brief on what the British Foreign Secretary Geoffrey Howe would be raising with Gorbachev which could then be rewritten as his own briefing for the Soviet leader.[45] All his briefs were written with the assistance of his youthful MI6 reports officer who was managing indirectly to brief both the British and Soviet senior leadership. Thatcher noticed 'just how well briefed Mr Gorbachev was about the West. He commented on my speeches, which he had clearly read.'[46] Gorbachev's trip was a success and an important one. Thatcher was convinced that he was someone she could do business with. After the visit, Downing Street sent a note to the White House on the possibilities of engagement. Gorbachev disliked nuclear weapons and wanted an end to the arms race but was determined to try and stop Reagan's missile defence initiative. Three weeks later, Thatcher gave Reagan a fuller account at Camp David, explaining that it was worth investing in getting to know Gorbachev. Reagan agreed. The combination of pressure in the early 1980s followed by relaxation and engagement in the latter half of the decade helped push the sclerotic Soviet system towards change, aiding a process of liberalisation which would unravel the Soviet Union from within.

Gordievsky's briefings also played well in Moscow – one reason why he was appointed resident-designate at the end of April 1985.

The prize was within his grasp. Then it slipped away. The cipher clerk brought the telegram into the Resident's office on 16 May. As Gordievsky read the handwritten message, he tried to hide the fear that had swept over him. 'In order to confirm your appointment as Resident please come to Moscow urgently in two days' time for important discussions.' This was not usual procedure, he knew. As if realising that it had been too blatant, the Centre sent a further telegram the next day explaining that the summons was to discuss British issues. There were difficult discussions within MI6 and between Gordievsky and his case officers about what to do. They sat down and asked him if he knew any reason why he should not return. He answered that he did not. They had not asked if he thought he should go back, a question which might have elicited a different answer. One part of Gordievsky was determined to keep going, especially with the pinnacle of his career in sight and a chance, with Gorbachev now in charge, to help engineer real change. But as Gordievsky looked at the faces in the room, one person thought they saw something else in his eyes – perhaps a hope for a reprieve and a wish that he would be told there was no choice but to defect immediately. He conducted his last assignment on a Saturday by taking his two small daughters to a park in Bloomsbury and leaving behind an artificial brick containing thousands of pounds for an agent to pick up, and then he headed off.

Everything was nearly normal in Moscow when Gordievsky returned. But not quite. Those tiny tell-tale signs were there, he thought, that something was amiss. The slight pause as the border guard at Moscow's airport studied the passport and the telephone call before allowing him to pass. The third lock on the door of his flat turned even though he no longer used that key. The sense that someone had been inside the apartment and the fear that every room might be bugged. Care and diligence are the hallmarks of the successful spy who stays alive, but when the heat is on, fear and suspicion can crowd out balanced judgement and warp the mind. Keeping cool – being able to maintain watchfulness without slipping into paranoia – is the hardest test. Tiny decisions about when to run and when to wait and call your opponents' bluff over what they know determine whether escape or a firing squad are the final destination. Philby kept his nerve time and time again as he was tested. Now it was Gordievsky's turn to run the gauntlet over the coming days as he met with KGB colleagues and tried to decipher what lay behind each glance and each question. In the eyes of colleagues he sensed fear and an eagerness for distance.

'Can you please come over?' a superior requested, knowing there was no choice in the answer. 'There are two people who want to talk to you about high-level agent penetration of Britain.'[47] He was taken to a small house. Only later did he remember that the other three men drank brandy out of one bottle, while he was served out of another. At the time, all he remembered was a strange out-of-body sensation overcoming him and then waking up in a bed in only his vest and underpants the next morning. He was probably supposed to have remembered nothing of the interrogation, but that morning he had taken a pill provided by MI6 to maintain alertness which may have counteracted at least some of the potency of the KGB drugs. 'You're a very self-confident man,' he remembered one of the men saying to him. But had he given anything away? 'We know very well that you have been deceiving us for years,' a KGB boss told him. 'And yet we've decided that you may stay in the KGB. Your job in London is terminated of course.' He knew they suspected him. But he also knew they did not have enough proof. If they did he would be a dead man. Slivers of memory began to rise to the surface from the drugged interrogation. There were the books and questions about why his daughter knew the Lord's Prayer. And then the accusation. 'We know who recruited you in Copenhagen,' they had said. 'That's not true,' he remembered saying. 'We know you were a British agent. You'd better confess.' Confess, the man said again and again. You've already done it, just do it again, he said, talking slowly as if to a child. 'No, I've nothing to confess.' Had he confessed? He did not think so. They had only the books for sure, and he went to Lyubimov's apartment in a sweat to talk about those. But they knew there was more. The surveillance was everywhere. It was time to run. 'If I don't get out, I'm going to die,' he told himself.[48]

An escape plan had first been devised when Gordievsky returned to Moscow from Copenhagen in the late 1970s. The plan was kept up to date by Joan, the officer who would attend some of the briefings in London. This was not easy. Brush contact and signalling sites had to be identified in Moscow by people based in London. Moscow in winter is a very different city from Moscow in summer, and so they had to be workable in both seasons. Contingencies had to be planned for – what if roadworks closed a designated site?

Details of Gordievsky's plan were kept on an LP sleeve in secret writing which he would then have to develop. The idea was to have a signalling spot which was available to Gordievsky every Tuesday night. That spot, near the Ukraine Hotel, had to be passed and watched at exactly the right time by someone from the small MI6 station every week, come rain come shine, and there needed to be a plausible reason for doing so. Even when Gordievsky was not in town it had to be watched. In fact precisely when Gordievsky was not in town it had to be watched in case the KGB had surveillance on the MI6 officers and associated a deviation from the pattern with the absence of Gordievsky. When he returned in May the KGB watched him every day. At first the surveillance was intense. His tall apartment block was inhabited mainly by fellow KGB officers. They all noticed the arrival of heavy surveillance – sometimes as many as fifteen cars or people outside the apartment and in nearby parking lots and markets. The fact that they were clearly observable was no doubt intended to put Gordievsky under more intense psychological pressure in the hope of forcing errors on his part. He would go jogging and shopping and act normally knowing that he had to be patient and wait for the surveillance to ease before making his move.[49] This lasted for weeks.

The signal Gordievsky was to give to MI6 when he was ready needed to be precise and sufficiently unusual in order to avoid the entire complex escape procedure being kicked off by some innocent action misinterpreted. In practice, this meant the signal was mildly absurd, which did not necessarily induce confidence on the part of Gordievsky. A man wearing a particular type of trousers, carrying a particular bag and eating a particular brand of chocolate would walk past Gordievsky to acknowledge that the signal had been received. The first time Gordievsky waited at the point, there was nothing. Had he left too soon? he wondered. He tried again the following Tuesday. This time a man, unmistakably British in his attire, carrying a Harrods bag and eating a Mars bar strolled past and looked him in the eye saying nothing.

One of Gordievsky's final acts in Moscow was to phone a friend.

He called Mikhail Lyubimov and said he would like to meet him on Monday. Lyubimov noticed a confidence to his friend's voice that was in sharp contrast to the nervous wreck who had appeared in his apartment only a few weeks earlier. They agreed to meet at Lyubimov's dacha in Zvenigorod an hour outside Moscow where he was taking a break. Gordievsky knew the phone was bugged but also asked an odd question. Did his old friend remember a short story by Somerset Maugham called 'Mr Harrington's Washing'? The reference was a risky joke. 'I knew the KGB was not bright enough to work it out.' The story by Maugham, a former British Secret Service officer, involved a plan to escape from Russia over the border with Finland.

The Gordievsky escape plan at the end of the Cold War mirrored the plan hatched during Harrington's escape during the days of the Bolshevik Revolution in that it required a risky crossing of the border into Finland. In case his family was coming, two cars were needed, each driven by one of the MI6 officers in the Embassy. They would leave Moscow on Friday and stay overnight in Leningrad before going over to Finland on Saturday. The pretext was one of the officers' wives needing some specialist, but not too serious, medical treatment in Helsinki which had led the two families to decide to make a weekend trip together. Phone calls were made to London to establish the cover story. The first problem was an unfortunate coincidence. A new British ambassador was due to fly in that very Friday and he was going to have a welcome reception for staff. Would two of his staff really miss the opportunity to attend? So they would have to leave afterwards and drive through the night to make the rendezvous. The Ambassador was also briefed on the escape plan, and he was highly reluctant. He could just see his first week in the job being marked not by the usual introductions but by a huge diplomatic row as two of his staff were caught smuggling a spy out of the country. It could be the shortest posting in Foreign Office history. But he was overruled. The plan required political clearance and this had gone to the highest level.

Getting an agent out of Moscow was about as risky an operation as one could ask for. Getting caught in the act could have major diplomatic repercussions at just the time when the Prime Minister was working hard to improve relations with Gorbachev. As a result, the decision on whether or not to go ahead was one for Margaret

Thatcher herself to take. The problem was that when the moment came she was not in Downing Street. She was up in Scotland staying at Balmoral Castle undertaking one of the Prime Minister's regular visits to the Queen. The conversation could not be held on the phone in case of interception, so Thatcher's Foreign Affairs Adviser Charles Powell had to race to Heathrow to catch a flight to Aberdeen and then take a car to Balmoral to seek approval. On arrival, the Queen's aides were none too amused when he explained that he could not tell them why he had come and what was so urgent. For all the risks, Thatcher had no doubt that the escape plan had to be put into action. 'We have an obligation and we will not let him down,' Thatcher remarked. The escape plan was always high risk. There were people at Century House who thought a trap would be waiting. Surveillance was heavy and the fear was that Gordievsky had been broken and it was a provocation, much like the arrest of the American after clearing Penkovsky's dead drop a quarter of a century earlier.

A stunning summer sunrise on Saturday morning greeted the two cars as they drove towards Leningrad. There was a mix of fatalism and excitement as the two officers set out with their families. There was the knowledge that, succeed or fail, it was the end of their time in Moscow. Expulsion was inevitable, but it would be faced either while basking in the glow of a daring escape or, more likely, having been caught in the act. The pessimists gave the plan about a one-in-twenty chance of working. Everything had to go right. Cumulatively the chances of one thing going wrong that would throw all the timings were high. Surveillance vehicles followed them almost all of the way. They had to reach the designated spot close to the Finnish border at exactly the right moment – not too early or too late, so when they had some time to kill they visited a monastery, still under surveillance. As they drove out of Leningrad, city surveillance handed over to provincial. They would need to be shaken off somehow. A stroke of luck helped. All the cars on the highway were stopped for ten minutes to allow a convoy of tanks to pass. Time was ticking by. Once the tanks had passed, the drivers floored the accelerator. A gap opened up with the surveillance cars behind still coming out of the queue of traffic.

The two cars pulled off the main road into a layby in a forest to have a picnic. The surveillance cars, now desperate to catch up, roared past. As the picnic items were unpacked and the tea was being poured, a smelly-looking tramp got out of a ditch. 'Which car?' he said.

Gordievsky had slept with the doors of his Moscow flat barricaded on Thursday night, fearing arrest. On Friday afternoon he had shaken off his surveillance on the way to the Leningrad station. Police were everywhere, inducing panic before he remembered there was a large festival taking place. He slept fitfully on the overnight train, eventually falling out of his bunk after taking sedatives. Next was another train taking him close to the border and then a bus journey before a walk. As he located the agreed spot, he waited among the tall conifers with mosquitoes gnawing at him. He was way too early and walked back into the nearby town to kill time before returning and sipping a bottle of beer hidden in the grass. These were the hardest moments. As he waited, he became nervous that he had missed the car. He knew it would not come back. He walked out on to the road. 'Stop, this is madness,' he told himself, and went back to wait in the heat and the undergrowth. At last came the sound of the cars and he peered at the people getting out. The last time he had seen one of them was eating a Mars bar on a Moscow street.

Gordievsky was bundled into the boot of the Ford Cortina (the smaller of the two cars), and a heat-reflecting blanket was put over him to fool any infra-red sensors. He was given a bottle to urinate into and some pills to calm him down. He gulped one down straight away. The cars made their way to the border crossing. As diplomatic cars, they should have been exempt from being searched. There had been despair a week before when a British military attaché had allowed his trunk to be searched for fear it had set a precedent. If a search was demanded, the cars would refuse and head back to Moscow. Later the team would realise they had forgotten even to lock the boot. No agent had ever been exfiltrated successfully from Russia since the start of the Cold War. At that moment in Century House in London, the Foreign Office adviser to MI6, gathered with senior staff, looked at his watch. 'Ladies and gentlemen, they're about to cross the border. I think it would be appropriate to say a prayer.'

A packet of cheese and onion crisps was opened as the team waited for their papers to be checked. They fed a few crisps to the dogs that sniffed vehicles for signs of life in a desperate attempt to throw them off the scent. Another unorthodox method was employed. One of the two families had a baby whom they had taken with them. The dirty nappy of the baby was changed on the car boot with Gordievsky underneath. Inside Gordievsky, unable to take off his jacket in the confined space, was drenched with sweat and struggling to breathe, listening to the odd fragment of Russian spoken in an official voice. As the barrier looked set to rise, the phone in the guard's booth rang. He walked slowly over to answer it. He glanced over at the car. Then he put the phone down and wandered slowly back to the car. More documents please, he said. He checked them and then walked back to the kiosk. The boom swung up and the car gratefully pulled out. A few moments later, Gordievsky heard the ominous, brooding opening notes of Sibelius's 'Finlandia' come on to the car stereo. He was over the border.

The relief dissipated minutes later when he felt the car stop and then reverse. The boot was flung open. Joan's face stared down on him with a smile. It had been her plan and it had worked. The first words Gordievsky spoke were: 'I was betrayed.' Five miles from the border, in what still felt like bandit country, a second team including Joan had been waiting for him. One of the officers who had helped deal with his reports in London, had reconnoitred the route while he had been posted to Moscow just before the escape and had now prepared the second half of the plan. Gordievsky changed clothes in the forest. If anyone tried to drive towards them the officer would block the road with his car. 'You must be very tired but we are so very glad to see you,' he said as he extended his hand to the agent whose reports he had worked on but whom he had never met face to face. Gordievsky shook it but remained quiet, the enormity of what had happened still dawning on him.

A team from Danish intelligence were also waiting. Gordievsky was placed in the boot of one of their cars which headed in one direction while an MI6 officer took the old clothes and documents away in a plastic bag. He signalled back to London from a payphone: 'Really enjoyed the fishing. It has been a successful trip. And we've had one guest.' There had always been an expectation that Gordievsky's family might be taken out with him and the reference to 'one guest' was supposed to convey that Gordievsky came out alone, although there was some confusion on the other end as to whether there was one guest in addition to their agent. The cars carrying the lone guest drove north through the night towards Norway without stopping. As they reached the Arctic Circle the summer sun disappeared for only a few hours before rising again. Eventually they came to Norway's north, and from there a flight to Oslo and then to London brought Gordievsky to his new home.

That morning, Mikhail Lyubimov arrived at Zvenigorod station in good time for the 11.13 a.m. train. His friend did not emerge from the last carriage as he had promised. After a while, he checked the timetable again to see when the trains departed from Moscow. Perhaps there had been some confusion. He waited some more, glancing at his watch. But his friend never came. Lyubimov was left alone on the platform. 'It was not so easy when you work with a man all your life and he is a traitor,' Lyubimov, who was interrogated over the following days, would reflect. 'It was not just betraying the Soviet Union. But he betrayed me.' The two friends would never meet or speak again.[50]

The escape was a humiliation for the KGB. After three or four days, whispered rumours and gossip had gone round its headquarters about the disappearance of the future London Resident. But there was no announcement.[51] A few days later the new British Ambassador was summoned to the Foreign Ministry in Moscow. A Soviet official produced a photograph taken just a few days earlier of the Ambassador in full ceremonial uniform surrounded by all his Embassy team as he presented his credentials. The Soviet official placed a finger on the faces of the two MI6 officers who had smuggled Gordievsky out of the country. The Ambassador played innocent but he was told that those two – and others – had forty-eight hours to leave the country.[52] Gordievsky was free, but he was not put out to pasture. On his second day in Britain, Chris Curwen – now C, the Chief of MI6 – flew by helicopter to the Midlands country house where Gordievsky had been put up to meet his prize catch. The formality of the country house with its butlers did not suit Gordievsky, who was next taken to the Fort, the service's training facility. The reports officer, who had been waiting in Finland, and others would listen in over a year as he drained his memory bank and talked through the documents he had smuggled out. Supervising the process were more senior officers including Shergy's Sov Bloc rising stars Colin McColl and Gerry Warner.

Margaret Thatcher began to treat Gordievsky as an occasional adviser. At their first meeting, she expressed her gratitude for his work and then began to ask what more he could tell her about Gorbachev, how to handle him and what the pressure points were. (The only time a meeting with Thatcher did not go well was in 1989 when she asked Gordievsky what he thought the Soviet position would be on the unification of Germany, and the Prime Minister, deeply hostile to it, did not like his answer that Moscow would find it hard to oppose.) Her views were not necessarily changed by Gordievsky, but he provided her with the ammunition and confidence to make her case for how to deal with the Soviet Union and how much pressure to apply.

Another visitor arrived by helicopter at the Fort in September. Bill Casey, the buccaneering head of the CIA, came down to the Fort specifically to see Gordievsky. Reagan was about to meet Gorbachev in Geneva for one of the superpower summits that dictated the course of the Cold War and wanted a breakthrough on arms reductions. Casey sat in front of Gordievsky with a yellow-and-blue CIA notebook scribbling away like a schoolboy until he asked if he could use a tape recorder. The American spoke in a thick accent and mumbled, which meant that C, also present, had occasionally to translate. He had come to take part in a role-playing game. 'You are Mr Gorbachev,' he said, pointing to Gordievsky, 'and I am Mr Reagan. We would like to get rid of nuclear weapons, starting with a large number of strategic weapons. To inspire confidence, we will give you access to Star Wars,' the latter comment referring to the Strategic Defense Initiative designed to shoot down missiles and the source of much Soviet angst. 'What do you say?' asked Casey.

Gordievsky leant back in his seat. 'Nyet.'

'Why, why?' asked Casey.

'I don't trust you. You will never give us anything,' Gordievsky replied. By chance the last meeting he had attended in Moscow was about the upcoming Geneva talks in which the KGB had said that there was no point trusting the US since it had no desire for serious agreement.[53]

'What should we do?' asked Casey. The Kremlin will believe you only if you drop Star Wars, Gordievsky explained. Impossible, said Casey, it was the President's pet project. Gordievsky, like many in MI6, held to a tough line and suggested keeping going with Star Wars, arguing that the Soviet Union would never be able to keep up technologically and would eventually be forced to give in. Later Gordievsky would also go to the Oval Office of the White House to meet Reagan in person and on a subsequent visit would meet President George H. W. Bush.

Gordievsky was the star turn at a conference at Century House for officials across Whitehall and spoke to senior military chiefs. He was a valuable tool for building MI6's reputation. The year of debriefing generated a set of extraordinarily detailed reports. A fifty-page briefing entitled 'Soviet Perceptions of Nuclear Warfare' had a particular influence.[54] Even the sceptics about intelligence in the Foreign Office sat up and listened. Rodric Braithwaite, the young private who had sat with headphones clamped over his ears in the cellar in Vienna in the early 1950s, had risen through the ranks of the Foreign Office to become ambassador to Russia by the closing years of the Cold War. He remained somewhat doubtful of the output of the organisation that he had declined to join but saw the value of its star agent. 'What Gordievsky described was the kind of terror the Russians felt facing us,' he explained. 'Something which if you have ever been in Moscow you would have perceived but if you are Prime Minister or President you hadn't the remotest idea of. You would have thought these villainous people are trying to nuke us tomorrow and you never thought they were terrified that we were going to nuke them tomorrow.' It was not so much the originality of Gordievsky's analysis that was influential, Braithwaite argues, as its provenance. Information acquired secretly is often privileged over the same information acquired openly – the sight of 'Top Secret' written across the top of a paper often leads the reader to assume it must be true and more true than something acquired openly. 'There was nothing mysterious about those Russian attitudes ... [but] it came from a source which they had to accept because of Gordievsky's personal background. Reagan and Thatcher were prepared to listen to it.'[55]

Gordievsky remained driven. All he cared about was his work and getting his family out. The latter proved a problem. The Soviets had no idea where Gordievsky had gone until MI6 decided to tell them a few weeks later. London was not a suitable location, it was decided, and so Gerry Warner went to Paris and asked his station chief to engineer a meeting with a non-KGB member of the Soviet Embassy at a plush club. The Soviet Scientific Counsellor duly arrived. On the manicured lawn, Warner was introduced. 'We've got a message for the head of your KGB station,' Warner began. The man went white as a sheet. 'You're looking for Gordievsky. We've got him. We'd like his family.' The poor counsellor staggered off in shock. The reply from Moscow was an emphatic no. A death sentence was passed *in absentia* against Gordievsky. Reuniting the former KGB man with his family became a priority for the British government right up to the Prime Minister, who would raise the issue regularly with Gorbachev at their summits.

The pressure would eventually work and his family would come to Britain as the Soviet Union collapsed in 1991, the final release brokered by Rodric Braithwaite. But it was too late. His decision not to tell his wife that he was working for British intelligence had shielded her when she was interrogated. But it had also left her bitter at never having known the truth. She left him as soon as she made it back to Britain. His daughters barely remembered him.[56] Gordievsky had followed his beliefs, but in doing so he had paid a heavy personal price.

As the Cold War began to draw to its unexpected close, MI6, like Gordievsky, remained sceptical about Gorbachev. Throughout the Cold War, it saw one of its roles as preventing political leaders being taken in by Soviet rhetoric. There was a desire to force politicians to face uncomfortable truths. 'It is always a temptation for anybody to choose the easier course and it is always a temptation if somebody is saying "I am a friend of yours and I don't mean any harm" to accept that,' argues Gerry Warner. 'But if you are being told all the time by a microphone in your ear that it is totally untrue and that he's holding a knife behind his back and he's about to kick you where it hurts, the temptation is less to trust him. And that is the kind of way in which I think it would have been very easy both for Conservative and Labour governments throughout the Cold War to choose the easy option if they hadn't been constantly reminded of what was going on.' As the politicians, and particularly the Prime Minister, started to invest more heavily in Gorbachev and his reforms, MI6 endeavoured to continue this function. Some critics felt that rather than reflecting the underlying intelligence it was the product of a deeply ingrained MI6 culture in which the service struggled to believe that the Soviet Union could change and be anything other than an implacable enemy.

Ammunition for its hawkish position of not being too quick to trust Gorbachev came from one defector right at the end of the Cold War. A very scared Vladimir Pasechnik contacted the British Embassy in Paris during a 1989 visit to France. The Foreign Office were eventually persuaded it was worth getting him out. A scientist who worked on the Soviet's secret biological weapons programme, he revealed that the USSR was secretly developing chemical and biological weapons such as VX, sarin and plague, including strains designed to survive Western antibiotics. The reports were met with intense resistance at first from the Foreign Office and Whitehall as they indicated that Gorbachev was evading treaty commitments. The Chair of the Joint Intelligence Committee, Sir Percy Cradock, personally came to speak to the defector to convince himself of the veracity of the information.[57] Cradock and others in the intelligence world remained sceptical that Gorbachev was really changing the Soviet Union, believing that his reforms were cosmetic and not perceiving the way in which they would start to gather a momentum of their own which took events beyond those planned by the leadership.

Gordievsky's first words out of the car boot – 'I was betrayed' – had also been enough to send shudders down the spine of a Secret Service which thought it had just emerged from the wilderness of mirrors of the molehunt. There was the question that is asked after every blown operation. Was there another traitor? Another Philby? It took a decade following the escape to understand that there was indeed another traitor. But he was not British. At the moment that Gordievsky was returning to his drugged interrogation in Moscow, the CIA was watching its own slow-motion horror movie. Its entire network of what the agency's more cynical operators called 'assets' was being rolled up one by one in the Soviet Union and Eastern Europe. Agents were being recalled back to Moscow or disappearing off its streets or having 'accidents'.

It had taken a few years to shake off the Angleton-induced paralysis that had hobbled the recruitment of Soviet spies, but by the early

1980s the agency had hoovered up a good selection of sources. Perhaps, however, Angleton and his fellow believers would, on one level, be proved right. For all their obsession with a mole within their garden, the CIA finally acquired one soon after it stopped looking.

On 16 April 1985, CIA officer Aldrich Ames walked into the Soviet Embassy in Washington DC. He had told his superiors he was trying to recruit an agent, but he was the one doing the betraying. By the time of a third meeting at a hamburger joint in Georgetown on 13 June, Ames was receiving a shopping bag of money. He was extremely well placed as the head of counter-intelligence in the Soviet division. He was the man who had identified Gordievsky for the CIA and who held exactly the same position in the agency that Philby once held in MI6. It meant he saw all the files and knew all the agents.

Ames's treachery seemed to explain Gordievsky's near-demise. Not everyone was sure. Ames claimed he did not give any agents' identities away until his 13 June lunch, by which time Gordievsky had already been recalled to Moscow. But he might have given away just enough to draw suspicion on to Gordievsky and it might explain why Gordievsky was interrogated but never arrested. The KGB may have had only a tip-off and not concrete evidence, making the situation similar to Philby's initial questioning in 1951 after Burgess and Maclean had fled, when the evidence was strong but essentially circumstantial. It may also have been that one of Gordievsky's sharper colleagues in London noticed that he was producing lots of reports during the Gorbachev visit but without meeting many contacts. A new head of division in Moscow who had never liked Gordievsky may have ordered an investigation.[58]

Ames's treachery was not discovered until 1994. Gordievsky and Ames even met face to face in 1989, Gordievsky not knowing that he was shaking hands at Langley with the man who might nearly have killed him. It had all been about the money – $2 million in all. Where the early British traitors had been ideological, the CIA's traitors were utterly venal. The damage was the same. When the Berlin Wall came down in 1989 the head of the CIA's Soviet division learnt everything from CNN because he had no agents left to report to him on what was unfolding.[59] Just like MI6 in the 1950s, the CIA was institutionally unwilling to accept the idea that it might be penetrated. Just as Angleton had warned, it was manipulated by KGB double agents and deception operations. But its failure to deal with the problem was itself a legacy of Angleton. The memory of what he had done was so painful that counter-intelligence had become a backwater for careers, and no one, but no one, wanted to start that whole mole-hunting business again. The result was inevitable and catastrophic. It was not just Ames either. Five current or former CIA officers betrayed their country in the decade after Angleton left.[60] Intelligence and counter-intelligence exist in a natural tension. If one dominates the other, then trouble arrives soon afterwards. The CIA was plunged into a bad place full of suspicion internally and was mistrusted around Washington.

Philby and Gordievsky bookended the Cold War – one side's hero, the other's villain. Recruiting an officer from the other side is always relished deeply because of the opportunities it provides for quickly uncovering the other side's secrets and subverting their work. But with Gordievsky there was also the sense of payback for the betrayal that had so scarred MI6 decades earlier. There were one or two other spies of an importance approaching that of Gordievsky but whose names have never come to light, insiders say. They maintain that over the course of the Cold War the British Secret Service ran somewhere between forty and eighty agents in Eastern Europe and the Soviet Union and lost only a handful, Penkovsky among them.

Gordievsky's afterlife was happier than Philby's in many ways. He was given the kind of status and access that Philby had craved but never received. He lived in a well-heeled suburban town with none of the cravings for home that plagued Philby, none of the complexities or doubts over his actions. In Moscow, their mutual friend Mikhail Lyubimov still celebrates the life of one old comrade by meeting on Philby's birthday with his widow and others who knew him. The ageing band gathers every year at Philby's old flat to drink vodka and whisky and celebrate his life. But the taste for espionage has long ago faded. 'When I started my career I liked espionage very much and I was enthusiastic,' Lyubimov recalls wistfully. 'But by the end of my career I became disappointed. I came to the conclusion that it does more harm than good.' The betrayer had become the betrayed.

Lyubimov will have no truck with those who liken the betrayal of Philby to that of Gordievsky. 'It is different because Philby never worked for the MI6 actually,' he argues, using a logic only a spy can really understand. 'He worked for the Soviet Union. He many times himself told me, "Look, they consider me to be a double agent. I am not a double agent. I worked only for the Soviet Union." How could he be a traitor if since from the very beginning he worked for the Communists? What did he betray? Gordievsky is a traitor. This is clear because he worked for the KGB, then he went to the British side.'[61] Gordievsky has no time for the accusations of a betrayal. 'The betrayal question is pointless because it was a criminal state,' is his answer. 'The most criminal element of the criminal state was the KGB. It was a gang of bandits. To betray bandits ... was very good for the soul.'[62]

Did it all matter? Did the spying and the lying and betraying make any real difference? Critics argue that all the spying accomplished was to raise the temperature by heightening the suspicions that fuelled the Cold War in which ignorant armies clashed by night. Those who believe in intelligence say it did make a difference by managing a hostility that was real and dangerous. 'The risk in the Cold War and the Cold War going very badly wrong was surprise,' argues Scarlett. 'What nobody wanted was to be surprised ... intelligence gave knowledge which greatly reduced that fear of a surprise attack. And as the Cold War developed, more confidence developed that the other side was understood, and that helped manage the situation and was a key reason why we got to the end without a blowout.'[63]

Much of the vast Cold War intelligence effort was precautionary and was never actually used. The counting of Soviet tanks was designed to watch for enemy activity and prepare a response should war come. The fact that such tactical intelligence was never needed does not mean it was not important in increasing confidence. On the strategic level, each side was desperate to mask its weakness and project strength. But neither truly understood how the other perceived its actions and how it misread its intentions. It was not *what* a country was doing which was misunderstood but the *why*. Spies, like Gordievsky, may have helped open a window into the reality beneath the rhetoric and provide a transparency which helped prevent miscalculation. But Gordievsky's contribution came late in the day; before then there was strategic blindness. 'Both sides were stumbling about with a vague idea of one another's capabilities but only a thin and mostly distorted idea of one another's intentions,' argues Rodric Braithwaite. And if the idea that Gordievsky's actions did help ease tension by revealing the mind of the enemy (just as Penkovsky had over the Berlin crisis in 1961), why is the same not true for Philby and his cohorts who spied the other way? The answer cannot hold for one side and not the other. Did Philby and his friends help Stalin calibrate his policy to avoid hostilities at the beginning of the Cold War and reduce his own paranoia about invasion? It is true they were never quite trusted and their intelligence was never exploited in quite the same way in Moscow because of a less rigorous analytical and assessment process. But the question still remains whether it would actually have been safer for both sides to have had more spies in the enemy camp and to have had more in their own. Some have wondered whether openness might negate the need for spies at all and make the world safer. 'Much better if the Russians saw the Cabinet minutes twice a week. Prevent all that fucking dangerous guesswork,' Harold Macmillan's private secretary once remarked.[64]

Western intelligence had expended enormous energy in counting missiles and tanks, often erring on the side of caution by over-estimating their numbers and never really understanding that the weight of the Soviet military machine masked a hollowness in the wider Soviet economy which was creaking ever more loudly under the strain. The Soviet Union had been able to match the West for military hardware through the 1970s but failed to keep pace in the field of consumer goods that would prove to people that life under Communism really was better than under capitalism. And then by the 1980s the Reagan arms build-up, encapsulated in the Star Wars concept, ensured that the US began to pull away here too, not least in the mind of the Soviets.[65]

No one saw the end of the Cold War coming as the 1980s began to draw to a close. Contrary to expectation, spies are often very poor at predicting change. The job of spies is to steal secrets. But the demise of the Soviet Union was not a secret locked away in a safe. 'It was inconceivable the killer piece of information could exist,' argues Rodric Braithwaite. 'Because the Russians themselves didn't know what they were up to or what was going to happen.'[66] The fall of the Soviet Union was the product of long-term social and economic trends, many of whose outworkings were in the open but which were never fully understood. Attempts by Gorbachev to create 'socialism with a human face' were part of the reason. But so were events in a landlocked country thousands of miles away where the latest chapter in a much older Great Game was being played out as the British Secret Service took on the Russians.

8

THE AFGHAN PLAINS

As they had done for a century and a half, British spies wound their way across the unforgiving terrain that joined Pakistan and Afghanistan. The horses and mules that Rudyard Kipling had used to cross the border in disguise had been replaced by sturdy, muddied Land Rovers but it still took the best part of a day to coil over the hills and around the mountains from Peshawar. This was the stark, beautiful terrain where the original Great Game in the nineteenth century had been played out and where the long intelligence duel between Britain and Russia had begun. Then the British spies, operating out of their offices in Peshawar, Kabul and Kandahar, had come to bully, bribe and barter with tribal chiefs to keep the Russians away from the imperial treasure chest of India. 'All sorts and conditions of men were made use of, high and low, rich and needy, mullahs and murderers, brigands, fugitives, anyone,' one officer remarked of the intelligence work of that time.[1] The quiet, walled compound in the Afghan capital Kabul – still known as the British cemetery – continues to bear witness to the human costs of imperial ambition with its roll call of those who fell as lonely garrisons were overwhelmed by wave after wave of religiously inspired mujahedeen. In February 1980, the successors to the spies of the past were arriving determined to ensure that the favour was returned to the Russians.

For most of the twentieth century Afghanistan had been a forgotten place, far away from the front lines of espionage and the Cold War. But as the 1980s opened it had been thrust back to the centre of geopolitics and intrigue. The Cold War was only the latest of many 'other people's wars' to be fought in the hills and plains of Afghanistan.

Six weeks before the Land Rovers struggled over the rough terrain, the Soviet war machine had thundered its way into Afghanistan. Now waiting for two MI6 officers was a gathering of tribal leaders, known as a loya jirga. The tribesmen had gathered in a school courtyard, a dusty, mud-and-brick compound, to hear from their British guests. The local men lined up with the younger fierce faces on the flank and the long, calmer white beards in the middle. Gerry Warner, who had taken over just six months earlier as the British Secret Service Controller for the region, addressed them through an interpreter while his head of station in Pakistan watched. London and Washington had decided that Soviet aggression would be confronted. But not directly. Instead it would be confronted through the men in front of Warner along with their sons, brothers and cousins. At what cost? he wondered. 'We are willing to help you. But if we do help you, I want to be sure you understand what this means. If we give you help you will be able to fight longer and more of your young men will be killed. And I still don't believe you can win this war,' he told them. There was a muttering from the gathered throng and then the longest beard spoke up. 'We are grateful for your help,' the man explained through the interpreter. 'But we will fight even without this help. And the Russians will leave in ten years.' He was wrong. They were gone in nine.

The Soviets had invaded after a succession of coups had eventually brought to power Hafizullah Amin, a hardline Communist whom the KGB (wrongly) thought might be a CIA agent. They had endeavoured to assassinate him, but neither poison nor snipers seemed to work. A KGB illegal had been infiltrated into the presidential palace as a cook to try and poison him, but it was unsuccessful.[2] In the end it was decided to kill him as part of a full-frontal assault on his country. In Moscow, Kim Philby watched in dismay. 'Was it essential to take up the military option?' he wrote to his friend Graham Greene. 'Wouldn't a quiet kinjal-thrust from behind an arras have done just as well?'[3] Invading was a decision which would contribute in no small part to the demise of the Soviet Union, the end of the Cold War and the beginning of a new struggle with terrorism. Afghanistan was the pivot from one era to the next.

For the Cold Warriors in London and Washington, the invasion of Afghanistan was an opportunity not to be missed. CIA officers had begun preparing the previous year. One senior officer addressed staff in Islamabad in August 1978 and said that when he saw that a Soviet-backed regime had taken over in a coup, he had turned to his wife and said, 'Honey, those Communist bastards are not going to screw with our Afghanistan like this. I'm going to overthrow that damn regime.' He told the four-man CIA team to get in touch with the nascent Afghan resistance, the mujahedeen groups, and see what they were made of.[4] A small programme providing humanitarian support as well as anti-Soviet propaganda had begun in mid-1979. By mid-December – before the Soviet invasion – a meeting of top officials, including the US Vice-President, had decided that the US would 'explore with the Pakistanis and the British the possibility of improving the financing, arming and communications of the rebel forces to make it as expensive as possible for the Soviets to continue their efforts . . . We will attempt to increase propaganda and pressure on the Soviets worldwide. We will recommend to our European allies that they encourage their press to pay more attention to the subject.'[5] The pitched battles of the Cold War had been fought not in Europe but through proxies in the developing world from the Congo and Cuba to Vietnam and now, following the invasion, to Afghanistan, which was next in line to be swept up into the maelstrom of super-power conflict. Afghanistan would also offer the Camel Drivers of MI6 a chance to engage in some of their most aggressive and direct covert action.

The Prime Minister took a helicopter to one of the refugee camps over the border in Pakistan into which millions of Afghans had spilled. Her speech would be interrupted as the Afghans rose to their feet. 'Allahu Akbar,' they chanted at the Iron Lady. Margaret Thatcher was deeply concerned by the idea that control of Afghanistan might allow the Soviet Union to thrust through Iran towards the Gulf and cut off oil supplies. The invasion had confirmed everything she had believed about the dangers of easing relations with the Soviets through the policy of détente. 'I knew the beast,' she would say. The Prime Minister told the refugees of her admiration for their refusal to 'live under a godless communist system which [was] trying to destroy [their] religion and [their] independence'.[6] Back home, her Secret Service was looking at the options. The Americans eventually settled on providing weapons to the mujahedeen. Stansfield Turner, President Jimmy Carter's cautious Director of the CIA, who had been appointed to clean the agency's house out after scandals and Congressional inquiries, initially had deep concerns about the efficacy and the morality of such an operation until he was persuaded by his more aggressively minded staff. 'Eventually they convinced me the guerrillas were going to fight even if they just had old British Enfield rifles from World War I.'[7] The British Foreign Office and, initially at least, the Ministry of Defence were also reluctant. 'They really had to be dragged kicking and screaming,' one official recalled.

The Chief of MI6, now Dickie Franks (who had once been Greville Wynne's handler), organised a dinner party of media editors. He explained to them that the mujahedeen were actually 'freedom fighters', not 'rebels' as the Soviets portrayed them. The first priority was information – not collecting it but shaping it in the public mind. Everyone had watched America lose public support for Vietnam as pictures of war were broadcast directly back into living rooms across the nation. This time there was a desire to determine the global outlook on the conflict from the outset. Television was what really mattered. Nothing was more picturesque and evocative than the sight of the Khyber Pass and the rugged farmer-soldiers resisting the steel and might of the Soviet bear. The problem was getting access to the land-locked country. It was suggested at the start of 1980 that Afghans could be found who could be equipped with small video cameras, rather than bulky film cameras, which they could take into the country. When this was done, a studio in London's East End converted the video taken by the smaller cameras. Out came shaky footage of a Soviet MiG fighter jet strafing a village against a blue sky. Women and children could just about be seen running away. It went around the world. MI6 used its contacts in Muslim countries to spread the pictures and keep the conflict in the headlines. But the quality of these pictures was relatively poor and editors quickly demanded better quality. Soon well-known journalists would start to make their own long trek into the hills, notably Sandy Gall from Britain's ITN who travelled on horseback with Russian jets streaking overhead. 'So far the West has stood idly by and done nothing to help the Afghans,' an Afghan commander told him. 'All we have had from the West is words not deeds.'[8]

Dressed in Afghan clothes, Gall's American equivalent Dan Rather first went into the country in 1980 for CBS News. His report was watched back in Washington by a Texan Congressman, Charlie Wilson, who, as well as enjoying sitting in hot tubs with pretty girls doing coke, sat on the Defence Appropriations Sub-Committee in Congress which funded covert action. He asked his staff how much was being spent on Afghanistan. Five million dollars, they said. 'Double it,' Wilson replied.[9] For Wilson and one faction of CIA officers, Afghanistan was simple. This was a chance to kill lots of Soviets, an opportunity for revenge for the open wound of Vietnam. Nothing more and nothing less. That required weapons and training. And a place from which to operate.

The dusty, dangerous city of Peshawar in Pakistan's North West Frontier Province, long the redoubt for spies and adventurers, was home to the leading political figures of the Afghan mujahedeen. The so-called Peshawar seven, who almost without exception despised each other and feuded incessantly, were to be the conduits for the money and weapons coming in. They would then distribute them to their field commanders, who were rooted in local villages and tribes. Six of the seven political leaders were Pashtuns, the tribe which straddled the Pakistan and Afghanistan border and which was closest to Pakistan and its military intelligence agency, the ISI. The ISI chief General Akhtar Abdur Rahman was a Pashtun. Only one leader, Burhanuddin Rabbani, a former law professor at Kabul University, was not Pashtun. He was a Tajik, from the group that made up about a third of the Afghan population. Pakistan was the key to the covert war. The mujahedeen's success relied on the sanctuary and training camps over the border. President Zia-ul-Haq of Pakistan had come to power in a military coup and was deeply religious and committed to the operation but also calculating in his approach. 'The water in Afghanistan must boil at the right temperature,' he told his top brass. Make it too hot and the Soviets might decide to punish Pakistan.[10] He wanted control over how the CIA's largesse was distributed and to whom. Everything would be done through the ISI.

With his jet-black hair and eyes, Gulbuddin Hekmatyar was a ruthless, violent fundamentalist. When they looked into his eyes the Americans sensed a dislike of them that could not be hidden. Yet he received more of the American money and arms than anyone else. The reason was simple. He was the most aggressive when it came to killing Soviets and he was the favourite of the ISI and Pakistan's

President. The CIA had tried to build their own contacts only from 1978 and so were dependent on the ISI (although MI6 did introduce one man called Abdul Haq who proved highly popular with the Americans and with the media who christened him 'Hollywood Haq' for his love of the camera).[11]

Long mule caravans snaked into Afghanistan carrying weapons. At first they were largely small arms of Soviet provenance in order to prevent the programme being traced back to the US. Large quantities from Egypt would be shipped up to Karachi in Pakistan and then trucked up the border by the ISI to be taken across (the mules were so important that the Soviets targeted them and the CIA shipped in more in response).[12] It was hardly the most covert operation in the world since it involved thousands of people. The mujahedeen would be trained in and recruited from the massive refugee camps, four near Peshawar and three around Quetta. They would also receive detailed satellite maps of Soviet positions courtesy of the CIA.

When the CIA officers running the programme visited Century House they would always have to hide their surprise at the shabbiness of their cousins' headquarters. Only when promoted to a certain level were the British officers allowed curtains and a desk which even vaguely looked like it was made of wood. Still, the British did their best to keep up the show. Some of the blue-collar CIA officers found the lunches and dinners in the stuffy old gentlemen's clubs and the introductions to tailors during their London visits a touch tiresome. They wanted to talk business. The British officers were forthright in saying they could not contribute any cash. The piggy bank was rather empty. Anything else we could help with? they would ask. Britain was supplying a few weapons and even winter coats from Ministry of Defence stores whose regimental buttons had been removed. How about ammunition? one American asked. In particular there was a need for more .303 ammunition for the old British Lee-Enfield rifle. The weapon had been first introduced in 1895 when Britain was still in Afghanistan the first time round and remained the staple of many a mujahedeen warrior partly because of its reliability. The CIA man explained they had swept the world for more stocks and wondered if the UK had some in reserve since it used to be their standard-issue weapon in Empire days. MI6 duly went away and checked with the Ministry of Defence. They said they had 2.25 million rounds but since the old rifles were a reserve weapon they could spare only a few thousand. Some bargaining ensued. When the CIA representative passed through town a few months later and checked up on the request, the British proudly said they had rustled up half a million. Thanks, the CIA man said, thinking to himself that the old Empire was not quite what it used to be.[13] His shopping list had a requirement to obtain 400 million rounds. The CIA's covert war was to be fought on a previously unimagined scale and no one else could compete when it came to resources. On another occasion, an MI6 officer explained to a CIA counterpart that there were not enough mine detectors to clear a particular route for supplies. 'How many could you use?' the CIA officer asked. 'Would ten be too much?' the MI6 man responded. The CIA provided twenty-five. They cost only $300 each.[14] The CIA's Afghan programme would eventually become a $700-million-a-year operation, dwarfing the entire budget not just of MI6 but of all Britain's intelligence agencies combined.

At the start of the conflict, Gerry Warner had asked his desk officer, a former soldier, to seek out the best commander to support. 'I want you to find Napoleon while he is still an artillery colonel,' Warner instructed him. Even though the scale of the American effort vastly overshadowed that of Britain, MI6 was able to do things the Americans could not because of a strict line in the sand drawn in Washington. It had been decreed that there should be no chance of Americans coming face to face with Soviets on the ground. That risked sparking a war, so CIA personnel were banned from going into the country. The British meanwhile were allowed in and out; they also were not locked into the same tight relations with Pakistan that the CIA enjoyed. So they began to seek out their own niche. Warner's desk officer examined reports from the field and intercepted Soviet communications. He looked all over the map, including at some individuals fighting in Helmand, but he kept coming back to one guerrilla leader who was giving the Soviets a bloody nose. Ahmad Shah Massoud's importance lay not just in his fighting skills but in the terrain into which he melted after each attack on the Soviets. The Panjshir Valley, beginning only fifty or so miles north-east of Kabul and running for nearly one hundred miles in all, was Massoud's home. A river wound through the valley with a dusty track and then verdant fields by its side and it was home to about 150,000 people.

The Soviets were pounding the countryside to try and drain support away from the mujahedeen but to no avail. The strategic importance came from its proximity to the Salang highway which snaked its way through the valley. This carried three-quarters of the ground traffic of Soviet supplies heading for Kabul. It offered a perfect target for hit-and-run guerrilla warfare.

The guide greeted four British men in the lobby of a Peshawar hotel. He had been asked by Massoud's brother to take them into the Panjshir. They told him and everyone else they met that they were freelance journalists reporting on the suffering of Afghan civilians. But the guide – who had spent some time in a military academy – noticed that the bearing and manner of the men was more typical of soldiers. They travelled for five days, mainly by night, covering ground quickly accompanied by packhorses carrying their equipment. By day the heat on the plains would be unbearable; at night up in the mountains the cold would penetrate even the thickest layers. The men – despite their training – struggled to keep up with their guide and a succession of stomach bugs slowed them down. Occasionally, they would pass so close to Russian soldiers that they could hear them talking. Sometimes they would be spotted and bullets would fly. They never fought back and simply kept moving. When they at last reached Massoud, their guide quickly realised from their reception and the large bundles of cash he glimpsed that these men were not normal journalists.[15]

The first British teams which had gone out to meet Massoud under journalistic cover were relieved to find him receptive, partly because he felt short-changed by the CIA–ISI operation. 'Massoud fought the enemy with empty hands,' argues Abdullah Anas, one of his commanders.[16] Massoud complained that the Pakistanis cheated him out of weapons. 'We get a top layer in each box of what we ordered. Then underneath them, the numbers are made up with old models,' he told a visiting (genuine) British journalist. 'We pay for our own arms from donations from workers in Kabul, and from money from emeralds. The rest we capture ourselves from the Russians.' He explained to the first British team to arrive that what he needed most was not regular weapons but specialist military training and supplies.

The British men who arrived were soon taken to see Massoud, who drove around in a captured Russian jeep with bullet holes in the windscreen and his short-wave radio always tuned to the BBC World Service. Massoud would be turned into an almost mythic character, a Che Guevara of the East, an image whose value he understood and which he carefully cultivated. He was from a well-off background and was well educated, having attended the lycée in Kabul where he learnt French. Slim with a wispy beard, he had a cool, quiet, almost feline manner and rarely became angry. He was an adept tactician and had become a student of the great thinkers of guerrilla warfare – including Che and Mao Tse-tung. He was deeply religious, always working closely with the mullahs in what he called a holy war. But he was not as radical as some other commanders like Hekmatyar, with whom a long feud had begun in the 1970s when the latter's men had failed to join Massoud as agreed for an uprising. Massoud barely left the valley for the rest of his life, moving from village to village night by night, usually sleeping beneath a tree or sometimes in a cave. His strength was also his weakness. In his home terrain of the Panjshir, he commanded undivided support and inspired a fierce loyalty; elsewhere he was seen as too rooted in one place and in one ethnic group ever to be a national leader.

The four men who arrived in the Panjshir were part of an annual mission that MI6 had begun organising. The SAS was keen to get involved but it was considered too dangerous for serving British soldiers to travel into the country. If they were captured they would not be deniable. So MI6 built on its existing paramilitary capability – known as the 'increment' – which consisted of soldiers who had 'officially' retired but were in fact available for special operations. Soldiers with the right skills would be interviewed in a London hotel and provided with false identity documents and training in intelligence techniques. A team consisting of seven or eight MI6 and increment officers would typically travel into Afghanistan twice a year, heading in through Chitral to the top end of the Panjshir on foot and horseback, dressed in the local shalwar kameez to blend in as far as possible. During their visits they would also teach English to Massoud's aides, such as Abdullah Anas. A secret training base was established in a small, narrow valley in the Panjshir with a large cave. At night, the men would communicate with London through satellite phones. They had brought with them laser binoculars and special sights for weapons. During their two- to three-week stay, the

Anatoly Golitsyn with his wife Svetlana at Coconut Grove in Los Angeles soon after he defected from the KGB in 1961.

Stephen de Mowbray joined MI6 in the wake of the Second World War and went on to play a key role in the molehunts within British intelligence.

Sir Dick White rose first to be director general of the Security Service, MI5, and then chief of the Secret Intelligence Service, MI6.

James Jesus Angleton was a deeply controversial head of counter-intelligence at the CIA. Many believed he never recovered from the betrayal of his close friend Kim Philby and would later obsess about the threat of Soviet moles.

Sir Roger Hollis, head of MI5, was investigated for being a possible KGB agent. A report would later conclude he was not working for the Russians, but its contents remain secret. (Getty)

Sir Maurice Oldfield leaving Buckingham Palace following his investiture. As a chief of MI6 he was widely admired, though the concealment of his homosexuality would cause a scandal after his death. (Corbis)

David Cornwell, better known as John le Carré, served with military intelligence in Vienna before joining MI5 and MI6, and later making his name as a writer. (Getty)

Admiralty clerk John Vassall was caught in a 'compromising situation' in Moscow and blackmailed over his homosexuality. He would spend years passing British secrets before being caught, partly thanks to leads from Anatoly Golitsyn. (Corbis)

Greville Wynne arriving back in Britain after being released as part of a 'spy-exchange' between Britain and the USSR. (Getty)

No man's land in Berlin: the moment in when Greville Wynne was exchanged for Gordon Lonsdale.

Kim Philby (left) with George Blake (right) in the Soviet Union. The two former MI6 officers had not known each other in Britain when they were both spying for the KGB. They were only briefly friends in Moscow before they fell out, although Blake did introduce Philby to his last wife, Rufina.

Gordon Lonsdale, whose real name was Konon Molody, worked as an undercover KGB officer, or 'illegal', in Britain until he was caught. (Getty)

Oleg Gordievsky preparing for an orienteering competition at a KGB holiday resort near Moscow in 1971. Gordievsky soon became one of MI6's most important agents.

Gordievsky (left) working the diplomatic circuit in Copenhagen and talking to the Danish Defence Minister. He was first approached by MI6 in Denmark although there were initial fears that he might be a double agent.

Oleg Gordievsky, Mikhail Lyubimov and their wives in Denmark. Gordievsky and fellow KGB officer Lyubimov were close friends until Gordievsky fled Moscow.

Ahmed Shah Massoud, known as the Lion of the Panjshir for his guerrilla war against the Soviet Union. MI6 built up close relations with him and sent undercover teams to train and support his fighters. (Getty)

Two future director generals of MI5, Stephen Lander and Eliza Manningham-Buller, shortly after they joined the service. They are pictured on a training course on the roof of a Security Service building on Gower Street.

Despite the reservations of her father (who had prosecuted George Blake), Eliza Manningham-Buller joined MI5 and worked on the Gordiesvky case and was later the head of the Security Service at the time of the 7 July 2005 attacks.

Sir Richard Dearlove, Chief of the Secret Service from 1999 to 2004, pictured after giving evidence into the inquest into the death Diana, Princess of Wales, in 2008. Dearlove led MI6 through the aftermath of the 11 September attacks and the Iraq war. (Getty)

Sir John Scarlett, who earlier in his career ran Gordiersky as an agent, was Chairman of the Joint Intelligence Committee in the run up to the Iraq War and Chief of MI6 from 2004 to 2009. (Andrew Crowley)

teams would train the mujahedeen on the use of explosives, sniper rifles, silencers and the manufacture of improvised explosive devices. They would also teach the use of mortars and accompany the Afghans out on attacks to help instruct them on their use.

The secure radios provided by the British team were particularly valuable since they allowed tactical co-ordination of attacks by different groups of fighters without the fear that the Soviets were listening in and preparing an ambush. These were still being used in the late 1990s. One of Massoud's commanders, Muslem Hayat, says that in his area of operations which covered two square miles and three villages, he was able to destroy 100 tanks and armoured vehicles and 400 trucks using improvised explosive devices. He personally laid a thousand devices over the years.[17] One substance popular with the Afghans looked like camel dung and if put in the petrol tank of a Soviet vehicle would damage the engine. The flow of weapons was not one way. The conflict provided a unique opportunity for the West to get its hands on the latest Soviet military technology, and MI6 and the CIA were both issued with collection-guidance lists from their defence ministries on what kit was wanted for closer examination. This ranged from small arms like the latest AK-47 assault rifle to the real prizes like the new avionics systems for Soviet helicopters. Both the CIA and MI6 managed to extract helicopters from the battlefield, MI6 taking one out in parts on the back of mules.

Leafy rural Britain as well as the Panjshir was the site of mujahedeen training. Massoud personally selected a small number of educated and reliable fighters who could be sent abroad. Some of these battle-hardened men were taken to the Gulf where perhaps they might be able to blend in. But others were deposited in the rather more unusual surroundings of Scotland and rural Sussex. They were trained at a facility run by a small security company. The locals, who might well wonder who the rather exotic new arrivals might be, were to be told that the company had a contract in the Gulf. Ten to twelve men would be instructed at a time, living in an old barn. 'They were well armed and ferocious fighters but they lacked battlefield organisation,' recalled one person involved in the training.[18] They were tutored in 'specialist skills' including planning ambushes and attacking aircraft on the ground before being taken back into Afghanistan via Pakistan where they could get on with killing Russians and coaching their comrades. Many of those who received this training would years later go on to prominent positions in the Afghan parliament and government.

The Americans and the Pakistanis did not buy into Massoud – the Pakistanis because he was a Tajik, not a Pashtun, the Americans because he had called a ceasefire with the Soviets in early 1983 which lasted around a year. In the previous two years he and his 3,000-odd men had fought off six Soviet assaults, including one comprising 15,000 soldiers accompanied by a massive bombing campaign.[19] The Soviets feared, admired and hated Massoud at once. His frustrating of their forces had led to his being christened 'The Lion of the Panjshir'. His ceasefire had been a tactical move to buy some time to regroup as supplies were running low. But the Americans, egged on by the Pakistanis, saw it as an unwillingness to fight. 'Massoud's biggest interest in life was Massoud. And he was particularly good at it,' argued one CIA chief in Islamabad.[20] 'He could have done a lot more than he did.' Massoud's own people were angered by America's aloofness. 'The Americans wanted to fight the Cold War. He wanted to fight for the Afghans,' declares Abdullah Anas.[21]

The British had a different view. They saw Massoud as an effective fighter and worked hard at meetings in Washington to persuade the Americans that they should back him – American buy-in, however reluctant, was important since the CIA would actually be funding much of the British support. The fact that the gargantuan CIA programme had left Massoud behind was something of an advantage to the British. He could be their man. It provided an opportunity for Britain to wield some influence and show that it knew best, an attitude the Americans were always aware of. The CIA thought the British popularised Massoud because he was the only contact they had. There was 'always an underlying prickliness about the come-lately Americans taking the lead in their old backyard', reckoned the Texan Milt Bearden, who ran CIA operations in Afghanistan in the second half of the decade.[22] Another senior CIA officer was aware of how the British were always trying to stay in the game. 'They probably thought they knew more about Afghanistan than we did and they could play Athens to our Rome. There was a certain desire to be involved. They didn't want to be missing out.'[23] The ISI meanwhile ignored the British. Why talk to them when you have the Americans? They thought the British were playing their own game. Like the inhabitants of many former parts of the British Empire, the Pakistanis remained convinced that the conniving British had a devious plan and were playing divide and rule, manipulating everyone else. MI6 was not to be trusted, they thought. That at least left some space in which the British could operate, a chance to play the Great Game.

Stuart Bodman was a British journalist who died in a firefight near Bagram airbase on 1 July 1983. Except he was not and he did not. The confusion was both deliberate and accidental, all part of the world of deniable operations. The Afghan Foreign Ministry held a press conference a few months after he died proclaiming that Bodman was a spy, his work evidence of the 'shameless interference of imperialist countries' and in particular of 'the hellish organisation of the intelligence service of England'. He had been identified by the passport and driving licence found by his body, they said. The documents showed he was working for a press agency called Gulf Features Service.

Enterprising Fleet Street reporters tracked Stuart Bodman down two weeks later to a pub near London. 'The closest I came to spies was when I caddied for Sean Connery at Kingston Hill Golf Club years ago,' explained the thirty-year-old, who worked in a warehouse.[24] Records at the Passport Office showed that someone had falsely applied for a ten-year passport under Bodman's name in November 1982. 'I've never been further than Jersey,' the real Stuart Bodman said.[25] Gulf Features had been set up just a few months earlier by a successful, well-respected British industrialist named Sir Edgar Beck. It was rather a strange venture for a man who had a long career behind him in the construction and maintenance of major public buildings in London, including the Foreign Office and Downing Street. He denied all knowledge of Bodman and Afghanistan, saying it was all 'a complete mystery'. So, no doubt, was the failure of his news agency to publish any stories.[26] 'We know absolutely nothing about it,' was the Foreign Office response to inquiries.

Bodman was a British spy, but he was not Bodman and he was not dead. The identity was one of those used by MI6 for the increment soldiers it smuggled into the Panjshir for the same mission as the four men who had travelled in with a guide. The fake Bodman had spent a few weeks training Massoud's men. As their time came to an end, Massoud turned to the Britons. 'The Russians know you are here,' he told them. 'Bodman' and two colleagues had slipped into a vast convoy that smuggled lapis lazuli through Logar to Peshawar in Pakistan. Hundreds of horses carried the motley band of travellers, which included a team of French doctors, one of whose female members a British soldier had taken rather a shine to. At local villages they would stop for water. The Soviet airbase at Bagram was close, but the mujahedeen controlled the countryside. At one point, they came across a group of wandering Afghan nomads who had pitched their own tents. The nomads appeared unusually anxious, the accompanying mujahedeen noticed. Half an hour later, they learnt why.[27]

It was the dead of night when flares lit up the sky followed by the sound of gunfire. They were on a plain not far from Bagram airbase and bullets whizzed past. Then helicopter gunships roared overhead. No one could see where the Soviets were coming from and the convoy scattered in a thousand directions. Horses were cut down. One of the Britons was half trampled by one of their animals panicking. An Afghan hauled him out. One guide crawled to a nearby river. He could see Russian tanks scouring the landscape and kept his head down until the next morning when he began to walk again. Eventually in the second village he visited, the guide found the British men. Battered and bruised, they resumed their journey, still hunted by the Soviets. Twice more they came close to being ambushed by commandos and changed their route to try and evade their pursuers. 'It was a very lucky escape for the British,' reckons one of Massoud's lieutenants. They finally made it over the border around two in the morning. Two of the British men, still dressed in Afghan garb, were barely able to walk and were virtually dragged by their guides.

The Russians, who had been tipped off about the route, had failed to capture their main prize. But in the chaos the team had abandoned their equipment including their secure radios, satellite phones and fake documentation. Within two hours, realising that they had a useful haul, the Soviets sent four helicopters from Kabul which took the equipment to Moscow. Some of the documentation was later put on display at a Kabul press conference in October when the Soviets through their Afghan clients decided to publicise the find. Stuart Bodman was dead, they said. In fact his body was that of a Panjshiri horseman.[28] They said he also had with him a video camera and a modern communications unit with a computer encoding system. There was also a diary, they said, which mentioned twenty-five time fuses, twenty-five electric fuses and fifty detonators for the manufacture of mines and bombs as well a list of chemicals and instructions on how to make explosives and where to place them. An explosives specialist named Tom may also have been part of the group, they said.[29]

The Afghan and Soviet press did their best to expose what the British were up to. 'A good pay is taken by the hired instructors training Afghan terrorists in Pakistan to carry out acts that are not worthy of gentlemen. One of the instructors ... is making remote-controlled high-explosive bombs that are launched on peaceful Afghan villages. It is an open secret that some important highways in Afghanistan have been blown up with British mines.'[30] At other times, the Afghans accused the CIA of sending in undercover spies with film cameras from Peshawar.[31] The CIA did run a programme which sent non-Americans, often Europeans, into the country posing as journalists on false passports and with communications and filming equipment to report back on what they saw.[32] Groups of private individuals and small charities providing medical and humanitarian aid would soon follow the journalists in the pilgrimage to see Massoud which caused some awkwardness for the secret MI6 teams which had to be careful not to run into them.

As well as being able to go into the country, the British were also able to support activities that the CIA could not. The Americans were still struggling under the burden of the Congressional inquiries of the mid-1970s into assassination and covert war. A few of the more wily CIA officers saw a way of getting round their own lawyers and restrictions by bankrolling the British to undertake certain actions. 'They had a willingness to do jobs I couldn't touch. They basically took care of the "How to Kill People" department,' one CIA officer claimed later in an account of the war. 'The Brits were eventually able to buy things that we couldn't because it infringed on murder, assassination, and indiscriminate bombings. They could use guns with silencers. We couldn't do that because a silencer immediately implied assassination – and heaven forbid car bombs! No way I could even suggest it, but I could say to the Brits, "Fadallah in Beirut was really effective last week. They had a car bomb that killed three hundred people." I gave MI6 stuff in good faith. What they did with it was always their business.'[33]

British officials involved at the time shy away from American talk of 'assassination' but say fighters were trained in the use of silencers and sniper rifles as well as in the manufacture and planting of impro-vised explosive devices to blow up Soviet convoys. Fortunately for the British, these fighters allied to Massoud would be on their side in 2001 and in the battles that followed. This was not the case for those the Americans worked with like Hekmatyar and Jalaluddin Haqqani who received the bulk of American aid.

For Margaret Thatcher it was all simple. They were freedom fight-ers not terrorists. Abdul Haq came to visit Downing Street, one of his feet having recently been blown off. He had subsequently admitted to being behind a bomb blast at Kabul airport that killed twenty-eight people. When questioned as to why the Prime Minister refused to meet members of the Palestinian PLO or Nelson Mandela's ANC, a spokesman for the Prime Minister said it was different as the Afghan rebels were fighting a foreign invader.[34] 'They were good terrorists so we supported them. The ANC were bad. That caused her no moral problem at all,' explains one of Thatcher's former officials. The Chief of MI6, and his Director of Operations Colin McColl, would occa-sionally brief the Prime Minister on operations, but contact was sporadic – perhaps a forty-minute meeting every six months. Just as there was little contact on the ground between MI6 and CIA teams in Pakistan, there was relatively little co-ordination at the level of political leaders. MI6 was left to get on with its own business.

The great terror for the mujahedeen remained the Mi-24 Hind gunships which flew out of Bagram airbase and which provided the Soviets with control of the skies. After four years it was clear that the Soviets were hurting, but not enough. They had also begun to use more special forces, their Spetsnaz troops, to carry out commando raids, often dropping on to hills by helicopter. There were those in Washington who wanted to escalate the covert war, to supply more advanced weaponry and to shift from just hurting the Soviets to trying to drive them out. Politicians like Charlie Wilson were pushing the CIA to send more advanced weapons systems, especially surface-to-air missiles, and to up the funding. The first attempt to counter

Soviet advantage in the air was a British-made device which London was keen to deploy. There had been resistance in some quarters to using more advanced weaponry because of a fear that the Western hand in the war would be made all too clear, but resistance in London and Washington was eventually overcome (Thatcher personally pushing it through in London).

The Afghan warriors employing the British-supplied Blowpipe missile quickly saw that their task required something approaching a death-wish. It was a shoulder-fired surface-to-air weapon but a pretty inept one. The user had to launch it while standing directly in front of an attacking aircraft and then guide the missile to the target by manipulating a joystick with his thumb as he stared death in the face, like playing some suicidal video game. The operator would be looking, literally, down the barrel of a gun. The general opinion of British soldiers who had used them in the Falklands was that they were 'a pile of crap' and they were being phased out in the British army in favour of the new Javelin weapon.[35] Still, hundreds were smuggled into Afghanistan via Pakistan. A British team came out to provide the extensive training required. The results, even when tried out on 'gently descending parachute flares', were miserable. Half of the first batch would not accept the command signal and went astray. After a British expert had flown over and agreed that something was wrong they were all taken back to England to be modified before being returned for action.[36] No one is able to recall a single aircraft being shot down using a Blowpipe.[37] At one battle, Pakistani officers tried to show the mujahedeen how to fire them and launched thirteen with no hits and with one Pakistani captain and an NCO severely wounded by the unscathed attacking aircraft.[38] The British military were mortified by the failure of their kit.

After the Blowpipe the Stinger arrived in Afghanistan. This was an American 'fire and forget' weapon that locked on to the heat source of an aircraft. In a sign of how much this had become a media war, the mujahedeen fighters given the privilege of firing the first missile were also given a video camera on which to record the event. They came, unsurprisingly, from Hekmatyar's party. The result of their foray into TV journalism was filmic chaos. At three in the afternoon on 25 September 1986, a group of Hind gunships came in to land. As they made their final approach, the words 'Allahu Akbar' could be heard repeatedly on the tape as three missiles blazed away. Two hit their target. The picture then shook as people, including the cameraman, jumped up and down in celebration. It then zoomed into the wreckage and on to the grisly image of the corpses. Mujahedeen began cursing and firing shots into a body before a final close-up of one deceased member of the Soviet aircrew barely out of his teens. The video would be shown by the CIA to President Reagan in the White House.[39] Massoud received almost none of the Stingers: only eight came his way at the end of the war out of 2,000 provided to the mujahedeen (600 of which were estimated to be still at large in 1996).[40] Abdullah Anas and others would occasionally purchase some on the black market from other corrupt Afghan commanders. The missiles certainly boosted morale, but even they were not as effective as sometimes claimed. Only 16 per cent actually hit their targets, according to one official involved at the time.[41] Soviet aircraft flew higher, and more of them remained in base for longer, although this also may have been due to a political decision. Journalists kept offering to pay money to see a Stinger being fired and bringing down a Soviet aircraft, but they never got the picture.[42]

Towards the end of the war, there was an element of theatre to proceedings, a sense that much of it was being played out for the now extensive audience of visiting journalists. Massoud was a master of the media. He understood its value. His soldiers also grew used to the presence of journalists. When the cameras came out, they would immediately strike a pose. The only way into the country was under the protection of a particular commander, so media accounts almost always tended to fête their protector. Massoud was widely glamorised even though he could be as brutal as any commander. Hacks paid for mujahedeen to attack a particular Russian post so that they could film it. There was talk that some had offered $10,000 for a picture of the execution of a Russian soldier. The Pakistanis had always been very adept at the theatrics. The performances had been well rehearsed for visiting dignitaries from Washington, including Congressmen like Charlie Wilson (who at one point introduced his latest girlfriend, who was called Snowflake, to Gulbuddin Hekmatyar, an unlikely meeting if ever there was one).[43]

When the custom-fitted, unmarked and blacked-out Starlifter air-craft pulled up at Islamabad airport it meant that the CIA Director,

Bill Casey, had travelled out to see the show. When Casey paid his first visit to the country he was made to believe he was being driven by jeep into Afghanistan. In fact that was considered far too dangerous and he was actually taken to a fake training camp in Pakistan. He cried tears of joy at the sight of so many willing warriors. Eventually he would be allowed to see a real camp.[44] The mumbling Casey, who had fought with the CIA's forerunner the OSS during the Second World War, was in many ways a throwback to the CIA of Frank Wisner and the early Cold War. He did not care much for intelligence analysis or Congressional oversight. He wanted the CIA to be a tool to wage a clandestine war against the Soviet Union. President Reagan's strategy was to pressure the Soviets on all fronts and all around the world, whether in Central America or Central Asia. It was the 1980s version of that old Cold War notion of rollback. Part of the idea was propaganda. The Soviets were worried about the spread of radical Islam in these years. The Americans were not. Ten thousand Korans were printed and distributed in Central Asia, religion being used to undermine the godless Soviets.[45] Casey also wanted to take mujahedeen operations into the Soviet Union itself, a step further than even the Albania operation of the early 1950s. He wanted to have strategic bridges and roads blown up to impede the movement of Soviet supplies into Afghanistan. This did happen, although the CIA always denied that it had authorised the attacks and said that the mujahedeen had acted on their own or with Pakistani support.

The ISI sent its own men undercover into Afghanistan to act as advisers and eyes and ears. Two-man teams would go in for three months, growing thick beards to blend in. They were told to deny any connection to the Pakistani government and to avoid being captured alive. The ISI's head of Afghan operations, Mohammad Yousaf, was explicit about the training provided for sabotage and assassination, including how to spot Soviet officers in order to kill them. 'These attacks could range from a knife between the shoulder blades of a Soviet soldier shopping in the bazaar to the placing of a briefcase bomb in a senior official's office.'[46] The attacks became more aggressive and less clearly military, more what most would call terrorism. A bomb under a dining table at Kabul University in late 1983 killed nine Soviets including a female professor. 'Educational institutions were considered fair game as the staff were all Communists indoctrinating their students with Marxist dogma,' according to Yousaf. Shots were fired at a Soviet cinema; remote-controlled car bombs began to go off; rockets were lobbed into Kabul killing civilians. Boats carrying supplies towards Afghanistan were also targeted. 'We required limpet mines that a small recce boat or a swimmer could carry, which could be clamped to the side of the boat just below the water line,' Yousaf recalled later. 'For these we turned to the British, via MI6. They obliged and it was the UK's small but effective contribution to destroying a number of loaded barges on the Soviet side of the Amu throughout 1986.'[47] CIA officials supplied electronic timers, plastic explosives and other items which could have military uses but which could also be deployed against civilians. They told the ISI never to use words like sabotage or assassination when Congressmen came through. No one wanted an inquiry.[48] Moscow began to issue warnings, hinting that it would strike training camps in Pakistan. The water was getting too hot and the temperature was soon turned down a notch.

The CIA chief in Islamabad, Milt Bearden, and his ISI counterpart, Brigadier Yousaf, increasingly began to argue as the decade came to a close. The ISI man had an abiding distrust of the Americans, a distaste for the fact that Yankee money was funding his jihad and tried to assert control, which Bearden resisted. The Americans began to perceive risks in their reliance on the Pakistanis and tried to go around the ISI's back to build their own relations with commanders. They engaged sources to provide reports on what weaponry was reaching the front line and find out whether the Pakistanis were actually passing on all the material they claimed (the CIA reckoned at least a third of the weaponry was siphoned off by the ISI for other projects). The CIA also tried building relations with Massoud, although officers did not see him face to face, instead working through intermediaries. One officer assigned to work with Massoud learnt that Hekmatyar had put word out to have him (the American) killed.[49]

In Moscow, a few in the Soviet leadership realised early on that they were not going to win the war in a conventional sense. But there were always voices calling for more troops and tougher tactics and there was an unwillingness early in the 1980s to accept that the intervention had become a war which was now being lost. As the decade stretched on and the coffins returned home and the mothers of the soldiers began to protest, the conflict increasingly became the Soviets' Vietnam. The leadership struggled to find a way to extricate itself from a war which sapped morale and underscored the decay of hardline Communist power and policy. Thatcher could see by the second half of the 1980s that Gorbachev was looking for a way to disengage from Afghanistan. He told her it would be easier to find a solution if she stopped supplying the rebels with weapons.[50] But Britain and the US did not stop. They were determined to drive home the advantage, to keep the pressure on the Soviet Union. They continued even after the Geneva accords were signed in 1988 when it became clear that the war-weary Soviets were pulling out.

As the end of the war approached, CIA and MI6 officers in Pakistan increasingly argued about what – and who – would come next. Senior Americans remained opposed to Massoud, the British supportive. When the dangers of backing certain commanders like Hekmatyar were explained by a British officer to visiting American Congressmen, a message came back from Downing Street through headquarters and out to the field: 'Don't rock the boat.' The British pushed for working with the UN to try and forge a political compromise between the different factions. A few in Washington agreed, but the CIA was determined to keep going. Milt Bearden pointed out that the British had lost two wars in Afghanistan already.

Soviet soldiers finally marched out of Afghanistan on 15 February 1989. General Boris Gromov was the last to leave, solemnly walking across the Friendship Bridge that connected the two countries. Fourteen thousand of his comrades had been killed in the preceding years. Perhaps a million, perhaps two million Afghans had died. No one had counted. Some 300,000 to 400,000 had been armed over the decade.[51] Milt Bearden sent a high-priority 'Immediate' cable back to Langley. Subject: 'Soviet Occupation of Afghanistan'. The content of the message was a page which spelt out the words 'We won' in Xs across an entire page. For the first time Bearden switched off the light in his office, which he had previously kept on every night to make the Soviets across the road think he never stopped working.[52] 'Vietnam avenged,' one person remembers Bearden saying with his fist in the air.

They had won. But had their Afghan allies won? No institutions had been built. That had never been the point of the war in Western eyes. And the Soviets might have gone, but their Communist government was still in place and would last until 1992, much longer than many expected. An attempt by the mujahedeen to take Jalalabad in a frontal assault failed dismally. ISI figures like Mohammad Yousaf became bitter and suspicious, believing that the Americans were trying both to sabotage Pakistan's interests and to spread disunity among the Peshawar seven, though they hardly needed American help for that.[53] Without American largesse to keep them on board, old feuds among the Peshawar seven predictably bubbled back up to the surface. Massoud and Hekmatyar squared off for a fight. For all his tactical skill, Massoud lacked the ability to transcend his narrow position. The Americans had lost interest in Afghanistan after 1989 and walked away. Job done. Having been swept up in the superpower conflict like many other parts of the world, Afghanistan was suddenly dropped to earth with a jolt. But, uniquely, the country would have its revenge for being jilted so swiftly.

Afghanistan fell off the requirement list for MI6 set by the Joint Intelligence Committee in Whitehall once the Soviets had left. In the new budget climate, that meant that even if someone told an MI6 officer something interesting or important about the country the officer would worry that pursuing a lead when there was no requirement would get them into trouble. Relationships atrophied. Just enough was done to keep contact with Massoud on life support. The CIA shut down its Afghan programme in 1992. Massoud was angry that the Americans had simply walked away. In later years when Afghanistan suddenly became important again, relationships would have to be rebuilt, often with money instead of trust. That would lead to the old familiar faces re-emerging, now as warlords, the kaleidoscope of allegiances shaken up only a little.

The war left a dark legacy not just in Afghanistan but also in Pakistan that would shape the country's path. There were the millions of Afghan refugees who came to Pakistan and stayed, along with their guns. There was the power of the military in society and of the ISI within the military. The US had turned a blind eye to Pakistan's acquisition of nuclear weapons during the years of their joint jihad.

CIA analysts who had criticised the policy of ignoring the sprawling black-market network in nuclear know-how run by Pakistani scientist A. Q. Khan found their careers suddenly taking a sharp turn south.[54] But then as soon as the war in Afghanistan was won, the US decided it did not need Pakistan any more. In 1990 long-deferred sanctions were imposed on Islamabad's nuclear programme. The Pakistanis were left high and dry. They would never trust the Americans again.

Pakistan also had to deal with a culture of jihad that had taken deep root in parts of the country. Saudi money, which matched CIA funding, helped build radical madrasas which offered free education for the poor but led to many young people coming out the other end enthused with the notion of jihad. That might be fine when it was jihad against the Soviets. It would become more problematic later. The Saudis had encouraged their own jihadists to head for Afghanistan, where they joined a small army of other volunteers or jihadists from across the Arab world and North Africa. Clustered around two of the Peshawar seven, Haqqani and Abdul Rasul Sayyaf, the 4,000-odd Arabs did not do much fighting. But when the war was over they looked for ways and means to continue their jihad. Some found an outlet in a new front in Kashmir promoted by the ISI. The Pakistani spy service had become adept at training in the techniques most would call terrorism and passed these skills on to a new generation of jihadists eager to fight against India. Other Arab jihadists looked further afield for an enemy.

Afghanistan would soon become the sanctuary for those who sought to attack the West. When the Communist government in Kabul fell in 1992, Hekmatyar and Massoud battled each other and Kabul was shelled to pieces and consumed in an orgy of rape and murder. The anarchy that resulted opened the way for a new force to emerge backed by Pakistan and the ISI in the form of the Taliban. These Muslim fundamentalists promised order and purity out of chaos and swept to power in Kabul in 1996. At the same time as the Taliban emerged triumphant, the Al Qaeda leader Osama bin Laden flew in on a small plane from Sudan, returning to the country in which he had fought in the 1980s. Training camps drew in recruits from around the world, some run by old mujahedeen commanders from the 1980s with ISI trainers still offering free tuition, others closer to bin Laden specialised in recruiting for operations abroad. The only significant region which did not fall to the Taliban was the Panjshir Valley and the north where Massoud held firm. In Peshawar, one of Massoud's brothers and closest aides met with his contact from MI6. 'We were right,' the British officer told him with a touch of smugness, thinking no doubt more of the arguments with the Americans than the fate of Afghanistan. 'Hekmatyar failed and Massoud succeeded.'[55]

The CIA had largely disengaged from the country. Its main operation was trying to buy back and recover its Stinger missiles. As it became clear that bin Laden was targeting the US, especially after the deadly 1998 attacks on its embassies in Africa, the CIA tried to rebuild its relationship with Massoud to get to bin Laden, hoping to reactivate the contacts it had developed at the end of the 1980s. Massoud was curious but wary. His sanctuary was being squeezed by the Taliban, but he could see little benefit in acting as the proxy for an agency which cared only about getting bin Laden. In the end, he was offered cash but no military assistance.

One of the reasons for wariness in dealing with Massoud was the new agenda being pursued by both the CIA and MI6. By the 1990s fighting drugs had replaced fighting Soviets, and everyone knew that heroin was coming into Europe from Afghanistan, including from Massoud's territory. The 'drugs and thugs' desk at MI6 which dealt with crime and narcotics knew that Massoud's people were involved and from 1997 the New Labour government made dealing with narcotics a top priority for MI6.[56] This could conflict with counter-terrorism, which was also rising up the agenda. MI6 officers tried to peer across the Afghan hills but saw little. It was taking time to build up sources to find out what was going on. The Pakistanis pressed for recognition of the Taliban, offering help to establish contacts. A few wonder if that might have been worth doing in order to gain some leverage over them to expel bin Laden, but in London a new government was in power which promised an ethical dimension to its foreign policy. Talking to the Taliban would not fit with that.

The same arguments were in play in Washington, where the CIA and others worried that some figures in the Northern Alliance (the umbrella group Massoud had created in 1996) were directly involved in drugs or human rights abuses. The CIA decided to remain largely neutral between Massoud and the Taliban, on the grounds that supporting Massoud might just perpetuate the civil war.[57] The CIA, during the Clinton administration, was going through one of its periodic swings away from aggressive activity and the main fear for officers was once again of being hauled before Congress. The gungho days of Bill Casey were a distant memory. Even when the CIA had bin Laden in its sights, it hesitated before pulling the trigger. It had been given the authority to capture but not explicitly to kill. To kill would break the ban on assassination which had once again been emphasised in the 1990s. A major plan to collect more intelligence in Afghanistan began in 1998 using eight separate tribal networks. Five times in the next two years, CIA teams deployed to the Panjshir Valley to meet with warlords including Massoud. The CIA would boast that it had accumulated a hundred sources and sub-sources. But most of these were low level. Officials would later protest that the intelligence was never quite good enough to launch a missile or a snatch operation directed at the Al Qaeda leader. It was either single sourced or else bin Laden was hunting with a group of sheikhs from the United Arab Emirates. Or he was near a mosque – what would the newspaper headlines look like the next morning if they blew it up? Those in the CIA unit tracking bin Laden, like its chief Mike Scheuer, fumed at the failure of their leadership and that of the White House for not taking more risks.[58]

On one occasion in 1998, MI6 believed it might be able to obtain 'actionable intelligence' which could help the CIA capture Osama bin Laden. But given that this might result in his being transferred or rendered to the United States, MI6 decided it had to ask for ministerial approval before passing the intelligence on in case the Al Qaeda leader faced the death penalty or mistreatment. This was approved by a minister 'provided the CIA gave assurances regarding humane treatment'. In the end, not enough intelligence came through to make it worth while going ahead.[59]

It was becoming clearer in 2001 that Massoud and his men were the best option for going after bin Laden. The priority for MI6 was developing intelligence coverage. The first real sources were being established, although no one penetrated the upper tier of the Al Qaeda leadership itself. The problem was not locating bin Laden but getting close to him – that would require an agent of some sort in place who could help either directly by himself passing through security or by facilitating access for a team coming in. As the year progressed, plans were drawn up and slowly worked their way up to the White House for discussion on 4 September 2001. They involved dramatically increasing support for Massoud. Britain and MI6 were involved. 'The posse was getting ready,' reckons one British official involved. 'But it wasn't ready in time.'

On 9 September 2001, two Arab journalists who had been waiting to interview Massoud were told they finally had their chance. The queue of those wanting to speak to the Northern Alliance leader was not quite what it had been, but he still liked to use the power of the media. His enemies had decided to exploit this. Their letter of introduction had come from something called the Islamic Observation Centre in London. The two visitors were shown into a large room and did what most TV journalists do and began rearranging the furniture to get the right shot. A coffee table and some chairs were shifted so that the interviewer sat next to Massoud while the cameraman positioned his heavy-duty camera on the tripod. These two were a bit amateurish, thought some of Massoud's aides. What are the questions, Massoud, ever the experienced interviewee, asked? 'We want to know why commander Massoud said that Usama bin Laden was a murderer and should be sent from Afghanistan and many more questions,' the interviewer said. Massoud frowned but told them to continue. The last thing the Lion of the Panjshir ever saw was the red light of the camera going on.[60]

9

OUT OF THE SHADOWS

The latest man to be known by the letter C would occasionally cross the river from MI6's drab headquarters in Lambeth to wander through the corridors of Whitehall where other government departments were still beavering away. The civil servants Colin McColl met would sometimes be surprised to see him. It was almost as if he was a largely forgotten uncle discovered in the corner at a family get-together. 'I'd meet people – intelligent, knowledgeable people in Whitehall – they'd see me and they'd say things like "Are you still here?"' McColl later recalled.[1] As it entered the 1990s, the Secret Service appeared a little lost without the comfort blanket of the Cold War. Spying on the Soviet Union had never taken up more than half of its effort, but nevertheless the work of MI6 had been defined in the public mind – and to some extent in its own – by the world of Moscow Rules, Smiley and Karla and doubling, tripling agents.

In a grand, high-ceilinged room near Downing Street, the Chairman of the Joint Intelligence Committee had offered a celebratory glass of champagne to toast the end of the Soviet Union in August 1991. And with that, the war was over. McColl, a Sov Bloc veteran whose youthful sense of humour masked a sharp mind, had presided over victory. From his office high up in the building with a view across London, he would tell new recruits that they had joined at a fascinating time in which MI6 could not take its eye off the old threats but also had to look out for new dangers while maintaining Britain's place in the world. The position of the service in government was also changing, he would explain. But he did not always succeed in reassuring all his staff that the service had a role in the new world. One of his younger officers remembers an encounter with the Chief at a reception in headquarters. McColl turned to him and said, 'Well, what do *you* think we should do?'[2] The question did not necessarily inspire confidence. With its old adversary seemingly out of action, those on the inside wondered what MI6 would find to do next. Those on the outside wondered whether it was even needed any more. An air of gloomy insecurity hung around the corridors of the British Secret Service.

The rabbit warren of Century House, with its peeling lino and Formica tables, had a forlorn air and the Treasury, like a lion circling a wounded beast, was on the prowl. There was distressing talk of even merging with 'the other lot' at MI5 (who were also looking for work and trying to wrestle responsibility for fighting the IRA away from the Metropolitan Police). The peace dividend, shaped as an axe, fell. The first compulsory redundancies were painfully served and poorly handled within MI6. Overall staff numbers of around 2,000 were to drop by 25 per cent, senior staff numbers by more.[3] Stations were closed in Africa and the Far East; more emphasis was placed on inserting officers into countries rather than having them based there permanently. Every piece of turf had to be fought for using every ounce of Smiley-like cunning. The Foreign Office decided to claw back some money from MI6 by estimating how much desk space was used by spies operating out of embassies abroad and then insisting it be paid for. MI6 retaliated by calculating how much work its staff did to maintain their cover as Foreign Office diplomats. This, of course, came to more than the desk space and a truce was called. In perhaps the most telling sign that the service was being dragged out of the past, that creature very much in vogue in the 1990s, the management consultant, was even brought in to sniff around. These consultants were all carefully vetted, but even so their arrival was watched with utter bemusement by many old-timers. The freebooting era of the 1920s, when the Chief could pull an armful of gold coins out of his desk and hand them over to fund an operation, was being replaced by one of audits and value for money. A small attempt at privatisation proved disastrous when a group of long-serving office cleaners were sacked. This was blamed on pressure from the Treasury to outsource their work to a private company but more likely resulted from a failure to realise that, with the Cold War gone, the willingness of people (whether cleaners or the press) to accept the traditional constraints of secrecy was eroding rapidly. To much embarrassment, the cleaners took the spies to the cleaners by winning an employment tribunal and a healthy pay-out (along with plenty of publicity). The insecurity surrounding all the intelligence agencies occasionally manifested itself even within the stately confines of meetings of the Joint Intelligence Committee as representatives of each intelligence agency competed to try and knock out references in reports to the other agencies' work and put in their own.[4]

Gerry Warner had risen to be deputy chief of MI6 and then the security and intelligence co-ordinator in the Cabinet Office, responsible for overseeing the community as a whole and its health. He found he needed to traipse round departments, even the Bank of England, and ask what they actually wanted. A performance-monitoring system was instituted in which policy-makers would tick a box if they found intelligence useful. Intelligence was becoming less precautionary than it had been in the Cold War when the focus was on looking for signs of conflict or having the tactical knowledge of how to fight the war if it started. In the old days an analyst could spend his whole career watching a Soviet tank division before receiving his pension. Intelligence was now drawing closer to day-to-day decision-making. 'In many ways the intelligence we were providing was of more immediate use to politicians than the intelligence we had provided during the Cold War, because most of the intelligence provided during the Cold War was mostly of background interest – very important, very interesting – but there wasn't anything we could do about it,' argues Warner.[5] And even when it came to the Russians, things were a little odd.

The British Ambassador in Moscow, Rodric Braithwaite, nearly choked on his breakfast when one morning he opened up a local newspaper to find an interview, carried on two successive days, with his chauffeur. For seventeen years Konstantin had driven the Ambassador's Rolls-Royce in and out of the grand, menacing pre-revolutionary mansion on the Moscow River with its view over to the Kremlin. He was now admitting that he had spied on Braithwaite and his predecessors for the KGB. 'You might have warned me because this could cause me serious trouble back home,' Braithwaite told Konstantin. 'You know, questions in the House about the limp-wristed Ambassador who failed to notice his driver works for the KGB. That sort of stuff.'

'I couldn't,' replied Konstantin. 'I'm a Russian patriot.'[6]

Times were changing. For a while in 1991 the old KGB was in disarray and appeared out of business. Braithwaite hosted a delegation of spy-hunters from MI5 who had come to meet their former adversaries. The group were greeted at Moscow's airport by a KGB officer bearing roses, before enjoying a meeting at the Lubyanka in which both sides felt 'like wild animals being presented with their prey in circumstances where they couldn't eat it'. The British asked politely if the surveillance and harassment of members of Embassy staff in Moscow could be reduced and asked if the level of Russian espionage within Britain might be limited. They received the distinct impression that these ideas were ridiculous.[7] Braithwaite also had a new MI6 head of station working in the secure bubble room in the cavernous Embassy-cum-Residence. It had not been the obvious choice for an ambitious officer but Moscow was embedded deep in John Scarlett's psyche and the chance to be the first station chief to be 'avowed' or declared to the Russians at such an interesting time was simply too good an opportunity to miss. The idea was that the two countries would normalise their intelligence relations and act like other countries where the head of station did not do any spying per se but acted as a liaison with the local services for the passing of agreed information. Scarlett's past running of Oleg Gordievsky, a traitor reviled deeply by KGB types, was either unknown to the Russians or conveniently overlooked. But the old world had not entirely passed.

Dressed in shabby clothes the Russian had knocked on the door of an American embassy in one of the Baltic States. He was turned away disappointed. Defectors whom Western intelligence would have fought tooth and nail for in the past were now appearing hopefully at their doors bearing armfuls of documents and expecting dollars and visas in return. They seemed ten a penny and most got nowhere. Next stop for this man was the local British Embassy where he explained to a female diplomat that he had top-secret KGB material. The British diplomat had been trained to deal with walk-ins and glanced at the material, which had lain among bread, sausages and clothes in his bag. Vasili Mitrokhin would be one of the select few considered valuable enough to warrant assistance. He was a former archivist for the KGB who had secretly copied out and then buried large chunks of the organisation's secret operational history in the garden of his dacha. Understanding its potential, the British diplomat told him to return again soon at an agreed date, when he would meet an MI6 officer who would come over from London. At that meeting Mitrokhin produced 2,000 pages of his notes which included details of KGB illegals. This was enough to swing the argument in London. Displaying the kind of cheek which the old Robber Barons would have enjoyed, MI6 organised for the clandestine exfiltration of Mitrokhin and his family on the seventy-fifth anniversary of the Bolshevik Revolution. Scarlett was kept out of the operation, but a young MI6 officer dug up Mitrokhin's voluminous files and carried them to the British Embassy where they were taken to Britain in six large trunks.[8]

The Russians talked about 'no spy' deals, but there was little trust on either side. A few of the old Cold Warriors at MI6 could not quite let go and continued to want to use the defectors to turn the SVR, the renamed foreign intelligence wing of KGB, inside out and to extract every last drop of blood in revenge for Philby. MI6 even recruited one junior Russian diplomat who appeared to be mentally ill. This was a result of ambitious officers hoping to hit their 'performance targets' and exaggerating their successes, one disaffected colleague thought.[9] As early as 1992, there were the first signs that the SVR was also up to its old tricks with a couple discovered at Helsinki airport travelling under false identity papers, claiming they had been born in Croydon and Wembley in London. They looked a lot like old-fashioned Russian illegals.[10]

Scarlett's time in Moscow did not end happily. The Russians nominated one of their senior officers to take up the counterpart position as declared head of station in London. MI5, still not quite able to come to terms with the new world, kicked up a fuss. He is a spy, they said. Of course he is a spy, the Foreign Office and MI6 replied, that is the whole point. But he has had shady dealings with Saddam Hussein's Iraq, MI5 responded. It would be more of a surprise if someone who had worked for the KGB did not have a shady past, came the reply. The Russian intelligence officer was suffering from cancer and Moscow was keen for him to get to London for medical treatment, but his visa was blocked thanks to MI5. Moscow was understandably furious and decided on revenge. Scarlett was expelled under the public pretext of having recruited an agent in a military metallurgical firm. The expulsion was carried out not quietly but in a blaze of publicity, a photographer capturing an image of the publicity-shy spy in a car at the airport.

In Eastern Europe events were in some ways even stranger as MI6 officers would walk gingerly into the office of former foes and politely ask exactly what they had got up to in the past. MI6 and MI5 began a low-key role in reorganising intelligence services across what had been the Eastern bloc. This involved civilianising their services and teaching them 'how to collect intelligence in a different environment without threatening to put someone against a wall', as one Briton involved puts it.[11] One issue was what to do with the twenty-odd illegal sleepers that the Czechs had secreted around the world. This included one or two who had been sent to Britain and now did not want to go home. It was agreed between London and Prague to leave them alone as they had never done any damage.[12] As far as anyone knows, they continue to live somewhere in suburban Britain, their neighbours none the wiser about their training in servicing dead drops and sending burst transmissions.

There were old debts to be repaid as well. Agents who had been spying in place had been paid by means of escrow accounts with an understanding that one day they would be able to draw on the funds (this was always preferred by MI6 to giving them money which they could flash around, drawing attention to themselves). One agent had read the *Financial Times* voraciously and insisted on telling his case officer exactly how he wanted his portfolio invested. Some came out of the Cold War with a million pounds for having betrayed secrets. The valuable agent codenamed Freed had died in Czechoslovakia of a heart attack in the mid-1970s. With warm relations now established with the Czech service, MI6 approached Václav Havel, the former dissident intellectual now running the country, and explained that there was a bank account with the money the agent had accumulated in his lengthy career spying for Her Majesty. Havel agreed to help find any remaining family. A daughter was eventually located and carefully approached. She had never guessed her father had been a spy for MI6. But, according to a British official present at a meeting, she did remember him once saying an odd thing to her: 'I hope you marry a British officer.' Now she understood why, and she was given details of the bank account containing 25 million Czech koruna.[13]

There was one final innovation, an intrusion of the modern world, welcome to some but disorienting, even terrifying to others. The Secret Service was not going to be secret any more. The timing, coming at the end of the Cold War, was largely coincidental. MI5 had already been avowed in 1989. The staff there had foisted the move on a reluctant government. They had been unhappy with having no real legal basis for their work tapping people's phones and bugging their houses in the UK, other than a minister's sign-off. They wanted to feel that they were working within the law, not around it. 'It was not comfortable to be engaged in operations for which there was no proper legal cover,' recalled Eliza Manningham-Buller. There was also the European factor. Individuals had tried to sue security services in Europe for their actions. The European Court of Human Rights had decreed that any security or intelligence service had to be on a legal footing and have a proper system of complaints. Britain had neither. MI6 would have to become 'legal'.

There was also the rather expensive new office that MI6 was having constructed at growing expense in Vauxhall Cross. Like Century House, the building was on the south side of the river physically separating MI6 from the rest of government. But that was about the only thing the new place had in common with the old. It was flashy and very unsubtle. Gerry Warner pointed out that it would be hard to move to something that looked like an Odeon cinema and expect people not to ask what it was. The problem with Century House had been security. Not the location, which was widely known to everyone including bus conductors ('spies alight here' they would say as they reached the stop outside), nor even access, with its security guards who would wave people in without asking for any ID unless they did not recognise them. It was the fabric of the building itself that kept those concerned with its safety awake at night. The largely glass headquarters of the British Secret Service was housed on top of a petrol station. 'God, we were really living on borrowed time,' says McColl. The station was owned by Q8, the Kuwaiti petrol company. When Iraq invaded Kuwait in 1990 there was a joke doing the rounds that all the Iraqis would have to do was light a fuse to destroy the entire British Secret Service. The new architect-designed home in Vauxhall, known as Legoland by some, was secure but also a touch sterile, befitting the new era. Staff attitudes towards it were perhaps best illustrated during a special premiere for the new James Bond film *The World is Not Enough* in 1999, hosted inside the new headquarters. The previous year Dame Judi Dench who played M had been invited to Christmas lunch by the real C to help her gain some insight into her role. The actress who played Miss Moneypenny introduced the viewing. When the scene arrived in which a large explosion rocked the new MI6 headquarters, the assembled staff issued a loud cheer.[14]

The legislation which placed MI6 on a statutory footing was piloted through the House of Commons by Foreign Secretary Douglas Hurd, a former diplomat who had turned down an invitation to join the service in the 1950s. Serving as a diplomat out in China, he had occasionally counted railways wagons for MI6 and gazed askance at his Embassy colleagues. 'They were odd folk by definition,' he later recalled. 'You found yourself maybe sitting alongside somebody who had a rather peculiar job description and you understood gradually what he or she was up to.'[15] The act was passed in 1994. It answered a profound insecurity in the service. Before then, since it did not actually exist, MI6 could have been wound up or merged by the stroke of a pen and by the whim of any minister. It now had a secure foundation and at last there were fewer pretences and ums and ahs from ministers and officials when explaining exactly what bit of government they were talking about. But was there also a cost to coming out of the shadows?

There was 'a little sorrow' from those who had lived beneath the shroud of secrecy for so long, according to McColl. A generational divide marked attitudes within MI6 to its emergence, blinking, into the light. 'The old people were used to the old system and they weren't anti-avowal but they simply weren't terribly interested in it really,' remembers McColl, a product of Shergy's Sov Bloc master race where secrecy was prized and something of a reluctant lifter of the veil. 'It was always the slippery slide that we were worried about. That once you got on to the slope and you started opening things up you would run into problems over secrecy. And secrecy was and is absolutely central to the whole of our work because our work is about trust. It is about trust between the government and people running the service. It is the trust between the service and the people all over the world who are working for it, and many of them are taking great risks ... they do that in the faith that we are really a secret service which means to say we are not talking and we're not going out into the public and declaring ourselves. And I've always felt that that was one of our advantages. We were – and have been always – a secret service.' The cautionary tale, McColl and others believed, was the American experience. They had watched the very public undressing of the CIA by Congress in the mid-1970s. 'There was a sort of shudder that went through the intelligence world and it went through many of the people who were working for the Americans or working for us, because they were coming to us and saying "For God's sake, look what's happening in America" and "Is it going to happen to us?"'[16] As MI6 stepped out, some of the older generation went around muttering to each other. 'It will all end in tears,' they said.

The fear was that avowal would strip the service of its mystique, a sheen of glamour and power built up largely by fiction. This had been sustained through secrecy since no one had any way of judging whether the fictional portrayal was on the mark or not. McColl traces its origins back to the late nineteenth century when Kipling and others wrote of brave British spies fighting the dastardly Russians in the Great Game over India, a tradition continued in John Buchan's stories about the plucky Brits now defending the realm against the cunning Krauts. And then came Bond. 'It keeps the name going doesn't it,' reckons McColl, who speaks freely about MI6 as a 'brand'. 'I mean, everybody watched Bond. And so why shouldn't a little Bond rub off on our reputation?' The brand, it is argued, does more than just make the service feel good about itself, it also helps with the recruitment of agents who are convinced they are dealing with an all-knowing and all-powerful organisation. If people in the Middle East want to believe that MI6 is pulling the strings behind the most unlikely events, is that really a problem if it means they will come to it when they need help (and do so in preference to another country)? Some believed that the myths of popular culture carried with them dangers. One former Foreign Secretary argued that the image of a service that always did exciting things, always won and was always right, created an exaggerated view of MI6's potential which in turn fed into government and skewed views, particularly of inexperienced ministers, of what was possible and what was not.

The bleaker world of le Carré divided the service. 'There were those who were furious with John le Carré because he depicts everybody as such disagreeable characters and they are always plotting against each other,' recalls McColl, perhaps thinking of Daphne Park and her distaste for him. 'We know we weren't always as disagreeable as that and we certainly weren't plotting against each other. So people got rather cross about it. But actually I thought it was terrific because, again, it carried the name that had been provided by Bond and John Buchan and everybody else. It gave us another couple of generations of being in some way special.' But with the end of the Cold War, even the old-fashioned spy thriller suddenly looked like a museum piece and the authors were having to search for new plotlines. Who were the bad guys now?

While MI6 did not mind the mythologising of its work in fictional literature, it was firmly determined that its own secrets should remain under lock and key. There was a strict rule that staff could not write memoirs. 'We have always put quite a big effort into discouraging our retired people from writing books,' explains McColl. 'I have a lot of sympathy for them, because if you have been banging round the world for most of your life, unless you have got a very big family or a lot of old friends in the UK you come back here, you retire to some little village somewhere and it is a lonely life. You haven't got many roots and it's very tempting to write up some of the adventures you were involved in.' There was one spectacular case where MI6 failed to discourage one of its own disaffected officers from talking. Richard Tomlinson had joined as a high-flyer (although those who recruited him would later rue failing to take up his references). He was eager and enthusiastic. Perhaps a bit too eager and enthusiastic, thought some of his superiors, who wondered if his notions of how to behave might display a little too much influence from the Bond films. He was also seen as something of a loner. Tomlinson himself believed he was badly treated and not given any due process before being turfed out, which is also more than plausible given the way MI6 operated. Both sides would have cause to regret the breakdown in relations, though, as Tomlinson wrote a book exposing the ins and outs of his time in the service, which caused real shock and damage.

The death of Princess Diana in 1997 in a car accident in a tunnel in Paris led to the surfacing of one of Tomlinson's most awkward allegations. He said he remembered a not dissimilar plan being discussed to get rid of Slobodan Milošević, the Serb leader, earlier in the decade, involving a bright light being flashed at the driver of a car to induce a crash. Could there have been a plot? Eventually an inquiry would be launched which would find no evidence for the claim that the crash was anything other than an accident. It did raise the question of whether there had been a plan for a murder in the Balkans. The inquiry found there had been only the flimsiest notion. A 'creative' officer had been worried about a particularly violent Serb (but not Milošević) being on the verge of riding an extreme nationalist agenda to power in elections and accelerating the genocide. The officer compared the situation to Adolf Hitler the year before he came to power, where many lives would have been saved had he been assassinated. 'It seemed to me that we might be in the months running up to this extreme radical nationalist politician taking power. It seemed to me there might be an analogy with 1932 in Germany. So the question I was posing is whether we should have a plan to take action before the Hitler option actually took place,' he later testified.[17]

A few ideas were put down in messy handwriting in the form of a contingency plan, including using special forces and internal Serbian elements to do the deed. 'It is true that the ethos of the service was against assassination,' the creative officer would later testify, amid evidence that new entrants to MI6 were told in their initial training that assassination was not countenanced and the subject was not up for debate. 'Suddenly here I am confronted by a situation where we are dealing with a bloody civil war in the centre of Europe, where tens of thousands of innocent people are being killed. So it seemed to me appropriate that we should at least revisit the dictum of the services and see if we felt obliged to revise it in an exceptional case.' When he handed the notes to his secretary, she typed them up with some surprise into a page and a half of A4. 'I had never read or seen anything like it before,' she later said. He decided to go round his immediate boss, whom he thought might be cold on the idea, and send it direct to the Controller for Eastern and Central Europe. His superiors stamped on the idea, hard. They told him MI6 was not in that business – it was unethical, they said, a view with which he disagreed – and instructed him to destroy all copies of the memo he had written. A senior officer stood over the secretary as she deleted it from the antiquated computer system and shredded paper copies. The days of Anthony Eden and George Kennedy Young planning to bump off Nasser were long gone. 'We do not have a licence to kill,' a Chief would later explain, although he hesitated when asked whether the service had ever had one.[18]

With a secure footing and a shiny new headquarters, MI6 just needed something to do. The shape of an intelligence service, in theory, should be dictated by the threats a country faces and by its concept of national security. But this is rarely the reality. Institutional inertia often means old structures persist even when the threats they were created for have long since passed. This was the case in the 1990s when it took a while for the contour of new threats to be discerned. The old world in which an intelligence service purely and aggressively served the 'national' interest by helping secure advantage against other states had not entirely passed away but was being complemented by more amorphous, less state-centric threats to security like international terrorism and groups smuggling and selling nuclear weapons technology.

The new agenda for the spies was in parts familiar and unfamiliar. The Balkans conflict caught MI6 off guard, but the service began to adapt, establishing small teams in the region and working more closely with the military and other partners. Secretly obtaining the negotiating positions of other countries was traditional territory, even if now the targets might be the Serbs in the Balkans or even European allies. Former MI6 officers claim that secret intelligence had a major impact in Britain's negotiations for the important treaties negotiated that decade. Unsurprisingly politicians refuse to comment on that rather awkward possibility.[19] Economic intelligence was a staple of the Cold War, trying to divine the reality of Soviet economic performance, but now it shaded into the greyer terrain of business and commercial secrets. What were the Germans planning when it came to interest rates and who was bribing whom for arms contracts in the Middle East? More time was spent on dealing with drug barons, working with Customs, and looking for those laundering money in the Caribbean. All of this meant dealing with other government departments and agencies and not just with the Foreign Office. In the old days, officers from MI6 would not even declare themselves within Whitehall, and the intelligence community sat at one side in its own clearly designated compartment. Now its officers were being seconded to other departments and MI6 was increasingly drawn away from pure intelligence gathering. The threats looked global, but MI6 had shrunk in size with the end of the Cold War so it was having to choose more carefully and work more closely with other countries and institutions and not just with the US. There were some Cold Warriors who simply could not make the transition, who could not see the point of it all and who could not operate without the old familiar bearings. In late 1993, McColl instituted what became known as the 'Christmas Massacre' in which a raft of older, senior directors were pushed out to be replaced with a younger generation. The following year a youngish new chief, David Spedding, who tellingly had risen through Middle East work rather than Sov Bloc, was appointed.

By the second half of the 1990s, a clearer sense of the new agenda was coming into view, one which occupied more comfortable terrain than the economic and commercial focus of the preceding years. The proliferation of weapons of mass destruction – biological, chemical and nuclear weapons – formed one part. This had been at the cutting edge of work within the service thanks to concerns over the Pakistani scientist A. Q. Khan. From the 1980s, a small group within MI6 had been tracking Khan, who had stolen plans for uranium enrichment while working in the Netherlands and then returned to his native Pakistan to build a vast procurement network to secure the specialised parts in order to build a bomb. Nuclear and other unconventional weapons programmes tend to inhabit the most secret nooks and crannies of reticent states. But the network of largely European businessmen supplying Pakistan offered one way for MI6 to try and get a handle on what Pakistan was up to. This also required talking to other countries, including some in Europe, about what they were seeing, as well as trying to piece together the bigger picture, a picture which looked alarming as the 1990s came to a close.

The second plank of the new agenda was the emergence of a new breed of international terrorism. Terrorism was not new. Palestinian hijackings and later Lockerbie had seen it rise on the agenda in the 1970s and 1980s. But it began to take on a new hue in the mid-1990s, and ambitious officers started to gravitate towards it as they would have done to Sov Bloc work before. There were studies of the threat of radical Islam, but few in MI5 and MI6 had a clear realisation of quite what was brewing, not least on their own doorstep. London, or as the French called it Londonistan, was becoming a home for dissidents and a hub for propaganda including for Osama bin Laden's allies (the Al Qaeda leader's claim of responsibility for the 1998 Embassy bombings in Africa came through a fax machine in North London). British officials claim they were alert to a looming threat. The more aggressive American officials dispute that, saying that Britain was only marginally ahead of other European states which showed little appetite for the issue and often seemed only to feign interest because of the American focus. 'They thought we were as mad as March hares,' recalls one CIA officer who frequently pushed European counterparts to do more.[20]

Richard Dearlove became chief of MI6 in 1999. With a few exceptions, the top job has usually gone to the most aggressive operational officers and Dearlove, always ambitious, fitted that mould. He had acquired a reputation as a moderniser keen to make MI6 relevant and to engage with the outside world and other departments. Intelligence had to be useful, he argued. It was no longer about collecting against static targets like the Russian military but had, in the new world, to be about doing things. 'My career was very much defined by the Cold War,' Dearlove later told an audience. 'I cannot really exaggerate the extent to which our preoccupations of national security, hitherto so very firmly anchored, were cut adrift when the Cold War ended.'[21] He had joined in 1966, a time when the wounds inflicted by Philby and Blake were all too clear. He had risen through Sov Bloc which tended to produce traditionalists, like John Scarlett, who emphasised the purity of intelligence gathering. But in 1987 Dearlove had secured the plum posting of Geneva. This was traditionally one of the key Sov Bloc observation and attack posts targeting the large number of Communists who passed through the city for international summits and UN meetings. During the years of transition at the end of the Cold War, Dearlove broadened out the targets for intelligence collection, integrating technology with human sources. One of Saddam Hussein's half-brothers was posted there and used the city as Iraq's European hub. The Libyans and Iranians were also very active, as were the Chinese. Many influential Middle Easterners had summer houses by the lake. This opened up new targets and issues, including the proliferation of weapons of mass destruction and international crime. Dearlove's strategy was recognised as a successful model of how to address a wider range of security threats. He began to be seen as a leading moderniser and was sent to be head of station in Washington. He encountered a CIA unsure of its mission and haemorrhaging talented officers. It was also penetrated in the form of Aldrich Ames and was soon to go through its own painful polygraph-led molehunts. Dearlove, who had been educated in part in the US, built close relations which would become important later. His ambition for the top job was clear. So, just behind him, was that of John Scarlett, and the two men did not get on.

Scarlett's and Dearlove's rivalry was more than personal, it was also cultural, reflecting two strands in the service's culture. 'Round-heads and Cavaliers' was how one colleague put it. The modernising against traditionalist divide had evolved from the time when Shergy was battling to instil a sense of professionalism against the haphazard, amateurish culture that had spawned Albania and the like. By the 1960s a divide emerged between Shergy's Moscow Men and the more adventurous Camel Drivers who focused on Africa and the Middle East and covert action rather than on pure intelligence gathering. To be successful, a Secret Service needs both types: operating in St Petersburg will always be different to operating in Oman, but there is also normally a dominant culture. At the end of the Cold War, there was some resentment at all the talk about the crisis that the Soviet bloc's passing had caused. It had only ever been less than half the service's work, grumbled those who plied their trade in the souks of Damascus or on the plains of Africa. Now the Sov Bloc master race came to be seen as relics of the past, relegated to the sidelines. They had become the traditionalists, and the modernisers were those who wanted to do things, work more closely with the rest of Whitehall and make sure their intelligence had impact rather than just collect it. Scarlett was a classic Moscow Man. 'The buccaneering spirit can be overplayed because that's part of the myth,' he later noted. 'Above all we need people who are disciplined.'[22] After ascending to the top job in 1999, Dearlove was beginning to change the service when the world around the service suddenly changed.

John Scarlett had been in his new role as chair of the Joint Intelligence Committee for six days on the morning of 11 September 2001.

His rivals at MI6 had hoped that his unusual appointment (unusual because a consumer rather than producer of intelligence normally occupied the post) would keep him out of the running to become chief of MI6 in the future. During a meeting in his office in neighbouring Downing Street someone walked in and told him to turn on the TV. The Twin Towers in New York were collapsing. The Prime Minister was already on his way back from the TUC conference in Brighton.

Within three hours of the attack, Scarlett and the head of MI5 Stephen Lander began to brief the Prime Minister at Downing Street (Dearlove was on his way back from Stockholm). Blair had already framed the attack in dramatic, almost apocalyptic terms in his own mind. It was, he thought, the first salvo in a battle over the future of the world between modernity and fanaticism.[23] He immediately asked to see all the intelligence produced on Al Qaeda in the last year. He was handed thirty reports. That night he told the nation that Britain would stand 'shoulder to shoulder with our American friends'.

Britain's spy chiefs had known something was coming. 'The fact that a large-scale terrorist event occurred was not a surprise,' Dearlove said later. 'The fear was that it would be an attack probably against American interests probably not in the mainland.'[24] 'We had prior intelligence that summer of Al Qaeda planning a major attack,' Eliza Manningham-Buller, then the number two to Stephen Lander, recalled. 'We didn't know, nor did the Americans, where it was going to take place.'[25] Nebulous reports had coagulated and then dissipated over the summer. In June, British and American intelligence held one of their joint summits. 'The primary topic of discussion was a major terrorist event,' according to Dearlove. 'That was a routine meeting which turned into something not routine ... There was an increase in chatter [intercepted communications], an increase in indicators.'[26] Everyone was fearful. It was as if they were walking through a long, pitch-black corridor knowing that somewhere around them an animal was preparing to pounce. That month, the British passed on details that a senior Al Qaeda figure was planning car-bomb attacks against US targets in Saudi Arabia in the coming weeks. Nothing happened.[27] A British report from 6 July read: 'The most likely location for such an attack on western interests by UBL

[Usama bin Laden] and those who share his agenda is the Gulf States, or the wider middle east.'[28] A JIC report that month said that attacks were in their final stage of preparation.[29] An attack had not been a surprise but its target and scale were.

At the Downing Street briefing on 9/11, Scarlett and Lander told Blair it was the work of Osama bin Laden and that no government would need to have been involved.[30] Blair and his press secretary Alastair Campbell pressed them on how they could be so sure. Blair immediately feared that President Bush would be put under pressure to respond aggressively and they all knew that Washington would be looking for any evidence that Iraq, Libya or Iran were involved. A 'ragged' meeting of the emergency committee, COBRA, followed in a secure basement room beneath Whitehall. London's airspace was closed and security at key buildings tightened.

Intelligence that flowed in overnight pointed even more strongly at bin Laden. The newly appointed Foreign Secretary Jack Straw said that the UK should not get ahead of the US. 'He felt our best role was to stay close and to try and exercise influence privately,' Alastair Campbell recorded in his diary.[31] In Washington, there was an awareness that Britain wanted to be involved in any military response in Afghanistan. 'Give them a role,' Bush said to his aides on 13 September.[32] The instinctive reaction of both Blair and his spies was the same: to get close to the Americans and find out what they were planning and to try and guide them away from any temptation towards unilateralism. Blair wrote the first of many private notes to the American President advising him on some of the diplomatic options.

A flock of spooks was despatched to Washington. Although US airspace would be closed for days, a special dispensation was made for a flight from Britain on 12 September. Richard Dearlove, Eliza Manningham-Buller and Francis Richards, head of GCHQ, all headed to an airbase where an old freight DC-10 was the only plane available to fly them across the Atlantic. The station commander would not allow it to take off. Airspace was closed, he explained. Dearlove let rip. The Prime Minister was calling the President to make sure it took off, he explained, and he would accept responsibility if there were any problems. It took off without clearance to land in the US and with the pilot keeping an eye on the fuel gauge in case he had to turn back. Some seats had been installed in the back, but the plane was largely empty. The small group of passengers remained silent over the journey, lost in their thoughts of what the previous day meant and where it would take them.

As they flew down the eastern seaboard the spies gazed out of the window at the smoke from the burning rubble of the Twin Towers curling up into the sky. When they arrived at Andrews Air Force Base outside Washington they were taken by motorcade to CIA headquarters at Langley. They were greeted at the doorstep by the normally ebullient but now sombre Director George Tenet. The delegation was too big to fit in Tenet's personal dining room and so they used another executive room, soulless with blue walls and tables covered in crisp white linen. 'There was an air of surrealism about the whole late-night gathering, as white-jacketed waiters moved quietly around the tables and served us food,' recalled an American who was present.[33] The Americans looked knackered, thought the British. There was not much intelligence to impart but the gesture of solidarity was appreciated by the Americans. 'The message I was sent to Washington by Tony Blair to deliver', Dearlove later said, 'was that we would stand by the United States in their hour of need and we would bring to the table our capability and our assets.'[34] Blair's Foreign Affairs Adviser David Manning, who had been stranded in New York, had joined the team. 'I hope we can all agree that we should concentrate on Afghanistan and not be tempted to launch any attacks on Iraq,' he said at the end of the dinner as the officials broke into small groups.[35] The relationship with the Americans, so close during the Cold War, had been fraying towards the end of the 1990s. The absence of a unifying threat and focus on more localised enemies like drug barons had meant that the intelligence services were not always pointing in the same direction. Britain had also edged closer to Europe. But with 9/11, old reflexes kicked back in. A CIA official told his counterpart that MI6 could play an important role in acting as a link to other European intelligence services.[36]

The British contingent returned to their Embassy in Washington to talk late into the night before moving on to the Four Seasons Hotel where they were staying. Among the other guests there was Mahmood Ahmed, the head of Pakistan's ISI, who had been in town by chance. He studiously avoided the British until they managed to doorstep him in the corridor. He seemed terrified by what it all meant, they thought. For the return journey they agreed to pick up some stranded VIPs. Among them were a group of parliamentarians including former Prime Minister John Major, who started asking why these Britons he did not recognise had a plane at their disposal. The spies drew the line, though, at picking up the Duchess of York, Sarah Ferguson, who was also stranded.

At CIA headquarters, a sense of unreality had haunted the empty corridors on 11 September as all but a small core of staff were evacuated into the car park amid fears of an incoming plane. Mike Scheuer, who had previously run the CIA's unit tracking bin Laden, had turned on his TV just as the second plane hit. 'We had a chance to stop this and we didn't,' was his reaction. Many who had worked on the Al Qaeda issue reflected that the day's carnage was the direct result of having been constrained for so long from going after bin Laden with all the aggression he showed in targeting the United States. The insiders were aware in a way that others were not just how much had been known about bin Laden and his plans. They were determined not to repeat past mistakes. These individuals took the attack hard, feeling a sense of personal responsibility. Aggression would be the watchword in their response. 'The analogy would be the junkyard dog that had been chained to the ground was now going to be let go and I just couldn't wait,' recalled the take-no-prisoners head of the CIA Counter-Terrorism Center, Cofer Black, who had personally had a run-in with bin Laden in Sudan. Later he would say, 'There was a before 9/11 and an after 9/11. After 9/11 the gloves came off.'[37]

Five days after the attack, Black and CIA colleagues went to the bland, modern British Embassy in Washington late in the afternoon to brief senior MI6 officers still anxious about the American response. The British officials had requested the meeting and they expressed caution about taking actions which might destabilise the Middle East. 'Our only concern is killing terrorists,' Black said in his characteristically blunt style during a bleak three-hour meeting. 'When we're through with them, they will have flies walking across their eyeballs,' he would tell President Bush, who relished the tough talk and the promise of swift retribution. 'All rather bloodcurdling, isn't it,' one person present said to another CIA officer as the meeting at the British Embassy ended. Cofer Black told the same CIA officer they would probably all get indicted for the things they were about to do. 'If you're going to be an officer of the CIA you're just going to have to appreciate that if you go on long enough and do a good enough job, at the end of your career, it should involve probably hiring a lawyer,' he later explained.[38] The colourful language and martial metaphors of Black and his cohorts jarred with the style of London's more old-school spies. Back in Whitehall, every morning the spy chiefs would traipse in, 'all in dark suits and carrying their battered briefcases,' noted Alastair Campbell.[39] For Blair himself, disaster also spelt opportunity. Members of his own cabinet told him he was seen around the world as the only person who could restrain Bush. A headline in an American paper described one of his speeches as 'a pitch for world leadership'. For the spy chiefs as well, the thrust into the centre of the action was enough to give them whiplash. Before 11 September 2001, the Prime Minister hardly saw his spy-masters and the Cabinet Secretary, Sir Richard Wilson, recalled doing his best to get them a slot in Blair's diary in order to build a rela-tionship. But now the position of the intelligence chiefs was trans-formed. Every day, the Prime Minister would turn to them first in the meetings. The chief of MI6 drew close. 'The Prime Minister was in the air a great deal of the time going round the world. At least that's what it felt like sitting at home,' recalled the Cabinet Secretary later. 'He had Sir Richard Dearlove with him. Richard Dearlove, who had previously, as it were, not had contact really with Number 10, seized his chance, quite understandably, and got to know the Prime Minister and the Prime Minister got to know him.'[40] Dearlove would become one of his closest advisers in the months to come, a reflection of the extent to which national security decisions surrounding ter-rorism and proliferation were informed by intelligence rather than the diplomacy of the Foreign Office, an institution that was seen as lacking the heft and agility required. Intelligence was now deter-mining government policy day to day. The argument seemed resolved in favour of the modernisers with their call for intelligence to be 'useful' and as close as possible to the decision-making The events of 11 September 2001 answered the insecurities felt so deeply since the end of the Cold War. For Britain's spies it was a chance to influence a prime minister directly and to be at the centre of power once more.

For that Prime Minister, it was a chance to influence an American president and walk the world stage. No one in London had any conception of where the American President would lead them or at what cost.

In Afghanistan, MI6's shadow warriors were returning to the fray but without their old partner. Massoud had been killed by the suicide bombers posing as TV crew two days before 9/11, the removal of their most troublesome adversary a gift from bin Laden to his Taliban allies. It was clear that the Taliban had not so much fought their way to power as bribed, bartered and intimidated their way. The coalition strategy would be to mirror that.

On 28 September, the Foreign Secretary approved the deployment of MI6 officers to the region.[41] The UK still had people who had been involved with the mujahedeen in the 1980s and who had the language skills and regional expertise. Insiders say the response showed an MI6 strength but also a weakness. When it moved, MI6 could move very quickly, but it moved with all it had and this was not that much. A handful of officers with a budget of $7 million landed in the north-east of Afghanistan at the end of the month. Passing the rusting Russian vehicles blown up during the last jihad, they met General Mohammed Fahim of the Northern Alliance and began working with other contacts in the north and the south to build alliances, to secure support and to bribe as many Taliban commanders as they could to change sides or leave the fight.[42]

Plucked overnight from retirement in the Cotswolds to be despatched to the wilds of the Panjshir, one of the Britons sent into Afghanistan after 9/11 to negotiate with the Northern Alliance was an old MI6 hand straight out of a John Buchan novel. Paul Bergne, then in his mid-sixties, was an expert archaeologist who spoke at least a dozen languages. He was a tall, gentle, veteran spy who had immersed himself in the culture of every country he visited. In the Foreign Office he was often referred to as 'Greenmantle' in reference to one of John Buchan's novels in which the gentleman-adventurer Richard Hannay investigates an uprising in the Muslim world. Bergne was the type of polymath who inhabits the nooks and crannies of the service often largely forgotten until the next crisis hits their region of expertise. With a detached, quizzical air and an independent streak he had joined MI6 in 1959, first serving overseas in Vienna before becoming the in-house expert on Islam and Central Asia. After he retired in 1992 he was appointed Britain's first ambassador to Uzbekistan and Tajikistan where he initially ran the Embassy from a messy, cheap hotel room. His second retirement, largely spent in academia, ended as he was asked to go to Afghanistan to persuade the Tajiks of the Northern Alliance to do more than use Western intervention to regain the upper hand in their old feuds, not least with the Pashtun. When the Northern Alliance took Bagram airbase, he had to intervene personally to stop them firing on British troops as they landed because no one had expected them. The Northern Alliance, he said, 'came within an ace' of opening fire on the Britons. 'I asked the foreign minister not to take any hasty action, because he was extremely angry,' Bergne later said. 'They had been sorely tempted to open fire.'[43]

At the CIA, Cofer Black's instructions to the team leader he was sending to Afghanistan were simple and grisly when it came to Al Qaeda's leadership. 'I want to see photos of their heads on pikes,' Black told Gary Schroen. 'I want bin Laden's head shipped back in a box filled with dry ice. I want to be able to show bin Laden's head to the President. I promised I would do that.' It was the first time Schroen had heard a direct order to kill. 'We can certainly kill bin Laden, but I don't know where we're going to find dry ice in Afghanistan,' he replied. The strictures put in place after Larry Devlin's testimony before Congress in the 1970s were gone, lifted by a president who demanded action and supported by an agency which did not want to let the American public down. 'The authorities had changed,' Black would explain. This was war. The pendulum was swinging once again for the CIA, this time violently.[44]

Schroen had been pulled out of a retirement programme because he had served in South Asia on and off since the late 1970s and had been the link man to Massoud in the late 1990s. He got hold of an ageing Russian helicopter and $3 million in hundred-dollar bills and headed towards Northern Afghanistan, one of the worries being the danger of being shot down by a shoulder-fired missile of the type that the CIA had supplied years earlier. He was joined by a team of CIA paramilitary officers. 'If they didn't do paramilitary actions for a living, they'd probably be robbing banks,' one CIA officer said of their ilk.[45] After they landed they hooked up with the Northern

Alliance, still shell-shocked from the brutal murder of their leader. There was no master plan to co-ordinate the work of the CIA and MI6 teams. Everything was moving too fast. Everyone just needed to do what they could and make sure they did not run into each other. Conversations were simply about who had assets where. Most British contacts were with the Northern Alliance but with a sprinkling in the south, where the Americans were also struggling to find viable allies. The failure to find a partner in the south was slowing plans and causing problems. Soon the US and British teams were providing intelligence reports on Taliban front-line positions and mapping their defences for a bombing campaign. 'Are you going to stay this time?' the Afghan allies repeatedly asked the CIA's overall Afghan commander when he arrived. 'Yes. We are staying this time,' he promised.[46]

At a meeting at a military bunker, the concerns of the Pakistani leadership were evident. The Taliban had been their proxy. The wily President Pervez Musharraf, who had seized power in a coup, told his assembled senior commanders that they had to make a choice. Abandon their old allies, the Taliban, or else they would be steam-rollered by the US. To make the choice easier he moved key generals, including his ISI chief Mahmood Ahmed, the man who had looked so worried at the Four Seasons. Ahmed had been particularly close to Mullah Omar, the Taliban's one-eyed leader, and wanted to pre-serve the group's influence. 'In terms of the policy, it really did turn 180 degrees,' recalls Bob Grenier, then the CIA chief in Islamabad.[47] But, with the decision made, the Pakistanis explained to Grenier that they were deeply worried that the Northern Alliance would rout the Taliban and take Kabul. They warned the Americans that this would cause bloodshed and risk excluding the Pashtun population of the south. Disputes raged in Washington and especially in the CIA over whether or not to listen to this advice and restrain the Northern Alliance. Post-Massoud, the collection of leaders at the top of the Alliance did not look appealing. Most looked like thuggish warlords because that was what they were. Washington agreed to hold back from bombing the Taliban front-line positions until a more coherent Pashtun resistance could be organised in the south to complement the largely Tajik Northern Alliance.

This was a chance for the ageing Afghan jihadists of the 1980s to choose sides – the Taliban or the Americans and the Northern Alliance. Old faces re-emerged from the woodwork seeking one more shot at glory. The one-legged Abdul 'Hollywood' Haq, once fêted in Downing Street, managed to garner some support from Afghan-American businessmen and rode into battle once more heading from Peshawar to Jalalabad with a group of twenty supporters. An unarmed US Predator drone watched as he was surrounded by Taliban forces and executed. Hamid Karzai, another Pashtun whose father had fought the Taliban, was nearly killed by a misdirected bomb. He would be one of the only Pashtun leaders to sign up with the Americans. That would stand him in good stead. Some of the other commanders the US had once backed now sided with their enemies, Gulbuddin Hekmatyar among them. Another was Jala-luddin Haqqani, who had been Congressman Charlie Wilson's favourite and yet became one of the most deadly adversaries of the new Afghan government and the closest local leader to Al Qaeda (while remaining so close to the ISI that it considered him one of its assets).

For a tense few days in October it looked as if air strikes were not having any impact and the bombers started to run out of targets. There was talk in the press about the 'Afghan Winter' approaching. But once fire was finally focused on the Taliban positions in the north they crumbled, allowing the Northern Alliance to sweep into Kabul. In all, only around 100 CIA and 300 US special forces were sent to Afghanistan, but within two and a half months of deploying on 27 September and by working with air power and local forces they were able to topple the Taliban. But where was the man whose head was supposed to be delivered on dry ice?

Britain's SBS alongside MI6 was sent into the wild, mountainous Tora Bora region to hunt for bin Laden alongside US teams. Several members of a SBS team listened to bin Laden speak to his fighters on shortwave radios that had been captured. Two of them at one point spotted a tall figure in a camouflage jacket move south-east with a fifty-man protective detail and enter a cave through a hidden entrance. The Americans and British, accompanied by Afghans of dubious loyalty, were few in number and their request to the Pentagon for back-up was turned down.[48] By failing to commit large numbers of ground troops to secure the border, the US allowed bin Laden to slip away into Pakistan. 'Massoud liberated Afghanistan from the Soviets,' declared his former aide Abdullah Anas. 'Osama bin Laden gave it to the Americans in two weeks and then fled.'[49] Bin Laden was able to regroup his organisation over the border in Pakistan.

Once again, the view in Washington was 'job done in Afghanistan'. Soon the US began withdrawing special forces teams and preparing them for their next war. Nothing much had followed behind the military, no great aid or development or attempt at institution building. Some in Washington, ignoring the key role played by Afghan allies, drew the over-confident conclusion that small teams combined with air power could win wars without a large body of ground troops.

The rout of the Taliban meant that prisoners were swept up into makeshift and ageing jails, including many foreign fighters who had trained in the camps and fought against the coalition. In mid-December the MI6 officers who had been deployed to the region began to interview prisoners held by the Northern Alliance. In January they turned to interviewing those held by the Americans. In neither case was the decision to interview referred up to ministers in London. On 12 December it had been agreed in London that MI5 officers should also be sent out to interview prisoners who might possess intelligence on attacks against the UK. The first MI5 staff arrived at Bagram on 9 January 2002. The following day an MI6 officer conducted his first interview of a detainee held by the US. He reported back to London that there were aspects of the way the detainee had been handled by the US military before the interview that did not appear consistent with the Geneva Conventions. Two days after the interview he was sent instructions, copied to all MI5 and MI6 staff in Afghanistan, about how to deal with concerns over mistreatment. 'Given that they are not within our custody or control, the law does not require you to intervene to prevent this,' it explained, referring to signs of abuse. It went on to say that the Americans had to understand that the UK did not condone such mistreatment and that a complaint should be made to a senior US official if there was any coercion by the US in conjunction with an MI6 interview. The instructions ended with a no doubt happily received lawyerly warning that '*acts carried out overseas in the course of your official duties [are] subject to UK criminal law. In other words, your actions incur criminal liability in the same way as if you were carrying out those acts in the UK.*[50] The instructions, it was later found, were inadequate, in that they failed to require officers to report their concerns immediately to senior US officials and to London. In the next three weeks before he came home the MI6 officer saw no other signs of mistreatment. But it had not been an isolated incident.

The gloves had come off. On 7 February President Bush made clear that the US did not consider the Geneva Conventions applied to detainees arrested in Afghanistan and they were to be sent to Guantánamo Bay in Cuba. There were more signs of abuse. In April an MI6 officer was present at an interview conducted by the US military and raised concerns with a US officer. In July an MI5 officer said he heard a US official talking about 'getting a detainee ready', which appeared to involve sleep deprivation, hooding and stress positions. When he reported it to his senior management they did nothing. It would not be surprising if officers in the field felt they were getting little support from back home.

Britain's closest ally was, as its vice-president Dick Cheney put it, working 'the dark side'. The top Al Qaeda prisoners who were picked up in the War on Terror were taken on a journey to 'black' sites, secret locations in Eastern Europe and Asia where pliant governments had allowed the CIA to harbour secret facilities. There the agency could engage in acts everyone but the administration itself would describe as torture. The CIA was becoming, in effect, a military command as well as an intelligence agency which would be engaged in everything from interrogation of detainees to firing guided missiles to killing Al Qaeda leaders, creating an awkward situation for an ally who worked closely with it.

How much did British intelligence know about their cousins' walk on the dark side? Very little, they claim, which in itself points to an intelligence failure. 'It took us longer than it should have done to find out,' accepts one former official. There were warning signs early on, however. 'I was worried by the reaction that one heard – which was a very emotional reaction – in the weeks after 9/11 from a number of American officials,' Dearlove said later. 'We tried even at that stage to point out we had lived with a serious, different type of terrorist threat. We had gone down a track which had caused great problems. I'm thinking of internment in Northern Ireland. And we had learnt many hard lessons ... our position was if you forfeit the moral high ground in confronting these types of problems you make it maybe much more difficult. You maybe gain a short-term advantage, you certainly lose long-term advantage.'[51]

Britain and America share most but not all secrets. The secret rendition programme in which high-value Al Qaeda suspects were tortured was highly classified, but it was still clear that *something* was happening to these prisoners in the years after 9/11 because they had disappeared. What's more, the UK was happily receiving intelligence reports based on their interrogation. A ream of very interesting reports began to reach Britain in 2003. The material was gold dust but the Americans were saying very little about its source. Was it a newly minted agent inside Al Qaeda's leadership? some in British intelligence wondered. Soon it became clear that material was coming from the self-confessed 'mastermind' of 9/11, Khalid Sheikh Mohammed, who was spewing out details of plans and plots and plotters. 'I said to my staff, "Why is he talking?" because our experience of Irish prisoners and terrorists was that they never said anything,' Eliza Manningham-Buller recalled.[52]

Another intelligence chief wondered if Mohammed had been turned to work with the West. What had really happened was that he had been waterboarded, a technique which makes the body think it is drowning, a total of 183 times. 'The Americans were very keen that people like us did not discover what they were doing,' Manningham-Buller said. 'One of the sad things is Cheney, Rumsfeld and Bush all watched *24*,' she added, referring to the TV drama in which an American spy uses extreme techniques to extract information and stop attacks.[53]

As they processed the leads supplied from Washington, MI5 was relieved to find that it already knew about half the people Khalid Sheikh Mohammed had identified in the UK. But the remaining half were new leads which were hurriedly pursued. An urgent hunt began for one of those he helped identify named Dhiren Barot, a key Al Qaeda figure in the UK, who proved well trained enough to lose his surveillance team temporarily. Eventually he was picked up, but the FBI was furious he was not handed over to it.

When MI5 officers interviewing detainees in Guantánamo Bay became concerned over mistreatment in 2004, protests travelled through intelligence channels and also through Downing Street and the Foreign Office.[54] But the spies also say that the leads that emerged out of torture in the black sites were important for national security (although not quite to the extent President Bush later claimed when he wrote that they directly prevented attacks on Canary Wharf and Big Ben). Ask them quietly and a few of those who have worked at the heart of the secret state will whisper that the idea that torture is never useful and always produces flawed intelligence is too easy a truth to cling to. They will say that Algeria, whose methods were brutal, was an important partner after 9/11, providing vital intelligence. They will say that you never really know how intelligence you are handed was produced. And, they ask, can you imagine the witch-hunt and the blame game if there was to be an attack on Britain tomorrow and it was found that intelligence on it from, say, Saudi Arabia had been declined because of concerns over its provenance? But while passive receipt of intelligence is one thing, the moral terrain becomes even more treacherous when you are watching interrogations on video monitors from neighbouring rooms (as Pakistani officials say occurred with some detainees) or sending questions over to the Americans to be put to someone you know has been spirited away somewhere secret, as happened with British resident Binyam Mohammed, held in Pakistan and then in a secret prison in Morocco. In his case there was sufficient concern over wrongdoing to justify opening a criminal investigation into complicity with torture. 'No torture and there is no complicity with torture,' John Scarlett said, defending MI6's actions. 'I have every confidence and always have had every confidence in the standards, the values, the integrity of our officers.' The relationship with the Americans had nonetheless experienced tensions, he acknowledged. 'Our American allies know that we are our own service, that we are here to work for the British interests and the United Kingdom,' Scarlett later said of the relationship. 'We're not here to work for anybody else and we're an independent service working to our own laws – nobody else's – and to our own values.'[55] Trust between the two countries' intelligence services began to erode as British inquiries unearthed and made public details of American techniques, breaching the 'control' principle in which a country which originates an intelligence report maintains control over where and how it is passed on or released. Some Americans fumed at the way in which European governments distanced themselves from American policy on detainees while at the same time using the intelligence produced. Speaking before Congress, Mike Scheuer, the former head of the CIA's bin Laden unit, lashed out at 'effete sanctimonious Europeans who take every bit of American protection offered them while publicly damning and seeking jail time for those who risk their lives to provide the protection'.[56]

The British and Americans have long had a classified no-spy agreement which says they do not collect secret intelligence on each other and do not recruit each other's citizens as agents. This is partly about sovereignty and partly about the problems of parallel intelligence operations pranging into each other as they go after the same agents. The British can, however, occasionally run unilateral operations inside the US against other nationals with US approval (approval which is extremely rare, although some US officials suspect that Britain may have run unilateral operations without approval against the IRA at various points). The US does not have the ability to run approved unilateral operations in the UK, much to the annoyance of some CIA officers (very occasionally they have been caught evading this). After 9/11, some senior American intelligence officials pushed hard to run their own operations inside the UK to collect intelligence. London resisted strongly, fearing not least that the Americans might end up carrying out rendition operations as they did in other European countries like Italy in which suspects were snatched off the street. One former CIA official recalls a meeting at which the head of MI5, Eliza Manningham-Buller, never one to be shy of expressing her opinion, resisted US unilateral operations particularly strongly. 'Try it and we'll arrest you,' the CIA man recalls her saying. Another CIA official at the same meeting came out irritated by what he saw as a patronising lecture about how Britain was a country of rules where the Magna Carta had been written and fumed to his colleague about being told what he could or could not do by a 'medium-sized power'.[57]

When a man in Birmingham is communicating with a terrorist planner in Karachi the distinction between foreign and domestic information quickly blurs. Streams of information from different sources need to be integrated and trails of data mined and manipulated to establish how someone might be linked to a network. Staff from MI5 and MI6 were thrown together in joint teams alongside colleagues from GCHQ who pluck terrorist communications out of the ether. MI5 found itself co-ordinating closely with the police with whom it used to have an often difficult relationship. The days of bitter rivalry between MI5 and MI6 had passed, although the odd clash still occurred. Most of the difficult entanglements, particularly the case of Binyam Mohammed, centred on the Security Service, MI5, rather than on MI6. After 9/11 senior MI5 officials had been keen to take the lead on all intelligence which related to threats to the UK. Even if detainees were held abroad, they wanted to carry out the interviews. In the past, MI6 officers used to joke that their counterparts should never be allowed beyond the Straits of Dover because their understanding of the ways of foreign intelligence services was so limited. There used to be a running joke about the telegrams MI6 officers in a faraway country received from MI5 in London which was looking for help from the local intelligence service in some investigation. 'Please instruct your liaison ...' the telegrams would begin before going into the details of the request. 'You weasel, you cajole, but you don't instruct liaison partners,' explained one old hand from MI6. But there was no *Schadenfreude* at the mounting allegations faced by its sister service, not least because it coloured the reputation of all of British intelligence. Paradoxically, public perception and reputation is remarkably important for those who work in the secret world. It is precisely because they cannot talk much about their work that they worry more about the ways in which it is perceived by the public.

MI5 also had to deal with its fictional portrayal in the BBC drama *Spooks*, which began broadcasting a few months after 9/11. 'I don't think the public think it's like *Spooks*. I think they realise *Spooks* is fiction in the same way as they know that James Bond isn't like MI6,' says Manningham-Buller, who claims not to have watched the programme since the first series and the unfortunate demise of a female officer in a vat of boiling chip fat (the programme was thought to have led to a drop in female applicants because of its violence). 'There are two regrets I have. One is that it portrays intelligence as simplistic, as a simple thing to be understood if you only do things in the right order – that things can be solved in forty minutes by six people. The second thing I regret about it is it portrays the service as having utter disregard for the law. Whereas we are very careful that everything we do has a proper legal basis.'[58] The hits to the MI5 website, and particularly its recruitment pages, surge after every episode of the drama, but insiders are less sure that the Bondish image of gun-toting, rule-breaking secret agents is as helpful to a domestic security service trying to investigate its own citizens as it is to a foreign intelligence service, like MI6, out trying to do bad things to foreigners. If *Spooks* was like real life, one MI5 officer explained, the camera would cut to the officer at 3 a.m. still filling in his warrant form and all the associated paperwork before being allowed out the door.

At times the pace of a counter-terrorist investigation is not far off that portrayed in *Spooks*. Intelligence gathering can involve some of the same techniques as were used in the old Cold War world – human motivations are much the same when it comes to recruiting agents who know the secret intentions of an enemy. But the differences are also stark. Intelligence is much more time-sensitive. Discerning the Soviet order of battle could be pieced together slowly. Intelligence about a planned terrorist attack or the location of a terrorist leader requires immediate action. The shelf life of good intelligence in counter-terrorism may be days rather than years. The shelf life of an agent in the badlands of Pakistan, whom it might have taken a long time to recruit, may be much shorter as well.

MI5 officers in early 2004 watched grainy surveillance of a terrorist cell inspecting fertiliser for a bomb in a storage facility and listened to the men in their bugged cars and flats talk of the nightclubs and shopping centres they were planning to attack. One night in March, they recorded the driver of a Vauxhall Corsa picking up the ringleader of the plotters and another man in Crawley and driving them around before taking them back. The driver was identified in the log as 'UM' – unidentified male.[59] It was clear that 'home-grown terrorism' had arrived on British shores. These were second-generation Britons of Pakistani descent. It was a trend that had not been appreciated in the immediate aftermath of 9/11. In the 1990s, the radicals who had found a home in Britain were seen as plotting against their homelands of Algeria, Egypt and Saudi Arabia. Arab intelligence services would privately describe the UK as a 'terrorist sanctuary' to CIA officers, but despite those complaints a blind eye was turned by the British as long as individuals were not breaking any law or plotting against Britain. The 2004 investigation, codenamed 'Crevice' by the police, revealed for the first time that Britons would attack Britain, in this case with support from an Al Qaeda which had been ejected from Afghanistan but had been able to regroup in the wilds of the tribal areas of Pakistan. 'Crevice was the moment when the lights went on and you could see the state of the kitchen,' explained one intelligence official soon afterwards.[60] There was worse to come. Home-grown radicalisation was now on the radar, but still no one expected British suicide-bombers to strike.

The first that staff at MI5 knew of what was happening on 7 July 2005 came as they watched their TV screens. Soon the images of a blown-apart bus opened like a tin can would be seared on their minds. The UK's threat level had been lowered a few days earlier. No one had seen the four young men with their rucksacks coming. 'We did not know it was a suicide bombing until the forensics began to come through,' recalled Eliza Manningham-Buller. 'So at the beginning we were trying to support the police in possibly finding the team who had done it, who for all we knew at that stage were still alive and capable of mounting another attack.'[61] The aftermath was chaos. At one point closed-circuit TV from Luton, where the bombers had passed through, made it seem as if there was another person carrying a rucksack. Should they tell the public? Someone from MI5 thought they saw the same person from the CCTV around Westminster and Buckingham Palace. Everywhere was locked down. 'It wasn't until the evening when I got home quite late that the emotional impact of that day hit me,' recollected Manningham-Buller later.[62]

Eliza Manningham-Buller addressed her staff the next day inside MI5 headquarters at Thames House in Millbank. She said it had been a day they had always feared would happen but hoped would not. Many had been up all night and she said she was proud of them. They needed to continue to do what they had been trained to do. Brace yourselves, she also warned; by the end of the week there would be speculation about whether we were to blame for allowing the attack to take place. Don't read the papers, get on with your job. The accusations would indeed come. The night of her speech, the credit card of Mohammed Siddique Khan was found close to where the bomb at Edgware Road tube station had detonated. MI5 investigators soon realised that they had come across him before. He was the unidentified male who had been driving the Vauxhall Corsa in March 2004. He had come under MI5 surveillance on multiple occasions as part of the Crevice investigation but had never been prioritised sufficiently to be followed up. There had been a number of leads dating back to 2001, including that Khan had attended training camps in the UK and Pakistan, but the different strands had never been woven together to understand that all the pieces of intelligence related to the same man. The explanation for not placing him higher up the list of targets was a lack of resources, especially as a new set of leads had arrived at Thames House in 2004 (including those generated by Khalid Sheikh Mohammed's waterboarding). 'We're not the Stasi, we can't cover everyone,' explained one official defensively.[63]

Two weeks to the day after 7/7, there was another attack. This time it failed. 'For me, it was worse,' recalled Manningham-Buller, who was having a regular lunch with her directors when news came through. 'Although nobody died, I had that feeling that if this is going to happen every fortnight, how are we going to be able to cope with this?'[64] The fear of an endless army of suicide bombers coming over the horizon filled everyone with apprehension. Authorities were unsure that they would be able to cope as they circled the date two weeks ahead and wondered if something would happen then. For the coming months and years, it felt like 'trench warfare'. 'It's like the old game of Space Invaders,' explained one person involved in the day-to-day work of counter-terrorism. 'When you clear one screen of potential attackers, another simply appears to take its place.'[65] The days of playing investigations long, watching them patiently in order to build up enough evidence, were disappearing. That was too resource intensive. Disrupt and move on to the next network was the only game-plan available. 'We had more than we could cope with and had to make some uncomfortable decisions on prioritisation,' explained Manningham-Buller. Government money soon came flooding in and MI5 more than doubled in size and expanded into the regions. A transformation from the old counter-espionage agency of Arthur Martin to a modern counter-terrorist organisation which had begun with the tackling of the IRA in the 1990s was now under way.

MI5 launched a blitz, recruiting new human sources on an 'industrial scale', working its way through lists of people who could be approached. 'We knew that we needed many more human sources and much greater coverage,' said Manningham-Buller. These agents remain the lifeblood of intelligence work. For all the talk of 'community intelligence', insiders say that there is no substitute for agents within the organisations themselves. 'Like the IRA you don't get it [the intelligence] from housewives. To get to terrorist planners you need people to get to people in the middle. The sort of detailed information to stop an attack isn't swilling around the mosque.'

After 7/7, Manningham-Buller approached the Chief of MI6 to ask him to lend her his best agent runners because running agents has traditionally been more of a domain of expertise for MI6 than MI5. At one point, the largest deployment of operational MI6 officers was not to any country overseas but within the UK. They would work alongside MI5 officers to try and recruit agents who could be sent into Pakistan's tribal areas and elsewhere to infiltrate Al Qaeda and its allies. Getting into the heart of networks takes time. The ambition, just as the KGB had for Philby, is to find someone who can survive inside the enemy's ranks, prosper and rise. The higher they rise, the more complex their moral choices may become. When does revealing a terrorist plan to your handler endanger your own life? When does going along with a terrorist plan involve innocent people dying? Agent motivation is infinitely variable. For some it is the desire to prevent violence in their community, for others it will be a grudge against someone they know. The approach to an agent is always the hardest moment. Typically an officer has between half a minute and a minute in which to keep someone interested or lose them for ever. A bit like an approach at a nightclub for a different type of assignation, a good opening line and the right manner can go a long way. When approaching someone to be an agent, the first ten seconds are typically lost anyway as the subject is in shock at the officer revealing their hand.

Amid the danger and excitement also lies the mundane. MI5 agents and their handlers can spend up to half a day conducting complex counter-surveillance routines to make sure they are not followed when they are preparing to meet. The initial thrill of feeling as if you are in your own spy film is quickly replaced by the boredom of having to jump on and off yet another bus but with the added edge that getting it wrong could cost someone their life. The process could end up with the agent climbing into a covert vehicle. These are hardly the height of luxury – some have no windows in the back and a small light illuminates what looks like carpet peeling off the walls. There are no seatbelts and no air conditioning or heating. In an emergency, a meeting can take place in a vehicle but otherwise the agent may be driven, by a circuitous route, to a lock-up somewhere where a half-dead yucca plant sits in one corner and his case officer waits with a cup of tea. The first question is always the same – 'How long have you got?' If the answer is only fifteen minutes then they will cut to the chase. If there is longer then there will be time to talk about the agent's welfare and whether they have any security concerns or other needs. The idea is to make them feel confident. 'The main aim is not to extract intelligence. If that is your top priority and all you do then it goes wrong,' explains one former agent handler. The art lies in building a relationship and establishing empathy and sympathy while always remaining in control.[66] A room full of MI5 agent handlers would look like a cross-section of British society from old men to young women, black and white, skinheads and men in suits, one for each occasion and for each type of agent.

In a modern warehouse somewhere in central London, a young Muslim man sits, observed by his MI5 handler. A small heater keeps the room warm and a cup of tea sits untouched on a coffee table. A driver stands by the vehicle just outside, ready to organise a fast getaway in case of any sign of trouble. 'I don't see myself as a spy in that sense anyway because I am just fulfilling my duty and my right as a Muslim citizen – you know keeping my eyes out,' the Muslim agent working for MI5 explains.[67] The bearded man could still recall his first nerve-racking meeting with MI5, the fear that he might be a suspect, the relief quickly followed by a new anxiety when he was asked to inform. 'I'm not going to go and spy on Mohammed buying halal sausages in the local store because that's not what I do. I would never do that. But if I know there is a bunch of Muslims who intend to do something and I hear about that or find out about that in whatever way then, yes, I was more than willing to see them again and talk about that and if they [MI5] ask me, to query more about these individuals. I felt that that's OK because these lads are not just the normal Mohammed or Abdullah praying in the mosque ... I don't want anyone to blow up a bomb next to me or blow my family up ... so I don't feel that this is against the Muslims in that sense. It is against the criminals.'[68] The agent meets maybe three or four times a month with an MI5 officer, sometimes for half an hour, sometimes for two or three hours with a twenty-four-hour number for emergencies. 'I never thought I would have personal contact with MI5 but it's not like the TV. It's not like the movies, yeah, so I don't feel like I'm in some kind of *Bourne Ultimatum* ... Some of them look a bit dodgy, some of them are ugly, some of them are nicer. You know, that's how it goes you know. Men and women, big and fat. You know. Thin, chubby. Black and white.'

The agent's work includes trying to stay close to people, although he maintained he was never pushed to do anything by MI5. 'The pressure is not really from them. The pressure is when you are out there on your own ... It's not comfortable sitting there with a terrorist or a criminal or whatever it is. You don't want to associate with these kind of people. So sometimes when you do sit there, yeah, it's a little bit of adrenalin kick there ... I don't really see them as practising Muslims. I see them like any other criminal, any other gangster out there who is just using the name Islamic or Muslim ... if someone's going to blow up a place and I find out about it, I'm going to make sure someone is going to stop it because that's harmful to Islam. Because that's what now people are going to think, "Ah Muslim, the terrorist, Muslims they're barbaric, Muslims they're this, Muslims are that," and that is not the true picture of Islam and if I can stop that before it happens then I am happy ... there are limits to what I am willing to do. If I was asked, and I mean that, if I was asked to do something specific against specific Muslims and they're not really any threat to society or threat to anyone then I would never do anything like that because that's not right, because that's not straight down like that. I would never do it.'[69]

The more agents it recruited and the harder it looked, the more threats MI5 found. In 2003, it was watching thirty networks linked to terrorism; by 2004 it was fifty. By November 2006 it had suddenly climbed to 200 groups with 1,600 individuals. Thirty of these groups were actively planning attacks.[70] There was no telephone directory of Al Qaeda officials outlining its structure of the type Penkovsky had

supplied decades earlier. The enemy was fluid and constantly evolving. It felt like chasing a will-o'-the-wisp.

At a lonely secret CIA base near the Afghan border with Pakistan,
the real dangers of agent running became clear in December 2009
along with the ability of Al Qaeda to learn the old games of double
agents. Al Qaeda is always on the look-out for plants from Western
intelligence and demands references from known radicals. Recruits
can be quickly exposed to extreme violence, perhaps witnessing the
beheading of someone carrying a mobile phone, to send a message.
Parts of Al Qaeda, especially those like the older generation of Egyptians who had grown up battling a state security service trained by
the KGB, were well versed in counter-intelligence and the organisation has tried to send some people into MI5 as penetration agents
(a greater concern might be someone who joins in good faith but is
then pressured due to family or personal ties). By late 2009, Al Qaeda
was able to replicate old-style Cold War techniques and run a double
agent against the CIA. Jordanian intelligence approached a well-
known radical asking him to go to Pakistan to contact Al Qaeda's
senior leadership. He was run jointly with the CIA, which had high
hopes he might be able to locate Al Qaeda's number two. But when
he came across the border from Pakistan to a meeting at the CIA's
base in Khost, Afghanistan, he blew himself up. Among those killed
was the commander of the CIA base, a brave, dedicated and experienced woman with a long track record of tackling Al Qaeda.

On 2 May 2011, the CIA would at least have its vengeance for her
death and the three thousand others killed nearly ten years earlier.
Osama bin Laden was tracked, through one of his couriers, to a
compound in Abbottabad, Pakistan, using a combination of human
and technical intelligence. A team of US Navy Seals landed by night
and killed the Al Qaeda leader; his body was disposed of in the sea a
few hours later. A man who had eluded western intelligence for so
long and who had been assumed to be hiding in the wilds of Wazir-
istan had been watching satellite TV in a comfortable house close to
a military garrison. Pakistan was not informed in advance for fear of
jeopardising the operation. The first MI6 knew of the mission was
when its Chief was called by his American counterpart to explain
what had just happened.

MI6 had reorganised after 9/11 and reshuffled its staff, opening new stations overseas, with Islamabad becoming its largest base. MI6's uptick in funding was not as large as that for MI5, but it still struggled to recruit fast enough. Old hands were rehired to help out. It took a while for it to be clear how it could help most effectively in countering terrorist threats to the UK. Eventually it focused on chasing leads overseas and upstream to relieve the pressure domestically. This included maintaining the intelligence coverage of suspects as they moved from the UK overseas, particularly to Pakistan. It was no good following someone every day in Britain if you lost them the minute they set foot in Karachi. But knowing what they were doing required the help of a sometimes already stretched liaison partner who had to be carefully massaged. This was always particularly difficult with Pakistan's mercurial ISI. Sometimes help could be enlisted overtly, sometimes through a secret relationship, having a local official on your payroll to check the records. One problem is reciprocity. A Pakistani general might offer his help in catching a British Al Qaeda suspect in his backyard – but only if a Baluchi nationalist in London is sent the other way in return. Working with the ISI was always complex, not least because it cared little for foreigners' concerns over human rights. 'We're not worried about that,' one Pakistani official explained when asked about the allegations of torture in the Western media. 'We're not afraid of the third degree.'[71]

The task of facing terrorism was daunting in terms both of scale and of the moral chicanes to be navigated. It required close working with allies, some of whom played by different rules. There were mistakes made and lessons learnt. It did though provide a new raison d'etre for the spies and seemed to answer the question of what they were for in the new world. But for British intelligence the years after 9/11 witnessed another crisis, one that shook them to the core and that exposed the deep and bitter tensions over their new role.

10

IN THE BUNKER

It was late on 24 September 2002 and the MI6 officer was wearily heading home. He took the lift down to the ground floor of the service's ziggurat headquarters at Vauxhall Cross and stepped through one of the airlock tubes at the main entrance. He was an old hand with a couple of decades of service behind him in the hot-spots of the world, but he had never quite got used to the new building. With a nod to the armed security guards, he stepped out into the spaghetti-like chaos of the Vauxhall interchange. As he navigated the buses and cars to make his way to the railway station, a placard heralding the headline for that day's *Evening Standard* newspaper caught his eye. '45 MINUTES FROM ATTACK', it warned in big, bold black letters. He stopped in his tracks. The government's dossier on Iraq's weapons of mass destruction had been launched that morning and he knew, in a way the public did not, precisely what the headline was referring to. Two thoughts hurtled through his mind in quick succession. 'That's not quite what the original intelligence report said,' was his first. His second thought, which quickly swamped the first, was: 'If this goes wrong, we're all screwed.'[1]

Two and a half thousand miles away in Baghdad, President Saddam Hussein was also perturbed. He had summoned his Revolutionary Command Council which, nominally, helped him run the country. Given that his management style consisted largely of fear interspersed with occasional violence, its members knew their lives depended on his favour, and Saddam realised this meant that they often lied to him. As he looked around the table and demanded answers he appeared 'stiff' and 'under pressure'. He had just read this new dossier published with much fanfare by the British government. It contained detailed information about his own military capabilities. There was even a claim that weapons of mass destruction could be fired in forty-five minutes. This puzzled him. He knew nothing of the capacity they described. Was there anyone in the room who was aware of any capabilities that the President himself did not know about? By turn, each member of the Revolutionary Command Council hurriedly said no, they did not. That would be impossible, they said, knowing a wrong answer could be costly. Anything they knew, he would know. Saddam Hussein remain puzzled. If his underlings really were telling the truth, what explained the confidence of those devils at British intelligence?[2]

If Saddam had known what had gone through the MI6 officer's mind outside Vauxhall Cross perhaps he might have had some inkling of the trouble that was heading his way. If the MI6 officer had known of Saddam's bemusement he too might have shared in that reaction. The service was about to go through a crisis which, according to one colleague with a historical bent, was to be its darkest hour since Philby's betrayal.

The direction that Britain's closest ally was heading in was always apparent. The night after the 11 September attack when British officials dined at CIA headquarters in Langley, the Downing Street Foreign Affairs Adviser David Manning had cautioned against striking Iraq, sensing that Washington's hawks already had Saddam within their sights. The following month CIA officers were over in London for the memorial service for the former MI6 Chief David Spedding. 'We should focus on Afghanistan,' an MI6 officer told a CIA counterpart. 'If you go into Iraq, it's really going to complicate things.'[3] 'Afghanistan first' was the message from London but by the first week of December, the chief of MI6 was in the White House with David Manning for talks with President Bush's top advisers. The British officials were delivering a paper entitled 'the second phase of the war against terrorism'.[4]

A few days earlier, at four o'clock in the afternoon on 30 November, a senior MI6 director, an Arabic speaker deeply versed in the Middle East, took a telephone call from Manning. The Iraq issue was building up apace, Manning explained. Could the officer do a quick paper on how to approach the subject by six that afternoon? 'If the US heads for direct action, have we ideas which could divert them to an alternative course?' the paper began. It warned of the dangers of planning to remove Saddam. 'This is not going to be simple or straightforward, and it doesn't have to pan out well,' was the message from the leading member of the service's 'camel corps'.[5] After the weekend more papers were sent over by the officer. Another paper took a completely different approach, outlining a set of broad motivations for action beyond just WMD. 'At our meeting on 30 November, we discussed how we could combine an objective of regime change in Baghdad with the need to protect important regional interests which would be at grave risk if a bombing campaign against Iraq were launched in the short term.' Where did the talk of regime change come from? 'It came out of the ground like a mist following the change of temperature on 9/11,' the officer later reflected. 'It became clear to all of us that nothing short of decisive intervention in Iraq was going to satisfy the Americans.' At this stage a bombing campaign in support of Iraqis trying to topple Saddam was perceived as a more likely strategy than an all-out invasion. These were technically private papers rather than 'policy papers' but the words regime change were all over them at a time when the Foreign Secretary was trying to head off such talk as a bad idea and illegal.[6] Downing Street had turned to MI6 and its experts – rather than the Foreign Office – and the service was offering a route map for the way forward, touching even on the need to provide a legal basis for any intervention.

Washington's hawks held back for a while. But by the spring of 2002 victory in Afghanistan seemed to have been achieved and London watched Washington's gaze turn resolutely back to Iraq. George W. Bush and members of his team had differing motives – unfinished business for some like Cheney who regretted not driving on to Baghdad in 1991, with an added personal twist for the new President whose father had led that first Gulf War. In neo-conservative eyes this was the once-in-a-lifetime chance to reshape the Middle East state by state, beginning with Iraq. America's intention was clear, although the means by which it would achieve its goal was not.

This provided an opening for Blair. He told President Bush he would stand by him in dealing with Saddam; the only issue was how the Iraqi leader would be dealt with. 'TB [Tony Blair] wanted to be in a position to give GWB [George W. Bush] a strategy and influence it,' wrote Alastair Campbell in his diary.[7] The Prime Minister had known what his mission was within three days of the attack. 'My job is to try and steer them in a sensible path,' Tony Blair had told his

Foreign Secretary.[8] For Blair, this was his moment on the world stage, the chance to harness the writhing anger of the United States and guide it on to a surer footing. He enjoyed being, in his words, 'a big player'.[9] In London, there was that reflexive instinct among spies, soldiers and wannabe statesmen to stay close to the Americans. Maintaining that relationship – and with it the flow of American intelligence and the self-perception of walking on the world stage (even if on someone else's coat-tails) – had become gospel. Staying close supported the often illusory notion of influence.

Blair also shared the view of a titanic struggle that could be fought by 'modernising' the Middle East through a dramatic act. 'Our enemy has an ideology. It does threaten us. The ultimate answer is in the spread of democracy and freedom.' 'In the choice between a policy of management and a policy of revolution, I had become a revolutionary.'[10] Crucially, the British Prime Minister also harboured the same nightmares as those in power in Washington, a dark vision of a world in which, without decisive action, terrorists and weapons of mass destruction were destined to join together with catastrophic consequences. That dread had become all-consuming in the upper reaches of the US government. Fearful of missing another attack, the spies were chasing shadows everywhere. An overheard conversation in a Las Vegas casino about a nuclear weapon obtained from Russia's stockpile heading for New York made it on to the CIA's Daily Threat Matrix which some days listed a hundred specific threats.[11] Then anthrax turned up in the post, killing five people, and the nightmare seemed to have become real. As Kabul fell, new intelligence emerged revealing that bin Laden himself had met with two former members of Pakistan's nuclear programme just weeks before 9/11. CIA Director George Tenet personally jumped on his plane to Pakistan to try to discover the truth. All this time, Bush and Blair were also receiving secret intelligence briefings about the Pakistani nuclear salesman A. Q. Khan offering countries, including Libya, instructions and parts to make a nuclear bomb. Saddam's weapons, such as they were, were no more of a threat after 9/11 than they had been before. What had changed was the tolerance in London and Washington.[12]

There was a commingling of calculation and belief in Tony Blair to the point where pulling them apart was impossible. In his view, a line needed to be drawn somewhere when it came to states developing weapons of mass destruction, and that somewhere was Iraq.[13] Blair was sure that Iraq was developing weapons of mass destruction because his spies believed it always had been. After the first Gulf War of 1991, MI6, the CIA and UN weapons inspectors had combed over the wreckage of Iraq and had been shocked to find Saddam had been much closer to building a nuclear bomb behind their backs. They vowed never to be caught out again, overlooking the fact that they had also over-estimated Saddam's stockpile of chemical agents.[14] As with Soviet military and economic power, it was safer to err on the side of caution because normally the costs of being wrong that way were lower. In 1995, a fleet of limos pulled up outside a hotel in the Jordanian capital, Amman. Inside were two of Saddam's daughters and their husbands. One of the men, Hussein Kamel, revealed that there had also been a larger biological programme than anyone had suspected before 1991 but said it was destroyed. The Iraqis then owned up and provided extensive documentation. Western intelligence had been deceived again. Saddam was clever and cunning, they decided, a master of deception. Through the 1990s, there had not been much need for independent intelligence gathering. The UN weapons inspectors became the eyes and ears of the CIA and MI6. In some cases this was done covertly, the US placing its own spies inside the inspection teams who collected military targeting information on sites.[15] MI6 also passed intelligence to and debriefed inspectors, twice in 1998 discussing with them how to publicise the finding of traces of VX on missile warheads (although Operation Mass Appeal, as it was called, was abandoned when the story leaked out independently).[16] Later that year, the inspectors were expelled by Saddam. With their dominant source of new information eradicated, intelligence analysts were left with history. Worst-case assumptions had become just assumptions, which were left unchallenged.

As America's objective became clear, a meeting at Chequers was called in April 2002. A minute of the meeting recorded that the Prime Minister wanted to lead and not just support the American process of regime change (although what precisely regime change meant remained unclear). Britain's two most senior spies, Richard Dearlove and John Scarlett, both argued for co-operation with the US planning. 'It's keeping our hands on what's going on and not letting the Americans run away with the ball,' Dearlove later said of the thinking.[17] The roles of these two rivals, Scarlett, as chair of the Joint Intelligence Committee, and Dearlove, as Chief of MI6, were central to the build-up to war. Scarlett, a graduate of Moscow Rules, was ever the details man. Dearlove was the forceful, big-picture visionary thinker, keen for intelligence to make an impact. Both would be accused of drawing too close to power.

Richard Dearlove was a frequent transatlantic traveller in the months after 9/11, commuting back and forth between London and Washington and meeting with the most senior American officials in the White House. Like all MI6 chiefs since Dick White he understood the importance of nurturing close relations with the US. But along with David Manning, he had now been given the specific task of tracking the development of US policy on Iraq and reporting back to Blair. The Americans were well aware of this. CIA officials noted how skilfully Dearlove, like the experienced case officer he was, cultivated his relationship with Tenet, who, like many CIA chiefs, came from a more political than operational background, in order to gain maximum access for Britain.[18] The British always did this (to the annoyance of the non-Anglophiles in the agency), but Dearlove did it particularly well. 'We used to joke that Tenet was Dearlove's best recruitment,' recalls one CIA officer.[19]

CIA officers had been surprised at just how upset the British were in the summer of 2002 when they heard that their annual summit was going to be cancelled. The CIA and MI6 would have regular meetings, often in Bermuda or somewhere far flung, to divide up the world, agreeing targets and identifying potential conflicts of interest. In the summer of 2002 Tenet explained that he was too busy for such a meeting. He was worried it would not look right for him to disappear for so long. In the end, it was agreed that a quick summit could take place, but only if it was in Washington and over the weekend. Dearlove and colleagues travelled over in July. After the regular discussion, Dearlove approached Tenet and asked to speak 'off-line'. They talked for close to two hours. According to Tenet, Dearlove came away with a clear perception that the US administration was determined to transform the Middle East, starting with Iraq. During the visit, Dearlove also had an argument with staff in Vice-President Cheney's office about their claim that Saddam was linked to Al Qaeda, which the British generally thought was 'bollocks'.

'[Dearlove] believed that the crowd round the vice-president was playing fast and loose with the evidence. In his view, it was never about "fixing" the intelligence itself but rather about the undisciplined manner in which the intelligence was being used,' Tenet later said.[20]

Dearlove headed straight to Downing Street on his return for a crucial gathering of Britain's national security nomenclatura on 23 July. Scarlett began by summarising the latest assessment of Saddam's regime. The regime was tough and based on fear and the only way of overthrowing it would be through massive military action which Saddam was not yet convinced would come. Dearlove was up next and reported back on his trip to Washington. In the draft minutes of the meeting, he was quoted as saying that there had been 'a perceptible shift in attitude. Military action was now seen as inevitable. Bush wanted to remove Saddam, through military action, justified by the conjunction of terrorism and WMD. But the intelligence and facts were being fixed around the policy.' When the draft minutes were circulated, Dearlove objected to that last sentence, saying it was not what he meant, and it was altered. The British Chief of Defence Staff then spoke up and outlined the possible contribution Britain could make. The military wanted in. They disliked the idea of a big war being fought by the Americans without their closest ally by their side. The Chief of Defence Staff told Blair later that he would have a real problem with his army if they were not properly involved.[21]

The Foreign Secretary, Jack Straw, piped up next with a note of caution and a line of argument he frequently deployed. 'The case was thin,' he said. 'Saddam was not threatening his neighbours, and his WMD capability was less than that of Libya, North Korea or Iran.' Libya had become an increasing worry as a new stream of intelligence through 2002 showed it acquiring components for a bomb. The intelligence was far stronger than anything on Iraq. Blair dismissed Straw's remarks by saying that there were other strategies for dealing with Libya and Iran. The best approach to deal with Iraq, Straw said, would be an ultimatum demanding the return of UN inspectors. 'This would help with the legal justification for the use of force,' he added. The UK, much more than the US, needed a legal rationale. Non-compliance with UN resolutions on WMD offered more chance of a rationale than regime change.

One person in the room was startled and taken aback by the nature of the discussion. 'What struck me was that some of the language used implied that we were closer to military action than I had imagined that we were,' recalled Sir Richard Wilson, the Cabinet Secretary. He also detected an underlying tension between Blair and his Foreign Secretary. Straw, Wilson believed, was trying to prevent Blair being too 'gung-ho about military action'. Wilson was about to retire and used his farewell meetings with Blair to warn him that 'he was getting into a position which could be dangerous'. He sensed Blair was serious about military action. 'There was a gleam in his eye which worries me,' he thought.[22]

The overall conclusion was that Britain should work on the assumption that it would join the US in military action. America's intentions were clear. So were Blair's to those around him After the meeting he wrote a private note to President Bush. His advisers were so worried by the opening line that they asked him to tone it down. 'What I was saying to President Bush was very clear and simple. It is: You can count on us,' Blair would later say of the content.[23] But selling a war to an unconvinced public would be tricky. Regime change did not cut it in Britain in the way it did in post-9/11 America, even though Blair believed that this would be the only way of dealing with the weapons.[24]

The decision was taken to rest the public case entirely on Iraq's possession of weapons of mass destruction in defiance of the United Nations. This would mean leaning heavily on intelligence. As far back as April, Scarlett had met with Alastair Campbell to discuss what would be needed 'communications-wise to set the scene for Iraq'. Early drafts were begun of a dossier on Saddam's weapons programmes. Some MI6 officers, including the senior Arabist director who had briefed Manning, were unhappy with the idea. 'All our training, all our culture, bias, would be against such a thing, and we were very relieved when we thought we had seen it off.' But when the officer returned from holiday in the first week of September, he was alarmed to find the idea had been resurrected and now appeared unstoppable. 'It was up and running like a racehorse . . . and we didn't feel that there was an opportunity, an occasion, when we could throw ourselves in front of it.'[25]

Every Wednesday afternoon, Britain's spy chiefs and those they work with from other departments gather in a cosy egg-shaped conference room. The select few always sit in the same seats and arrive without aides or assistants. With no politicians present it is a useful time to catch up on gossip, but the collegiate atmosphere turns sober and serious as they get down to business reviewing the latest, carefully drafted assessments that have been produced for them. The Joint Intelligence Committee has acquired something of a mystique. Some former members believe this was not always well founded, but nevertheless it was precisely that mystique which politicians wanted to tap into when they asked the JIC to take the unprecedented step of publishing a dossier for public consumption. No one on the committee demurred. 'We weren't asked would we like to produce this. We were told we will produce this,' recalled Sir David Omand, Security and Intelligence Co-ordinator and member of the JIC at the time. 'Now, in my position, I could have phoned up Downing Street and I could have asked to see the Prime Minister and said, "This is a terrible idea. Why do you want to do this?" I didn't do that because I didn't think it was such a terrible idea at the time.'[26] Campbell told Scarlett and others that the dossier had to be 'revelatory and we needed to show that it was new and informative and part of a bigger case.'[27] The JIC prides itself on its ability to come to an agreed collective decision with no dissent. 'All have to dip their hands in the blood of collective judgement, however unwelcome that may be', as Omand describes the process.[28]

Scarlett was in charge but working closely with Downing Street. The fact that Alastair Campbell could talk of the Chair of the Joint Intelligence Committee as a 'friend' and 'a very good bloke' was indicative of the informality of the Blair government and the willingness of the spies to work with it.[29] At times of crisis, Downing Street takes on the sense of a bunker under siege, its residents hunkering down as the artillery rounds lobbed by the press, parliament and diplomacy explode all around. In this heady atmosphere, it can be hard to resist when the Prime Minister asks for help. Former chairs of the JIC have argued that the committee entered the 'the Prime Minister's magic circle' over Iraq and was engulfed by the heady atmosphere, failing to keep its distance and objectivity.[30]

As the drafting process took place, Scarlett received comments from the Prime Minister as well as from Alastair Campell and

Jonathan Powell, his Chief of Staff, and he attended meetings chaired by Campbell to look at the presentation of the dossier.[31] Intelligence was drawn closer to policy than it had ever been before. Politicians and their advisers would never normally comment on JIC drafts. The dossier, those at the top would claim, was not designed to make the case for war. It was just putting information in the public domain so that people could make up their minds. 'In no sense, in my mind, or in the mind of the JIC, was it a document designed to make a case for anything,' Scarlett later asserted.[32] That claim was disputed by some of those just below him. 'We knew at the time that the purpose of the Dossier was precisely to make a case for war,' one senior military intelligence officer, Major General Michael Laurie, later complained. 'During the drafting of the final Dossier, every fact was managed to make it as strong as possible ... It was clear to me that there was direction and pressure being applied on the JIC and its drafters.'[33] A line had been crossed. Intelligence, some would argue, was being used as a tool for political persuasion.

Scarlett was the meticulous briefer at formal meetings but the man who had more informal access to the Prime Minister was Dearlove. What was discussed between the two men remains their secret. Dearlove was a confident, can-do character. Blair was also more forward leaning on Iraq than many of his advisers, including David Manning. Manning watched the Foreign Office, where he had come from, struggling with the demands placed on it while MI6 began to provide more policy advice than it had in the past.[34] Dearlove, like Blair, was a liberal interventionist. 'The case for going to war with Iraq was only, as it were, partially supported by the intelligence,' he later told an audience. 'I think the case for going to war in Iraq was a moral one ... I take the liberal interventionist view of foreign policy. That's my personal view as a citizen of this country. The reasons for looking at Iraq as a problem that might justify military action were very broad-ranging. And in a way I think the most difficult issue for a British prime minister facing the possibility that the United States were going to invade Iraq was the dilemma any British prime minister would face – do you support the United States in this venture, or, and the alternative – there probably was no alternative – do you go with Russia, France and Germany and as it were oppose US policy?'[35]

Dearlove, his critics say, relished being at the epicentre of power, briefing Blair and even President Bush in the Oval Office. But this was the culmination of not so much a personal as an institutional desire, an urge to show that the Secret Service was still needed despite all those questions after the end of the Cold War. 'One of the cultural weaknesses of SIS [MI6] is that it is too eager to please,' one former senior official reckons.[36] For all the Bondish bravado, an insecurity had always haunted the service since its inception in 1909, a fear that it would no longer be needed and that one day it might simply be disposed of, its cherished traditions and war stories consigned not even to the history books but just to the fading memory of a few. The post-9/11 era had offered deliverance from those fears. Iraq was its apotheosis. Dearlove developed a relationship which was far, far closer to the Prime Minister than to the Foreign Secretary to whom a Chief normally reports. He was among the Prime Minister's closest advisers and, in the eyes of other officials, enjoyed a 'privileged relationship'.[37] Dearlove disputes the idea that he was too close as 'complete rubbish'. 'I wasn't sipping Chardonnay in the evenings with Tony Blair, or nipping off to have breakfast with him to Chequers. I was going to meetings, as the head of SIS, to discuss SIS business in relation to the development of national security policy . . . A lot of people were jealous of my position, and therefore, I think, motivated to talk about it, including the Foreign Secretary of the day.'

Politicians and spies frequently have one personality trait in common with each other which they do not share with the civil servants with whom they work – they both have an appetite for risk-taking. Dearlove was acutely aware that the Prime Minister was relying on him by deploying intelligence as the central plank of the argument for intervention. This, he knew, was a 'fragile and dangerous position'. At one point Blair turned to his spy chief. 'Richard, my fate is in your hands,' he said.[38]

The problem with making the public case about the threat posed by Iraq's possession of weapons of mass destruction was that even though everyone, including the spies, was convinced by the intelligence that said Saddam had the weapons, they were not sure it looked strong enough to win the argument. The intelligence was 'sporadic and patchy', as a Joint Intelligence Committee report of March 2002 indicated (the assessment was even less confident about the weapons than a paper from the previous May).[39] A war could not easily be justified on sporadic and patchy intelligence. What the Prime Minister needed was clear. Would MI6 be able to step up to the plate and deliver?

Before September 2001, Iraq had been a graveyard slot for MI6 officers, a backwater where you were sent if your career was sloshing around in the shallows. 'The intelligence picture on Iraq was, I would say, neglected,' Dearlove later admitted of the decade between 1991 and 2001.[40] Gathering secrets on Saddam Hussein's weapons of mass destruction ranked way down the list of priorities set by the Joint Intelligence Committee, twentieth by some accounts. The intelligence base was 'thin'.[41] After 11 September, Iraq would roar up the top twenty faster than one of the guided missiles Saddam was suspected of hiding. But, even once it had become a priority-one target, it takes time to build up intelligence sources. Good human intelligence cannot be switched on and off like a tap. Potential agents have to be spotted, researched, cultivated, approached and their veracity and good faith validated. It can take years to establish proper intelligence coverage against a hard target; eighteen months is a minimum. That was not the time-frame on offer. 'If we had clear options, we wouldn't have felt the pressure so much,' one senior officer recalled. 'There was undoubtedly considerable pressure to generate new sources, new insights, and we were, in all honesty, not well placed to do that. Our access to Iraq was no better than it was,' another senior officer later recalled.[42]

MI6 had a small stable of agents reporting from within Iraq. One or two of these were agents of long standing and reliability. One in particular had been reporting since the time of the first Gulf War in 1991. He had some personal disgruntlement with Saddam and disliked his regime. His reports had been impressive on certain specific areas where he had access, such as Iraq's air defences. These reports had proved vital in helping administer the No Fly Zone over Iraq in the 1990s. The problem is that neither this agent nor any of the others had any first-hand, inside knowledge of Iraq's WMD programme; their expertise lay elsewhere. But they could see which way the wind was blowing and they knew exactly what MI6 was looking for. And so they managed to find it. Much of the crucial – and controversial – evidence would come from these agents, though not directly. They would find their own agents (or sub-sources) who in turn provided the goods – cash bonuses were on offer. Much of it would be inferential, sourced from their circle of contacts in Baghdad or people they had met and recruited (or at least claimed to have done). There was no point, these agents thought, in reporting on the rather large number of people who knew nothing about special weapons or who were doubtful of their existence. That was not what was wanted.

And so in August and into September 2002 the magicians at MI6 were able to pull a rabbit or three out of their hat. With their customary flourish, they produced new intelligence, in the nick of time, that seemed to save the day. The new sources would be vital in adding colour to the dossier and would allow Scarlett to instruct the assessments staff to 'firm up' the dossier's conclusions and dispose of the caveats.[43]

Walking through Baghdad at the end of August, the Iraqi was nervous. He had been risking his life for many years by spying on his own country as an agent for the British Secret Service. At an agreed location he activated a tiny transmitter, smaller than a packet of cigarettes, to send an encrypted message to his contact. At the receiving end was another undercover source operating for MI6 in Baghdad (not an MI6 officer but an intermediary), who could eventually get the information back to Vauxhall Cross. One of the Iraqi agent's sources had produced a rather vague and ambiguous report saying that biological and chemical munitions could be with military units and ready for firing within twenty to forty-five minutes. Quite what the weapons were he could not say. The report seemed to have come originally from someone who was just talking to a colleague casually, unaware that they would pass on the information to a foreign secret service. The source was untested but he was named and seemed to be in a position to know the information.

The dossier was being drawn up in a rush, far faster than usual for a JIC document. Emails whizzed back and forth, some pleading for more information. 'Has anybody got anything more they can put in the dossier?' was the plea Sir David Omand recalled. 'I wouldn't interpret that as meaning people saying there isn't enough intelligence in substance, but this isn't going to look very convincing if we are not allowed to show more of it. That's my personal explanation of why, as it were, people fell on the forty-five minutes. At least that was something the Secret Service would allow to be used. With hindsight, one can see that adding a bit of local colour like that is asking for trouble. But we didn't really spot that at the time.'[44] MI6 officers were feeling the pressure to come up with the goods. '[T]eams were wrestling with all this, having a very difficult time,' according to the senior MI6 director.[45]

Not everyone was convinced by the 'local colour'. Expert analysts found MI6's description of the new sub-source not as straightforward or as clear as they would have expected. When they asked MI6 'their response was unusually vague and unhelpful'.[46] The problem with the claim that munitions could be deployed in forty-five minutes was the absence of the type of collateral and corroborating intelligence an analyst would expect. Where were these chemical weapons being produced and by whom? What kind of chemicals were they? It was just a lonely piece of intelligence floating in a sea of uncertainty. It was 'a disturbing moment', an MI6 officer later told the Iraq Inquiry.

There was a debate about how this new intelligence should be worded. An original draft talked about Iraq 'probably' having dispersed its special weapons and stating that they 'could' be with military units and ready for firing within forty-five minutes. Alastair Campbell pointed out that in one draft of the dossier the use of the qualifier 'may' in the main text was weaker than the language used in the summary. Scarlett replied that the language had been 'tightened'. Scarlett would later say this followed a re-examination of the original intelligence. A few of the experts inside Whitehall remained unhappy with the claim but consoled themselves with the thought that at least the press or parliament would probe it carefully. They never did.

What did the report actually mean? The source did not seem to know much about chemical or biological weapons or even about the difference between them. And the issue of timing was also perplexing. If it related to battlefield shells, as the JIC's drafters in the assessment staff believed it probably did, then forty-five minutes to move munitions from storage places to the units which would fire them was not particularly surprising. In fact it was pretty pathetic rather than scary if it took forty-five minutes to fire a shell. If it was referring to a ballistic missile then that would be rather too quick. Ministers say the difference was never explained to them. Nor was it explained to the public. When he heard about it, the Director of the CIA had his own view. His people thought it did not fit with what they knew about the artillery capabilities of the Iraqis. He thought the original source questionable and referred to it privately as the 'they-can-attack-in-45-minutes shit'.[47]

But this was not the most important piece of intelligence that rode, like the cavalry, to the rescue. The most welcome of the new sources galloped over the horizon just as the sun was setting on the dossier. MI6 had managed to bag what looked like an important new agent. Dearlove personally mentioned the good news to David Manning at a meeting on 10 September and a copy of the report was duly despatched to Downing Street. The next day Dearlove informed Scarlett on the phone and MI6 formally issued its new report. An agent claimed that the production of biological and chemical weapons was being accelerated. The agent promised more critical intelligence soon. The source was still untested but Dearlove believed the information was too important to sit on.[48] But while those people at the top in London had learnt about this new source before even the intelligence report was formally issued, others – the ones who could judge the technical credibility of the information – remained in the dark.

Dearlove had a scheduled meeting with the Prime Minister on 12 September to update Blair on MI6 operations in Iraq. Accompanied by a senior officer, he went through all of MI6's sources with Blair one by one, including the new source. The aim was to give Blair a 'flavour' of what was happening on the ground. Dearlove made clear just how important the new source promised to be but added that the case was developmental and the source unproven. Some inside MI6 believed this process was emblematic of what had gone wrong. Too much unproven intelligence, hot off the printer, was walked too quickly into the welcoming arms of Downing Street, they argued. This, traditionalists claimed, was the logical end point of the desire of modernisers within the service to make it useful, relevant and close to policy. There is a reason, they say, why intelligence gets assessed by experts carefully and placed into context and put down on paper rather than orally briefed to policymakers. But that was not the style of the Blair government. In truth, this was not a new debate. There is a rich pedigree of intelligence officers walking their successes round to Downing Street, particularly during times of conflict. 'Everything is supposed to go through the assessment staff,' one member of that staff at the time of Iraq recalls in discussing how the process worked in general terms. 'Often we got it half an hour after it had gone to Downing Street with it post-dated to cover their back.' Observers of the relationship believed this desire to make an impression has long reflected the insecurity of MI6 and the way in which its leadership has sought to win over political leaders.

The new source talked not just about accelerated production but also the building of further facilities and the employment of so-called dual-use facilities. Strangely there was no satellite imagery nor intercepted communications to confirm this.[49] The new source promised another consignment of crucial intelligence in the next three to four weeks, including details of WMD sites. This, it was hoped, might be the eagerly sought 'silver bullet'. The key 'new source on trial' was said to have direct access. He may have been in the Iraqi Special Security Organisation which was responsible for protecting key sites and individuals. A source from the SSO was reporting on Iraq's plans to confuse UN inspectors and bug their rooms, and on how scientists were to be kept away from them if there were any suspicions about their loyalty. Those who later saw reports reflected that this was all actually standard Iraqi behaviour that anyone who had been an inspector in the 1990s would recognise. However, these security precautions were taken to indicate that there must be some-thing to hide and this source reported that he was sure there was. But would a security official actually know much about what that was? Saddam had in fact ordered key military units to check methodically and scrub themselves of anything that could be suspicious (for instance, traces relating to pre-1991 equipment), fearing that the US would use it as a justification for war, and to hide sensitive materials unrelated to unconventional weapons.[50]

Dearlove and senior officers around him were bullish. They were delivering the goods. One officer went so far as to utter the immortal words: 'We've got another Penkovsky.' A third new sub-source over the summer had delivered what looked like confirmation of mobile biological labs. In all, three reporting streams produced six new reports at the crucial moment. But further down the food chain there were rumblings in some corners of Vauxhall Cross. A few members of staff felt uncomfortable that fresh, untested intelligence was being taken to Downing Street; two people asked to be moved because of their misgivings. The 'new source on trial' was particularly controversial at the time, 'a cause celebre' an officer told the Iraq Inquiry. People felt the chain of command had been 'disenfranchised' because of 'senior people who reach down into the machinery and try moving the cogs'. Those at the operational level 'were genuinely annoyed and concerned,' he said. Another described the report as 'based in part on wishful thinking'. 'Here was a chap who promised the crock of gold at the end of the rainbow.'[51]

Brian Jones returned from a holiday in Greece on 18 September just as the dossier neared completion. He was in charge of a team of analysts of weapons of mass destruction in the Defence Intelligence Staff of the Ministry of Defence, the home of much of the government's residual knowledge and in-depth expertise. His staff told him that their work in his absence had been dominated by the dossier. His expert on biological weapons was not completely happy with the dossier but felt he could live with it; his expert on Iraq's chemical weapons was very unhappy, especially since his suggested changes to drafts were being ignored. 'The trouble is I have absolutely no reliable intelligence that Iraq has produced significant quantities of any chemical warfare agent or weapons since the Gulf conflict of 1991,' Jones said he was told by his colleague. 'I have been making this point in comments on every draft of the dossier,' he said. 'But we are just being ignored.'[52]

What bothered Jones and his staff was the certainty being expressed. How was such confidence possible? That was when he heard the first whisperings of a new source so sensitive that only a few could be let into the details, the one that had just arrived in mid-September (and which was describing accelerated production). His antennae went up and he went to see his boss.

'This dossier business,' his superior began. 'DCDI [Deputy Chief of Defence Intelligence] wants me to tell you that there is some new intelligence, very sensitive, can't be shown to many, that clears up this business your chaps have been worrying about. OK?'

Jones complained that this was not good enough.

'But an officer from MI6 has reassured me that it is OK,' his boss replied.

Had he seen it personally?

'No. But MI6 have told me it was good stuff.' He told Jones he had been reassured by MI6 that the report was sound even though he had not seen it.

Jones privately contacted someone who had seen the MI6 report and explained his concerns. Should he take the unusual step of writing a formal minute outlining these concerns or was it really as good as claimed? 'Write the minute,' he was told.[53] His Chemical Weapons analyst also recoded his concerns on paper. 'The 20 September draft still includes a number of statements which are not supported by the evidence available to me,' it read.[54]

The information from the new source on trial was not included directly in the dossier because Dearlove wanted to protect the source, but knowledge of it was crucial in hardening up the judgements and overcoming the concerns within DIS. The new source, with its talk of accelerated production, seemed to confirm what had been only implied in the August report and helped overcome the last remaining qualms, including over forty-five minutes.[55] 'We were told at the time that it did clinch it, and that we should bury our concerns,' Jones later said.[56] How could reports be so sensitive that they could not be revealed to the experts but could be shown off to the Prime Minister and used to harden up a dossier designed for public consumption?

'They weren't seen by experts. You forget this is a Secret Service. We have to protect our sources. We can't allow documents like that to reach anyone who really knows.' That was how the fictional MI6 employee in Graham Greene's *Our Man in Havana* explained to the vacuum-cleaner salesman why no one had noticed that his technical diagrams for a new super-weapon were actually enlarged versions of a two-way nozzle and double-action coupling from an 'Atomic Pile' vacuum cleaner. 'We haven't shown them the drawings yet,' the Chief explained in the 1958 novel, referring to the experts outside the service. 'You know what those fellows are like. They'll criticise points of detail, say the whole thing is unreliable, that the tube is out of proportion or points the wrong way.'[57]

By mid-September the dossier, stiffened by MI6's new sources, was nearly ready to face the outside world. Scarlett maintained that while he was in charge of the main text, the foreword was overtly political and therefore not under his control. Downing Street officials say it would have been important for Blair to have felt his JIC Chair was comfortable with it.[58] Scarlett did make a few small changes and then, in the words of one member, 'flashed it round the JIC', some members of which paid relatively little attention.[59] The language was stark. 'What I believe the assessed intelligence has established beyond doubt is that Saddam has continued to produce chemical and biological weapons, that he continues in his efforts to develop nuclear weapons,' Blair assured the reader in his foreword. The idea that there were limits to the intelligence and even major gaps had been lost, along with so many of the other caveats.[60] The dossier's foreword implied that there was more that the public could not see and had to be kept under wraps because of security. The reality was that the dossier 'may have left with readers the impression that there was fuller and firmer intelligence behind the judgements than was the case.'[61]

Blair rose to present his case before an expectant House of Commons on 24 September 2002. 'I am aware, of course, that people will have to take elements of this on the good faith of our intelligence services, but this is what they are telling me, the British Prime Minister, and my senior colleagues. The intelligence picture that they paint is one accumulated over the last four years. It is extensive, detailed and authoritative. It concludes that Iraq has chemical and biological weapons, that Saddam has continued to produce them, that he has existing and active military plans for the use of chemical and biological weapons, which could be activated within forty-five minutes.' Thanks to MI6 riding to the rescue with its new sources, the intelligence that in March had been 'sporadic and patchy' could now be claimed as 'extensive, detailed and authoritative'.

In the land of intelligence, like that of the blind, the one-eyed man is king. The trickle of MI6 sources amounted to more than the Americans had managed and the fresh intelligence, including the new source of September, was quickly passed over the Atlantic. 'Did this information make any difference in my thinking?' asked CIA Director George Tenet when he later tried to explain why he had got things wrong. 'You bet it did.'[62] The Bush administration was preparing to make its case both to its own public and to the world and British intelligence would be closely involved.

An American National Intelligence Estimate was hastily cobbled together reflecting the fact that no one had assessed Iraq's programmes properly for a long time. One officer said he could count the number of sources on one hand and still pick his nose. None of the four sources the US had on Iraq were inside the WMD programme. 'How come all the good reporting I get is from SIS?' Tenet asked one of his staff once – music to British intelligence's ears with their long-standing desire to show they could always bring something to the party.[63] Each side would lean on the other, sometimes more than they realised.

The CIA and its Director George Tenet's experience mirrored that in Britain. 'Don't worry, it's a slam dunk,' Tenet told President Bush when he worried that the public case for Saddam's weapons was not strong enough ('The two dumbest words I ever said,' he later reflected). Tenet would see himself as the fall guy when it all went wrong, arguing that the dilemma for the spies was that if they did not get involved the intelligence would be misused, but when they did involve themselves they were drawn into a messy, political process of advocacy.

Tenet had the White House on his back, constantly pushing and probing, and Vice-President Cheney visiting Langley to check up on progress. No one, on either side of the Atlantic, could easily put their finger on direct pressure on analysts to come to certain conclusions. But it is also naive to think that analysts can close themselves off from their surroundings and the political context, however hard they try. How likely is it that junior staff will challenge assumptions to which they know their superiors have committed themselves in their relationships with politicians? The analysts also complained they were not told enough about the intelligence sources to understand their motivation and reliability or to realise that some of the material was going round in circles between different countries and being repackaged to look as if it was new when in fact it was old. The case for Iraq having developed mobile biological weapons was emblematic of much that what went wrong.

In an upmarket but anonymous hotel room in Amman, Jordan, a well-built, olive-skinned man nervously chain-smoked cigarettes, the ashtray overflowing as the hours passed. He was, he said, a former major in the Mukhabarat, the feared Iraqi intelligence service. He could talk in ghastly detail about the methods he and his colleagues used to maintain Saddam's grip on power. But there was more, he explained. He knew something about biological weapons labs. His rapt audience consisted not of spies but two journalists. His back-story sounded plausible, but there was something in the way he glanced downwards when he talked about the mobile labs that did not quite feel right. And there was the fact that he had been introduced by the Iraqi National Congress, an émigré group run by the mercurial Ahmed Chalabi, dedicated to Saddam's overthrow. So the story about the mobile labs languished through a lack of confidence in the source.[64]

A few weeks after that Amman meeting US Secretary of State Colin Powell stood before the United Nations, George Tenet literally and metaphorically covering his rear. 'One of the most worrisome things that emerges from the thick intelligence file we have on Iraq's biological weapons is the existence of mobile production facilities used to make biological agents,' he explained. 'Iraq has at least seven of these mobile biological agent factories,' he claimed, before out-lining the four sources that backed up the case. 'A fourth source, an Iraqi major, who defected, confirmed that Iraq has mobile biological research laboratories.'[65] While one of the journalists listening won-dered, but only for a few weeks, if he had missed a story, Powell did not know that parts of his own intelligence community had a year earlier deemed the major to be a fabricator. They had issued a 'burn notice', but never recalled his reports or amended the work based on them. Nor did Powell know that CIA officers had also been warned that the crucial main source about mobile labs, on whom so much in America and Britain depended, might also be a fabricator. 'Curveball' was the fitting codename for that main source.

In November 1999 a young Iraqi had arrived at Munich airport and requested asylum from the German government. It was well known in the barbed-wire-encrusted holding camp in which he was placed that one way out was by convincing German intelligence you had something they wanted. Streams of Iraqi defectors pimped their stories to the intelligence agencies. Many were entirely made up or wild assertions based on fragments of what they had heard or seen back home. Most, but not all, were weeded out. Like Golitsyn and the Cold War defectors, Curveball knew he needed something of value to avoid being discarded. He appeared reserved and calm as he told his interrogators that not only did he have details about Saddam manufacturing biological weapons on mobile grey metal trailers but that it was being done with German equipment. The Germans clumsily debriefed Curveball, asking him leading questions. Within a few months he had his own apartment and had been granted political asylum. The Germans passed the intelligence to allies including Britain's MI6 and American military intelligence, the DIA, but not the CIA with whom relations were less close. The DIA introduced the stream of reporting into the American system – a total of 100 reports in less than two years. It was agreed the material was technically credible, but that was different from determining whether it was actually true. Because of the potential embarrassment centring on the involvement of their companies, the Germans decided not to allow direct access or reveal his true identity to their allies. He did not speak English and he hated Americans, they lied. They also, truth be told, were not too sure about him. Little did they know the vast edifice that would be built on the shifting sands of his meagre, unreliable intelligence. And it was not just America. 'The vast majority' of Britain's case for believing in biological weapons production came from Curveball.[66]

No one likes being dependent on a source without knowing much about it, so MI6 did its best to get around German reticence and find out who Curveball really was. The Americans were angry that their 'closest ally' was not keeping them in the loop, at least initially, of their investigation. 'People were really pissed off that the Brits were talking to the Germans about the case and they didn't share it all with us,' a CIA officer said afterwards.[67] CIA officials say that they later learnt that some MI6 officers began to have doubts about Curveball in 2002, saying they were not convinced he was a 'wholly reliable source' and 'elements of [his] behaviour strike us as typical of individuals we would normally assess as fabricators'. But despite these concerns, MI6 was never willing to reject completely his reliability (largely due to his apparent technical knowledge) and continued to use his reports, which would become crucial to the dossier.[68] From 2002, Curveball was also backed up by the major from the Mukhabarat, providing false reassurance, and MI6's third new source, from an agent known as Red River. Red River, a long-standing MI6 agent, reported a new 'sub-source' in the summer of 2002 who talked of the possible use of fermenters on trailers and railway trucks. These were suspected of being for biological weapons production but the source could not be sure of their purpose. In London, it was said that this confirmed the Curveball account; in truth it was complementary rather than confirmatory, a subtle but important difference.

The CIA division chief rolled into lunch fifteen minutes late at the Sea Catch restaurant overlooking the canal in Georgetown. His lunch partner, an ever-prompt German spy, had been waiting. After small talk the CIA officer asked if his agency could meet Curveball. 'Don't ask,' was the reply. 'He hates Americans.' That was not enough of a reason, the CIA man responded. 'You do not want to see him because he's crazy,' the German said. 'I personally think the guy may be a fabricator,' he added.[69] The Germans had begun to realise that Curveball might be critical to the American case for a war and that worried them. The CIA officer says he passed on these concerns at a number of meetings with senior officials. But some in the CIA and Washington did not seem to want to have a major source knocked out from under them.

A few months later the same CIA division chief received a late-night phone call from George Tenet. It was early February 2003 and Colin Powell was preparing to address the UN on the case for war. The Secretary of State and his aides had spent days and nights sweating over the files at CIA headquarters in Langley with officials scurrying around them trying to tie down loose ends. Twenty-eight items had been removed from his speech because they were too weak.[70] Powell wanted it to be accurate but he also saw this as his 'Adlai Stevenson' moment, a reference to the Secretary of State during the Cuban Missile Crisis who had brandished conclusive proof of Soviet actions inside the UN Security Council. Among the intelligence Powell wanted to use was some of the new material collected by MI6. An exhausted Tenet called the CIA officer who had met the German contact to get Dearlove's home number to negotiate clearance. That officer says he told Tenet personally that there were problems with Curveball. Tenet says he does not remember being told this. The next afternoon, Curveball's intelligence was in the Security Council chamber. 'Mein Gott,' a German intelligence official exclaimed as he watched Powell speak on TV. 'I thought you said it wasn't going to be used,' the German officer in Washington said to the division chief the next day.[71]

On 28 January President Bush had walked up to the dais in

Congress for his annual State of the Union message. A year before, he had warned of an 'axis of evil'. This time he outlined the case as to why Iraq needed to be dealt with first. Among the charges was one that he leant on the British to substantiate. 'The British government has learnt that Saddam Hussein recently sought significant quantities of uranium from Africa,' the President stated. This became the American equivalent of the British forty-five-minutes claim – the lightning rod for all the arguments over mistaken intelligence and how it had been used by politicians (the Americans always made more of the nuclear case, the British made more of the chemical/biological). The CIA had already carried out a quick investigation of the claim using a retired American ambassador, Joe Wilson, who was married to a CIA officer. He said he thought there was nothing to it. The British held the faith though, arguing that their own sources, separate from fabricated documents later found in Italy and including intercepted communications, suggested that on a trip to Niger an Iraqi ambassador had at least discussed uranium sales (even if no deal was actually done). The CIA never agreed and pushed the White House to keep the issue out of presidential speeches. They were none too pleased to hear it turn up in the State of the Union address, even if cleverly attributed not to them but to the British. Some in London felt the same. 'If desk officers in the Service had had their way, [the Niger intelligence] probably would never have seen the light of day,' an MI6 officer later testified. But, as with Curveball, doubts were buried.

On 27 November 2002, the UN inspectors strode through the doors of one of Saddam's presidential palaces on the Tigris River. They had arrived in Iraq clutching valuable intelligence, much of it supplied by Britain, indicating potential sites housing the weapons programmes. The demand for their entry had been part of a British strategy. If Saddam refused to allow them in, the case for war, especially at the UN, would be stronger. If he did let them in, they would either disarm him or find something which could be used to justify regime change. Hawks in Washington, such as Dick Cheney, thought inspections might be a trap to divert them away from war, but the British plan, backed by Colin Powell, won out. Then came the problem. The inspectors were not finding anything. They scoured the presidential palace for stores of suspicious items and documents.

They found only marmalade in the refrigerators.[72] And so it went on as they went to site after site. No one in London seemed worried at first. That cunning Saddam is good at deception, they all agreed. It was his typical cat-and-mouse game. 'When the inspectors started to report that they weren't finding what we all thought was going to be found, the response, for example, in SIS, was simply to turn up the volume control to say, "That just proves how devious and duplicitous Saddam Hussein is, and how incompetent the inspectors are," recalled Sir David Omand.[73] Nothing significant came of the British leads.[74] 'We inspected a lot of chicken farms,' one former inspector said later of the whole process. On closer examination they were, indeed, chicken farms.[75] The inspectors began to harbour doubts. Iraq was in a state of near collapse and it seemed unlikely that it could sustain and hide the necessary infrastructure. Hans Blix, the head of the UN inspecting body, told Blair he was grateful for the intelligence that had been provided, but 'it had not been all that compelling'.[76] At another meeting between the two men over crumpets at Chequers, Blair told Blix that without 'honest co-oper-ation' from Iraq there would be a decision to act by the start of March. Blix sensed that the brutal nature of Saddam's regime weighed heavily on Blair's thinking.[77] The US had begun to spy on Blix as they were convinced he was not aggressive enough. Even though he believed there were weapons and generally agreed with the con-clusions of the British dossier, there were concerns that he was avo-iding strong conclusions in order to prevent his reports being used as a justification for war. The distrust of the UN and its intentions meant that Washington saw no point in letting inspections run their course, even though this might have encouraged other allies to join the coalition.[78]

By February 2003, the inspectors had conducted 400 inspections at 300 sites and found nothing. In London, they moaned that the inspectors were naive and were botching the process. Jokes started to go around British intelligence about how the inspectors had forgotten their spades. But as time went on a shade of fear began to attach itself to the humour. There was particular anger that the inspectors had failed to take the proper equipment, including ground penetrating radar, when they visited a bunker beside a military hospital based on a British tip-off. 'There were some quite breathless moments when intelligence was rushed in saying "We found it", a Downing Street official recalled, yet nothing materialised, despite the intense interest of a prime minister who was 'desperate' to see whatever there was.[79] 'The Prime Minister was interested in a silver bullet,' recalled the Arabist MI6 director. 'If there was a gleam of a silver bullet anywhere, he would want to know about it, and he would want to see the product.'[80] Meanwhile, the three to four weeks in which the new source on trial had promised to deliver intelligence on WMD sites came and went. Tony Blair and Jack Straw kept pressing MI6. What was holding it up? they asked.[81] But nothing more was heard. The MI6 director, who believed any WMD would be no larger than something that could fit on a petrol truck, was now becoming increasingly pessimistic about the chances of finding anything. He knew it was now too late to change the argument for going to war. 'We were on the flypaper of WMD, whether we liked it or not.'[82]

Moving each day, sleeping in a different place every night, Saddam Hussein was in a bind. Like Khrushchev with his missiles in 1961, the secret Saddam was keeping from the world was that he was weaker than he appeared. He was conscious of Iran next door developing its own weapons and of the danger of seeming frail. Viewed from his isolated bunker deep underground, Iran always felt a more immediate threat than the US.[83] But at the same time Saddam was not quite bluffing about his ability since he was also telling the US and UK privately and publicly that he had no weapons (consistency is not necessarily required if you are a dictator). The problem was that he did not know how to convince them. After the 1991 Gulf War, the nuclear facilities had been damaged and Saddam had decided the country did not have the resources to continue while under sanctions. Orders had come down to Jaffar Dhia Jaffar, the erudite British-trained leader of the nuclear programme, to hand over everything to the Republican Guards so they could destroy it all. 'Saddam decided to terminate the programmes in July of 1991, hoping that sanctions would be lifted soon because it was just far more important to lift sanctions than to continue with these programmes,' Jaffar later explained.

The Iraqi leader had not given up all ambitions. Getting rid of weapons, he believed, would end inspections and lead to the lifting of the sanctions. Then he might be able to restart his programmes.

There was an unexpected flaw to his master plan though. He could not convince people he really had got rid of the weapons. He would reflect that his crucial mistake had been to destroy the weapons unilaterally after 1991 without UN supervision.[84] In order to maintain the illusion of power, only a handful of Iraqis had known of the destruction in 1991 – a decision which would ultimately cost Saddam. There was a push by Iraq to try and close the file with the UN in 1997 and 1998, according to Jaffar. But when it failed, Saddam concluded that whatever he told the US they would not lift sanctions so he might as well remove the humiliating burden of inspections. 'Why have both sanctions and the inspectors? We'd rather have the sanctions and not the inspectors.'[85] He also never believed, right to the end, that the US would actually invade; air strikes were the most he expected. Had it not been for the 11 September attacks his gamble might have paid off, as the appetite for sanctions had begun to crumble.

Saddam's regime was characterised, like many dictatorships, by a mixture of fear and incompetence. It was so chaotic that no one really knew what anyone else knew, including Saddam himself, which was why he called a Revolutionary Command Council meeting after the British dossier. Every general knew he did not have the special weapons but thought his counterpart down the road did. This has led to the Byzantine argument that intelligence agencies could never have known that Iraq did not have weapons. 'There was clearly a great deal of confusion among the Iraqi leadership about what their own capability was,' Richard Dearlove reflected later. 'I am certainly of the view that there were probably no human sources in Iraq who could have told us authoritatively that they did not have WMD.'[86] In other words, no source telling the truth could have been believed.

Saddam summoned his Revolutionary Command Council and top military aides again in December. This time he told them that there were no WMD. Some of his generals were stunned by the news. Up until then he had always implied he had something up his sleeve. Morale plummeted (although he later dropped hints that led some commanders to believe there was still some kind of capability).[87] The Iraqi leader was now trying his best to convey to the outside world what had happened, though he never offered total co-operation, fearing it could be used to undermine his grip on power. That month he offered a vast declaration of what had happened to the weapons, as had been demanded. It was dismissed in Washington and London as offering nothing new, the critics not realising that this was because there was not a lot new to offer. 'I don't think that anyone would have been satisfied unless they had come up with a report that said "Here are the weapons,"' noted Hans Blix. Blix's approach, on chemical weapons particularly, was to focus on the so-called 'unaccounted for' materials, items which Iraq could not prove had been destroyed.[88] 'There were the reasons for that,' explains Jaffar. Books were not kept properly and production and procurement were exaggerated to secure one's position. 'So when you come to these reports later you find that there's a difference between what was said was produced and what actually exists. That was called material unaccounted for. That doesn't mean it actually exists. It exists on paper perhaps. But it doesn't exist in practice.'[89] Jaffar himself grew so angry with the failure of the UN to give Iraq a clean bill of health over its nuclear programme that when he met Hans Blix and Mohammed ElBaradei, the official in charge of nuclear inspections, in May 2002 in New York, the Iraqi had to be calmed down by another of Saddam's close aides who had accompanied him. Blix would wonder if rumours that US intelligence agencies had approached Jaffar as he arrived to try and persuade him to defect might have contributed to his irritation.[90]

There were explanations for everything, but no one was listening. The aluminium tubes the US (and for a while the UK) said were for centrifuges to make a nuclear bomb were for rockets. The trip to Niger was not for uranium – 'We had 500 tons of Yellow Cake in Baghdad at the time, so why should we go and buy another 500 tons from Niger?' explains Jaffar.[91] Part of the problem, former inspectors argue, was the past behaviour of officials including Jaffar. 'The failure to give Iraq a clean bill of health really relates to Jaffar's own behaviour,' argues David Kay who led inspections of the nuclear programme in the early 1990s. 'They did not come forward with the evidence of their programme. We had to discover it, they lied, cheated and tried to deceive us, they tried to cover up and they tried to retain portions of that programme ... So you can never be sure that you'd gotten everything because the Iraqis failed to be honest about it. They started out lying, they continued lying and so consequently the attitude among the inspectors developed: they never tell the truth, and so there must be something more there.'[92]

Iraq was saying the same thing secretly as it was saying publicly. One of MI6's tasks is to conduct back-channel contacts when the British government does not want it known openly that it is talking to someone. This was the case with the first contacts with the Provisional IRA when the British government maintained a public policy of not talking to terrorists. The same kind of back-channel contacts also took place with Saddam's regime (with British ministerial knowledge). The Controller for the Middle East met a senior Iraqi intelligence official secretly a number of times as war approached (it remained unclear to MI6 whether this was with or without Saddam's agreement). The Iraqi official told him there were no weapons and there was nothing more to say. This was not the lost opportunity to avoid war, as some would later claim. The official was saying in private exactly what Saddam was saying in public. At the time everyone considered this statement, like those of Saddam in public, to be simply rhetoric and 'just what he was expected to say' and therefore deception.[93] '[He] failed to persuade his British interlocutors that he had anything new to offer ... and the British – on their own – elected to break off contact,' George Tenet later said.[94] The bar for intelligence that suggested there were no weapons was far higher than for any evidence of their existence.

At the same time in the margins of the UN General Assembly in New York, a strange sideshow was taking place. The Iraqi Foreign Minister, Naji Sabri, had been in contact with French intelligence for some time through an Arab journalist intermediary and was now passing information indirectly to the US in response to questions. Even though he was Foreign Minister, Sabri was never in the tightest circle around Saddam and he may well have not known the truth. What he said and how it was reported remains contentious. By one account, he said that Jaffar had been summoned in to see Saddarn earlier in the year and told him he could build a nuclear bomb within eighteen to twenty-four months of receiving fissile material – a fairly meaningless statement since obtaining the material is arguably the hardest part of the process. Sabri is also supposed to have said that chemical weapons may have been dispersed but there were no serious biological programmes. Former CIA officers have suggested the reports of the contact were rewritten to strengthen the conclusions and imply that Iraq was still aggressively pursuing a WMD programme including a nuclear weapon. This was technically true but only at a real stretch since it was a long-term aspiration rather than a current project. In George Tenet's later account he says (without naming Sabri) that the source said Iraq was stockpiling material for chemical weapons, had mobile launchers and was dabbling with biological weapons, though not with sufficient success to constitute a real biological weapons programme. That last point conflicted with Curveball and so was ignored while the more gloomy parts were highlighted. A more alarmist account of the Sabri intelligence was passed to MI6 which fed into their analysis. A CIA officer chased Sabri around the world to try and meet him and get a direct answer to questions but only got close to him just before the war. By then, he was told, it was too late to bother.

The train had left the station in London and Washington. 'The books had been cooked, the bets placed,' reckoned one CIA official.[95] The accretion of scraps of intelligence had become impossible to disprove. This was the same error as the molehunters made. Every piece of evidence which seemed to contradict a deeply found belief was treated as a masterful act of deception by the other side. Or to put it another way, how do you prove a negative? How do you persuade someone that you are not hiding something? Donald Rumsfeld expressed this strange view best when he said 'the absence of evidence is not absence of evidence.'[96] But what if sometimes the absence of evidence really is a sign that something is not there? Reports arrived late in the day saying that most members of the Iraqi leadership were not convinced that it would be possible to use chemical or biological weapons and that chemical weapons had been dispersed and would be hard to reassemble. The fact that intelligence now suggested Iraq did not have usable weapons able to attack, let alone in forty-five minutes, was never revealed to the public (although some ministers had been told by Blair). The intelligence picture now looked far more contradictory and complex than the public knew.[97]

At 12.35 p.m. on 18 March, Tony Blair stood up in parliament. He had just failed in a desperate attempt to secure a second UN resolution to authorise war explicitly, one in which he had enlisted MI6 to brief swing members of the Security Council and try and convince them. He now needed to explain to an anxious parliament – and especially to his own Labour Party – why war was about to start when some voices called for more time for inspections, especially as there were signs the Iraqis were providing more co-operation. As he spoke, the first planeload of inspectors was arriving in Cyprus following a phone call Hans Blix had received two days earlier from US officials telling them it was time to get out. If Blair had lost the vote he would have resigned. An anxious President Bush called privately to offer him the chance to back down, and Jack Straw had told him a few days earlier that it was still not too late to change course, but Blair was committed. 'The truth is that our patience should have been exhausted weeks and months and even years ago,' he told parliament before reaching for an analogy with the appeasement of Hitler in the 1930s.[98] Blair also went on to place Iraq within the frame of his wider fears. He said he knew of some countries or groups trading in nuclear weapons technology and that he knew of some dictatorships desperately trying to acquire such technology. 'Some of those countries are now a short time away from having a serviceable nuclear weapon.'

As the bombs were about to fall on Baghdad, a phone call came into MI6 headquarters at Vauxhall Cross. It was from a Palestinian who was an occasional contact for the service. He had a message from the Libyan leader Colonel Gaddafi. The leader's son, Saif, was ready to deliver it. The rendezvous took place in the private room of an upmarket hotel in London's Mayfair. Present were two MI6 officers. Saif was nervous. He had not met with anyone from the British Secret Service before and had been brought up to think of its officers as a breed of half-man half-devil intent on destroying his father. He explained that Gaddafi senior wanted to talk about weapons of mass destruction. The MI6 officers called David Manning at Downing Street who told them to keep talking. On the day the first bombs fell on Baghdad, a plane took off for Libya.[99]

The two British intelligence officers on board the plane headed for Sirte, desert headquarters of the Libyan leader, where the eccentric colonel held court in a huge Bedouin tent with camels roaming outside. Gaddafi was worried about being next on the list after Saddam and wanted to see if he could buy his way back into the international community by giving up a weapons programme that he thought no one knew about. What he did not realise was that MI6 already knew all about his secret nuclear weapons programme. It had been supplied by the Pakistani salesman A. Q. Khan and his network had been penetrated by MI6 for a number of years. Gaddafi told the leader of the MI6 team, Mark Allen, that his Libyan counterpart for the negotiations would be the intelligence chief Musa Kusa.[100] It was made clear that the Libyans wanted the Americans on board and saw the British as the best way of achieving that goal.

Mark Allen went with Dearlove to Washington a few days later to discuss the offer. Dearlove briefed the President personally. Steve Kappes was assigned by the CIA to work with Allen on talking to Gaddafi. The mercurial Gaddafi would make it a difficult process. The Libyans were nervous about revealing what they had purchased from A. Q. Khan (even though it was still far from operational) because they feared that their old enemies could simply walk away from the secret negotiations and use the information as a pretext to attack. Libya's evasiveness in turn inspired distrust from MI6 and the CIA, who knew how much the Libyans were hiding even as they kept on insisting they had to come clean. At one point, a retired British military figure had to be sent out as a gesture of good faith with the message that a deal was on the table. As months passed, Gaddafi may also have been watching the 'victory' in Iraq turn sour as roadside bombs began to detonate and he may have started to wonder if the appetite was still there for another war.

By the summer, a nervy, frustrating impasse had been reached. Plans to take down the A. Q. Khan network had been stalled in order not to compromise the Libyan negotiations. A risk needed to be taken. A source inside the Khan network revealed that a consignment of nuclear parts was going to be shipped to Libya. The boat carrying them, the BBC *China* (which had nothing to do with the BBC or with China) was diverted in the middle of the night to an Italian port, where a team quickly identified five cargo containers and opened them with considerable relief. Allen called Musa Kusa and confronted him. The Libyans folded. They agreed to allow a team of CIA and MI6 inspectors into the country to examine their sites.

A small unmarked plane carrying a joint CIA–MI6 team departed from Northolt airfield on 19 October for Libya. Only a handful of officials on each side of the Atlantic knew about the trip. The team, which consisted of specialists in nuclear programmes, chemical and biological weapons as well as missiles, was taken around previously clandestine sites by Libyan guides during the day and then filed reports back to Langley and Vauxhall Cross by night. But the Libyans continued to prove evasive on key details. After ten days, the group returned home frustrated. The enigmatic Musa Kusa (whose past links to international terrorism and especially in arming the IRA were well known to the British and American officials) was invited to Britain to discuss the problem with Allen and Kappes. Intelligence was literally laid out on the table before him to highlight the differences between what Libya was claiming and what was known to be true. This included playing a tape of a recording between A. Q. Khan and Libya's nuclear chief from February of the previous year.

Kusa agreed a second inspection visit which began on 9 December. This time there was more co-operation but still not quite enough. The scale and ambitions of the nuclear programme were the main stumbling block. Rain fell on the last full day as the possibility of failure hung over the visiting team. In the dark before dawn the next morning, the team headed to the airport and their thirty-two-seat plane. As the British and American intelligence officers prepared to board, the Libyans announced that they had something for them. A stack of brown envelopes about a foot high was handed over. When the team opened the envelopes on board the aircraft they found inside the design for a nuclear weapon that had been given to Libya by A. Q. Khan. It was what they had been waiting for.

The final outlines of the deal were hammered out on 16 December in an all-day session in a private room at the Travellers Club on Pall Mall, a favourite haunt of Secret Service officers. Those Libyans who had forgotten to wear ties were quickly hustled inside before a doorman could stop them. Libyan resistance over just how much they would publicly admit proved the last stumbling block, along with questions over whether Gaddafi would humble himself by making the announcement. The Libyans continued to fear being double-crossed. Saddam Hussein had just been captured in Iraq and Gaddafi seemed to fear meeting the same fate. Blair spoke by telephone with the Libyan leader two days later to finalise plans. On 19 December the secret diplomacy finally became public, although only after a bizarre delay when Gaddafi decided to wait to make his announcement because a football match being shown on television ran over schedule. Within weeks, President Musharraf was pressurised to put A. Q. Khan out of business. These were crucial victories, but they were only a sideshow to the problem that was preoccupying London and Washington, as Saddam's weapons proved to be a Banquo's ghost, haunting them long after his regime had been crushed.

The war in Iraq had been won swiftly, the peace was another matter. The non-existent weapons of mass destruction were not the only intelligence failure. The political reporting before the war was paltry. Few, apart from some academics whose advice was ignored, were aware of the country's tribal and social structures. Not only had there been a failure to understand Saddam's mindset and ask if he was bluffing, but the focus on the weapons meant not enough work was done on how the country would stand up to invasion and what would come after. There was, however, a warning that war would lead to more terrorism against the UK and serve the narrative of Al Qaeda by providing a justification for more attacks.[101] 'Arguably we gave Osama bin Laden his Iraqi jihad so he was able to move into Iraq in a way he wasn't before,' Eliza Manningham-Buller later reflected. Iraq, she said, 'increased the terrorist threat by convincing more people that Osama bin Laden's claim that Islam was under attack was correct. It provided an arena for the jihad which he had called for . . . and our involvement in Iraq spurred some young British Muslims to turn to terror.'

As the war had unfolded, a few people had also begun to wonder why Saddam had not used any of his 'special weapons', especially as troops approached Baghdad. Perhaps deterrence had worked or command and control had been disrupted, the military explained.[102] When the war was over, the question of the missing weapons could no longer be ignored. 'We were being warned of the possibility that Saddam had got rid of WMD and certainly most of the documentation, before the conflict,' Alastair Campbell wrote in his diary as the war ended. A month later the panic grew as Donald Rumsfeld said weapons might not be found and his deputy dismissively stated that the focus on WMD had been a 'bureaucratic convenience'.[103] When a BBC report claimed that the intelligence on the forty-five minutes had been included against the wishes of the spies and despite knowledge that it was wrong, Blair was angry. A struggle began between Downing Street and the BBC. The source for the story, weapons inspector David Kelly, would be caught in the crossfire and killed himself within weeks.

For a tense few days, the spies and politicians eyed each other nervously. Each wondered if the other side would break ranks and try to pin the blame on them. Every hint that this nuclear option might be pursued sent tremors through the system. Campbell called Scarlett on 1 June as stories of unhappiness among the spooks proliferated. Scarlett said the 'agencies were pushing back and denying all this, but there was precious little sign of that in the Sundays,' wrote Campbell.[104] 'He [Scarlett] said we were being made to accord to our stereotypes – you are the brutal political hatchet man and I am the dry intelligence officer. It's not very nice but I can assure you this is not coming from the people at the top. He was clear I had never asked him to do anything he was unhappy with. I said it was really bad, all this stuff.' Three days later, government ministers were talking about 'rogue elements' in the intelligence services and 'skulduggery'. This time it was the spies' turn to worry. Campbell's phone lit up with messages from Dearlove, Scarlett and Omand.[105] Staring into the abyss of mutually assured destruction, the spies and politicians came to a fretful peace.

As time went on, and site after site was searched and hope after hope of finding weapons of mass destruction was dashed, an air of panic began to consume Vauxhall Cross. 'People were going round saying "For Christ sakes, just find something",' recalls one individual.[106] Everyone understood how important this was politically. In Number 10, the Prime Minister became increasingly agitated.[107] The men given the job of finding something were drawing a blank. David Kay went out first, convinced there were weapons. The first warning sign came when he was briefed on the intelligence. Is that all there is? he thought. He had asked to see the underlying material behind the British dossier. The sources, it seemed, had been over-interpreted, perhaps misinterpreted. 'I thought it was a pretty thin gruel.'[108] A couple of mobile trailers were heralded as a big find but then had to be discounted. There was excitement about containers on a river-bed but they disappeared. Some old chemical shells were discovered buried in the desert which the White House wanted to publicise but they were told they dated back to before 1991. Jaffar was among those interviewed by Kay's team. He told them everything had been in the 7 December declaration. Tensions emerged between allies. At a meeting one person present recalls Tenet asking Dearlove outright if he could see the intelligence that lay behind the British claim on Niger. Dearlove declined, but said MI6 still believed it to be true. Tenet told colleagues later that Dearlove was no more forthcoming in private. The refusal was most likely based on the control principle, meaning the original intelligence was not Britain's to share without permission.

Kay returned within a few months to tell a stunned Washington they had been 'almost all wrong'. The US and British administrations had wanted Kay to keep quiet and were furious. British officials had even gone to see the CIA head of station in London to complain about him. The CIA man had cabled Washington but Kay himself was copied into the traffic and asked the MI6 station chief in Baghdad to intervene. This led to another complaint from London to Washington, with Kay again copied in. Charles Duelfer was next up to lead the hunt, passing through London on the way where an eager Blair wanted to hear his plans.[109]

Those working on inspection reports sensed the anxiety in London. How can you be sure there isn't anything when you haven't covered the whole of the country? British officials kept asking. The inspectors explained they had not just visited sites but interviewed captive Iraqi scientific, military and intelligence officials who all said the same thing. Scarlett was among those keen to make sure that any report was as robust as possible. He emailed a series of 'nuggets' to Duelfer asking if they would be included. These were unresolved items from an older classified report. Details had been unearthed of Iraqi intelligence doing work on poisons but inspectors said it would be disingenuous to describe this as work on chemical weapons. 'I could not believe my eyes,' thought Rod Barton, one of the senior inspectors, when he saw the email. He told Duelfer it was unacceptable to include the nuggets since there was no evidence. Over a video conference, Scarlett backed away. 'The nuggets were fool's gold,' Duelfer reflected. 'It was obvious the game was up,' Barton, who soon quit, thought. 'There was no WMD there. They were going to have to bite the bullet and say so.'[110] Letting go was not easy.

One by one MI6's prized sources were melting away like mirages in the desert heat. As each oasis was approached, the weary travellers of the MI6 validation team sent out to check the sources, often escorted by special forces soldiers, discovered only sand slipping through their fingers. Some of the key sources did not last long. Just three months after the fall of Baghdad, MI6 interviewed the cherished new source in whom so much had been invested and who had dispelled so many doubts. He denied ever having said anything about accelerated production of biological and chemical weapons.[111]

With the forty-five-minutes claim, MI6 visited the military officer alleged to have supplied the report, who denied any knowledge of having ever said such a thing. So they went looking for the main source who had passed on the information claiming it was from the military officer. He proved hard to track down. 'There was a lot of umming and aahing,' remembers one of the people involved. It was clear he had simply made it all up. He was the Baghdad equivalent of Graham Greene's Havana's vacuum cleaner salesman with an over-active imagination. MI6 reported the bad news back to London in 2004. 'I particularly remember the moment when the Prime Minister was told that the forty-five-minutes intelligence was false,' one individual later recalled. 'That felt like a pretty big moment in terms of the Prime Minister's trust of SIS and intelligence. Privately, I felt that he felt let down.'[112]

When an American team went to a key facility looking for Curveball's mobile trailers they found a seed-purification plant. They went back six times to make sure. A six-foot-high wall made it impossible for trailers to move in and out at the location he had described. A confused site manager said there had never been any doors where Curveball indicated.[113] Curveball's own travel records revealed he could not have been in Iraq to witness an accident as he had claimed. His former boss admitted he had been fired from his position in 1995. A CIA team who finally got access to Curveball found that he simply refused to answer any more questions when they confronted him with the holes in his account. They also thought the British were doing their best to hold on to his intelligence. Perhaps the mobile laboratories were there just in case Saddam wanted a capacity to produce material in the future, MI6 argued defensively. The Germans and the British disagreed over who had introduced the disputed technical details into the reporting. It transpired that Curveball had got much of his material by reading inspectors' reports off the internet and piecing it together with the little he knew.[114]

The British and Americans turned to each other. But we thought you had other intelligence to back everything up? Each realised the other side's material was less substantial than they had believed, and not just on Curveball. They had shared much but never everything. On the Sabri case and Curveball it was only after the war that each realised that the other side had doubts about intelligence the other had thought cast-iron. 'If only you'd told us everything and we'd told you everything, maybe we could have pieced it together,' one officer told his American counterparts wistfully after the war. The American agreed, but would later wonder whether that would really have made any difference.[115]

The shutters at Vauxhall Cross came down. 'It was like drawing teeth,' a Whitehall official said of the long-drawn-out process of MI6 rowing back on its sources (far slower than validating them in the first place). The nuclear and missile sources were not too bad, it was argued, but the latter in particular were never relevant to the public debate. Those senior officers who had invested most in the sources continued to argue they had not been wrong. They said the weapons, particularly mobile rocket launchers with weaponised VX, must have been moved to Syria before the war. They said their multiple sources (human and technical) on this were never disproved and were 'very compelling'.[116] But this was thoroughly investigated by the inspectors of David Kay and Charles Duelfer's Iraq Survey Group after the war. They interviewed Iraqi pilots and ground crew to see if anything could have been smuggled on flights; they looked at the routing of trucks. They found no hard evidence. The absence of a clear Syrian motive for accepting such dangerous consignments and the failure of even the Israelis to push the line added to the case against. Some still cling to the fading hope that something will be proved to have gone over the border.

With the exception of the forty-five-minutes claim, Lord Butler's inquiry said the original intelligence had not been misreported. There was no distortion, he concluded. The original intelligence was simply wrong. This, in many ways, is a far more damning conclusion for MI6 than the notion that the politicians had 'spun' the intelligence against the wishes of the spies. The politicians may have pushed and pressed, but ultimately, the problem was that MI6's reporting was dud.

Bureaucratic explanations were proffered. For instance, the posts of requirements officers at headquarters, who were supposed to act as a quality control on reporting from the field, had been staffed by inexperienced officers because of cuts and their role had become subordinate to the production officers, whose job was to get as much intelligence to customers as possible.[117] But few believed this really explained the disaster that had befallen the service.

'There was a sense in which, because of past success – very, very considerable successes supporting this government – that SIS [MI6] overpromised and under-delivered,' David Omand later reflected. 'We were getting the promise,' a Downing Street official agreed, 'but it was only ... after the military invasion that we realised just how much of their product was false.'[118] The argument that they had overpromised is disputed by some who maintain that they always made clear the intelligence was scanty. Clandestine weapons programmes are the most closely guarded secrets of a state, their intimate details known only to a handful, the hardest target for a secret service. But stealing secrets from such a target is exactly what the service is there for.

A few of the spies implicated in the whole affair argued they had been left exposed by the politicians. 'We got dumped on and we took it,' is how one puts it. Their argument is that the intelligence was never the reason that Britain went to war. The decision was a political choice by a prime minister who settled on intelligence as the best means by which to sell that choice to parliament and the public. Their failing, these spies argue, was not to see the risk to the service's reputation and get more political cover. 'Blair promised to look after you and then dropped you in it,' one said. 'But he had never quite promised to do so nor quite dropped you in it directly. His DNA was never on the murder weapons.' Secret services though are supposed to be smart enough to play these games and not get caught with their trousers down.

Dearlove, who continued to believe that war was the right decision, took a more nuanced line. 'The policy was made to be over-dependent on the intelligence particularly in presenting the case in parliament, when in reality there were many others factors contributing to policy decisions,' he told an audience a few years after the war. 'I think it was feared those other factors would not carry the day with the parliamentary opponents of the war. This calculation turned out to have very undesirable consequences for the intelligence community. There were obvious risks involved, but at the time [they] appeared manageable.'[119] It was the overemphasis on intelligence that was the mistake, in his eyes, and the failure to make more of the moral argument for removing Saddam. 'I agreed with the policy. I still do. I still think it was the right decision to take at that time in the circumstances. But the reasons for going to war were not specifically intelligence based.'[120]

One of the reasons that Blair and others made the decision for war in the first place, though, was because they believed the intelligence they had been told about weapons of mass destruction in Iraq. The two sides – politicians and spies – were so closely conjoined in the run-up to war that separating them requires an almost impossibly delicate operation. Blair was taking a risk, utterly confident in his own judgement. Icarus-like, the service had flown a little too close to the sun, it was said by many. It was an analogy rejected by those at the top of MI6. 'The Icarus metaphor is used time and again,' argued the Arabist MI6 director who had observed Dearlove work so closely with the Prime Minister. 'It has limited applicability because Tony Blair was not the sun and Dearlove was not a child with wax wings. They were consenting adults, wrestling with unprecedented policy riddles.' Was there another way? 'I would have done it differently. I believe in a Chief who stays south of the river and is not so easy to get hold of,' he also said, before adding that this might not have been so easy to carry out in practice. 'That's my daydream. But that's a ... daydream. Real life ... is different.'[121]

A few might have believed they had been left swinging by Number 10 but many more inside MI6 believed the organisation itself was to blame. Some simply acknowledged that their sources had been wrong. Others thought it was their own leadership who had left them exposed by getting too close to power. The unhappiness was palpable. During the Suez Crisis the official machinery of intelligence was largely ignored and bypassed; this time, in an attempt to avoid a similar fate, it had been sucked deep into the maelstrom. 'The vehicle of WMD as an argument for the war was incapable of sustaining the weight put upon it, given that we didn't have all the answers and we didn't have the sources,' reflected an MI6 director who had worried for the morale and integrity of his service.[122] The impact on MI6's reputation – and its self-perception – was calamitous. The use of intelligence to sell a war to the public might not have mattered much if it turned out to be true. But once it was proved to be wrong, it left the public, and especially those who had been persuaded by the intelligence, feeling bitter, not least towards the spies.

With the service still reeling, the appointment of John Scarlett as the new Chief was viewed with distinctly mixed feelings in some quarters. Dearlove, who was due for retirement, was well-known to be opposed and pushed his own number two forward for the job. A few others believed Scarlett was too much the quiet professional and lacked the vision to lead the service. The disquiet in some quarters at Scarlett's appointment was expressed at staff forums. As one person remembers, it was strongest among the old-school 'Tory back-woodsmen' who thought a New Labour placeman getting the job was another sign of the service being subordinated to Downing Street and as a return favour for delivering the dossier. The response was that he was the best man for the job. One of the reasons Scarlett was appointed was that he was a traditionalist by instinct, a man who was seen as capable of restoring a focus on the core task of gathering intelligence. He was also seen as a hawk on Iraq's weapons compared to some of the other candidates.

Two weeks before he left MI6 in the summer of 2004, Dearlove addressed staff in the Vauxhall Cross auditorium. Those who expected a fulsome apology would be disappointed. He gave a robust, even militant, defence of his approach. Don't think you can keep away from Whitehall, he warned. Just because we were caught up in a controversial war does not mean the whole modernising approach was wrong. A couple of weeks before that address, he had been in Washington for a farewell dinner at the CIA on a hot summer's evening. People who judge us have not done what we have done, he told the assembled spies with a nod to George Tenet, who would resign soon after. One CIA officer at the party thought the two spymasters looked 'defeated'.[123] His supporters believe Dearlove had been taking MI6 in the right direction and had been the right man for the moment in the period after 9/11. It was only Iraq which blew the exercise off course. Others believed the direction itself was wrong, drawing the service too near to power.

On taking over, Scarlett knew he had to convince the sceptics and adopted a strategy of holding meetings and sandwich lunches with staff to listen to their concerns. Egged on by colleagues, a veteran asked at one of these whether Scarlett had any regrets over Iraq. Neither then, nor when asked publicly, would he explicitly say that he did.[124] 'It was a difficult time for the service obviously,' he admitted in an interview. 'The worry clearly at the time was that the reliability of our reporting had been brought into question ... We had to carry on doing a good job, responding to the criticisms where you have to, put things right where it has been pointed out they've been wrong and over the passage of time the quality of your work will ensure that those questions move away.'[125]

Scarlett was told by some staff that they wanted to keep their distance from policy, their fingers having been burnt by Iraq. A few who had been close to Dearlove worried that their careers were finished, but most of them stayed and adapted. They believed that, as time went on, Scarlett realised how much the service's work had changed since his departure for the JIC before 9/11 and he began to restore the shift towards a more integrated approach with other services and other parts of Whitehall to cope with the challenges of terrorism and nuclear proliferation. The old Cold War world of gathering intelligence on static targets had largely but not totally passed away.

Scarlett also began edging the service once again into the public eye. The process had begun in the 1990s with avowal, and Dearlove had pushed the pace harder until the whole process was subsumed beneath the tidal wave of Iraq. With MI6's reputation battered by Iraq and British intelligence as a whole deeply worried by allegations of complicity in torture, it was time to put aside a concern for maintaining the air of mystery. For its centenary in 2009, Scarlett went so far as being interviewed in his office, a Union Jack fluttering outside the window and a clock built by the founder of the service, Mansfield Cumming, tick-tocking steadily in the corner. A degree of openness was now necessary, but it had its limits, he explained. 'What we brought out of the shadows rightly in my view is the fact that we exist when for the majority of my career we didn't even admit the fact that Britain has a secret intelligence service ... The role which we play in government ... is also there for discussion; the kinds of people that we employ, the way in which we recruit our staff ... But what we actually do, the operations we conduct, the particular intelligence we produce, the sources with whom we work, the people with whom we work, that remains secret. And those are the key secrets, the operational secrets, which have always remained secret and must remain secret.' Scarlett's traditionalism still shone through in some areas, particularly a deep-seated belief in old-fashioned patriotism. 'If you wish to serve your country, and many people do, then this is a pretty good way of doing it,' he said. Along with the armed services, the intelligence service was one of the few places where patriotism was still talked about openly in contrast to the more modern vogue for 'shared values' and the like. Spies, like soldiers it seems, are asked to do difficult things for the country that others might shy away from and so still need that deep-seated emotional sense of national interest and working for the Crown.[126]

At other times, the failure over Iraq might have raised questions about what the service was really for, but the continued threat from international terrorism provided an answer. A third of MI6's work focused on the new world of terrorism. But there would have been offices in Vauxhall Cross whose work would have been familiar to Shergy as well as to Scarlett. Russians talk about a 'third round' in the duel between the two countries (the first being MI6's 'war' against the Bolsheviks from 1917, the second being the Cold War) and continue to see MI6 as bent on subverting their country. The Russians for their part continue to try and penetrate Britain, never with quite the success of Lyubimov's time, but still with plenty of vigour. 'Since the end of the Cold War we have seen no decrease in the numbers of undeclared Russian intelligence officers in the UK at the Russian Embassy and associated organisations conducting covert activity in this country,' Jonathan Evans, the head of MI5, announced in November 2007. Between a third and a half of staff at the Russian Embassy in London are thought to have some kind of intelligence role.

The Russians' prime target remains government and military secrets but also energy, bio-tech and high-tech industries. Their intelligence officers continue to look for individuals with access and some frailty or vulnerability. None will share Philby's motivation. 'Ideology doesn't wash any more. It's the far more human motivations,' a present-day spy-hunter explains – usually money, sometimes ego, occasionally blackmail. Targets will be patiently cultivated and first asked to pass something innocuous like a trade magazine before the pressure is increased. Meetings will be arranged in person and not by phone, all straight off the pages of the 1960s warning booklet 'Their Trade is Treachery'. Sensitive agents will not be run by diplomats but met abroad or by visiting officers using the old le Carré era techniques of brush contacts and dead-letter drops. The illegals still ply their trade, travelling the world on a stack of false passports with no diplomatic cover to protect them. In 2010, a large network of illegals run by the Russian Foreign Intelligence Service, the SVR, was rolled up in the United States including one member, Anna Chapman, who had previously lived in London. MI5's concentration on its new core mission of counter-terrorism meant it had fewer resources than it used to have to find out what exactly she had been doing. By 2008, it was spending only a paltry 3.5 per cent of its budget on trying to catch all the Russian (and other) spies running around Britain, many of whom target dissidents who have made London their home.[127] The murder, using polonium-210, of a former officer of the FSB (Russia's domestic security service) Alexander Litvinenko, who had been on the MI6 payroll at one point, was a reminder of old methods, but the investigation into his death also revealed how far the KGB's successor had become intertwined with business and criminality, making it hard to know who exactly it was working for at times.

The 'compromising situations' of old were still in play, with some new twists. In the summer of 2009, the US Ambassador in Moscow lodged a formal protest about a covertly filmed video showing one of his diplomats on a darkened Moscow street, then alone in his underwear in a hotel room. The video then cuts to the same room with the lights dimmed and with two people apparently having sex in the near-dark. The individual concerned was adamant it was a fake and experts in Washington agreed. A month earlier, another video had surfaced showing a British diplomat caught *in flagrante* with two blonde women while drinking champagne. That diplomat failed to deny anything and promptly resigned. The speculation was that he had turned down an approach from the Russians.

It would be naive to think the traffic was all one way. The Russians cite the 2006 discovery of an MI6 'spy rock' in a Moscow park containing a secret transmitter. An agent would walk past and press a button on a hand-held electronic device to transfer information. A British intelligence officer could later walk past with his own device and upload data. The Russians said that this was a sign that the old enemy had not lost its appetite. And so, alongside all the talk about collective security and globalisation, the old national games of power politics and spying persist. 'The Cold War is long over,' Scarlett said in 2009 with a hint of exasperation. 'And it is important for everybody to take a realistic view of what the other side is doing.'[128] In Moscow, George Blake, living in his four-bedroom flat, still lectured to new recruits of Russia's intelligence services. He had finally developed a taste for vodka but conceded that life in the Soviet Union had 'little to do with the idealised Communist society that I had dreamed of'. There were no regrets though. 'I am 87 years old and to tell you the truth, it is no longer of particular importance to me whether my motivations are generally understood or not,' he said defiantly when asked to reflect on how it had all begun.[129]

At the end of 2009, Scarlett passed his green-inked pen to John Sawers. Sawers had joined MI6 at the start of his career but opted early to switch to the regular Foreign Office; he rose fast through senior positions there and in Number 10 and as ambassador to the United Nations. In MI6 terms he was an outsider. For decades, one of the prime responsibilities of a chief during his tenure was 'succession planning' to prevent an outsider being brought in to take over the club. Past chiefs had even delayed retirement in order to make sure a crown prince could be groomed. MI6 has a strong sense of its own culture and traditions and of being somehow different. It was felt that outsiders did not understand the rules and that their appointment sent the wrong signal. But Sawers's arrival was a sign that the rest of government wanted to continue to draw MI6 into the mainstream. Sawers is smooth, in the Foreign Office manner, and is skilled in the ways of Whitehall and relaxed in the public eye. Given the choice between being a Moscow Man and a Camel Driver, he may opt for the latter description, perhaps reflecting a career spent in part in the Middle East, including Cairo and Baghdad, but also exhibiting a desire to do things rather than just to collect intelligence quietly and build up the files.

Sawers's vision, befitting his background, was for a service more closely aligned with Whitehall. In the old days, it is said, the spies were like labradors dropping their bones of intelligence at the master's feet and asking what they should do next. Now 'customers' in Whitehall want more than just intelligence and to be informed of a problem. They want to know what can be done to deal with it. It is about having impact, not just offering intelligence. It is not just about saying 'Yemen is a risk' but offering help to build up the capacity of the Yemeni government to deal with the problem. It is not just about saying 'Iran is this close to a nuclear weapon' but offering a way of slowing it down, perhaps by sabotaging some of its centrifuges which spin to enrich uranium (strangely, about half of them were breaking down in 2009, although a number of intelligence agencies might privately like to take the credit). Secret intelligence, Sawers explained, is 'information that gives us new opportunities for action'.[130]

Sawers also believed that restoring reputation and public confidence as well as internal morale was a first-order priority. He found a climate of doubt among the public, unsure of the service's efficacy and ethics, which in turn risked putting a brake on its work. Inside, he found staff still nursing their wounds. 'Put two officers in a room together and the conversation quickly turns to Iraq,' says one of his officers, although those two people will rarely agree on exactly what went wrong. An undercurrent of anger still flowed beneath the calm surface.

'The most draining aspect of my job is reading, every day, intelligence reports describing the plotting of terrorists who are bent on maiming and murdering people in this country,' Sawers said in his debut speech (and the first by a chief to be televised).[131] Terrorism and proliferation may top the agenda but the notion of national security has now moved beyond the old ideas of preserving and protecting the state to encompass broader notions of cyber security and human security. Should an intelligence service be looking at banking crises or whether another country is trying secretly to evade its responsibilities under some future treaty to prevent climate change? In an era in which the post-9/11 year-on-year budget increases were becoming a memory, showing that intelligence had concrete value became a priority again, as it had done in the early 1990s. The threats were unpredictable and corrosive, Sawers warned. Economic intelligence returned to the agenda. If the taxpayer could be shown to have saved money through the service providing intelligence on threats to the financial system, then that would keep Treasury wolves at bay.

Afghanistan had also become a dominant focus for MI6, one which some feared risked tilting the balance of its culture too far. MI6 was criticised in some quarters for giving insufficient warning of what lay in store for the pitifully small force Britain sent to Helmand in 2006. The province had been quiet only because there had been no foreigners there before and it was quickly evident that narcotics, corruption and the insurgency offered a potent witches' brew. In the 1980s, the covert war that Gerry Warner had initiated in Peshawar had been a sideshow to the bigger war against the Soviet Union; by Sawers's time, support for military operations had become a dominant strain of work in which enormous resources were invested. This was not the world of long-term, patient agent handling but of quickly providing real-time tactical intelligence to the troops out in the muddy fields and dirt compounds. Human sources still needed to be recruited, but the security situation was so tight that different forms of tradecraft had to be used. There were also clandestine, back-channel talks with Taliban commanders to try and bribe or persuade those considered vulnerable to leave the fight, a move exposed when President Karzai angrily expelled two European officials for working with MI6 on a deal that he disliked and when it was claimed that MI6 had managed to facilitate the travel to Kabul for talks of a top Taliban leader who turned out to be a grocer from Quetta. There would be worry in some quarters that it would be harder later to switch away from such a large, static target and focus on new, emerging threats which could suddenly crop up elsewhere, as well as on more traditional targets like Russia and China which would require less rough-and-ready fieldwork and more of the old Moscow Rules.

Afghanistan certainly proved the success of a newly integrated form of operations in which MI6 worked closely with the military delivering tactical information and working in small cells alongside Special Forces, surveillance teams and colleagues from GCHQ to track individuals from the Taliban and Al Qaeda (a methodology pioneered in the Balkans in the 1990s to hunt for Serbian warlords). But it did also raise broader questions about the provision of intelligence and whether, in particular, secret intelligence had been overvalued in contrast to other forms of cultural and social knowledge. It is that latter type of knowledge that might allow you to know what farmers in Helmand might really think of the Taliban or of the arrival of thousands of British troops or alternatively what kinds of tribal and sectarian divisions existed in Iraq prior to 2003. These were not secrets in the classic sense of requiring spies to steal them. But it is precisely this kind of knowledge that government has frequently lacked and which has been ebbing away from a Foreign Office that increasingly values management skills over deep cultural knowledge. The days of the 'Sovbloc master race' and the 'Camel Drivers' are now long passed in the culture of MI6. But would it have been better for the remaining Arabists of the Secret Service Camel Corps to spend less time sitting down with Arab rulers and sheikhs in their palaces and more time talking to the young people who ended up using Facebook and social media to organise the removal of President Mubarak from power in Egypt?

Sir John Sawers is less rooted in the service's history than his predecessor. The clock belonging to the first Chief, Mansfield Cumming, was removed from the Chief's office when he took over, along with some of the other memorabilia, a visible sign of a desire to move forward rather than look to the past. But Sawers also had to contend with the messy aftermath of his service's past dealings with Colonel Gaddafi's Libya. What had once seemed like an unalloyed triumph came back to haunt MI6. Gadaffi had become disillusioned with the 2003 deal. Western oil and gas companies might have welcomed him with open arms, and Tony Blair might have visited his tent, but Gadaffi never felt he got as much as he expected. The deal had only ever been about survival from his point of view so when that was threatened by the arrival of domestic protest in Spring 2011, he responded, characteristically, with a savage and brutal crackdown. If he was now a problem once again, at least he no longer had chemical weapons or nuclear weapons in development, Britain's spies argued as the shooting began.

In early March came the first problem. As government troops

made their way towards the rebel-held town of Benghazi, MI6 tried to send in two officers by helicopter to open up communications and co-ordinate with rebel fighters. The team – protected by Special Forces – landed at night but immediately aroused suspicion from locals and were captured. To add to the embarrassment, a phone call from a British diplomat pleading for their release was intercepted and broadcast by the Libyan regime.

As the pressure grew on the regime and NATO air strikes began, Musa Kusa began to look for a way out. As the interlocutor on the 2003 deal, Gadaffi's disillusionment had affected his relationship with his long-time spy chief, who was shifted to become Foreign Minister (in most countries a promotion but not in repressive regimes). In 2011, Kusa did not flee straightaway, instead waiting until it was clear which way the wind was blowing. Britain was not his first port of call as he sought an escape. The French had established a special cell to encourage defections and had approached him at a conference in Ethiopia and then at the end of March. But just as Kusa made his move to Tunis on the pretext of a medical visit, Paris upped the stakes. It wanted a public denunciation of Gadaffi to intensify the sense of a regime collapsing. That was a step too far and Kusa suddenly found himself stuck in Tunis – one foot in and one foot out of the regime – a dangerous place to be. At that point, Kusa turned to the British and requested an immediate exit. Events moved extremely quickly. In less than twenty-four hours, he was flown to Britain on a private plane (it was so quick that not all the paperwork was ready for him on his arrival). Kusa was taken off for debriefing, but as word emerged of his appearance in the UK critics began asking why the government appeared to be now protecting a man said to have blood on his hands not just for his role in Libya but also because of knowledge or complicity in events such as the shooting of WPC Yvonne Fletcher and the Lockerbie bombing. Officials stressed that there had been 'no deal' to give him immunity from prosecution and it was promised that police would be allowed to interview him.

Kusa was well protected by British security officers when he decided to make a statement in Arabic to the BBC a few days after his arrival. He turned up wearing a flat cap, thick glasses and a scarf (whether for disguise or fashion was unclear). Ever the controlling spymaster, he was cool and detached as he tried to position himself as a dealmaker between the regime and opposition. The following day he fled the country. The political temperature was too hot, the headlines about being the 'fingernail puller in chief' and 'up to his eyeballs in murder and torture' too much. Using the pretext of meeting opposition groups, he made his way to Qatar. British officials weakly claimed that they expected he might return soon but that never seemed likely.

Kusa had one more parting gift for the British, although he may have delivered it unwittingly. When Tripoli finally fell a few months later to the rebels, his office was ransacked. Among the papers discovered were a series of letters that would prove devastating for the British Secret Service. 'Dear Musa,' one dated 25 December 2003 opened before expressing regrets that the Libyan would not be joining a colleague for lunch in London the next day and ending 'Happy Christmas' and then – handwritten – 'your friend Mark'. Another letter ended with an offer of best wishes to all the people of 'his service' and noted how the British official had 'enjoyed' working with Kusa 'greatly', stating 'my admiration and every congratulation' and offering lunch at MI6 headquarters.

Such warm, personal greetings between an MI6 officer – widely presumed to be Mark Allen – and his Libyan interlocutor in the wake of the 2003 deal might in itself have been only marginally awkward. But the detail of the other letters was dynamite. They revealed that Britain appeared to have played a role in the transfer of two members of the Libyan opposition to Colonel Gadaffi, whose regime, the men say, tortured them. In one, signed 'M', the MI6 officer congratulates Kusa on the 'safe arrival' of a figure known as Abu 'Abd Allah Sadiq. 'This was the least we could do for you and for Libya to demonstrate the remarkable relationship we have built over recent years.' The letter goes on to offer thanks for helping an officer who had just been out seeking information from the detainee. 'Amusingly, we got a request from the Americans to channel requests for information from Abu 'Abd Allah through the Americans. I have no intention of doing any such thing. The intelligence about Abu 'Abd Allah was British. I know I did not pay for the air cargo. But I feel I have the right to deal with you direct on this and am very grateful for the help you are giving us.' The letter, dated 18 March 2004, is signed 'M'.

The organisation that had actually organised and paid for the 'air cargo' of not just Sadiq but also his pregnant wife less than two weeks earlier had been the CIA. But as the MI6 officer noted, it had been British intelligence that had facilitated the transfer.

Abu 'Abd Allah Sadiq's real name was Abdelhakim Belhadj and he had once been a leading figure in the Libyan Islamic Fighting Group, or LIFG. In early 2004, Belhadj was in China but worried about his security and decided to see if he could seek asylum in the UK, and through interlocutors made contact to discuss the possibility. He and his wife took a flight to Malaysia, where, after questioning, they were told they would be able to travel to the UK via Bangkok. But in Bangkok they were detained and handed over to US authorities. Belhadj has claimed that in between interrogation sessions he was hung by his wrists from hooks in a cell and was beaten. On 8 March 2004, the couple were then sent to Libya on an American private flight (but with Libyan intelligence officers on board). A hooded Belhadj was shackled to the floor on the seventeen-hour flight, including the two hours it is thought to have stopped to refuel on the British territory of Diego Garcia. A CIA memo does include a demand for assurances that his human rights would be respected. However, Belhadj claims he was beaten in Libyan jails before finally being released in 2010. He then went on to become a leading military commander in the rebel grouping fighting Gadaffi's regime.

The stash of documents, which include the provision of extensive information on Libyan suspects in the UK, also seemed to show British complicity in the transfer of another member of the LIFG called Abu Munthir, also known as Sami al-Saadi. He had fled Afghanistan in 2001 and had also ended up in China before, like Belhadj, he approached British officials through an interlocutor. He says that it was intimated that he and his family would be allowed to return to Britain, where they lived in the 1990s (back then British intelligence had often had relationships with LIFG members because they opposed Gadaffi, a sign of how alliances had shifted so much). He and his family were placed on a flight to Hong Kong, where he was then held for two weeks. During this time, plans were being cooked up between London, Washington and Tripoli. Had it all been a trap?

A CIA memo to Libyan intelligence during these weeks read: 'We are also aware that your service had been co-operating with the

British to effect Abu Munthir's removal to Tripoli.' The memo details the precise procedures required to ensure a plane could pick him up and get him to Libya. On arrival, the family were unloaded into three cars, the parents hooded, and taken to a prison. The rest of the family were released after a few weeks but Munthir was held. The transfer happened just days before British Prime Minister Tony Blair arrived to meet the Libyan leader.

In a later interview, Abu Munthir recalled being visited by Musa Kusa in jail in Libya. 'You've been running from us,' he recalled the Libyan spymaster telling him. 'But since 11 September I can pick up the phone and call MI6 or the CIA and they give us all the information we want on you.'[132] Abu Munthir says after a few months the torture began, including with an electrified hose. He says Kusa himself was a frequent participant in the interrogations. At other times he says both American and British officials visited him. He says he was cleaned up and told to co-operate with them or else face more torture. When one British man and woman arrived, he says he was placed in a less squalid interrogation room but tortured before and after. He says it was impossible for him to tell the British visitors that he was being mistreated because a Libyan agent was present and watching him, although at one point he has said he tried to signal to the visiting Britons that he was being mistreated and felt that they understood what he was trying to communicate.

The memos and accounts of the men were profoundly damaging for MI6. In January 2012, the Police and Crown Prosecution Service announced that while they would not be charging any individual from MI5 with regards to the treatment of Binyam Mohammed or from MI6 in relation to a case the service itself had referred (involving a detainee held by the US at Bagram airbase in January 2002), the information from the Libyan memos was 'so serious' that it was in the public interest for the two cases to be investigated. This, in turn, forced the collapse of a planned government inquiry which was intended to draw a line under the wider issue of complicity in torture.

British officials say that after the complicity issue had arisen a few years earlier, they had searched the records for any further cases of concern but say they had somehow missed the Libyan cases. They also say they had no record on file of Belhadj claiming mistreatment when he was visited by MI6 officers to check on his conditions. The

Munthir case shows the risks in relying on assurances from the Libyan officials and verbal checks with detainees to be sure that torture is not taking place.

The relationship with Libya was one being pushed at the highest level by Tony Blair and number 10 Downing Street at the time. Disarming Gaddafi was perceived as a great success. But was too much given in return and did Britain, and especially MI6, get too close? Some at the highest levels of British intelligence suggested this might have been the case. 'I do not think it was wrong in principle,' Eliza Manningham-Buller said of the rapprochement in her 2011 BBC Reith lecture before adding that 'there are clearly questions to be answered about the various relationships that developed afterwards and whether the UK supped with a sufficiently long spoon.'

The crucial issue will be how far MI6's dealings with Libya were 'authorised' by ministers (including Jack Straw as Foreign Secretary) and how detailed those authorisations were when it came to counterterrorist co-operation. 'It was a political decision, having very significantly disarmed Libya, for the government to co-operate with Libya on Islamist terrorism,' Sir Richard Dearlove argued publicly after the revelations. 'The whole relationship was one of serious calculation about where the overall balance of our national interests stood.' He denied the relationship was 'cosy', instead emphasising that 'it has always been pretty clear that our governments in the UK have accepted that danger and difficulty and have given political clearance for that sort of co-operation.'

Sawers was said to be furious when he learnt of the Libyan operations at the same time as the public. In all previous examinations of the issue, including by parliamentary committees, nothing had emerged of these operations. The revelations inevitably raised questions outside the secret service over what else might have remained hidden. This had the potential to be damaging not only with the public but also with the Secret Service's political masters, who were said to be angry about what had emerged.

A concern inside the service was whether the erosion of public and political trust would restrict the ability of MI6 to operate and make it more risk averse.

A few operational officers had felt that there had been too much caution starting from John Scarlett's tenure, too much concern over the dangers of something going wrong. Whilst many agents spying for MI6 have died (like Penkovsky), as far as anyone knows publicly no MI6 officer has died as a result of hostile action (in stark contrast to the CIA). Is this a sign of success or one in which the balance of risk has gone awry?

There have been close calls – bullets picked out of flak jackets in Iraq and Afghanistan. And there are certainly still people doing dangerous things and taking risks, but when Sawers goes overseas to visit officers one of the first questions his staff ask is 'How do I know in dealing with terrorism I won't one day be hauled before the courts back home?' This is a question about legal risk that would have been unimaginable in the days of Anthony Cavendish and Daphne Park and reflects the legacy of the accusations over complicity in torture. The answer to the question is that everything with the slightest element of political or legal risk is now signed off by the Foreign Secretary or other officials. It becomes their responsibility to decide if the intelligence that might be produced (to meet requirements set by them) is worth the consequences of things going wrong. The threshold for those authorisations has lowered so much that now there are about 500 authorisations a year compared to 50 in the 1990s. This would have been a shock to George Kennedy Young and his robber barons, who would have laughed the idea out of the Broadway bar.

'Torture is illegal and abhorrent under any circumstances, and we have nothing whatsoever to do with it,' Sawers said in a televised speech (before the Libya revelations). 'If we know or believe action by us will lead to torture taking place, we're required by UK and international law to avoid that action. And we do, even though that allows the terrorist activity to go ahead.' It was a message designed not just to draw a line under the past publicly but also to signal to ministers that they had to understand what their decisions would mean in practice.

In recent years, the public has watched with curiosity as Chiefs of MI6 occasionally emerge from the imposing confines of Vauxhall Cross into public view and now even before the cameras. The work of the Secret Service is painted by its leadership as one of a modern, professional bureaucracy – playing by the rules and not that different from the rest of the civil service in its care for procedure and pensions.

Occasionally, glimpses of what secret work really involves bubble up from the subterranean world. Sometimes, as with Libya, they contradict the sanitised public presentation.

Another incident which cast a harsh light was the death of Gareth Williams, a brilliant GCHQ code-breaker who was on attachment to MI6. His body was found in a locked bag in his London bathroom. A private man who had been happy and successful at GCHQ, Williams did not settle well in London and asked for an early return to Cheltenham. 'He disliked the office culture, post-work drinks, flash-car competitions and the rat race. He even spoke of friction in the office,' his sister told the inquest into his death. 'The job was not quite what he expected. He encountered more red tape than he was comfortable with.' Even if the death was linked to his private life, as some thought, the fact that it took a week for his line-manager at MI6 to report him missing from Vauxhall Cross raised serious questions about the organisation and led to an unreserved apology by Sir John Sawers. The line manager's evidence to the inquest stretched the 'bounds of credibility', according to the Coroner, and other irregularities in the investigation meant that questions continued to surround the death.

There are those who still argue that what the service has lost in recent years is that air of mystique, the élan and sense of being different and perhaps even a touch dangerous. Without this, 'it will look just like a sub-committee of the Department of Work and Pensions,' fears one former officer with a wistful look in his eyes. There are those who wish to see exactly this outcome. 'I don't believe in intelligence any more than I believe in little green men,' Rodric Braithwaite, former Ambassador and JIC chair argues. 'It is much better to look at intelligence as if it were another branch of government like the Inland Revenue doing a job which has to be done and is necessary but not particularly glamorous and which goes wrong from time to time – just like the Inland Revenue.'[133] Old-time spies shiver at such thoughts.

If the layers of myth and mystique are stripped away, what would the public see and would they want to see it? In the Cold War, the spies, as John le Carre recently put it, were there to 'clean the drains so we can have clean water'. In the modern era, the public still want the benefits spies produce – particularly in terms of security. But there are those who may be less comfortable when they are shown precisely what methods are used to produce those benefits and gather intelligence – especially from hard places and difficult partners. The fears over where openness might lead which were voiced at the time of avowal remain in some quarters of the secret world, not least the fear of being stripped bare by court cases.

In the modern era of accountability and transparency, one in which anything hidden is distrusted, how secret does a secret service have to be? Sawers argued that removing too many layers of secrecy will undermine the trust of agents and 'partners' (especially, of course, the Americans) in providing information to MI6. 'Secrecy is not there as a cover up. Secrecy plays a crucial part in keeping Britain safe and secure,' he has argued. To critics of the secret world, such concerns are simply a means of covering up mistakes or avoiding embarrassment. Only a credible system of accountability offers the chance to bridge the gap between MI6's demand for secrecy and the public concerns over ethics and efficacy. But the decade from 2001 found the existing system of oversight widely viewed as inadequate – largely as a result of its failure to get to grips with issues such as Iraq and mistreatment of detainees.

The relationship with the Americans altered. It remained closer than with any other country but with subtle changes. The British remained not entirely sure of where the Americans were heading. There were concerns on the British side over legality and account-ability – for instance, being drawn into supporting a programme of CIA drone strikes that even killed British and American citizens. These concerns were interpreted by some Americans as a sign their old allies were not quite up for the fight. In some cases, the US would pass on intelligence about threats but without detail on the source for fear that it might end up being revealed by British courts (as happened with the Binyam Mohammed case), forcing MI6 to try and find it out themselves as occurred in the context of intelligence about a Mumbai-style Al Qaeda attack in Europe in 2010. Concerns about the security of information were not all one-way though. In May 2012, reports emerged out of Washington of an agent having infiltrated Al Qaeda in Yemen for up to a year before leaving and bringing with him an underwear bomb that he was supposed to use to blow up a flight to the USA. A few days later it was reported that even though the agent's family was from the Middle East, he had been holding a British passport and had been recruited in a joint MI5/MI6 operation. British officials declined to confirm the reports, but while the operation might appear to have been a success on one level, it also raised concerns in London about the amount of sensitive intelligence which was leaking out of Washington. As has been the case for decades, MI6 cannot offer potential agents the money that the CIA can put in front of them, but it likes to think it has an edge in being able to offer them a greater guarantee of secrecy. Leaks about the identity of an agent are therefore seen as especially damaging because of the fear it will make it much harder for MI6 to recruit such individuals in the future. Such ebbs and flows in the relationships have certainly occurred before, though the wider shift of American focus towards Asia and away from Europe may presage a more profound shift.

For Britain also there was a deeper question of whether an age of austerity, coupled with a weariness induced by the costly engagements of Iraq and Afghanistan, would lead to a reassessment of the country's ambitions and, in practice, their downgrading. But the old reflexive instinct of wanting to walk the global stage remains among the political class and as long as it does they will look to Britain's spies to support them and to act as a tool in wielding influence. Sawers runs a service operating in more than one hundred countries and which still aspires, despite the years of empire being long gone, to have a global reach. That was what politicians told him they wanted. But it is becoming harder. The focus on terrorism has made coverage patchy, even in areas such as Daphne Park's old hunting ground of Africa. As resources became more stretched, hard decisions are required over where to focus.[134]

But there are still only a handful of secret services which aggressively practise the recruitment and running of human sources around the world. The Americans, Russians, Chinese, the Israeli, the French and the British. Others make do with analysing what they get from liaison partners and dealing with the odd defector and the like. But the game is also changing. The dividing line between technical collection and human collection is increasingly blurred thanks to cyber-techniques and complex eavesdropping. MI6 may now present itself as a modern, professional bureaucracy integrated with other departments and closer to policy-making, focused on 'knowledge management'. But beneath the shiny new exterior, the world of Daphne Park and Vienna, of Wynne and Penkovsky, of Philby and Shergy, is still there if you look hard enough. Somewhere there is the agent and his handler alone in the room wondering if each can trust the other.

EPILOGUE

The crowd gathering at St Margaret's Church in Westminster Abbey hoisted their umbrellas and turned up their collars as autumn rain fell from grey skies on to the streets around. They had come to bid farewell to one of their own. Some had come, in spirit, from Broadway, barely a hundred yards to the north where Daphne Park had begun her career in her beloved Secret Service; others from Century House just over the river where she had risen through the ranks; a few came to remember her from Vauxhall Cross further west down the river where her successors continued their work for the country she had served. Eliza Manningham-Buller was there towards the front while the chiefs of MI6 sat separately – Scarlett close to her, McColl a few rows behind him, Sawers over the aisle, his security detail discreetly, and perhaps unnecessarily, eyeing the assembled marquises, field marshals, foreign secretaries and assorted great and good of a fading British establishment. At one side, immobile and weathered, sat Anthony Cavendish who, like Daphne Park, had walked the streets of Vienna after the war. Addressing them was the man who had sat in a tent with Gadaffi a few years before. In the pews listening was the man who had helped deliver Gordievsky from Moscow. Old habits dying hard, others preferred the dimmer recesses of the church, their stories still unspoken.

Shergy's ghost hung over them, his name invoked in the address as the guiding mentor of the young Daphne Park and of many others who had gathered and still others absent. The smiles were instinctive, but also perhaps wistful, as the story was told of the search in her flat a few months earlier for the gun she had somehow mislaid and the surprise when it turned out to be a pearl-handled revolver personally built by the armourer of the Special Operations Executive during the Second World War. There was a colourful account of the African upbringing of a child of Empire and the story of her passing secret messages to her Ambassador in Moscow in the 1950s on the dance-floor – the safest place if one wished not to be overheard and the only time he could not get away, Park had explained. There was a reference to her fascination with the riddle of power but also with the most ordinary of people. A stillness of remembrance, coloured by loss, settled over the congregation and eyes gazed into the middle distance as the final words of Alfred, Lord Tennyson's epic poem 'Ulysses' were read, calling forth one last adventure:

> Though much is taken, much abides; and though
> We are not now that strength which in old days
> Moved earth and heaven; that which we are, we are;
> One equal temper of heroic hearts,
> Made weak by time and fate, but strong in will
> To strive, to seek, to find, and not to yield.

ACKNOWLEDGEMENTS

This book has grown out of a decade of reporting on intelligence and security issues and, in particular, from a number of programmes made for BBC Radio looking at British and American intelligence agencies. It owes much to the willingness of individuals to share their knowledge and experience, many of whom have understandably requested anonymity but they have my gratitude. Among those who I can thank for advice and assistance over the years are Abdullah Anas, Christopher Andrew, Elizabeth Bancroft, Rodric Braithwaite, Anthony Cavendish, Rod Barton, Peter Earnest, Michael Goodman, Oleg Gordievsky, Franek Grabowski, Paul Greengrass, Muslem Hayat, Peter Hennessy, Alan Judd, Mikhail Lyubimov, Eliza Manningham-Buller, Stephen de Mowbray, the late Daphne Park, Bob Steers, Prokop Tomek, Nigel West and William Hood. I would also like to thank the trustees of the Liddell Hart Centre for Military Archives at King's College, London, for permission to quote from the papers of Anthony Courtney and the Imperial War Museum for access to its sound library. My thanks also to Svetlana Golitsyn for permission to cite her late husband's as yet unpublished manuscript. Particular thanks to my Radio 4 producer Mark Savage for his guidance over the years, to Peter James for his insightful comments on the manuscript, to my editor Bea Hemming for her faith and guidance and to George Capel for her support and enthusiasm. Last but not least, my thanks to Jane, Joseph and Samuel for their patience and support.

NOTES

INTRODUCTION

1 Interview with former Chief Sir Colin McColl for BBC Radio 4, 2009
2 'A Century in the Shadows', BBC Radio 4, August 2009
3 John Scarlett, Channel 4 News, 21 September 2010

CHAPTER 1: INTO THE SHADOWS

1 *On the Cold War Front – Czechoslovakia 1948–1956* exhibition catalogue, Prague, 2009, http://www.ustrcr.cz/data/pdf/vystavy/katalog-na-fronte-en.pdf
2 Bob Steers, 'Jan Mašek', *Intelligence Corps Journal*, 2005; interview with Bob Steers.
3 National Archives FO 1007/309, British Field Security Reports for Vienna
4 Information from Prokop Tomek and *On the Cold War Front*. The ten years were 1950–60. Additional private information on the penetration of Measure
5 Bob Steers, 'Jan Mašek', *Intelligence Corps Journal*, 2005; interview with Bob Steers.
6 National Archives DEFE 21/33: a 1950 report by Philip Vickery reflects the British view of the importance of Vienna. The American view can be found in 'The Current Situation in Austria, CIA', 31 August 1949, declassified and available at www.cia.gov
7 Suzanne St Albans, *Mango and Mimosa*, Virago, London, 2001, p. 318
8 Martin Herz, *Understanding Austria*, Wolfgang Neugebauer,

Salzburg, 1984, p. 42

9 John Dos Passos, *Tour of Duty*, Riverside Press, Cambridge, 1946, p. 291

10 MI6 officers had called for caution before taking the side of the locals straight away, reminding others that the Russians had been allies and had made great sacrifices. National Archives FO 1020/1272, Note from H. B. Hitchens

11 National Archives FO 1007/306, Secret Field Security Report for 17–23 August 1945

12 National Archives FO 1007/309, Field Security Reports for Vienna for the first months of 1948

13 Ian Fleming, *Thrilling Cities*, Jonathan Cape, London, 1963

14 Norman Sherry, *The Life of Graham Greene*, vol. 2, Jonathan Cape, London, 1994, p. 252

15 Ibid., p. 250

16 Ibid., p. 84

17 Graham Greene, *Ways of Escape*, Penguin, Middlesex, 1982, p. 227; Sherry, *Life of Graham Greene*, vol. 2, p. 127

18 Smollett may have been the source for this part of the story as well as others, but his full role may have been masked by Greene and the film-makers in a deal

19 Reference to Philby's visit is made in passing on a tape by John Bruce Lockhart who was very briefly based in Vienna after the war. The tape has since been withdrawn from the Imperial War Museum

20 Barbara Honigmann, *Ein Kapitel aus meinem Leben*, Hanser, Munich, 2004, p. 59

21 E. H. Cookridge, *The Third Man*, Arthur Barker, London, 1968, p. 21

22 Patrick Seale and Maureen McConville, *Philby: The Long Road to Moscow*, Hamish Hamilton, London, 1973, p. 64; Cookridge, *Third Man*, p. 28

23 National Archives KV 2/1012–4, Edith Tudor-Hart's MI5 file; KV2/1604–5, Alex Tudor-Hart's file

24 John Bruce Lockhart in Nigel West (ed.), *The Faber Book of Espionage*, Faber & Faber, London, 1993, p. 238

25 Quoted in Miranda Carter, *Anthony Blunt: His Lives*, Macmillan, London, 2001, p. 153

26 Genrikh Borovik, *The Philby Files*, Little, Brown, London, 1994, pp. 55 and 38–9

27 Honigmann, *Ein Kapitel aus meinem Leben*, p. 62

28 Borovik, *Philby Files*, pp. 55 and 137

29 Borovik in ibid., p. 251, claims that Philby saw Litzi in Vienna. Other accounts talk of Paris or say the end of the marriage was agreed through letters. Litzi at the time was living in Berlin

30 Honigmann, *Ein Kapitel aus meinem Leben*

31 Marie-Françoise Allain, *The Other Man: Conversations with Graham Greene*, The Bodley Head, London, 1983, pp. 18–19

32 Rufina Philby, Mikhail Lyubimov and Hayden Peake, *The Private Life of Kim Philby*, St Ermin's Press, London, 1999, p. 174

33 The similarities have been commented on, for instance, in Michael Shelden, *Graham Greene: The Man Within*, Heinemann, London, 1994, pp. 322–3; Siegfried Beer, 'The Third Man', *History Today*, 1 May 2001, vol. 51, p. 45

34 John H. Richardson, *My Father the Spy*, Harper Perennial, New York, 2005, p. 92

35 John le Carré, 'We still need spies', *Guardian*, 2 March 1999

36 John le Carré, *A Perfect Spy*, Coronet, London, 1987, p. 447

37 John le Carré, 'The Madness of Spies', *New Yorker*, 29 September 2008; John le Carré, 'A service known only by its failures', *Toronto Star*, 3 May 1986

38 Le Carré, 'Madness of Spies'

39 Le Carré, 'A service known only by its failures'; Graham Greene, *Our Man in Havana*, Vintage, London, 2001, p. 79

40 Peer de Silva, *Sub Rosa*, Times Books, New York, 1978, pp. 42–52

41 Anthony Cavendish, *Inside Intelligence*, HarperCollins, London, 1997, p. 64. This may also be the incident referred to in Tom Bower, *The Perfect English Spy*, Heinemann, London, 1995, p. 206

42 Interview with Anthony Cavendish

43 National Archives FO 1007/309

44 National Archives FO 1020/1272, Secret Field Security Report

45 National Archives FO 1020/8 (72), Importance of Vienna for the exploitation of intelligence regarding the countries adjacent to Austria and especially the Russians, Top Secret, 10 November 1945

46 John Whitwell, *British Agent*, John Kimber, London, 1966, p. 26

47 Interview with Anthony Cavendish

48 Bob Steers, 'There were Two in this Squad', *Intelligence Corps Journal*, February 2007

49 Keith Jeffery, *MI6: The History of the Secret Intelligence Service 1909–1949*, Bloomsbury, London, 2010, pp. 670–3

50 Percy Cradock, *Know your Enemy*, John Murray, 2002, London, p. 50

51 Peter Hennessy, *The Secret State*, Penguin, 2002, London, p. 13

52 Jeffery, *MI6*, pp. 705–6

53 Cradock, *Know your Enemy*, p. 52

54 *The Heart of the Matter*, BBC TV, 22 September 1985

55 Cavendish, *Inside Intelligence*, p. 189

56 George Kennedy Young, *Who is my Liege?* Gentry Books, London, 1972, p. 31

57 George Kennedy Young, *Masters of Indecision*, Methuen, London, 1962, p. 26

58 National Archives FO 1007/327, Allied Control Commission Austria – Joint Intelligence Committee Report, 18 April 1946, Russia's Intentions in Austria

59 Richardson, *My Father the Spy*, p. 98

60 National Archives FO 1020/3464, Top Secret memo 23 March 1950

61 National Archives DEFE 28/31

62 Bower, *Perfect English Spy*, p. 186; Cavendish, *Inside Intelligence*, p. 188

63 Jeffery, *MI6*, p. 671

64 Ibid., pp. 669–71

65 National Archives DEFE 21/33 contains the list of JIC priorities for Austria and also reflects frustrations in London in some areas. The extra resources are mentioned in Jeffery, *MI6*, pp. 669–71

66 National Archives DEFE 21/33

67 James Critchfield, *Partners at the Creation*, Naval Institute Press, Annapolis, 2003, p. 64

68 James V. Milano and Patrick Brogan, *Soldiers, Spies, and the Rat Line*, Brassey's, Washington DC, 1995, pp. 1–2 and 46

69 Ibid., p. 201

70 Asher Ben Natan, *The Audacity to Live*, Mazo Publishers, Jerusalem, 2007, p. 34

71 National Archives FO 1007/309

72 National Archives FO 1020/99; Robin Steers, *FSS: Field Security Section*, published by Robin Steers, 1996, p. 23

73 The Soviet intelligence services used a number of different names until being reorganised as the KGB in 1953. For ease of understanding, the KGB is used for the organisation throughout this period

74 Jeffery, *MI6*, pp. 690–3

75 Critchfield, *Partners at the Creation*, p. 69; Ben Natan, *Audacity to Live*, pp. 37 and 55

76 Critchfield, *Partners at the Creation*, p. 69; Milano and Brogan, *Soldiers, Spies, and the Rat Line*, pp. 1–2 and 73

77 Ian Black and Benny Morris, *Israel's Secret Wars*, Hamish Hamilton, London, 1991, p. 188

78 All material about Daphne Park from an interview conducted by the author unless otherwise noted

79 National Archives ADM 223/500

80 National Archives FO 1020/1272 and FO 1020/14

81 National Archives FO 1007/307

82 National Archives FO 1032/1459

83 National Archives WO 232/92; Tony Geraghty, *Brixmis*, HarperCollins, London, 1997; Iain Cobain, 'How the T-Force abducted Germany's best brains for Britain', *Guardian*, 29 August 2007

84 National Archives DEFE 21/33

85 Interview with Daphne Park

86 Daphne Park, 'Licensed to Kill?', Ian Fleming Centenary Lecture, Royal Society of Literature, London, 12 May 2009

87 Tom Bower, *The Paperclip Conspiracy*, Michael Joseph, London 1987

88 Daphne Park, 'Licensed to Kill?'

89 Details of kidnapping are scattered through Martin Herz, *Understanding Austria*

90 National Archives FO 1020/99 34

91 Herz, *Understanding Austria*, pp. 401–3

92 Milano and Brogan, *Soldiers, Spies, and the Rat Line*, p. 173

93 De Silva, *Sub Rosa*, pp. 4–5

94 Allen Dulles, *The Craft of Intelligence*, Weidenfeld & Nicolson, London, 1963, p. 213

95 Pontecorvo fled Britain to the USSR. In 1953, when he was supposed to attend a scientific congress there was an attempt to lure him back, offering forgiveness in return for information about the Soviet programme. A meeting was offered in Vienna with Field Security men waiting, guns at the ready, in the British district, but he never showed up. Steers, *FSS: Field Security Section*, pp. 157–8

96 Caroline Alexander, 'Vital Powers', *New Yorker*, 30 January 1989

97 Interview with Daphne Park

98 National Archives FO 945/376

99 Christopher Andrew and Vasili Mitrokhin, *The Mitrokhin Archive*, Allen Lane, London, 1999, pp. 177–9

100 This account taken from Paul Gorka, *Budapest Betrayed*, Oak Tree Books, Wembley, 1986, p. 78

101 Márta Pellérdi, 'Their Man in Budapest: James McCargar and the 1947 Road to Freedom', *Hungarian Quarterly*, vol. XLII, no. 161, Spring 2001

102 William Hood, *Mole*, Weidenfeld & Nicolson, London, 1982, p. 115

103 Jeffery, *MI6*, p. 671

104 Christopher Felix, *The Spy and his Masters*, Secker & Warburg, London, 1963, p. 132

105 Tim Weiner, *Legacy of Ashes*, Allen Lane, London, 2007, pp. 9, 17

106 Richardson, *My Father the Spy*, p. 106

107 Hood, *Mole*, p. 28

108 Clarence Ashley, *CIA Spymaster*, Pelican, Gretna, 2004, p. 82

109 John Limond Hart, *The CIA's Russians*, Naval Institute Press, Annapolis, 2003, p. 178; David E. Murphy, Sergei A. Kondrashev and George Bailey, *Battleground Berlin*, Yale University Press, New Haven, 1997, p. 268

110 Hart, *CIA's Russians*, p. 38

111 Hood, *Mole*, p. 74

112 Richardson, *My Father the Spy*, p. 111

113 All details of Golitsyn taken from Volume One of his unpublished memoir, a copy of which was provided to the author. A further

copy is lodged with the Library of Congress, Washington DC.

114 Murphy, Kondrashev and Bailey, *Battleground Berlin*, p. 25

115 Peter Deriabin and Frank Gibney, *The Secret World*, Ballantine Books, New York, 1982, pp. 286–9

116 Reference to the kidnap plan is also made in Christopher Andrew and Oleg Gordievsky, *KGB: The Inside Story of its Foreign Operations from Lenin to Gorbachev*, Hodder & Stoughton, London, 1990, p. 346

117 Ashley, *CIA Spymaster*, p. 102

118 Ibid., p. 103; Hood, *Mole*, p. 152. Deriabin's intelligence was also passed on to the British and is referred to in National Archives KV 5/107

119 National Archives KV 5/107, Effects of recent Soviet defections and desertions, 8 May 1954. The Chief of MI6 asked for the memo to be shown to the head of MI5

120 Hood, *Mole*, p. 73

121 National Archives FO 1020/99

122 Milano and Brogan, *Soldiers, Spies, and the Rat Line*, pp. 101–3

123 Ibid., pp. 111–12

124 Nicholas Elliott, *With my Little Eye*, Michael Russell, Norwich, 1993, p. 49

125 David Stafford, *Spies beneath Berlin*, Overlook Press, New York, 2003, p. 16

126 Bower, *Perfect English Spy*, p. 180

127 Tape recording provided by Bob Steers

128 Interview with Sir Rodric Braithwaite

129 Stafford, *Spies beneath Berlin*, p. 23; interview with Anthony Cavendish

130 Bower, *Perfect English Spy*, p. 84

131 George Blake, *No Other Choice*, Jonathan Cape, London, 1990, pp. 17–18; Bower, *Perfect English Spy*, p. 84; *Blake – the Confession*, BBC Radio 4, 1 August 2009; private information from a CIA officer serving with Blake and from British sources

132 Golitsyn memoir

133 De Silva, *Sub Rosa*, p. 93

134 Hood, *Mole*, p. 116

135 National Archives KV 5/107 includes Kholkov's intelligence on these networks in Austria

136 Andrew and Mitrokhin, *Mitrokhin Archive*, p. 467

137 Michael Smith, *The Spying Game*, Politico's, London, 2003, p. 192

CHAPTER 2: THE COST OF BETRAYAL

1 Interview with Anthony Cavendish; Anthony Cavendish, *Inside Intelligence*, HarperCollins, London, 1997, pp. 54–9

2 Anthony Courtney, *Sailor in a Russian Frame*, Johnson, London, 1968, pp. 1–55

3 Liddell Hart Archives, Papers of Anthony Courtney, GB99 KCLMA Courtney

4 Ibid.

5 Tom Bower, *The Red Web*, Aurum Press, London, 1989, p. 101

6 Ibid., p. 113

7 National Archives KV 5/106 includes detailed British intelligence reports on the Baltic coast and its security

8 Bower, *Red Web*, p. 115

9 Ibid., p. 2

10 Interview with former SIS officer

11 Keith Jeffery, *MI6: The History of the Secret Intelligence Service 1909–1949*, Bloomsbury, London, 2010, pp. 705–6

12 Christopher Andrew and Oleg Gordievsky, *KGB: The Inside Story of its Foreign Operations from Lenin to Gorbachev*, Hodder & Stoughton, London, 1990, p. 317; Bower, *Red Web*, p. 60

13 'Latvian former counter-intelligence officers recall interaction with Britain', BBC Summary of World Broadcasts, 11 March 1988

14 Bower, *Red Web*, pp. 131 and 139

15 David Smiley, *Irregular Regular*, Michael Russell, Norwich, 1994, p. 191

16 *The Cost of Treachery*, BBC TV 30 October 1984

17 National Archives HW 75/60–3 includes intercepted Albanian security communications discussing the arrival of British teams

18 David Smiley, Imperial War Museum Sound Recording 10340

19 James McCargar interview, 'Frontline Diplomacy', Manuscript Division, Library of Congress, Washington DC; Peter Grose, *Operation Rollback*, Houghton Mifflin, Boston, 2000, p. 159

20 Obituary of Johnnie Longrigg, *The Times*, 14 March 2007

21 Percy Cradock, *Know your Enemy*, John Murray, London, 2002, pp. 26–9

22 Grose, *Operation Rollback*, pp. 124–5

23 Anthony Verrier, *Through the Looking Glass*, Jonathan Cape, London, 1983, p. 67

24 Christopher Felix, *The Spy and his Masters*, Secker & Warburg, London, 1963, p. 140

25 Tim Weiner, *Legacy of Ashes*, Allen Lane, London, 2007, p. 53

26 The Hoover Commission quoted in ibid., p. 252

27 Grose, *Operation Rollback*, p. 117

28 Ian Fleming, *Casino Royale*, Penguin, London, 2006, pp. 54 and 91–2; Simon Winder, *The Man Who Saved Britain*, Picador, London, 2006, p. 84

29 Kim Philby, *My Silent War*, MacGibbon & Kee, London, 1968, p. 117

30 Felix, *The Spy and his Masters*, p. 51

31 Quoted in Roderick Bailey, *The Wildest Province*, Jonathan Cape, London, 2008, p. 318

32 Ibid., p. 328

33 Jeffery, *MI6*, pp. 712–14; Patrick Seale and Maureen McConville, *Philby: The Long Road to Moscow*, Hamish Hamilton, London, 1973, p. 202

34 Imperial War Museum Sound Recording 10340; and Smiley, *Irregular Regular*, p. 4

35 David Smiley, *The Albanian Assignment*, Chatto & Windus, London, 1984

36 Obituary of Colonel David Smiley, *Daily Telegraph*, 12 January 2009

37 Eric Walton, Imperial War Museum Sound Recording 13626

38 Ibid.

39 Obituary of Tony Northrop, 'Covert Cold Warrior made it hot for Hoxha', *The Australian*, 6 September 2000

40 *The Cost of Treachery*, BBC TV, 30 October 1984

41 Quoted in Stephen Dorril, *MI6: Fifty Years of Special Operations*, Fourth Estate, London, 2000, p. 401

42 Cavendish, *Inside Intelligence*, p. 191

43 Peer de Silva, *Sub Rosa*, Times Books, New York, 1978, p. 55

44 Genrikh Borovik, *The Philby Files*, Little, Brown, London, 1994, p. 265

45 *The Cost of Treachery*, BBC TV, 30 October 1984

46 Tom Mangold, *Cold Warrior*, Simon & Schuster, London, 1991, p. 50; Philby, *My Silent War*, pp. 112–17

47 *The Cost of Treachery*, BBC TV, 30 October 1984

48 Bruce Page, David Leitch and Phillip Knightley, *Philby: The Spy Who Betrayed a Generation*, Sphere, London, 1977, p. 211

49 Yossi Melman and Dan Raviv, *The Imperfect Spies*, Sidgwick & Jackson, London, 1989, p. 82

50 Philby, *My Silent War*, p. 120

51 Bower, *Red Web*, p. 127

52 Verrier, *Through the Looking Glass*, p. 77

53 John Limond Hart, *The CIA's Russians*, Naval Institute Press, Annapolis, 2003, p. 6. Hart worked on the Albanian operation

54 David Smiley, Imperial War Museum Sound Recording 10340

55 Miles Copeland to Bruce Page, quoted in Phillip Knightley, *Philby: KGB Masterspy*, André Deutsch, London, 1988, p. 1

56 Hart, *CIA's Russians*, p. 6

57 National Archives KV 3/301

58 Borovik, *Philby Files*, p. 369

59 Knightley, *Philby: KGB Masterspy*, p. 128

60 The re-use of Albanian drop points from the war was also clearly madness since they were compromised: Bailey, *Wildest Province*, p. 328

61 Philby's reluctance is recounted in Miranda Carter, *Anthony Blunt: His Lives*, Macmillan, London, 2001, p. 161

62 Philby, *My Silent War*, p. 131

63 Ibid., p. 138

64 Private information. Harvey's memo has not been found in the CIA archives despite repeated attempts

65 Christopher Andrew, *The Defence of the Realm: The Authorized History of MI5*, Allen Lane, London, 2009, p. 504

66 A copy of an interview note written by Arthur Martin is located in National Archives KV 2/1014, which is Edith Tudor-Hart's MI5 file

67 Ibid.

68 Ibid.; Chapman Pincher, *Treachery*, Random House, New York, 2009, p. 398
69 A spy talking to Phillip Knightley recounted in *The Heart of the Matter*, BBC TV, 22 September 1985
70 Page et al., *Philby: The Spy who Betrayed a Generation*, p. 148
71 Interview with a former SIS officer
72 Nicholas Elliott, *With my Little Eye*, Michael Russell, Norwich, 1993, p. 16
73 Seale and McConville, *Philby: The Long Road to Moscow*, p. 135
74 Ibid.
75 Christopher Andrew and Vasili Mitrokhin, *The Mitrokhin Archive*, Allen Lane, London, 1999
76 Philby, *My Silent War*, p. xviii; Graham Greene, *The Confidential Agent*, Vintage, London, 2002, pp. 67–71
77 Philby, *My Silent War*, p. xvi
78 Quoted in Knightley, *Philby: KGB Masterspy*, p. 148
79 James McCargar interview, Foreign Affairs Oral History Program, Georgetown University
80 Philby, *My Silent War*, p. 148
81 Peter Wright, *Spycatcher*, Heinemann, Melbourne, 1987, p. 44
82 Video of Philby being interviewed at the press conference can be found at http://www.youtube.com/watch?v=N2A2g-qRIaU
83 Knightley, *Philby: KGB Masterspy*, p. 198
84 National Archives PREM 111/2077 and ADM 1/29241
85 National Archives PREM 111/2077; although Peter Wright (*Spycatcher*, p. 73) claims a bugging operation at Claridge's did take place
86 Elliott, *With my Little Eye*, p. 23
87 Tom Bower, *The Perfect English Spy*, Heinemann, London, 1995, p. 159
88 National Archives PREM 11/2077
89 Robert Rhodes James, *Anthony Eden*, Weidenfeld & Nicolson, London, 1986, p. 436
90 Anthony Eden, *Full Circle*, Cassell, London, 1960, p. 365
91 Bower, *Perfect English Spy*, p. 347
92 National Archives ADM 1/29240
93 'Russian says he killed Cold War UK diver to prevent explosion on ship', BBC Monitoring, 16 November 2007. The account

remains unverified and previous explanations included Crabb
running out of air or becoming caught up in the propeller of the
ship

94 *The Heart of the Matter*, BBC TV, 22 September 1985

95 Bower, *Perfect English Spy*, pp. 165–6

96 Quoted in George Blake, *No Other Choice*, Jonathan Cape,
London, 1990, p. 168

97 Verrier, *Through the Looking Glass*, p. 4

98 Percy Cradock, *Know your Enemy*, John Murray, London, 2002,
p. 117

99 Bower, *Perfect English Spy*, p. 186; Young's comments in *The
Heart of the Matter*, BBC TV, 22 September 1985

100 W. Scott Lucas, *Divided We Stand*, Hodder, London, 1991, p. 195

101 Private information

102 Bower, *Perfect English Spy*, pp. 192 and 201; Christopher Andrew
and Vasili Mitrokhin, *The Mitrokhin Archive II: The KGB in
Europe and the West*, Allen Lane, London, 2005, p. 148

103 George Kennedy Young, *Who is my Liege?* Gentry Books,
London, 1972, pp. 77 and 79

104 Chester Cooper, *The Lion's Last Roar*, Harper & Row, New York,
1978, p. 70

105 Cradock, *Know your Enemy*, p. 111

106 George Kennedy Young, *Masters of Indecision*, Methuen,
London, 1962, p. 28

107 Lucas, *Divided We Stand*, p. 193; obituary of John McGlashan,
Daily Telegraph, 10 September 2010

108 Peter Hennessy, *The Prime Minister*, Penguin, London, 2000, p.
232

109 Cooper, *Lion's Last Roar*, pp. 178 and 211–12

110 Hennessy, *Prime Minister*, p. 226

111 G. K. Young, *Subversion and the British Riposte*, Ossian Publishers, Glasgow, 1984, p. 146

112 Cooper, *Lion's Last Roar*, p. 212

113 Paul Gorka, *Budapest Betrayed*, Oak Tree Books, Wembley, 1986,
pp. 124–7

114 Cavendish, *Inside Intelligence*, pp. 90–1; interview with Anthony
Cavendish

115 The Clandestine Service Historical Series – Hungary vol. II

External Operations 1946–1955, written May 1972 and classified Secret, declassified March 2005, available through the National Security Archive, George Washington University

116 De Silva, *Sub Rosa*, p. 123

117 Hennessy, *Prime Minister*, p. 243

118 Weiner, *Legacy of Ashes*, p. 132

119 De Silva, *Sub Rosa*, p. 123

120 Cavendish, *Inside Intelligence*, p. 98

121 Felix, *The Spy and his Masters*, pp. 13–15; Peter Hennessy, *The Secret State*, Penguin, London, 2002, pp. 36–7

122 Young, *Masters of Indecision*, pp. 20–1

123 Michael Smith, *The Spying Game*, Politico's, London, 2003, p. 197

124 Anatoly Golitsyn's unpublished memoir

125 Eleanor Philby, *The Spy I Loved*, Hamish Hamilton, London, 1968, p. 39

126 Interview with Anthony Cavendish; Cavendish, *Inside Intelligence*, pp. 119 and 138

127 Interview with Anthony Cavendish

128 Bower, *Perfect English Spy*, p. 293

129 Knightley, *Philby: KGB Masterspy*, p. 211

130 Andrew Lycett, *Ian Fleming*, Weidenfeld & Nicolson, London, 1995, p. 376

131 Nicholas Elliott, *Never Judge a Man by his Umbrella*, Michael Russell, Salisbury, 1991, p. 188

132 Eleanor Philby, *The Spy I Loved*, p. 46

133 Elliott, *Never Judge a Man*, p. 188

134 Bower, *Perfect English Spy*, p. 296

135 The conversation has been reconstructed from different sources. Philby's account is in Borovik, *Philby Files*, pp. 3 and 344. The MI6 end, which may or may not be more likely to be truthful since it is based on the recordings, comes from Bower, *Perfect English Spy*, p. 297, and Elliott's final line is also quoted in Andrew Boyle, *The Climate of Treason*, Coronet, London, 1980, p. 465

136 Andrew, *Defence of the Realm*, p. 435

137 Ibid., p. 436

138 Borovik, *Philby Files*, p. 346. There are many discrepancies between Philby's account and that of his former employers.

Philby does not mention the second meeting and the partial confession and says his signal to the Soviets came on the first night rather than the second

139 National Archives FO 953/1697; Philby, *The Spy I Loved*, pp. 2–4

140 Knightley, *Philby: KGB Masterspy*, p. 219

141 Philby, *The Spy I Loved*, p. 176

142 Knightley, *Philby: KGB Masterspy*, p. 254

143 Bower, *Perfect English Spy*, p. 304

144 Derek Bristow, *A Game of Moles*, Little, Brown, London, 1993; Knightley, *Philby: KGB Masterspy*

145 Richard Deacon, *C: A Biography of Sir Maurice Oldfield*, Macdonald, London, 1984, p. 140; Bristow, *Game of Moles*, p. xi

146 Wright, *Spycatcher*, p. 194

147 Weiner, *Legacy of Ashes*, pp. 153 and 262

148 Bower, *Perfect English Spy*, p. 132

149 John Bruce Lockhart in 'The Role of the Intelligence Services in the Second World War', seminar held 9 November 1994, Institute of Contemporary British History, 2003, http://www.ccbh.ac.uk/witness_intelligence_index.php, p. 29

150 Private information

151 Anthony Cave Brown, *The Secret Servant*, Sphere, London, 1989, p. 720

152 John le Carré's introduction to Page et al., *Philby: The Spy Who Betrayed a Generation*, p. 27

153 John le Carré, *Tinker, Tailor, Soldier, Spy*, Sceptre, London, 2009, p. 406

154 Phillip Knightley, *The Second Oldest Profession*, W. W. Norton, New York, 1987, p. 271

155 Knightley, *Philby: KGB Masterspy*, p. 259

156 Malcolm Muggeridge quoted in Boyle, *Climate of Treason*, p. 502

CHAPTER 3: A RIVER FULL OF CROCODILES – MURDER IN THE CONGO

1 Unless otherwise indicated all material about Daphne Park comes from an interview by the author in 2009

2 Information compiled for Baroness Park's memorial service; Caroline Alexander, 'Vital Powers', *New Yorker*, 30 January 1989

3 National Archives FO 371/14665; 'Who Killed Lumumba?', BBC Correspondent, 21 October 2000, transcript available at http://news.bbc.co.uk/hi/english/static/audio_video/programmes/correspondent/transcripts/974745.txt

4 National Archives DO 35/8804, Africa: The Next Ten Years, May 1959, memo originally drawn up at request of Foreign Secretary but distributed to the Cabinet, 2 July 1959

5 National Archives PREM 11/2585. The memo is dated 11 December 1959 and was most likely written by John Bruce Lockhart, Controller for the Middle East and Africa

6 Ibid.

7 Interview with Baroness Park

8 Comment of not being sexy from author interview; latter comment about appearance from Rachel Sylvester, 'A licence to kill? Oh heavens, no!', Daily Telegraph, 24 April 2003

9 Sylvester, 'A licence to kill? Oh heavens, no!'

10 John Whitwell, British Agent, William Kimber, London, 1966, p. 169

11 John Bruce-Lockhart quoted in Keith Jeffery, MI6: The History of the Secret Intelligence Service 1909–1949, Bloomsbury, London, 2010, p. 598

12 Quoted in Tom Bower, The Perfect English Spy, Heinemann, London, 1995, p. 224

13 National Archives DO 35/8804, Africa: The Next Ten Years, May 1959, memo originally drawn up at request of Foreign Secretary but distributed to the Cabinet, 2 July 1959; Bower, Perfect English Spy, p. 220

14 Jeffery, MI6, p. 678

15 Interview with Sir Rodric Braithwaite, former Ambassador to Moscow, for BBC Radio 4, 2009

16 The conversation is recalled by Daphne Park. She did not name Scott, but details of his time in the Congo are in obituary of Sir Ian Scott, Daily Telegraph, 11 March 2002, http://www.telegraph.co.uk/ news/ obituaries/ 1387342/ Sir-Ian-Scott.html

17 Adam Hochschild, King Leopold's Ghost, Macmillan, London, 1999; Michela Wrong, In the Footsteps of Mr Kurtz, Fourth Estate, London, 2000, p. 46

18 Hochschild, *King Leopold's Ghost*, p. 301; Georges Abi-Saab, *The United Nations Operation in the Congo 1960–1964*, Oxford University Press, Oxford, 1978, p. 6

19 Marie-Françoise Allain, *The Other Man: Conversations with Graham Greene*, The Bodley Head, London, 1983, p. 101

20 National Archives FO 371/146630

21 *Foreign Relations of the United States 1958–1960*, vol. XIV: Africa, p. 263

22 'Who Killed Lumumba?', BBC Correspondent, 21 October 2000

23 Ian Scott, *Tumbled House: The Congo at Independence*, Oxford University Press, London, 1969, p. 90

24 National Archives FO 371/146635, Note from Ian Scott, 5 July 1960

25 Ludo de Witte, *The Assassination of Lumumba*, Verso, London, 2001, p. 2; Hochschild, *King Leopold's Ghost*, p. 301

26 'Who Killed Lumumba?', BBC Correspondent, 21 October 2000

27 National Archives FO 371/146635

28 Scott, *Tumbled House*, p. 109

29 Larry Devlin, *Chief of Station, Congo: Fighting the Cold War in a Hot Zone*, PublicAffairs, New York, 2007, p. xiii

30 Ibid., p. xv

31 Richard Beeston, 'Old Memories of Chaos in the Congo Stirred Up', *The Times*, 16 November 1996

32 National Archives PREM 11/2883; Harold Macmillan, *Pointing the Way*, Macmillan, London, 1972, p. 263

33 National Archives PREM 11/2585

34 Georges Abi-Saab. *The United Nations Operation in the Congo 1960–1964*, p. 21

35 *Foreign Relations of the United States 1958–1960*, vol. XIV, p. 574

36 Wrong, *In the Footsteps of Mr Kurtz*, p. 61

37 Devlin, *Chief of Station, Congo*, p. 88

38 Kenneth Young, *Sir Alec Douglas-Home*, J. M. Dent, London, 1970, p. 125

39 Brian Urquhart, 'The Tragedy of Lumumba', *New York Review of Books*, 4 October 2001

40 *Foreign Relations of the United States 1958–1960* vol. XIV, p. 294; Charles Cogan, *Avoiding the Breakup: The US–UN intervention in the Congo, 1960–1965*, Harvard University Kennedy School of Government Case Program

41 Christopher Andrew and Vasili Mitrokhin, *The Mitrokhin Archive II: The KGB and the World*, Allen Lane, London, 2005, p. 426

42 Bower, *Perfect English Spy*, p. 221

43 National Archives CAB 128/34, Cabinet minutes, 19 July 1960

44 Douglas Dillon testifying before the Church Committee, 2 September 1975, p. 24

45 National Archives FO 371/146639

46 Devlin, *Chief of Station, Congo*, pp. 259 and 23

47 *Foreign Relations of the United States 1958–1960*, vol. XIV, p. 373

48 4 August 1960 diary entry quoted in Macmillan, *Pointing the Way*, pp. 264–5

49 National Archives FO 371/146701

50 Devlin, *Chief of Station, Congo*, p. 23

51 Ibid., p. 47

52 *Foreign Relations of the United States 1958–1960*, vol. XIV, p. 426

53 Devlin, *Chief of Station, Congo*, p. 48

54 Revealed by Soviet spy Oleg Penkovsky, Meeting #14, p. 14, declassified and available at www.cia.gov

55 Wrong, *In the Footsteps of Mr Kurtz*, p. 66

56 *Church Committee Report; Foreign Relations of the United States 1958–1960*, vol. XIV, p. 338

57 *Foreign Relations of the United States 1958–1960*, vol. XIV, p. 356

58 Frank Carlucci who served in the US Embassy in the Congo during the crisis is quoted making these comments in Cogan, *Avoiding the Breakup*

59 Devlin, *Chief of Station, Congo*, p. 132

60 Urquhart, 'Tragedy of Lumumba'

61 Devlin, *Chief of Station, Congo*, pp. 66 and 85

62 Untitled (Believe Congo experiencing classic communist effort), CIA cable, 18 August 1960, declassified and available www.cia.gov

63 *Foreign Relations of the United States 1958–1960*, vol. XIV, pp. 421–2

64 Ibid., p. 424

65 Madeleine G. Kalb, 'The CIA and Lumumba', *New York Times*, 2 August 1981; Martin Kettle, 'President "ordered murder" of Congo leader', *Guardian*, 10 August 2000

66 Peter Grose, *Gentleman Spy: The Life of Allen Dulles*, Houghton Mifflin, Boston, 1994, p. 502; *Alleged Assassination Plots Involving Foreign Leaders: Interim Report*, 1975, hereafter known as the *Church Committee Report*, http://www.history-matters.com/archive/contents/church/contents_church_reports_ir.htm

67 Tim Weiner, *Legacy of Ashes*, Allen Lane, London, 2007, pp. 162–3; *Church Committee Report*

68 Devlin, *Chief of Station, Congo*, pp. 63–8

69 Ibid., pp. 77–84

70 De Witte, *Assassination of Lumumba*, p. 27

71 Scott, *Tumbled House*, p. 78

72 National Archives CAB 128/34, Cabinet minutes, 15 September 1960

73 Bower, *Perfect English Spy*, pp. 222–3

74 Devlin, *Chief of Station, Congo*, p. 85

75 Scott, *Tumbled House*, p. 81

76 *Foreign Relations of the United States 1958–1960*, vol. XIV, p. 528

77 Ibid., pp. 511 and 528

78 Ibid., p. 497

79 Devlin, *Chief of Station, Congo*, p. 94

80 Grose, *Gentleman Spy*, p. 392; Ted Gup, 'The Coldest Warrior', *Washington Post*, 16 December 2001

81 *Church Committee Report*

82 Ibid.

83 *The Interview*, BBC World Service, 1 January 2009

84 CIA cable to headquarters from Leopoldville, cited in *Church Committee Report*

85 *Church Committee Report*

86 Description from ibid.

87 Ibid.

88 *Foreign Relations of the United States 1958–1960*, vol. XIV, p. 495

89 Quoted in D. R. Thorpe, *Supermac: The Life of Harold Macmillan*, Chatto & Windus, London, 2010, p. 484

90 National Archives FO 371/146646

91 National Archives FO 371/146650

92 National Archives PREM 11/3188 includes a top-secret memo on concerns that Nkrumah and Egypt would declare an African high command in the Congo

93 Daphne Park recounted the story in 'Licensed to kill?', Ian Fleming Centenary Lecture, Royal Society of Literature, London, 12 May 2008

94 De Witte, *Assassination of Lumumba*, pp. 71 and 83

95 *Church Committee Report; Foreign Relations of the United States 1958–1960*, vol. XIV, p. 503

96 De Witte, *Assassination of Lumumba*, p. 53

97 Abi-Saab, *United Nations Operation in the Congo, 1960–1964*, p. 91

98 'Who Killed Lumumba?', BBC Correspondent, 21 October 2000

99 Ibid.; De Witte, *Assassination of Lumumba*, p. 57; Urquhart, 'Tragedy of Lumumba'

100 National Archives FO 371/146779

101 Devlin, *Chief of Station, Congo*, pp. 128–9

102 Interview with Charles Cogan, who later succeeded Devlin in the Congo

103 13 January 1961, declassified cable available www.cia.gov

104 De Witte, *Assassination of Lumumba*, pp. 95–7

105 Ibid., p. 79; 'Who Killed Lumumba?', BBC Correspondent, 21 October 2000; Cogan, *Avoiding the Breakup*

106 'Who Killed Lumumba?', BBC Correspondent, 21 October 2000.

107 Richard Beeston, *Looking for Trouble*, Tauris Parke, London, 2006, p. 60

108 De Witte, *Assassination of Lumumba*, p. xxiv

109 Wrong, *In the Footsteps of Mr Kurtz*, p. 79

110 John Stockwell, *In Search of Enemies*, André Deutsch, London, 1978, p. 105

111 Devlin, *Chief of Station Congo*, p. 225

112 Stockwell, *In Search of Enemies*, p. 136

113 Wrong, *In the Footsteps of Mr Kurtz*, p. 3

114 Weiner, *Legacy of Ashes*, p. 303

115 Gup, 'The Coldest Warrior'

116 Private information; John Colvin, *Twice around the World*, Leo Cooper, London, 1991, p. 69

117 Sylvester, 'A licence to kill? Oh heavens, no!'

118 Bower, *Perfect English Spy*, p. 351

CHAPTER 4: MOSCOW RULES

1 Meeting #1 London, 20 April 1961, transcript declassified by CIA and available at www.cia.gov

2 Clarence Ashley, *CIA Spymaster*, Pelican, Gretna, 2004, p. 110

3 Jerrold L. Schecter and Peter S. Deriabin, *The Spy Who Saved the World*, Macmillan, New York, 1992, p. 20

4 'Reported Provocation Attempt', declassified CIA communication, 30 December 1960, available at www.cia.gov

5 Greville Wynne, *Wynne and Penkovsky*, Corgi, London, 1984, p. 27. The MI6 man is named as Franks in Schecter and Deriabin, *Spy Who Saved the World*

6 Wynne wrote a number of books about his life but by far his most revealing account is in an interview with Anthony Clare, *In the Psychiatrist's Chair*, BBC Radio 4, Imperial War Museum 16196

7 Quoted in Schecter and Deriabin, *Spy Who Saved the World*, p. 311

8 National Archives FO 181/1155

9 Wynne, *Wynne and Penkovsky*, p. 27

10 Ashley, *CIA Spymaster*, pp. 150–1

11 Wynne, *Wynne and Penkovsky*, p. 68

12 Ashley, *CIA Spymaster*, p. 151

13 Tom Bower, *The Perfect English Spy*, Heinemann, London, 1995, p. 274

14 National Archives WO 208/3465

15 Peter Hennessy, *Having It So Good*, Penguin, London, 2006, p. 318

16 John le Carré, *Tinker, Tailor, Soldier, Spy*, Sceptre, London, 2009, p. 228

17 *Blake: The Confession*, BBC Radio 4, 1 August 2009

18 Ibid.; Bower, *Perfect English Spy*, pp. 264–5

19 George Blake, *No Other Choice*, Jonathan Cape, London, 1990, p. 198

20 Among those who remember deciphering the telegram was Daphne Park in the Congo

21 Bill Harvey quoted in Bower, *Perfect English Spy*, p. 269

22 Schecter and Deriabin, *Spy Who Saved the World*, p. 44

23 Meeting #1

24 This quotation is from Meeting #2, p. 20

25 Meeting #1 and Meeting #2, p. 1

26 Huw Dylan, 'Britain and the Missile Gap', *Intelligence and National Security*, volume 23, December 2008

27 John Limond Hart, *The CIA's Russians*, Naval Institute Press, Annapolis, 2003, p. 88

28 Schecter and Deriabin, *Spy Who Saved the World*, p. 94

29 Penkovsky Operation, Parts 3 and 4, Tapes 22 October 1966, declassified by CIA and available at www.cia.gov

30 Ibid.

31 Meeting #4, 23 April 1961

32 Ashley, *CIA Spymaster*, p. 191

33 Meeting #1, p. 22

34 Meeting #5, 24 April 1961

35 Professor Stephen Kotkin, 'Soviet Capitulation', lecture at the London School of Economics, 20 May 2010

36 Meeting #5

37 Meeting #7

38 Meeting #12

39 Meeting #13

40 Bower, *Perfect English Spy*, p. 272

41 Ibid., p. 275

42 The fact that it had never been done before was mentioned by MI6 station chief Gervase Cowell in 'The Role of the Intelligence Services in the Second World War', seminar held 9 November 1994, Institute of Contemporary British History, 2003, http://www.ccbh.ac.uk/witness_intelligence_index.php, p. 45

43 Interview with Baroness Park

44 'Baroness Park of Monmouth: Lives Remembered', *The Times*, 3 April 2010

45 Ashley, *CIA Spymaster*, p. 197

46 Penkovsky Operation, Parts 3 and 4, Tapes 22 October 1966

47 Meeting #16

48 Schecter and Deriabin, *Spy Who Saved the World*, p. 175

49 Ibid., p. 178

50 Obituary of Janet Chisholm, *Daily Telegraph*, 6 August 2004

51 Gordon Barrass, *The Great Cold War*, Stanford University Press, Stanford, 2009, p. 132

52 Christopher Moran, 'Fleming and CIA Director Allen Dulles' in Robert G. Weiner, B. Lynn Whitfield and Jack Becker (eds), *James Bond and Popular Culture*, Cambridge Schools Publishing, Newcastle upon Tyne, 2010; Andrew Lycett, *Ian Fleming*, Weidenfeld & Nicolson, London, 1995, pp. 383 and 367

53 http://www.jfklibrary.org/Historical+Resources/Archives/Reference+Desk/Speeches/JFK/003POF03BerlinCrisis07251961.htm

54 ASSESSMENT OF [BLANK], 13 July 1961, declassified and available at www.cia.gov

55 Richard Deacon, *C: A Biography of Sir Maurice Oldfield*, Macdonald, London, 1984, p. 131

56 Meeting #15

57 Ashley, *CIA Spymaster*, p. 224

58 Meeting #19

59 Penkovsky Operation, Parts 3 and 4, Tapes 22 October 1966

60 Ibid.

61 Hart, *CIA's Russians*, p. 99

62 Schecter and Deriabin, *Spy Who Saved the World*, p. 217

63 Bower, *Perfect English Spy*, pp. 272 and 277

64 Wynne, *Wynne and Penkovsky*, pp. 128 and 131

65 Ibid., p. 76

66 Schecter and Deriabin, *Spy Who Saved the World*, p. 221; Wynne, *Wynne and Penkovsky*, p. 140

67 Penkovsky Operation, Parts 3 and 4, Tapes 22 October 1966

68 See Chapter 7

69 Penkovsky Operation, Parts 3 and 4, Tapes 22 October 1966

70 Ashley, *CIA Spymaster*, p. 212

71 Ibid., p. 211

72 Ibid., p. 212; Schecter and Deriabin, *Spy Who Saved the World*, p. 262

73 See, for instance, Meeting #4, p. 6

74 Meeting #15, p. 5

75 Meeting #35

76 Schecter and Deriabin, *Spy Who Saved the World*, p. 257. Wynne would receive $213,700 jointly from the CIA and MI6 after he was released from prison

77 There is a note in the transcript reading: 'There is no question that subject both wittingly and unwittingly can be most trying in his often capricious demands and handling him on the part of all concerned requires great patience even if understanding is not always possible.' This appears to refer to Wynne, although it might refer to Penkovsky

78 Meeting #36

79 Peter Hennessy, *The Secret State*, Penguin, London, 2002, pp. 6–7

80 Michael Herman quoted in ibid., p. 12

81 National Archives CAB 159/34, Minutes of meeting of 29 September 1960

82 Meeting #37

83 Meetings #1 and #33 include discussions

84 Meeting #33

85 Bower, *Perfect English Spy*, p. 281

86 Memorandum for the record, 11 January 1962 (misdated at top 1961), declassified and available at www.cia.gov

87 See, for instance, CIA memo 'Discussion between SR/COP, CSR/9, DCSR/9, (blank) Re: SR/COP's European Trip February', 6 February 1962

88 Schecter and Deriabin, *Spy Who Saved the World*, p. 292

89 Bower, *Perfect English Spy*, pp. 398–9

90 Translation of letter dated 10 April 1962, declassified by CIA and available at www.cia.gov

91 Gervase Cowell in 'The Role of the Intelligence Services in the Second World War' seminar, p. 45

92 Ibid.

93 Ibid.

94 Hart, *CIA's Russians*, p. 119

95 Ibid.

96 See, for instance, Meeting #11, 1 May 1961

97 Dino Brugioni, *Eyeball to Eyeball*, Random House, New York, 1992

98 Schecter and Deriabin, *Spy Who Saved the World*, pp. 334–6

99 Ibid., p. 336

100 Len Scott, 'Espionage and the Cold War: Oleg Penkovsky and the Cuban Missile Crisis', *Intelligence and National Security*, vol. 14, no. 3, Autumn 1999

101 *Profession of Intelligence*, BBC Radio 4, 23 August 1981

102 Hennessy, *Secret State*, p. 44

103 Schecter and Deriabin, *Spy Who Saved the World*, p. 341

104 Tape No. 4, Friday afternoon 9 November 1962, declassified by CIA and available at www.cia.gov

105 Ashley, *CIA Spymaster*, p. 234

106 Joe Bulik in a 1998 interview published on the website of the National Security Archive, George Washington University

107 Penkovsky case memorandum, 16 June 1963, declassified by CIA and available at www.cia.gov

108 Bower, *Perfect English Spy*, p. 278

109 Schecter and Deriabin, *Spy Who Saved the World*, p. 409

110 Christopher Andrew and Oleg Gordievsky, *KGB: The Inside Story of its Foreign Operations from Lenin to Gorbachev*, Hodder & Stoughton, London, 1990, pp. 393–4

111 *Fatal Encounter*, BBC TV, 1991

112 Schecter and Deriabin, *Spy who Saved the World*, p. 410

113 2 November 1962, from Wynne, *Wynne and Penkovsky*, p. 9

114 Ibid., p. 13

115 Ibid., p. 41

116 National Archives FO 181/1155; private information

117 Memorandum for Chief SR Division from Joe Bulik, 10 May 1963, declassified by CIA and available at www.cia.gov

118 Bower, *Perfect English Spy*, p. 286

119 Schecter and Deriabin, *Spy who Saved the World*, p. 35

120 Ibid., p. 361

121 Frank Gibney (ed.), *The Penkovsky Papers*, Collins, London, 1965, p. 283

122 Ibid., p. 110

123 Schecter and Deriabin, *Spy Who Saved the World*, p. 356

124 Ibid., p. 358

125 Gibney (ed.), *Penkovsky Papers*, p. 125

126 Schecter and Deriabin, *Spy Who Saved the World*, p. 414

127 Interview with Sir Gerry Warner for BBC Radio 4, 2009

128 S-jak SZPIEG Case of Radio Operator Adam Kaczmarzyk, Polish TV documentary, 2004; *The Times*, 10 January 1969 and 8 August 1967, and additional private information

129 Details of the Freed case and Dearlove's role come from the

Czech archives and the work of Prokop Tomek. The issue of the payments to Freed is covered in Chapter 9

130 Martin L. Brabourne, 'More on the Recruitment of Soviets', *Studies in Intelligence*, vol. 9, Winter 1965, originally classified secret, declassified and available at www.cia.gov

131 Wilhelm Marbes, 'The Psychology of Treason', in H. Bradford Westerfield (ed.), *Inside CIA's Private World*, Yale University Press, New Haven, 1995, p. 71

132 Interview with Sir Colin McColl for BBC Radio 4, 2009

CHAPTER 5: THE WILDERNESS OF MIRRORS

1 The account of Golitsyn's defection comes from the first volume of his unpublished memoir. It concurs closely with the account provided from the American side – for instance in David Wise, *Molehunt*, Random House, New York, 1992

2 Friberg's reaction is recounted in Wise, *Molehunt*, p. 3, and Tom Mangold, *Cold Warrior*, Simon & Schuster, London, 1991, p. 50

3 Wise, *Molehunt*, p. 5

4 Wise, ibid., says there was a security alert regarding a bomb and that Golitsyn was allowed to remain on the plane at his request

5 Jerry D. Ennis, 'Anatoli Golitsyn: Long Time CIA Agent?', *Intelligence and National Security*, vol. 21, no. 1, February 2006, p. 32

6 Richard Deacon, *C: A Biography of Sir Maurice Oldfield*, Macdonald, London, 1984, pp. 121 and 167

7 Obituary of the Reverend Vivian Green, *Daily Telegraph*, 26 January 2005, http://www.telegraph.co.uk/news/obituaries/1481995/The-Reverend-Vivian-Green.html

8 Interview with Charles Allen for BBC Radio 4, 2009

9 National Archives PREM 11/4463

10 Mangold, *Cold Warrior*, p. 68

11 Christopher Andrew and Oleg Gordievsky, *KGB: The Inside Story of its Foreign Operations from Lenin to Gorbachev*, Hodder & Stoughton, London, 1990, p. 490

12 Peter Wright in *Spycatcher*, Heinemann, Melbourne, 1987, and Tennent Bagley in *Spy Wars: Moles, Mysteries, and Deadly Games*, Yale University Press, New Haven and London, 2007, are both of this view

13 Deacon, *C: A Biography of Sir Maurice Oldfield*, p. 190; Chapman Pincher, *Treachery*, Random House, New York, 2009, p. 571

14 Christopher Andrew, *The Defence of the Realm: The Authorized History of MI5*, Allen Lane, London, 2009, p. 435

15 Miranda Carter, *Anthony Blunt: His Lives*, Macmillan, London, 2001, p. 451

16 Anthony Blunt in his unpublished memoir held in the British Library and opened to the public in 2009

17 Andrew, *Defence of the Realm*, p. 438

18 Yuri Modin, *My Five Cambridge Friends*, Headline, London, 1994, p. 43; Genrikh Borovik, *The Philby Files*, Little, Brown, London, 1994, p. 365

19 Unless otherwise indicated, material regarding Stephen de Mowbray is drawn from an interview by the author

20 Andrew Boyle, *The Climate of Treason*, Coronet, London, 1980, pp. 210 and 323

21 Wright, *Spycatcher*, p. 54

22 Ibid.

23 Ibid., p. 243

24 Ibid., p. 264

25 Michael Shelden, *Graham Greene: The Man Within*, Heinemann, London, 1994, p. 41

26 Tom Bower, *The Perfect English Spy*, Heinemann, London, 1995, pp. 314–15

27 Wright, *Spycatcher*, p. 170

28 Andrew, *Defence of the Realm*, p. 506

29 Bower, *Perfect English Spy*, p. 316

30 Andrew, *Defence of the Realm*, p. 507

31 Golitsyn unpublished memoir

32 Jerrold L. Schecter and Peter S. Deriabin, *The Spy Who Saved the World*, Macmillan, New York, 1992, p. 379

33 Ibid., p. 390

34 Wright, *Spycatcher*, p. 208

35 Golitsyn, unpublished memoir

36 Golitsyn, *New Lies for Old*, Dodd, Mead & Co., New York, 1984, goes into more detail on this

37 Yuri Nosenko speech to the CIA in 1998. Previously available as

a podcast by the Centre for Counterintelligence and Security Studies, Alexandria. Also Bagley, *Spy Wars*

38 John Limond Hart, *The CIA's Russians*, Naval Institute Press, Annapolis, 2003, p. 129

39 Bagley, *Spy Wars*, p. 14

40 Ibid., p. 88

41 Ibid., p. 18

42 Clarence Ashley, *CIA Spymaster*, Pelican, Gretna, 2004, p. 271

43 Mangold, *Cold Warrior*, p. 147

44 Ibid., p. 149

45 Richards J. Heuer, 'Nosenko: Five Paths to Judgment', in H. Bradford Westerfield (ed.), *Inside CIA's Private World*, Yale University Press, New Haven, 1995, p. 398

46 Bagley, *Spy Wars*, p. 85

47 Ashley, *CIA Spymaster*, p. 277

48 Yuri Nosenko speech to the CIA

49 Walter Pincus, 'Yuri I. Nosenko, 81: KGB agent who defected to the U.S.', *Washington Post*, 27 August 2008; Hart, *CIA's Russians*, p. 144

50 Bagley, *Spy Wars*, p. 216

51 Hart, *CIA's Russians*, p. 160

52 Yuri Nosenko speech to the CIA

53 Details taken from ibid.

54 Pincus, 'Yuri I. Nosenko, 81: KGB agent who defected to the U.S.'

55 Heuer, 'Nosenko: Five Paths to Judgment', p. 383

56 Ibid.

57 References to this in 'The Family Jewels', p. 23, a CIA document which consists of almost 700 pages of responses from CIA employees to a 1973 directive from Director of Central Intelligence James Schlesinger asking them to report activities they thought might be inconsistent with the Agency's charter. Declassified and available at www.cia.gov

58 Ashley, *CIA Spymaster*, p. 284

59 Warren Richey, 'A cold-war case of CIA detention still echoes', *Christian Science Monitor*, 8 January 2008; Bagley, *Spy Wars*

60 Pincus, 'Yuri I. Nosenko, 81: KGB agent who defected to the U.S.'

61 Andrew, *Defence of the Realm*, p. 507

62 Pincher, *Treachery*, p. 393

63 Bower, *Perfect English Spy*, p. 338

64 Robert M. Hathaway and Russell Jack Smith, 'Richard Helms as Director of Central Intelligence', p. 124, internal CIA publication, originally classified secret, available at www.cia.gov

65 Wright, *Spycatcher*, p. 290; Andrew, *Defence of the Realm*, p. 511

66 Bower, *Perfect English Spy*, p. 135

67 Obituary of Andrew King, *Daily Telegraph*, 15 November 2002

68 Obituary of Donald Prater, *The Times*, 12 September 2001

69 Pincher, *Treachery*, p. 539

70 John le Carré, 'A Service known only by its failures', *Toronto Star*, 3 May 1986

71 *The Times*, 20 July 1984

72 Barrie Penrose and Roger Courtiour, *The Pencourt File*, Secker & Warburg, London, 1978, p. 238

73 Mangold, *Cold Warrior*, p. 75

74 See David Omand, *Securing the State*, Hurst, London, 2010, p. 252

75 Chapman Pincher, *The Truth about Dirty Tricks*, Sidgwick & Jackson, London, 1991; and Stephen Dorril and Robin Ramsay, *Smear!*, Grafton, London 1992, p. 264.

76 Hathaway and Smith, 'Richard Helms as Director of Central Intelligence', p. 101

77 Haviland Smith quoted in Tim Weiner, *Legacy of Ashes*, Allen Lane, London, 2007, p. 326

78 The officer was David Murphy: David Wise, *Molehunt*; David C. Martin, *Wilderness of Mirrors*, Harper & Row, New York, 1980, p. 199

79 Wright, *Spycatcher*, p. 308

80 Mangold, *Cold Warrior*, p. 279

81 Christopher Andrew and Vasili Mitrokhin, *The Mitrokhin Archive*, Allen Lane, London, 1999, pp. 242 and 477

82 Mangold, *Cold Warrior*, p. 305

83 Wise, *Molehunt*, p. 256

84 See introduction to Heuer, 'Nosenko: Five Paths to Judgment'

85 Bower, *Perfect English Spy*, p. 372

86 Pincher, *Treachery*, p. 545

87 Bower, *Perfect English Spy*, p. 372

88 Wright, *Spycatcher*, p. 378

89 Penrose and Courtiour, *Pencourt File*, p. 321

90 Ibid., p. 9

91 Deacon, *C: A Biography of Sir Maurice Oldfield*, p. 251

92 Le Carré, 'A Service known only by its failures'

93 John le Carré in the introduction to Alec Guinness, *My Name Escapes Me*, Penguin, London, 1997, p. viii

94 Private information

95 Dr Christopher R. Moran and Dr Robert Johnson, 'In the Service of Empire: Imperialism and the British Spy Thriller 1901–1914', *Studies in Intelligence*, vol. 54, no. 2, June 2010

96 Bower, *Perfect English Spy*, p. 270

97 Donald Rumsfeld speaking on weapons of mass destruction at a press conference in June 2002, http://www.defense.gov/transcripts/transcript.aspx?transcriptid=3490

98 Heuer, 'Nosenko: Five Paths to Judgment', p. 412

99 Wright, *Spycatcher*, p. 2

100 Ibid., p. 3

101 Letter to *The Times*, 18 July 1984; further letters relating to the subject on 19 July and editorial 23 July 1984

102 De Mowbray first spoke out in the wake of the authorised history of MI5. See Gordon Corera, 'Former mole-hunter speaks out', 26 January 2010, BBC News website, http://news.bbc.co.uk/1/hi/uk/8479807.stm

103 In *Treachery* Chapman Pincher brings together all the evidence that he believes points to Hollis having been a Communist spy

CHAPTER 6: COMPROMISING SITUATIONS

1 Interview with Mikhail Lyubimov, Moscow 2009. Further material on Lyubimov's time in London is drawn from Rufina Philby, Mikhail Lyubimov and Hayden Peake, *The Private Life of Kim Philby*, St Ermin's Press, London, 1999, part 3; Alexander Norman, 'Lunching with the Enemy', in John le Carré, *Sarratt and the Draper of Watford*, Village Books, Sarratt, 1999; Mikhail Lyubimov, 'London', in Helen Womack (ed.), *Undercover Lives*, Weidenfeld & Nicolson, London, 1998; David Leppard, 'With smiles and cash', *Sunday Times*, 19 February 1995

2 Philby et al., *Private Life of Kim Philby*, p. 272

3 Lyubimov, 'London', p. 158

4 Ibid., pp. 158 and 165

5 National Archives PREM 15/1935; Christopher Andrew, *The Defence of the Realm: The Authorized History of MI5*, Allen Lane, London, 2009, pp. 565–87; Peter Wright, *Spycatcher*, Heinemann, Melbourne, 1987, pp. 49–51

6 Anthony Courtney, *Sailor in a Russian Frame*, Johnson, London, 1968, p. 53

7 Liddell Hart Archives, Papers of Anthony Courtney, GB99 KCLMA Courtney; Courtney, *Sailor in a Russian Frame*, p. 55

8 Liddell Hart Archives, Papers of Anthony Courtney, GB99 KCLMA Courtney

9 Courtney, *Sailor in a Russian Frame*, pp. 126–7

10 National Archives PREM 13/483

11 National Archives PREM 15/582

12 Christopher Andrew and Vasili Mitrokhin, *The Mitrokhin Archive*, Allen Lane, London, 1999, p. 531

13 National Archives PREM 15/582

14 Liddell Hart Archives, Papers of Anthony Courtney, GB99 KCLMA Courtney

15 National Archives CAB 129/113, The Radcliffe Tribunal on Vassall

16 Andrew and Mitrokhin, *Mitrokhin Archive*, p. 531

17 Ibid., p. 443

18 The following account is drawn from John Vassall's confession and police reports (National Archives CRIM 1/4003) and the report of the Radcliffe Tribunal on Vassall (National Archives CAB 129/113)

19 National Archives CAB 129/113, Radcliffe Tribunal on Vassall

20 National Archives CRIM 1/4003

21 The case of the woman is mentioned in passing in National Archives CAB 129/113, Radcliffe Tribunal on Vassall

22 'MP friends of ex-spy are still in public life', *The Times*, 27 January 1975; Christopher Andrew and Oleg Gordievsky, *The KGB: The Inside Story, of its Foreign Operations from Lenin to Gorbachev*, Hodder & Stoughton, London, 1990, p. 364

23 Wright, *Spycatcher*, p. 166

24 National Archives CRIM 1/4003; D. R. Thorpe, *Supermac: The*

Life of Harold Macmillan, Chatto & Windus, London, 2010, p. 539

25 Interview with Sir Gerry Warner for BBC Radio 4, 2009

26 Wright, *Spycatcher*, pp. 310–11

27 Interview with Sir John Scarlett for BBC Radio 4, 2009

28 Christopher Andrew and Oleg Gordievsky, *Instructions from the Centre*, Sceptre, London, 1993, p. 94

29 National Archives ADM 1/30088; Harry Houghton, *Operation Portland*, Granada, London, 1972, p. 18

30 Houghton, *Operation Portland*, p. 31

31 Nigel West and Oleg Tsarev, *The Crown Jewels*, HarperCollins, London, 1999, ch. XI

32 Ibid., p. 264

33 National Archives ADM 1/30088

34 Houghton, *Operation Portland*, p. 71

35 West and Tsarev, *Crown Jewels*, p. 270

36 National Archives ADM 1/30088, The Romer Report

37 Andrew, *Defence of the Realm*, pp. 486–7; Wright, *Spycatcher*, pp. 130–1

38 Wright, *Spycatcher*, p. 132

39 Ibid., p. 136

40 National Archives ADM 1/30088

41 Thorpe, *Supermac: The Life of Harold Macmillan*, p. 527

42 Tom Bower, *The Perfect English Spy*, Heinemann, London, 1995, pp. 265–7

43 George Blake, *No Other Choice*, Jonathan Cape, London, 1990, p. 213

44 National Archives FO 953/2264

45 Gordon Lonsdale, *Spy: Memoirs of Gordon Lonsdale*, Mayflower-Dell, London, 1966; Greville Wynne, *Wynne and Penkovsky*, Corgi, London, 1984, p. 191

46 Blake, *No Other Choice*, p. 264

47 Quoted in Miranda Carter, *Anthony Blunt: His Lives*, Macmillan, London, 2001, p. 447

48 Andrew, *Defence of the Realm*, p. 499

49 Interview with Mikhail Lyubimov

50 National Archives PREM 15/582 includes a copy of the booklet

51 Peter Wright details the new strategy in *Spycatcher*, pp. 123–4

52 Norman, 'Lunching with the Enemy', p. 56

53 Leppard, 'With smiles and cash'

54 Oleg Kalugin, *Spymaster*, Smith Gryphon, London, 1994, p. 131

55 'I arrested a KGB superspy', BBC News website, http://news.bbc.co.uk/onthisday/hi/witness/september/30/newsid_2523000/2523457.stm

56 National Archives PREM 15/1935

57 Ibid.

58 This account derives from an interview with Mikhail Lyubimov and from Philby et al., *Private Life of Kim Philby*, part 3

59 Ibid., p. 274

60 Ibid., p. 280

61 Eleanor Philby, *The Spy I Loved*, Hamish Hamilton, London, 1968, p. 78

62 Philby et al., *Private Life of Kim Philby*, pp. 30–1

63 Ibid., p. 245

64 Kalugin, *Spymaster*, p. 142

65 Genrikh Borovik, *The Philby Files*, Little, Brown, London, 1994, p. 371

66 Norman Sherry, *The Life of Graham Greene*, vol. 2, Jonathan Cape, London, 1994, pp. 488–9

67 Borovik, *Philby Files*, p. 245

68 Michael Shelden, *Graham Greene: The Man Within*, Heinemann, London, 1994, p. 323

69 Marie-Françoise Allain, *The Other Man: Conversations with Graham Greene*, The Bodley Head, London, 1983, pp. 183–4

70 Philby et al., *Private Life of Kim Philby*, p. 175

71 Borovik, *Philby Files*, p. 234

72 Norman Sherry, *The Life of Graham Greene*, vol. 3, Pimlico, London, 2004, p. 749

73 Olga Craig, 'John le Carré: Espionage is an accident, like love', *Sunday Telegraph*, 29 August 2010

74 Sherry, *Life of Graham Greene*, vol. 2, p. 487

75 Ibid., p. 494

76 Yuri Modin, *My Five Cambridge Friends*, Headline, London, 1994, p. 270

CHAPTER 7: ESCAPE FROM MOSCOW

1 This account is drawn from interviews with Mikhail Lyubimov and Oleg Gordievsky

2 Interview with Mikhail Lyubimov; Christopher Andrew and Oleg Gordievsky, *KGB: The Inside Story of its Foreign Operations from Lenin to Gorbachev*, Hodder & Stoughton, London, 1990, p. 453

3 Oleg Gordievsky, *Next Stop Execution*, Macmillan, London, 1995, p. 336

4 Helen Womack (ed.), *Undercover Lives*, Weidenfeld & Nicolson, London, 1998, p. 190

5 Gordievsky discusses his family life and motivations in an interview with Dr Anthony Clare, *In the Psychiatrist's Chair*, BBC Radio 4, 1995, IWM 15628

6 Womack (ed.), *Undercoverr Lives*, p. 188

7 Rufina Philby, Mikhail Lyubimov and Hayden Peake, *The Private Life of Kim Philby*, St Ermin's Press, London, 1999, p. 290; Womack (ed.), *Undercover Lives*, p. 184

8 Interview with Oleg Gordievsky

9 Letter from Oleg Gordievsky to *The Times*, 18 August 2008

10 Interview with Oleg Gordievsky

11 Ibid.

12 Gordievsky, *Next Stop Execution*, pp. 198–206

13 Ibid., p. 219

14 The only time Gordievsky has ever publicly discussed these doubts was in an interview with Dr Anthony Clare, *In the Psychiatrist's Chair*, BBC Radio 4, 1995. Also additional private information

15 'Literary world applauds Rushdie knighthood', *Guardian*, 16 June 2007, http://www.guardian.co.uk/society/2007/jun/16/books.politics

16 Interview with Sir John Scarlett for BBC Radio 4, 2009

17 See 'MI6 versus KGB/FSB: The Battle in Moscow', 30 January 2006, Axis Information and Analysis, http://www.axisglobe.com/article.asp?article=634

18 Interview with Sir John Scarlett for BBC Radio 4, 2009

19 Gordievsky, *Next Stop Execution*, p. 239

20 Interview with Oleg Gordievsky

21 Christoper Andrew and Oleg Gordievsky, *Instructions from the Centre*, Sceptre, London, 1993, p. 77

22 Christopher Andrew, *The Defence of the Realm: The Authorized History of MI5*, Allen Lane, London, 2009, pp. 441 and 712

23 Ibid., p. 724 has the details of the drop

24 Eliza Manningham-Buller interviewed on *Desert Island Discs*, BBC Radio 4, 23 November 2007

25 'War secrets pigeon trainer dies', BBC News website, 1 April 2004, http://news.bbc.co.uk/1/hi/england/northamptonshire/3589853.stm

26 Interview with Baroness Manningham-Buller for BBC Radio 4, 2009

27 Interview with Sir Stephen Lander for BBC TV, 2009

28 Interview with Baroness Manningham-Buller for BBC Radio 4, 2009

29 Interview with Dame Stella Rimington for BBC TV, 2009

30 Interview with Baroness Manningham-Buller for BBC Radio 4, 2009

31 Ibid.

32 Andrew, *Defence of the Realm*, pp. 716–20

33 Gordon Barrass, *The Great Cold War*, Stanford University Press, Stanford, 2009, p. 278

34 Quoted in Andrew and Gordievsky, *Instructions from the Centre*, pp. 31–3

35 Ibid., p. 122

36 Ibid., pp. 45 and 129

37 Barrass, *Great Cold War*, has the best analysis of Ryan and Able Archer, pp. 299–300

38 Interview with Sir John Scarlett for BBC Radio 4, 2009

39 Private information

40 Barrass, *Great Cold War*, pp. 304–5

41 Interview with former CIA analyst indoctrinated into the information at the time

42 Quoted in Barrass, *Great Cold War*, p. 305

43 Milt Bearden and James Risen, *The Main Enemy*, Century, New York, 2003, p. 47; the British reaction comes from private information

44 Gordievsky, *Next Stop Execution*, p. 310
45 Ibid., p. 311
46 Margaret Thatcher, *The Downing Street Years*, HarperCollins, London, 1993, pp. 87 and 461
47 Gordievsky, *Next Stop Execution*, p. 328
48 Ibid., p. 343
49 Private information
50 Interview with Mikhail Lyubimov
51 Private information
52 Bryan Cartledge, interview for the British Diplomatic Oral History Programme, Churchill College, Cambridge. Available at http://www.chu.cam.ac.uk/archives/collections/BDOHP/Cartledge.pdf
53 Interview with Oleg Gordievsky and former British officials
54 James Adams, *The New Spies*, Pimlico, London, 1995, p. 35
55 Interview with Sir Rodric Braithwaite for BBC Radio 4, 2009
56 Gordievsky interview with Dr Anthony Clare, *In the Psychiatrist's Chair*, BBC Radio 4, 1995
57 Private information
58 Ibid.
59 Bearden and Risen, *Main Enemy*; Tim Weiner, *Legacy of Ashes*, Allen Lane, London, 2007, p. 416
60 James Robarge, 'Deceptions: James Angleton and CIA Counter-intelligence', *Journal of Intelligence History*, vol. 3, no. 2, Winter 2003
61 Interview with Mikhail Lyubimov
62 The author put each man's comments to the other. They did not speak directly
63 Interview with Sir John Scarlett for BBC Radio 4, 2009
64 Quoted in Phillip Knightley, *The Second Oldest Profession*, W. W. Norton, New York, 1987, p. 285
65 Professor Stephen Kotkin, 'Soviet Capitulation', lecture at the London School of Economics, 20 May 2010
66 Interview with Sir Rodric Braithwaite for BBC Radio 4, 2009

CHAPTER 8: THE AFGHAN PLAINS

1 National Archives WO 106/6148, Lecture on the Secret Service

from early in the twentieth century by a British officer to the Staff College in Quetta

2 Vladimir Kuzichkin, *Inside the KGB*, André Deutsch, London 1990, p. 316

3 Rufina Philby, Mikhail Lyubimov and Hayden Peake, *The Private Life of Kim Philby*, St Ermin's Press, London, 1999, p. 87

4 Gary C. Schroen, *First In*, Ballantine Books, New York, 2005, pp. 38 and 43

5 Special Co-ordination Committee Meeting on Afghanistan, 17 December 1979, available through http://www.margaret thatcher.org/document/D5EE99CO3C4147B091AE83160A8085 FF.pdf

6 Margaret Thatcher, *The Downing Street Years*, HarperCollins, London, 1993, pp. 87 and 168

7 Interview with Stansfield Turner, 29 November 2004

8 Sandy Gall, *Behind Russian Lines*, Sidgwick & Jackson, London 1983, p. 150

9 George Crile, *My Enemy's Enemy*, Atlantic Books, London, 2003, p. 18

10 Quoted in Brigadier Mohammad Yousaf and Mark Adkin, *Afghanistan: The Bear Trap*, Leo Cooper, Barnsley, 1992, p. 20

11 Steve Coll, *Ghost Wars*, Penguin, New York, 2004, pp. 52–4

12 Crile, *My Enemy's Enemy*, p. 354

13 Private information from US and British sources

14 Crile, *My Enemy's Enemy*, p. 199

15 Interview with guide who became one of Massoud's fighters

16 Interview with Abdullah Anas

17 Interview with Muslem Hayat

18 Ken Connor, *Ghost Force*, Orion, London 1993, p. 420

19 Mark Urban, *War in Afghanistan*, Macmillan, London, 1990, pp. 101–2

20 Private information

21 Interview with Abdullah Anas

22 Milt Bearden and James Risen, *The Main Enemy*, Century, New York, 2003, p. 218

23 Interview with retired CIA official who requested anonymity

24 'British and US "subversion" against Afghanistan', BBC Summary of World Broadcasts, 12 October 1983; 'Man named as

British spy killed in Afghanistan found in pub', Associated Press, 16 October 1983

25 'Dead UK spy alive and well', *South China Morning Post*, 17 October 1983

26 Obituaries of Sir Edgar Beck, *The Times*, 3 August 2000, and *Daily Telegraph*, 3 August 2000

27 Interview with guide who accompanied the convoy

28 Interview with Muslem Hayat

29 'Kabul news conference on British "spy"', BBC Summary of World Broadcasts, 4 October 1983; 'Death of British "spy" in Afghanistan: Britain's involvement', BBC Summary of World Broadcasts, 19 October 1983; 'Swede accused by Kabul of spying, possibly a journalist', BBC Summary of World Broadcasts, 6 October 1983

30 'Death of British spy in Afghanistan: Britain's involvement', BBC Summary of World Broadcasts, 19 October 1983

31 Soviet report of career of CIA spy in Afghanistan, 24 November 1984

32 Coll, *Ghost Wars*, p. 130

33 Crile, *My Enemy's Enemy*, pp. 197 and 201

34 'Reagan meets rebel leaders', Facts on File World News Digest, 1 August 1986

35 Colin Berry, *The Deniable Agent*, Mainstream Publishing, Edinburgh, 2007, p. 116

36 Yousaf and Adkin, *Afghanistan: The Bear Trap*, p. 88

37 Ibid.

38 Lester W. Grau and Ali Ahmad Jalali, *The Campaign for the Caves: The Battle for Zhawar in the Soviet–Afgan War*, Foreign Military Studies Office, Fort Leavenworth, Kansas, http://fmso.leavenworth.army.mil/documents/zhawar/zhawar.htm

39 Yousaf and Adkin, *Afghanistan: The Bear Trap*, p. 176; Coll, *Ghost Wars*, p. 150; Bearden and Risen, *Main Enemy*, pp. 248–52

40 Coll, *Ghost Wars*, pp. 11–12

41 Private information from former intelligence official working on Afghan campaign in the late 1980s

42 Urban, *War in Afghanistan*, p. 271

43 Crile, *My Enemy's Enemy*

44 Coll, *Ghost Wars*, p. 100

45 Ibid., p. 104; Yousaf and Adkin, *Afghanistan: The Bear Trap*, p. 193

46 Yousaf and Adkin, *Afghanistan: The Bear Trap*, pp. 113–14 and 146

47 Ibid., p. 198

48 Coll, *Ghost Wars*, p. 133

49 Schroen, *First In*, p. 46. The officer who had the hit put on him by Hekmatyar was Marc Sageman (private information)

50 Thatcher, *Downing Street Years*, p. 773

51 Crile, *My Enemy's Enemy*, p. ix

52 Bearden and Risen, *Main Enemy*, p. 358

53 Yousaf and Adkin, *Afghanistan: The Bear Trap*, pp. 198 and 233

54 Gordon Corera, *Shopping for Bombs: Nuclear Proliferation, Global Insecurity and the Rise and Fall of the A. Q. Khan Network*, Hurst, London, 2006

55 Coll, *Ghost Wars*, p. 237

56 Jason Bennetto, 'Boost for MI6 in war on drugs trade', *Independent*, 29 August 1997

57 Coll, *Ghost Wars*, p. 466

58 Details of intelligence collection plan from George Tenet, *At the Center of the Storm*, HarperCollins, London, 2007, p. 120. Mike Scheuer of the Bin Laden unit has frequently complained of the failure to take more aggressive action

59 Intelligence and Security Committee, *Rendition*, HMSO, 2007, Cm 7171

60 The best account of Massoud's final minutes is in Schroen, *First In*, pp. 5–6

CHAPTER 9: OUT OF THE SHADOWS

1 Interview with Sir Colin McColl for BBC Radio 4, 2009

2 Private information

3 Philip H. J. Davies, 'A Critical Look at Britain's Spy Machinery', *Studies in Intelligence*, vol. 49, no. 4, 2005

4 Private information from former member of Joint Intelligence Committee in the 1990s

5 Interview with Sir Gerry Warner for BBC Radio 4, 2009

6 Interview with Sir Rodric Braithwaite for BBC Radio 4, 2009;

Rodric Braithwaite, *Across the Moscow River*, Yale University Press, New Haven and London, 2003

7 Stella Rimington, *Open Secret*, Arrow, London 2002, pp. 234 and 238

8 Mitrokhin's story is recounted in Christopher Andrew's foreword to *The Mitrokhin Archive II: The KGB and the World*, Allen Lane, London, 2005, pp. xiii–xxiv; the detail of the young MI6 officer comes from additional private information

9 Richard Tomlinson, *The Big Breach*, Cutting Edge, Edinburgh, 2001, p. 110

10 James Adams, *The New Spies*, Pimlico, London, 1995, p. 10

11 Interview with former British official, 2009

12 Milt Bearden and James Risen, *The Main Enemy*, Century, New York, 2003, p. 427

13 Private information

14 Private information and obituary of Sir David Spedding, *Guardian*, 14 June 2001

15 Interview with Lord Hurd of Westwell for BBC Radio 4, 2009

16 Interview with Sir Colin McColl for BBC Radio 4, 2009

17 Information comes from evidence at the inquiry into the death of Diana Princess of Wales, 2008, transcripts available on National Archives website

18 Interview with Sir John Scarlett for BBC Radio 4, 2009; private information

19 Interview with Lord Hurd of Westwell for BBC Radio 4, 2009. An exchange on the subject was broadcast in *A Century in the Shadows*, BBC Radio 4, August 2009

20 Interview with former CIA official

21 Sir Richard Dearlove, 'Our Changing Perceptions of National Security', lecture at Gresham College, London, 25 November 2009

22 Interview with Sir John Scarlett for BBC Radio 4, 2009

23 Tony Blair, *A Journey*, Hutchinson, London, 2010, p. 346

24 Sir Richard Dearlove speaking at the Hay-on-Wye book festival, 31 May 2009

25 Interview with Baroness Manningham-Buller for BBC Radio 4, 2009

26 Sir Richard Dearlove speaking at the Hay-on-Wye book festival, 31 May 2009

27 Tenet, *At the Center of the Storm*, HarperCollins, London, 2007, p. 146; Joint Summit mentioned in Intelligence and Security Committee, *Annual Report 2001–2002*, HMSO. Available online at https://www.mi5.gov.uk/ output/intelligence-and-security-committee-annual-reports.html

28 Christopher Andrew, *The Defence of the Realm: The Authorized History of MI5*, Allen Lane, London, 2009, p. 809

29 Intelligence and Security Committee, *Annual Report 2001–2002*

30 Account of this meeting from Alastair Campbell, *The Blair Years*, Random House, London, 2007, p. 561

31 Ibid., p. 562

32 Bob Woodward, *Bush at War*, Simon & Schuster, New York, 2002, p. 62

33 Tyler Drumheller, *On the Brink*, Politico's, London, 2007, p. 30

34 Sir Richard Dearlove speaking at the Hay-on-Wye book festival, 31 May 2009

35 Drumheller, *On the Brink*, p. 31

36 Ibid., p. 33

37 Interview with Cofer Black by the author for *Secret Wars: The CIA since 9/11*, BBC World Service, 2006; statement of Cofer Black, Joint Congressional Inquiry into September 11th, 26 September 2002, http://www.fas.org/irp/congress/2002_hr/092602black.pdf

38 Woodward, *Bush at War*, p. 52; Drumheller, *On the Brink*, p. 35; interview with Cofer Black by the author for *Secret Wars: The CIA since 9/11*, BBC World Service, 2006

39 Campbell, *Blair Years*, p. 568

40 Sir Richard Wilson, evidence at the Iraq Inquiry

41 *The Handling of Detainees by UK Intelligence Personnel in Afghanistan, Guantanamo and Iraq*, Intelligence and Security Committee, March 2005, https://www.mi5/.gov.uk/output/intelligence-and-security-committee-special-reports.html

42 Michael Smith, *The Spying Game*, Politico's, London, 2003, p.1

43 Evidence of Paul Bergne to House of Commons Foreign Affairs Committee, 22 January 2002; obituaries of Paul Bergne, *The Times*, 19 April 2007, *Daily Telegraph*, 16 April 2007, and Craig

Murray's blog, 17 April 2007, http://www.craigmurray.org.uk/archives/2007/04/paul_bergne.html

44 Interview with Cofer Black and Gary Schroen by the author for *Secret Wars: The CIA since 9/11*, BBC World Service, 2006; Gary C. Schroen, *First In*, Ballantine Books, New York, 2005, p. 26

45 Drumheller, *On the Brink*, p. 48

46 Interview with Hank Crumpton

47 Interview with Bob Grenier

48 'Tora Bora Revisted: How We Failed to Get Bin Laden and Why it Matters Today', Report to the Foreign Affairs Committee, US Senate, 30 November 2009

49 Interview with Abdullah Anas

50 Account drawn from Intelligence and Security Committee, *The Handling of Detainees by UK Intelligence Personnel in Afghanistan, Guantanamo and Iraq*, March 2005, http://www.cabinetoffice.gov.uk/media/cabinetoffice/corp/assets/publications/reports/ intelligence/treatdetainees.pdf

51 Sir Richard Dearlove speaking at the Hay-on-Wye book festival, 31 May 2009

52 Baroness Manningham-Buller, lecture at the House of Lords, 10 March 2010

53 Ibid.

54 Intelligence and Security Committee, *The Handling of Detainees by UK Intelligence Personnel in Afghanistan, Guantanamo and Iraq*

55 Interview with Sir John Scarlett for BBC Radio 4, 2009

56 Statement before the House Committee on Foreign Affairs, 17 April 2007, http://foreignaffairs.house.gov/110/sch041707.htm

57 Private information from a number of officials

58 Interview with Baroness Manningham-Buller for BBC Radio 4, 2009

59 Evidence to the inquest into 7 July bombings

60 Private information

61 Interview with Baroness Manningham-Buller for BBC Radio 4, 2009

62 Eliza Manningham-Buller interviewed on *Desert Island Discs*, BBC Radio 4, 23 November 2007

63 Gordon Corera, 'Analysis: MI5 and the Bomber', BBC News web-

site, 30 April 2007, http://news.bbc.co.uk/1 /hi/uk/ 6477777.stm

64 Interview with Baroness Manningham-Buller for BBC Radio 4, 2009

65 Rosie Cowan and Richard Norton-Taylor, 'Britain now No 1 al-Qaida target', *The Guardian*, 19 October 2006

66 The author attended a meeting with an MI5 agent and his officer for the making of *The Real Spooks: MI5 since 9/11*, BBC Radio 4, December 2007

67 Interview with an MI5 agent for *The Real Spooks: MI5 since 9/11*, BBC Radio 4, December 2007

68 Ibid.

69 Interview with an MI5 agent for *The Real Spooks: MI5 since 9/11*, BBC Radio 4, December 2007

70 Baroness Manningham-Buller, speech at the Mile End Group, 9 November 2006, and private information

71 Interview with Pakistani official

CHAPTER 10: IN THE BUNKER

1 Private information from an individual who, unsurprisingly, requested anonymity

2 The meeting of the Revolutionary Command Council is in Charles Duelfer, *Hide and Seek*, PublicAffairs, New York, 2009, p. 390. Saddam Hussein also makes reference to asking this question of his ministers a number of times in conversations with his FBI interrogator, 13 May 2004. (Transcript at http://www.gwu.edu/~nsarchiv/NSAEBB/NSAEBB279/23.pdf). See also *Iraq Survey Group Comprehensive Report*, vol. 1, which details Saddam's demeanour at meetings in September 2002

3 Tyler Drumheller, *On the Brink*, Politico's, London, 2007, p. 53

4 Jack Straw evidence to the Iraq Inquiry

5 SIS4 evidence to the Iraq Inquiry

6 Jack Straw evidence to the Iraq Inquiry

7 Alastair Campbell, *The Blair Years*, Random House, London, 2007, p. 612

8 Ibid., p. 567

9 Tony Blair, *A Journey*, Hutchinson, London, 2001, p. 410

10 Ibid., pp. 369, 388 and 408–9

11 Bob Woodward, *Bush at War*, Simon & Schuster, New York, 2002, pp. 197 and 111

12 *Butler Review of Intelligence on Weapons of Mass Destruction*, p. 70

13 Blair, *Journey*, p. 385

14 *Butler Review of Intelligence on Weapons of Mass Destruction*, p. 45

15 Interview with former UN inspector Bill Tierney

16 The work, under the codename Operation Rockingham, is discussed in the *Butler Review of Intelligence on Weapons of Mass Destruction*. Scott Ritter identified the men he met with as from MI6

17 Sir Richard Dearlove evidence to the Iraq Inquiry

18 James Risen, *State of War*, Free Press, New York, 2006, p. 113; Drumheller, *On the Brink*, p. 32

19 Private information

20 George Tenet, *At the Center of the Storm*, HarperCollins, London, 2007, p. 310

21 Campbell, *Blair Years*, p. 645

22 Sir Richard Wilson evidence to the Iraq Inquiry

23 Tony Blair evidence to the Iraq Inquiry

24 Campbell, *Blair Years*, pp. 630–1

25 SIS4 evidence to the Iraq Inquiry

26 Sir David Omand evidence to the Iraq Inquiry, available online at www.iraqinquiry.org.uk/transcripts.aspx

27 Campbell, *Blair Years*, p. 634

28 David Omand, *Securing the State*, Hurst, London, 2010, p. 39

29 The 'mate' comment came in the Hutton Inquiry; the 'good bloke' in Campbell, *Blair Years*, p. 618

30 Sir Rodric Braithwaite, 'Defending British spies: The Use and Abuses of Intelligence', speech at Chatham House, 5 November 2003

31 Sir David Omand and Sir John Scarlett evidence to the Iraq Inquiry

32 Scarlett evidence to the Hutton Inquiry, quoted in *Butler Review*, p. 78

33 Michael Laurie's comments came in an email written to the Iraq Inquiry on 27 January 2010 in response to seeing Alistair

Campbell's testimony that the dossier was not designed to make the case for war. His email was released by the Inquiry in May 2011. Alastair Campbell then wrote to the Inquiry disputing his account.

34 Sir David Manning evidence to the Iraq Inquiry

35 Sir Richard Dearlove speaking at the Hay-on-Wye book festival, 31 May 2009

36 Private information

37 Matthew Rycroft evidence to the Iraq Inquiry

38 Sir Richard Dearlove evidence to the Iraq Inquiry

39 *Butler Review of Intelligence on Weapons of Mass Destruction*, p. 67; Julian Miller evidence to the Iraq Inquiry

40 Sir Richard Dearlove speaking at the Hay-on-Wye book festival, 31 May 2009

41 Evidence suggesting it was 20th was provided in the Iraq Inquiry but was challenged by another witness. The witness SIS4 described the intelligence base as 'thin' in his evidence

42 SIS2 and SIS4 evidence to the Iraq Inquiry

43 Sir John Scarlett evidence to the Iraq Inquiry

44 Sir David Omand evidence to the Iraq Inquiry

45 SIS4 evidence to the Iraq Inquiry

46 Brian Jones, *Failing Intelligence*, Dialogue, London, 2010, p. 85

47 Quoted in Bob Woodward, *Plan of Attack*, Simon & Schuster, New York, 2004, p. 190

48 Sir Richard Dearlove evidence to the Iraq Inquiry

49 Jones, *Failing Intelligence*, p. 234; and private information

50 Private information and Iraq Survey Group Comprehensive Report, vol. 1

51 Private information and evidence of SIS3 and SIS1 to the Iraq Inquiry

52 Jones, *Failing Intelligence*, p. 82

53 Written evidence of Brian Jones to the Hutton and Butler Inquiries; *Butler Review of Intelligence on Weapons of Mass Destruction*; Jones, *Failing Intelligence*, p. 89

54 The minute was published as part of the Hutton Inquiry and is available at http://www.the-hutton-inquiry.org.uk/content/cab/cab_33_0114too115 .pdf

55 Jones, *Failing Intelligence*, pp. 191 and 198

56 Brian Jones interview on the *Today* programme, BBC Radio 4, 20 July 2004

57 Graham Greene, *Our Man in Havana*, Vintage, London, 2001, pp. 189 and 78

58 Matthew Rycroft evidence to the Iraq Inquiry

59 Sir David Omand evidence to the Iraq Inquiry

60 Joint evidence of Sir John Scarlett and Julian Miller to the Iraq Inquiry

61 Quotes drawn from the *Butler Review of Intelligence on Weapons of Mass Destruction*

62 George Tenet speech at Georgetown University, 5 February 2004, https:// www.cia.gov/news_information/speeches_testimony/ 2004/tenet_georgetownspeech_02052004.html

63 Woodward, *Plan of Attack*, pp. 106–7

64 The author was the journalist present in the room along with a BBC colleague. Sections of the interview were broadcast as part of a programme profiling Saddam on BBC Radio 4 but a planned story on the mobile labs by the author never made it to air

65 Colin Powell speaking at the UN, 5 February 2003

66 'The Real Story of Curveball', *Der Spiegel*, 22 March 2008; Bob Drogin, *Curveball*, Ebury, London, 2007; Drumheller, *On the Brink;* and *Butler Review of Intelligence on Weapons of Mass Destruction*

67 Drogin, *Curveball*, pp. 92–3

68 *The Commission on the Intelligence Capabilities of the United States regarding Weapons of Mass Destruction*, 31 March 2005, p. 91 available online at www.gpoaccess.gov/wmd/index.html; Drumheller, *On the Brink*, p. 246; Drogin, *Curveball*, p. 131; and private information

69 Statement of George J. Tenet, former Director of Central Intelligence, 1 April 2005, available online at www.fas.org/irp/ offdocs/wmd_tenet.pdf

70 Michael Gordon and Bernard Trainor, *Cobra II*, Atlantic Books, London, 2006, p. 133

71 See Tenet, *At the Center of the Storm*, p. 377; statement of George J. Tenet, former Director of Central Intelligence, 1 April 2005 and Drumheller, *On the Brink*, p. 100; and Drogin, *Curveball*,

pp. 158–9

72 Hans Blix, *Disarming Iraq*, Bloomsbury, London, 2004, p. 96

73 Sir David Omand evidence to the Iraq Inquiry

74 Interview with former weapons inspector Rod Barton

75 Quoted in Bob Drogin, 'Spy work in Iraq riddled by failure', *Los Angeles Times*, 17 June 2004

76 Hans Blix, *Disarming Iraq*, p. 194

77 Ibid., pp. 129–30

78 Woodward, *Plan of Attack*, pp. 240 and 294

79 Matthew Rycroft evidence to the Iraq Inquiry

80 SIS4 evidence to the Iraq Inquiry

81 SIS4 evidence to the Iraq Inquiry

82 SIS4 evidence to the Iraq Inquiry

83 Saddam made references to his concerns over seeming weak to Iran in a casual conversation with his FBI interrogator, 11 June 2004, www.gwu.edu/~nsarchiv/NSAEBB/NSAEBB279/24.pdf

84 Interview with Jaffar Dhia Jaffar; and transcript of FBI interview with Saddam Hussein, Session 4, www.gwu.edu/~nsarchiv/NSAEBB/NSAEBB279/05.pdf

85 Interview with Jaffar Dhia Jaffar

86 Sir Richard Dearlove, talk at the London School of Economics, 31 October 2007

87 *Iraq Survey Group Comprehensive Report*, vol. 1

88 Hans Blix evidence to the Iraq Inquiry, 27 July 2010

89 Interview with Jaffar Dhia Jaffar

90 Blix, *Disarming Iraq*, pp. 229 and 62

91 Interview with Jaffar Dhia Jaffar

92 Interview with David Kay

93 Ron Suskind in *The Way of the World*, Simon & Schuster, London, 2008, identified the Iraqi as Tahir Jalil Habbush. This is incorrect according to multiple sources with knowledge of the events

94 Statement by George Tenet, 4 August 2008, http://www.georgejtenet.com/ TENETAUG4STATEMENT.html

95 Drumheller, *On the Brink*, p. 98

96 Rumsfeld speaking at a 2 February 2002 US Department of Defense news conference

97 *Butler Review of Intelligence on Weapons of Mass Destruction*; and

Scarlett evidence to the Iraq Inquiry. Former Foreign Secretary Robin Cook says he was briefed in his memoir

98 Hansard, 18 March 2003

99 Gordon Corera, *Shopping for Bombs: Nuclear Proliferation, Global Insecurity and the Rise and Fall of the AQ Khan Network*, Hurst, London, 2006, ch. 8; additional private information; material from Tenet, *At the Center of the Storm*. Mark Allen's role was revealed in a number of newspaper articles, for instance, 'Ex-spy is BP's Lawrence of Arabia', *Mail on Sunday*, 6 September 2009

100 Mark Allen is named as the MI6 officer in 'Ex-Spy is BP's Lawrence of Arabia', *Mail on Sunday*, 6 September 2009, and Douglas Frantz and Catherine Collins, *The Nuclear Jihadist*, Twelve, New York, 2007, p. 307

101 Sir David Omand evidence to the Iraq Inquiry, referring to a December 2002 JIC paper; and Eliza Manningham-Buller evidence to the Iraq Inquiry

102 Remarks of Major General Stanley McChrystal at the Foreign Press Center, Washington DC, 3 April 2003

103 Campbell, *Blair Years*, p. 693

104 Ibid., p. 700

105 Ibid., p. 701

106 Private information

107 Blair, *Journey*, Hutchinson, London 2010, p. 451

108 Interview with David Kay

109 Duelfer, *Hide and Seek*, p. 293

110 Interview with Rod Barton, former ISG Inspector; Duelfer, *Hide and Seek*, pp. 356 and 361

111 *Butler Review of Intelligence on Weapons of Mass Destruction*

112 Anonymous evidence to the Iraq Inquiry. Available online at www.iraqinquiry.org.uk/media/50706/Anonymous-Extract-1.pdf

113 *The Commission on the Intelligence Capabilities of the United States regarding Weapons of Mass Destruction*, ch. 1

114 Drogin, *Curveball*, p. 269; *Butler Review of Intelligence on Weapons of Mass Destruction* and *Commission on the Intelligence Capabilities of the United States regarding Weapons of Mass Destruction*, chapter 1

115 Private information

116 Sir Richard Dearlove evidence to the Iraq Inquiry

117 *Butler Review of Intelligence on Weapons of Mass Destruction*

118 Matthew Rycroft evidence to the Iraq Inquiry

119 Sir Richard Dearlove, talk at the London School of Economics, 31 October 2007

120 Sir Richard Dearlove speaking at the Hay-on-Wye book festival, 31 May 2009

121 SIS4 evidence to the Iraq Inquiry

122 Ibid.

123 Drumheller, *On the Brink*, pp. 202–3

124 The author put the question to Sir John Scarlett in an interview broadcast in 'A Century in the Shadows', BBC Radio 4, August 2009

125 Interview with Sir John Scarlett for BBC Radio 4, 2009

126 Ibid.

127 *Intelligence and Security Committee Annual Report for 2007–2008*

128 Interview with John Scarlett for BBC Radio 4, 2009

129 George Blake in an email to the author in 2010; 'Spy Blake enjoying comfortable old age in Russia', Agence France-Presse, 11 November 2010

130 Speech to the Society of Editors, 28 October 2010

131 Ibid.

132 Former Islamic Group official thanks NATO for sparing Libyan blood, Al Hayat 2 September 2011. Other information from copies of the documents found in Tripoli. Also 'How MI6 deal sent family to Gaddafi's jail', *The Guardian*, 9 September 2011

133 Rodric Braithwaite interview with the author for BBC Radio 4, 2009

134 See, for instance, *Intelligence and Security Committee Annual Report 2003–2004*

INDEX